THE BUMPER BOOK OF CROSSWORDS

THE BUMPER BOOK OF CROSSWORDS

H.W. MASSINGHAM
ALEC ROBINS
A.D. SCOTT

TREASURE PRESS

First published in Great Britain by Octopus Books Ltd
in two separate volumes entitled *The New Book of Crossword Puzzles* and *Challenging Crosswords.*

This one-volume edition published in 1988 by
Treasure Press
Michelin House
81 Fulham Road
London SW3 6RB

ISBN 1 85051 232 9

Printed in Great Britain

CONTENTS

INTRODUCTION

The crosswords in this book are intended to cater for a wide variety of tastes and solving ability, ranging as they do from the plain and simple to the less easy and more challenging. They are presented in ten separate Parts, each with its own style and character, and graduated in difficulty within each batch of puzzles.

Most of the clues are of two conventional kinds. One, the definition kind, presents a direct challenge. It consists of a word or phrase for which the solver has to find either an equivalent or a synonym; alternatively the required answer might be a proper name. The other, the cryptic kind, is not quite so straightforward. This kind of clue consists of two distinct parts: (a) a definition, as above, which indicates the answer required; and (b) a subsidiary and indirect piece of information which leads to the same answer. Note also that, in any cryptic clue, the definition may come first, followed by the cryptic part, or vice versa.

The different types of crosswords that you will meet are divided into ten Parts and are called Plain, Slightly Cryptic, Beat the Clock, Thematic, Double Trouble, Bars Not Blanks, Fully Cryptic, Cryptic and More Cryptic, Novelty and Jumbos, and it may be helpful to say something here about each Part.

Part 1 consists of plain puzzles of the kind that are sometimes known as 'quickies'. The answers are all words which almost everybody knows, and the clues are all perfectly straightforward, with no attempt to mislead you by way of verbal trickery. They are either synonyms, such as 'Come in (5)' (answer, ENTER), factual definitions, like 'A famous sea-battle (9)' (answer, TRAFALGAR), or descriptions of people or places, as 'US politician (7)' (answer, SENATOR) or 'Italian lake (4)' (answer, COMO). You will soon discover that your speed of solving gradually increases as you get into the swing of things, but be prepared to find, as you reach the last dozen or so, that the answers are becoming a shade less obvious and you are having to think a little harder before writing them in!

Parts 2, 3 and 4 are cryptic puzzles. Solvers who are unfamiliar with cryptic clues can be assured that they do not suddenly have to become geniuses in order to solve them! In these sections, the cryptic clues are restricted to eight basic types, examples of which are given below. Furthermore you will always know that a clue in these Parts is cryptic because, a dash or comma is used to separate the two distinct elements of the clue; and, also the 'anagram' type of clue has been made very obvious by the presence of '(anag)' in the clue itself. However, in the rest of the book, the dash appears only as an appropriate punctuation, and it will be up to solvers to spot the anagram indicators (i.e. a word or phrase indicating some sort of mixture of letters). The following are the eight types of cryptic clues, each accompanied by a clue of the kind that you will find in Parts 2, 3 and 4:

Two meanings. Two different definitions of the same word are given: e.g. 'A fish – you stand on it!' SOLE is a fish, and also the part of the foot that you stand on.

Pun. The answer sounds like a different word: e.g. 'Stir up – quarrels, by the sound of it!' ROUSE (stir up) also sounds like ROWS (quarrels).

Hidden. The answer is hidden inside the wording of the clue: e.g. 'Leading actor – among the first arrivals' STAR (leading actor) is hidden among 'firST ARrivals'.

Reversal. The answer becomes another word when reversed, or written backwards: e.g. 'Prevent – vessels turning over'. STOP (prevent) becomes POTS (vessels) when turning over.
Anagram. The answer is made up of the letters of another word, or words, when jumbled up: e.g. 'Change – later (anag)'. ALTER (change) is a mixture of the letters of LATER.
Charade. The answer is split into two or more parts: e.g. 'Girl is given mineral – in abundance!' GAL (girl) is given ORE (mineral), to make GALORE (in abundance). Some parts of a charade clue may be abbreviations, like N (North), C (a hundred), etc.
Ins and Outs. The answer will have one word inside another: e.g. 'The fellow's in debt? Put in custody!' REMAND (put in custody) is formed by MAN (fellow) inside RED (i.e. in debt).
Bits and Pieces. Sometimes the subsidiary part of the clue has to deal with a stray item like an individual letter, and this often calls for the use of abbreviations: e.g. 'Make an arrangement to go East in an aircraft' PLANE (an aircraft) is formed from PLAN (make an arrangement) with the addition of the single letter E (East).

It is worth noting some special areas of the book – particularly Part 4. This consists of 30 thematic puzzles, some of whose answers are connected with specified topics and which also contain the conventional clues described above. The solver's attention is drawn to the 'preambles' in this Part; they are explanations of the solving methods required. Preambles are also given in Part 5. As for Part 6 all the puzzles are based upon diagrams containing heavy bars instead of the more usual blocks. Part 7 is a collection of 50 crosswords which are fully cryptic. In Part 8, the first ten puzzles contain a mixture of definition and cryptic clues; the clues for the remaining 14 puzzles are all cryptic.

The puzzles in Part 9 have one feature in common: novelty. Each of them is different in some way from the 'normal' crosswords of the book's other Parts, perhaps because of some small gimmick in an otherwise familiar pattern, or maybe through its unusual appearance. Several of the shapes used here are original, notably the ruined castle, passenger-ship, pin-table, central-heating radiator and umbrella. Despite these unfamiliar features, however, you will find solving most of them just as easy as the puzzles in the first Parts with only a few that are more difficult. Every crossword in this Part has been given a title and, wherever necessary, a clear statement of the novelty or gimmick involved and the method of solving that is required.

Part 10 ends the book with three jumbo puzzles. In the first and the last jumbos, all the clues are of the conventional cryptic kind, while in the second puzzle, both definition and cryptic clues have been used, and also a number of straightforward clues (like definitions) whose answers belong to the area of general knowledge.

Solutions are provided at the back of the book for every crossword. The answer to each cryptic clue is designed to explain exactly how it was arrived at from the original wording.

THE PUZZLES

PART 1

PLAIN PUZZLES

1

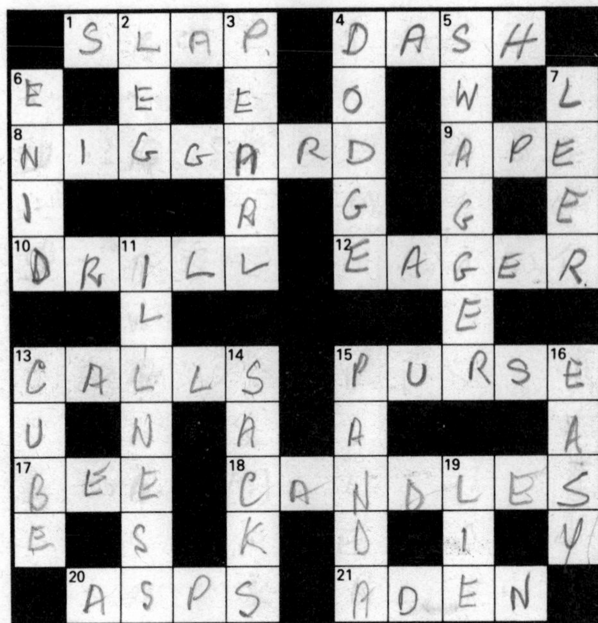

ACROSS

1. Strike with the palm (4)
4. To rush (4)
8. Miserly person (7)
9. To mimic (3)
10. Boring tool (5)
12. Keen (5)
13. Cries out (5)
15. Money container (5)
17. An insect (3)
18. Wax cylinders (7)
20. Serpents (4)
21. Middle-Eastern port (4)

DOWN

2. A limb (3)
3. A gem (5)
4. Evade (5)
5. Strut arrogantly (7)
6. Girl's name (4)
7. Sly sidelong glance (4)
11. Ailment (7)
13. Geometrical solid figure (4)
14. Dismisses from a job (5)
15. Kind of bear (5)
16. Simple (4)
19. Untruth (3)

2

ACROSS

6. Dog's house (6)
7. A regulation (4)
8. Semi-precious stone (4)
9. Larger (6)
10. A signal light (5)
12. To revile (5)
15. Horrified (6)
17. Magnitude (4)
19. A settee (4)
20. An Apache, for example (6)

DOWN

1. Army vehicle (4)
2. Stag's horn (6)
3. A sphere (5)
4. Boast (4)
5. Armadas (6)
11. Roman military force (6)
13. Next to (6)
14. To dye (5)
16. Boy's name (4)
18. Enthusiasm (4)

3

ACROSS

1. A wall painting (5)
4. Correct (5)
7. Restricted (7)
8. Scrap of cloth (3)
9. Building for horses (6)
11. List of actors (4)
13. To carry (4)
14. Concealed (6)
17. A snake (3)
18. Becoming liquid (7)
20. Precise (5)
21. To drive back (5)

DOWN

1. Stubborn animals (5)
2. A strong drink (3)
3. Small (6)
4. Went on horseback (4)
5. Wreath (7)
6. Taut (5)
10. American state (7)
12. Murderer (6)
13. Holy Book (5)
15. Boy's name (5)
16. A speck of soot (4)
19. Mischievous child (3)

4

ACROSS
1. To amuse (9)
8. Choices (7)
9. Biblical priest (3)
10. Untrue (5)
12. Break in pieces (5)
13. A finger (5)
15. Loaded (5)
16. Egg of a louse (3)
17. Small stones (7)
19. Shopkeeper (9)

DOWN
2. Meshed fabric (3)
3. Eat away (5)
4. Elephant's teeth (5)
5. A northern country (7)
6. Self-assured (9)
7. Fraudulent (9)
11. Not so heavy (7)
14. Drank heavily (5)
15. Parts of ears (5)
18. Meadow (3)

5

ACROSS

1. Male cat (3)
3. Chess pieces (7)
7. Encouraged (5)
8. Oily fruit (5)
9. Strike repeatedly (6)
10. Minute particle (4)
12. An entrance (4)
14. Church attendant (6)
18. Gleaming (5)
19. Sketched (5)
20. Died (7)
21. Neckwear (3)

DOWN

1. A digit (5)
2. Power (5)
3. Teasingly deceived (6)
4. A metal (4)
5. Raise with pulleys (5)
6. Water vapour (5)
11. Repaired (6)
12. A tomb (5)
13. A flower (5)
15. Student's allowance (5)
16. Chain of mountains (5)
17. Large jug (4)

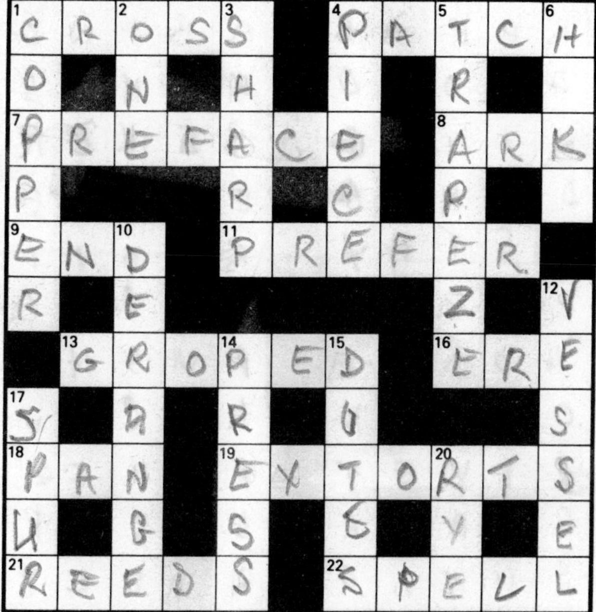

6

ACROSS

1. To traverse (5)
4. Piece stitched on (5)
7. A book's introduction (7)
8. Noah's ship (3)
9. Finish (3)
11. To like better (6)
13. Searched blindly (6)
16. Before, poetically (3)
18. Greek woodland god (3)
19. Obtains by force (7)
21. Tall marsh grasses (5)
22. A witch's charm (5)

DOWN

1. Reddish metal (6)
2. A single (3)
3. Keen-edged (5)
4. A fragment (5)
5. Circus apparatus (7)
6. A fish (4)
10. To make mad (7)
12. A ship (6)
14. Newspapers, etc. (5)
15. Shows excessive fondness (5)
17. A stimulus (4)
20. Kind of grain (3)

7

ACROSS

1. To knock (3)
3. Quivering (7)
7. Cake topping (5)
8. Bread maker (5)
9. Remain (4)
10. Spokes (5)
13. A steed (5)
15. Shove (4)
17. A bolt (5)
19. Temporary stop (5)
20. Ice-creams with fruit (7)
21. Wily (3)

DOWN

1. Sudden incursion (4)
2. A hunting-dog (7)
3. Sodden (5)
4. Shade of yellow (5)
5. Writing fluid (3)
6. Desert rodent (6)
11. To debate (7)
12. Tedious tasks (6)
14. Additional (5)
15. They are smoked (5)
16. Exceedingly (4)
18. Commercial vehicle (3)

8

ACROSS

1. Nunnery (7)
5. Kind of meat (3)
7. Boy's name (5)
8. A tooth (5)
9. To cut out (6)
11. Coastal inlet (3)
13. Commercials (3)
14. Protruded (6)
17. An instant (5)
18. Italian city (5)
20. Male pig (3)
21. A monarch's domain (7)

DOWN

1. Hidden treasure (5)
2. Nothing (3)
3. Boy's name (6)
4. Sepulchre (4)
5. A fish (7)
6. To wed (5)
10. Shedding (7)
12. A clothing fastener (6)
13. An aspirate (5)
15. A cotton fabric (5)
16. To yank (4)
19. A stick (3)

9

ACROSS

5. A meal (6)
7. The first murderer (4)
8. Wan (4)
9. Unlocked (6)
10. Great river (4)
12. Very short distance (4)
15. Royal residence (6)
17. Animal's hind quarters (4)
18. Old stringed instrument (4)
19. Soup-holder (6)

DOWN

1. Continue to hold (6)
2. Strong wind (4)
3. A partition (6)
4. Fruit with acid taste (4)
6. An implement (4)
11. Sprang up (6)
13. East Yorkshire river (6)
14. A nuisance (4)
16. A shivering fit (4)
17. Uncommon (4)

10

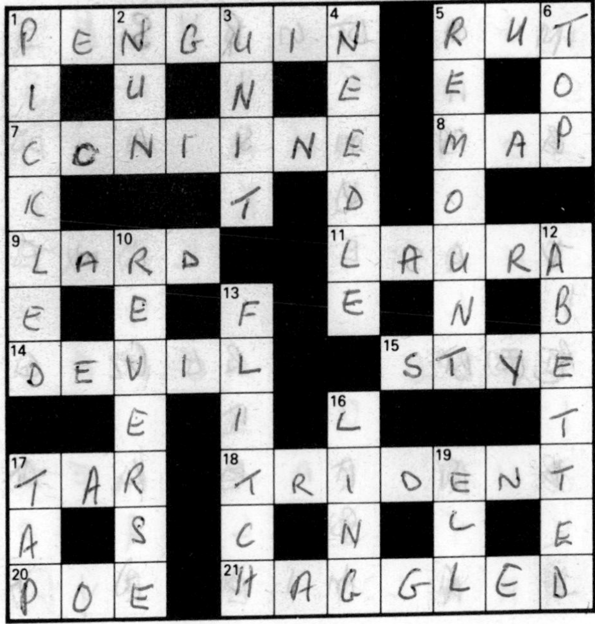

ACROSS

1. Antarctic bird (7)
5. A groove (3)
7. To imprison (7)
8. Chart (3)
9. Cooking-fat (4)
11. Girl's name (5)
14. Satan (5)
15. Inflammation on the eye-lid (4)
17. A sailor (3)
18. Three-pronged fork (7)
20. US author of horror stories (3)
21. Bargained (7)

DOWN

1. Preserved in brine (7)
2. Religious woman (3)
3. A single thing (4)
4. Sewing implement (6)
5. Climb into the saddle again (7)
6. Spinning toy (3)
10. The opposite (7)
12. Assisted (7)
13. A side of bacon (6)
16. Heather (4)
17. To hit lightly (3)
19. An old cloth measure (3)

11

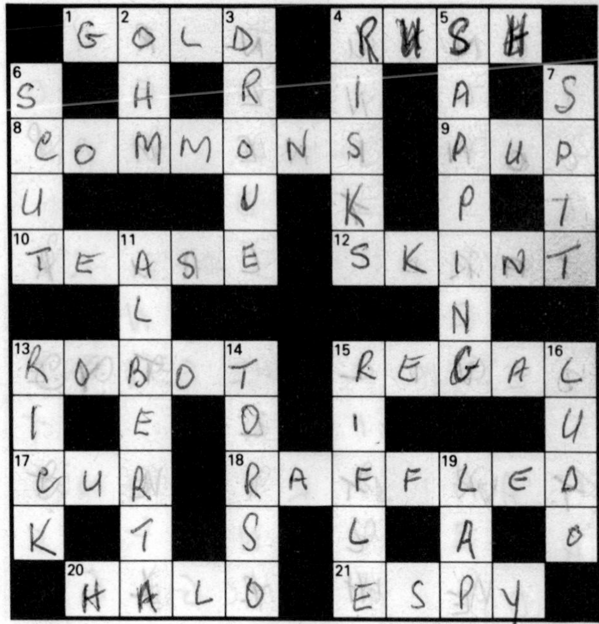

ACROSS
1. Precious metal (4)
4. To hurry (4)
8. Lower House of Parliament (7)
9. Young dog (3)
10. To tantalise (5)
12. Completely broke (5)
13. Mechanical car-maker (5)
15. Royal (5)
17. A worthless dog (3)
18. Disposed of by lottery (7)
20. Ring of light (4)
21. To notice (4)

DOWN
2. Unit of electrical resistance (3)
3. Motored (5)
4. Hazards (5)
5. Draining (7)
6. Hare's tail (4)
7. Saliva (4)
11. Canadian province (7)
13. Haystack (4)
14. Trunk of the body (5)
15. A fire-arm (5)
16. A board-game (4)
19. Circuit of a race-track (3)

12

ACROSS

6. Small shellfish (6)
7. Eject (4)
8. A graceful bird (4)
9. Ripe (6)
10. Removed by theft (5)
12. Musical instrument (5)
15. Unit of electric current (6)
17. Part of a church (4)
19. Expensive (4)
20. Swerved (6)

DOWN

1. Chinese breed of dog (4)
2. Boy's name (6)
3. Sea-spray (5)
4. Young horse (4)
5. Arrange in groups (6)
11. Wood (6)
13. To tarry (6)
14. Depart (5)
16. A nobleman (4)
18. Contended in rivalry (4)

13

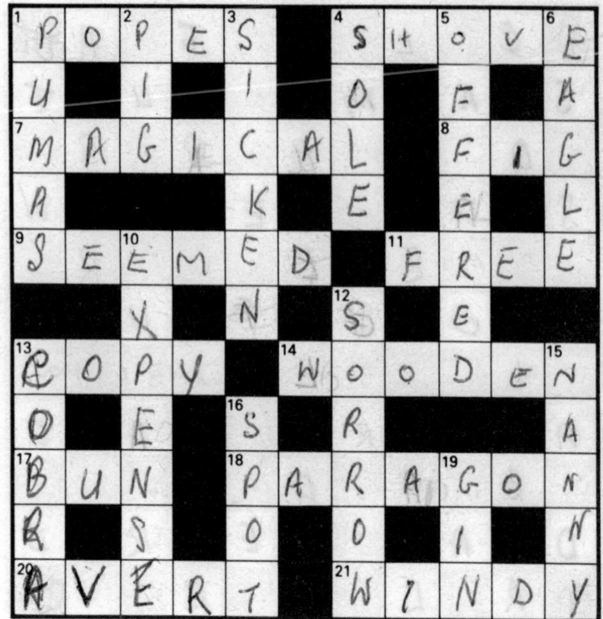

ACROSS

1. Pontiffs (5)
4. Push (5)
7. Occult (7)
8. Dried fruit (3)
9. Appeared (6)
11. Without cost (4)
13. To imitate (4)
14. Made of timber (6)
17. Small cake (3)
18. Model of excellence (7)
20. Ward off (5)
21. Breezy (5)

DOWN

1. Cougars (5)
2. A swine (3)
3. To nauseate (6)
4. A flat-fish (4)
5. Tendered (7)
6. Bird of prey (5)
10. Cost (7)
12. Grief (6)
13. Poisonous snake (5)
15. Child's nurse (5)
16. Catch sight of (4)
19. Alcoholic drink (3)

14

ACROSS

1. Throttled (9)
8. Traveller's baggage (7)
9. An insect (3)
10. Small room in ship (5)
12. Performing (5)
13. Buckets (5)
15. Part of a carpenter's joint (5)
16. Frequently, poetically (3)
17. Yearly publications (7)
19. Guardian (9)

DOWN

2. To pull (3)
3. Once more (5)
4. Avarice (5)
5. High spirits (7)
6. Lancashire resort (9)
7. Theatrical quality (9)
11. A bubble on the skin (7)
14. To slope (5)
15. Coat of uniform (5)
18. Since (3)

15

ACROSS

1. Type of aeroplane (3)
3. Flower-seller (7)
7. Jumbled (5)
8. Drive out (5)
9. Supernatural (6)
10. Extra runs (4)
12. A slight quarrel (4)
14. An outlaw (6)
18. A feather (5)
19. Organ of the body (5)
20. Pampered (7)
21. To regret (3)

DOWN

1. Name for an elephant (5)
2. Poisonous (5)
3. Violin (6)
4. Cattle (4)
5. To insinuate (5)
6. Speaks (5)
11. Narrative poem or song (6)
12. A theme (5)
13. Discovered (5)
15. English seaport (5)
16. A number (5)
17. A Lakeland mountain (4)

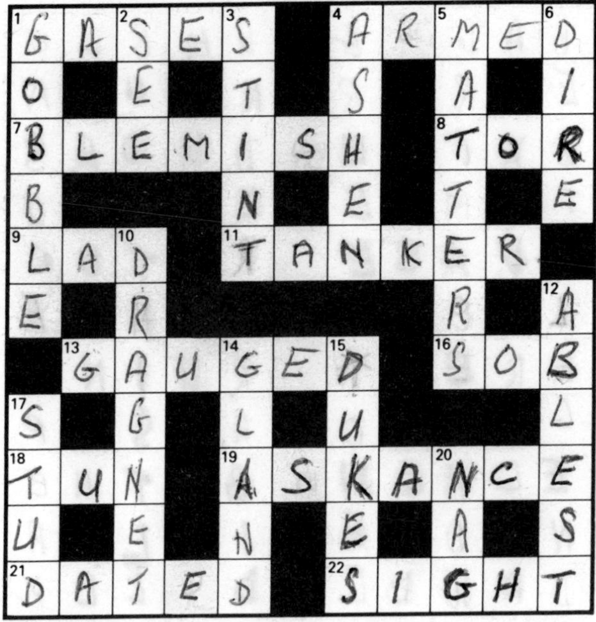

16

ACROSS

1. Oxygen, hydrogen, etc. (5)
4. Equipped with weapons (5)
7. A flaw (7)
8. A hill (3)
9. A youth (3)
11. Oil-carrying ship (6)
13. Measured (6)
16. Weep convulsively (3)
18. Wine-cask (3)
19. Sideways (7)
21. Outmoded (5)
22. Vision (5)

DOWN

1. Swallow hastily (6)
2. Behold (3)
3. Allotted amount of work (5)
4. Very pale (5)
5. Affairs (7)
6. Dreadful (4)
10. Dredging device (4-3)
12. Most skilful (6)
14. The pancreas is one (5)
15. Highest noblemen (5)
17. Horse farm (4)
20. Inferior horse (3)

17

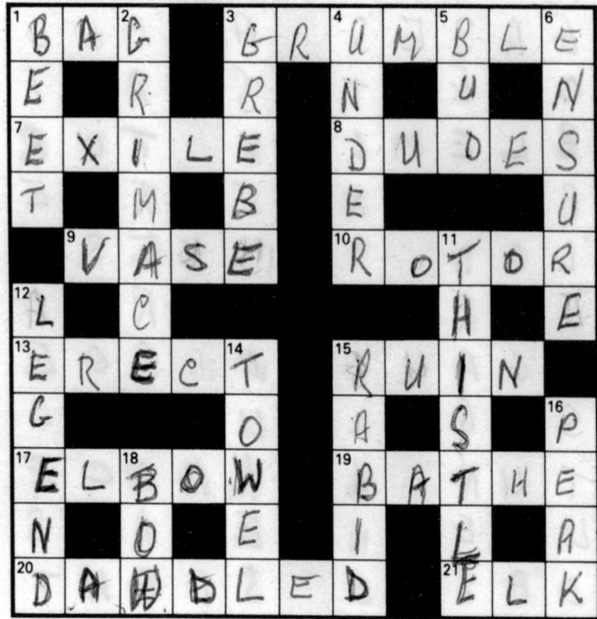

ACROSS

1. A sack (3)
3. To grouse (7)
7. Banishment (5)
8. US dandies (5)
9. A flower jar (4)
10. Spinning part of dynamo (5)
13. To build (5)
15. Destroy completely (4)
17. Joint of the arm (5)
19. To wash oneself (5)
20. Dilly-dallied (7)
21. The moose (3)

DOWN

1. A source of sugar (4)
2. A wry face (7)
3. Diving bird (5)
4. Beneath (5)
5. Flower not yet open (3)
6. Make certain (6)
11. Emblem of Scotland (7)
12. Mythical story (6)
14. A drying cloth (5)
15. Fanatical (5)
16. Mountain top (4)
18. Neckwear (3)

18

ACROSS

1. A shoemaker (7)
5. Dense mist (3)
7. One who gives (5)
8. Girl's name (5)
9. Native of Troy (6)
11. Climbing plant (3)
13. A curve (3)
14. To secure with a rope (6)
17. To elude (5)
18. A special skill (5)
20. Edward, in short (3)
21. Obstacles (7)

DOWN

1. A future officer (5)
2. Refuse container (3)
3. Caterpillars, for example (6)
4. Precious stone (4)
5. To provide (7)
6. Fielding position in cricket (5)
10. Enclosure with fruit-trees (7)
12. Drinking-mug (6)
13. Skilful (5)
15. Garden tools (5)
16. Network (4)
19. To be ill (3)

19

ACROSS
5. Edible root (6)
7. A story (4)
8. End of a cigarette (4)
9. Putrid (6)
10. Moist (4)
12. Poems (4)
15. Type of hound (6)
17. Hold tightly (4)
18. Smoothing implement (4)
19. To frolic (6)

DOWN
1. Endured (6)
2. A shellfish (4)
3. Asserted (6)
4. A vent for smoke (4)
6. Conservative (4)
11. Schoolteacher (6)
13. Seaman (6)
14. Male deer (4)
16. Parched (4)
17. Umbrella (4)

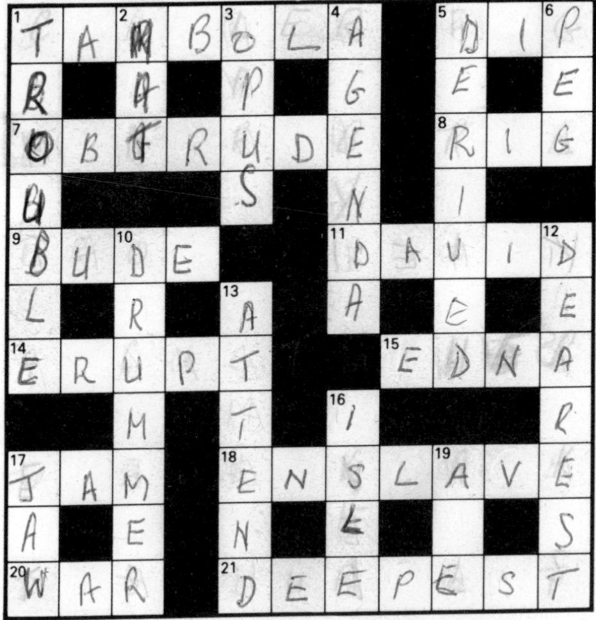

20

ACROSS

1. A form of bingo (7)
5. A short swim (3)
7. Thrust oneself forward (7)
8. Oil-drilling installation (3)
9. Cornish resort (4)
11. Patron Saint of Wales (5)
14. Explode like a volcano (5)
15. Girl's name (4)
17. A preserve (3)
18. To put in bondage (7)
20. Military hostilities (3)
21. Most profound (7)

DOWN

1. Bother (7)
2. Floor covering (3)
3. Musical work (4)
4. Items for discussion (6)
5. Drawn from a source (7)
6. Kind of pin (3)
10. A tympanist (7)
12. Darling (7)
13. To be present at (6)
16. Area cut off by water (4)
17. Part of the head (3)
19. High card (3)

21

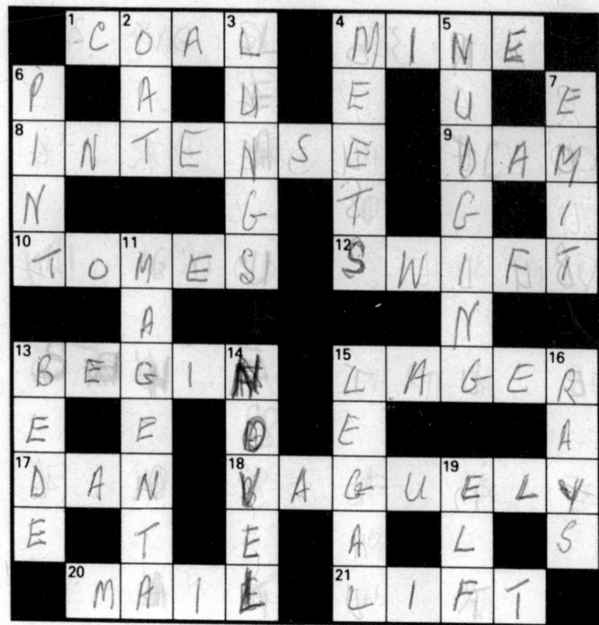

ACROSS

1. Type of fuel (4)
4. A pit (4)
8. Extreme (7)
9. Mother of animals (3)
10. Large books (5)
12. Speedy (5)
13. Commence (5)
15. Light ale (5)
17. Biblical tribe (3)
18. Imprecisely (7)
20. Chain armour (4)
21. Hoist (4)

DOWN

2. Type of cereal (3)
3. Organs of breathing (5)
4. Encounters (5)
5. Elbowing gently (7)
6. Liquid measure (4)
7. Issue forth (4)
11. Reddish purple (7)
13. Venerable old historian (4)
14. Fictitious tale (5)
15. Lawful (5)
16. Beams of light (4)
19. Mischievous fairy (3)

22

ACROSS

6. Type of straw-hat (6)
7. Dutch cheese (4)
8. Slide sideways (4)
9. Kind of meat (6)
10. Fragrant herb (5)
12. Web-footed birds (5)
15. Hot remains of a fire (6)
17. Type of bean (4)
19. Modern dwelling (4)
20. Type of overcoat (6)

DOWN

1. A sudden tug (4)
2. Bicycle for two (6)
3. Tropical trees (5)
4. English county (4)
5. Lords (6)
11. Picnic basket (6)
13. Naval flag (6)
14. Former Russian rulers (5)
16. A way out (4)
18. Period of time (4)

23

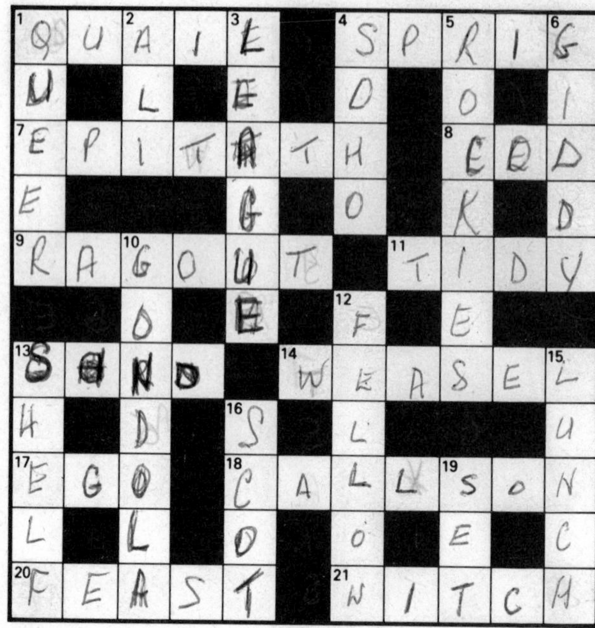

ACROSS

1. Bird of partridge family (5)
4. Ornamental spray (5)
7. Gravestone inscription (7)
8. A fish (3)
9. Kind of goulash (6)
11. Neat (4)
13. Granular substance (4)
14. The stoat is a large one (6)
17. The self (3)
18. Visits (5,2)
20. Banquet (5)
21. A hag (5)

DOWN

1. Strange (5)
2. Ex-champion boxer (3)
3. Nautical measure (6)
4. Part of London (4)
5. North American mountains (7)
6. Dizzy (5)
10. Venetian boat (7)
12. University don (6)
13. A ledge (5)
15. Midday meal (5)
16. A Glaswegian, for example (4)
19. A group (3)

24

ACROSS

1. Plentiful amount (9)
8. Shelter for ships (7)
9. Wonderment (3)
10. A clan (5)
12. Reasoning power (5)
13. English race-course (5)
15. Explode (5)
16. Loud noise (3)
17. To fawn upon (7)
19. Large speaking-trumpet (9)

DOWN

2. A piece of soap (3)
3. Loop with movable knot (5)
4. Pertaining to the ear (5)
5. A blunder (7)
6. Scottish islands (9)
7. A woodland plant (5-4)
11. Infuriate (7)
14. Jewelled head-dress (5)
15. Turn red (5)
18. Girl's name (3)

25

ACROSS

1. Domestic pet (3)
3. Horrific creature (7)
7. A colour (5)
8. Period of rule (5)
9. Fit of ill-humour (6)
10. To engrave (4)
12. Farm storehouse (4)
14. Yapped (6)
18. A lid (5)
19. Tests of knowledge (5)
20. To perplex (7)
21. A fool (3)

DOWN

1. First appearance (5)
2. Stable-boy (5)
3. Trough for fodder (6)
4. The accepted standard (4)
5. To contort (5)
6. A stock-farm (5)
11. To fondle (6)
12. Salted meat (5)
13. A crow (5)
15. Australian bear (5)
16. Writing-tables (5)
17. Spoken (4)

26

ACROSS
1. Girl's name (5)
4. Unit of weight for gems (5)
7. A glass (7)
8. Cutting-tool (3)
9. To steal from (3)
11. A colour (6)
13. Obstructs (6)
16. Organ of sight (3)
18. Japanese monetary unit (3)
19. Wander aimlessly (7)
21. A happening (5)
22. Frozen dew (5)

DOWN
1. One's inborn character (6)
2. The total (3)
3. A mixture of metals (5)
4. Christmas song (5)
5. Bring back to former state (7)
6. Place larger than a village (4)
10. Weighing instrument (7)
12. Animal that unearths rabbits (6)
14. Heavenly body (5)
15. Warm neckwear (5)
17. Tube round a wheel-rim (4)
20. A twosome (3)

27

ACROSS
1. A sudden thrust (3)
3. Grooves (7)
7. Beast of the desert (5)
8. Staple food (5)
9. A lot (4)
10. Block of metal (5)
13. Hell (5)
15. Listen! (4)
17. Sharp-edged implement (5)
19. Mediterranean island (5)
20. Suffer from the heat (7)
21. A high mountain (3)

DOWN
1. A hoisting apparatus (4)
2. Attack with artillery (7)
3. A young mare (5)
4. Jewish religious leader (5)
5. To be in debt (3)
6. Staid (6)
11. Large ape (7)
12. Counties (6)
14. A small fish (5)
15. Greek epic poet (5)
16. A fresh-water fish (4)
18. Girl's name (3)

28

ACROSS

1. Bird with large beak (7)
5. Strike gently (3)
7. To dispute (5)
8. A group of eight (5)
9. Complete (6)
11. A tree (3)
13. Prohibition (3)
14. An emergency (6)
17. Angry (5)
18. Less good (5)
20. A passing craze (3)
21. Of a white metallic colour (7)

DOWN

1. A smoothing tool (5)
2. Fall behind (3)
3. A fruit (6)
4. A niche (4)
5. They make earthenware (7)
6. Emblem of Red Indian tribe (5)
10. Drinking-mug (7)
12. Bricklayer's tool (6)
13. Short (5)
15. Out of sorts (5)
16. Not as much (4)
19. Fish-eggs (3)

29

ACROSS
5. Type of pepper (6)
7. Wander (4)
8. Ingredient of medicine (4)
9. Composition for church choir (6)
10. Identical (4)
12. White flakes (4)
15. Opportunity (6)
17. Raw hide (4)
18. Renown (4)
19. Of neither sex (6)

DOWN
1. Enchants (6)
2. To thrash (4)
3. Native of Great Britain (6)
4. London gallery (4)
6. A former tsar (4)
11. A primate (6)
13. Case for banknotes (6)
14. To signify (4)
16. High temperature (4)
17. A stoned fruit (4)

30

ACROSS
1. Crops gathered in (7)
5. Drunkard (3)
7. Ingredient of milk-pudding (7)
8. Girl's name (3)
9. Yorkshire city (4)
11. God of love (5)
14. Short nails (5)
15. An East European type (4)
17. Enemy (3)
18. Bandits (7)
20. Writing implement (3)
21. Intertwined (7)

DOWN
1. Small axe (7)
2. Travelling salesman, in short (3)
3. Public School (4)
4. Sleeplike state (6)
5. Surgeon's knife (7)
6. A plaything (3)
10. Church reading-desk (7)
12. Invented (7)
13. Accompany protectively (6)
16. To stupefy (4)
17. A dandy (3)
19. Boring tool (3)

31

ACROSS

1. Frigid (4)
4. Labyrinth (4)
8. Permitted (7)
9. A label (3)
10. Hues (5)
12. Give way (5)
13. First Greek letter (5)
15. Sat for an artist (5)
17. Australian bird (3)
18. Protected (7)
20. Dread (4)
21. Level (4)

DOWN

2. To lubricate (3)
3. Daybreaks (5)
4. Covered with wet earth (5)
5. Plucked instruments (7)
6. Dray (4)
7. Old (4)
11. Sea-god (7)
13. Highest point (4)
14. Wrath (5)
15. Location (5)
16. Extinct bird (4)
19. Female deer (3)

32

ACROSS

6. Wild dog-like animal (6)
7. Aid (4)
8. Gusto (4)
9. Bundle of firewood (6)
10. To tilt in a tournament (5)
12. A residence (5)
15. Busy (6)
17. A set piece of work (4)
19. Handle of a sword (4)
20. Lime-tree (6)

DOWN

1. Mistiness (4)
2. Slides on ice (6)
3. High steep rock (5)
4. A brutal ruffian (4)
5. Blossoms (6)
11. Hot-house plant (6)
13. Belgian port (6)
14. Food often served with custard (5)
16. A mere jot (4)
18. To ooze (4)

33

ACROSS

1. A canal boat (5)
4. East Europeans (5)
7. Legal experts (7)
8. Tip of a pen (3)
9. To anger (6)
11. A home for doves (4)
13. Treaty (4)
14. Easter headwear, perhaps (6)
17. It propels a boat (3)
18. Blown up with explosives (7)
20. Stale-smelling (5)
21. Very recently (5)

DOWN

1. A swelling (5)
2. Uncooked (3)
3. Vigour (6)
4. An upright pillar (4)
5. Cathedral city (7)
6. Type of fur (5)
10. Chronicles (7)
12. Realm (6)
13. Indisputable evidence (5)
15. Hot drink, like punch (5)
16. To follow an order (4)
19. To pull with a rope (3)

34

ACROSS

1. Defective (9)
8. SE coastal resort (7)
9. Receptacle for ashes (3)
10. Valued (5)
12. Male duck (5)
13. Poetry (5)
15. To reside (5)
16. Centre of the solar system (3)
17. Exempted from duty (7)
19. Uprightness (9)

DOWN

2. To spoil (3)
3. Kind of antelope (5)
4. Demon (5)
5. Campaign against Infidels (7)
6. Produce offhand (9)
7. Interval (9)
11. Boy's name (7)
14. Vote into office (5)
15. An old coin (5)
18. Piece of turf (3)

35

ACROSS

1. Youngster (3)
3. Know beforehand (7)
7. South American mountains (5)
8. A board-game (5)
9. Sulky (6)
10. A cry of woe (4)
12. Kind of meat (4)
14. Desires (6)
18. A fruit (5)
19. Animal's skin disease (5)
20. Type of cathedral (7)
21. Nevertheless (3)

DOWN

1. Alloy of copper and zinc (5)
2. Sing like Alpine people (5)
3. Quicker (6)
4. Instrument of torture (4)
5. Home of a Biblical queen (5)
6. Support for a canvas (5)
11. To boil gently (6)
12. Religious song (5)
13. North Yorkshire town (5)
15. Sweet thick fluid (5)
16. Mixture of rain and snow (5)
17. A girdle (4)

36

ACROSS

1. Sinks teeth into (5)
4. Domestic cock (5)
7. Event arranged in advance (7)
8. A thick covering (3)
9. To moo (3)
11. Hold in custody (6)
13. Device for turning lights down (6)
16. Not strict (3)
18. Decay (3)
19. Pin for twisting thread (7)
21. Religious belief (5)
22. To throw out (5)

DOWN

1. To bewilder (6)
2. Contribution imposed by state (3)
3. Uninjured (5)
4. Top of a wave (5)
5. Biased (7)
6. Close at hand (4)
10. Shrill sound (7)
12. An adept (6)
14. Meditated (5)
15. German river (5)
17. Boy's name (4)
20. To pass away (3)

37

ACROSS

1. Child's protection when eating (3)
3. A pistol-case (7)
7. Later (5)
8. Tediously commonplace (5)
9. Cathedral dignitary (4)
10. To feel longing (5)
13. To imagine (5)
15. Shrub (4)
17. An anaesthetic (5)
19. Male singing voice (5)
20. Treachery (7)
21. To sever (3)

DOWN

1. Sound of a donkey (4)
2. In an intermediate space (7)
3. One of the Great Lakes (5)
4. A corridor (5)
5. A weight (3)
6. Become less severe (6)
11. A poison (7)
12. Result of an action (6)
14. Short distances (5)
15. Conductor's stick (5)
16. To worry (4)
18. To weed (3)

38

ACROSS

1. A spear (7)
5. Nocturnal creature (3)
7. Classical language (5)
8. Middle part of the body (5)
9. An American (6)
11. Attempt (3)
13. Item of headwear (3)
14. Plan (6)
17. Girl's name (5)
18. Customary (5)
20. Scheduled to arrive (3)
21. Water-tank (7)

DOWN

1. Jovial (5)
2. Tub (3)
3. Songbird (6)
4. Small amphibian (4)
5. Stiff hair (7)
6. Shabby (5)
10. Plant producing dry fruit (3-4)
12. Happens (6)
13. Damp (5)
15. Girl's name (5)
16. Cosmetic powder (4)
19. Yorkshire river (3)

39

ACROSS

5. Liquid measures (6)
7. Seethe (4)
8. Mate (4)
9. Mounted (6)
10. A flower (4)
12. Turned up (4)
15. Season (6)
17. Confined (4)
18. Cutting tool (4)
19. Tanned (6)

DOWN

1. Dry measure (6)
2. Tot (4)
3. Procure (6)
4. Flex (4)
6. Ornamental band (4)
11. Move clumsily (6)
13. Standard (6)
14. Dreary (4)
16. Eastern language (4)
17. Supplicate (4)

40

ACROSS

1. Famous astronomer (7)
5. Morass (3)
7. Modified (7)
8. Grave (3)
9. Jealousy (4)
11. Difficult (5)
14. Heating apparatus (5)
15. A monster (4)
17. Natural mineral (3)
18. Italian dish (7)
20. Coin (3)
21. Withdraw from contest (7)

DOWN

1. Types of beards (7)
2. Destiny (3)
3. Piece of mischief (4)
4. Most ancient (6)
5. Sun-bathing (7)
6. Object of worship (3)
10. Intense (7)
12. European language (7)
13. Spikes on barley (6)
16. Finished (4)
17. Regal symbol (3)
19. On strike (3)

41

ACROSS

1. Thick slice of cake (4)
4. Try to achieve (4)
8. Violent storm (7)
9. Vegetable case (3)
10. Unyielding (5)
12. A sewer (5)
13. Strips off (5)
15. Connects (5)
17. Related (3)
18. React (7)
20. Become ragged at the edge (4)
21. Weak-minded (4)

DOWN

2. To beat (3)
3. Harmonise (5)
4. Replete (5)
5. Elucidate (7)
6. Agitate (4)
7. Paradise (4)
11. Gatherer of left-overs (7)
13. Long weapon (4)
14. Gruff and grumpy (5)
15. Heels over (5)
16. Splash (4)
19. No longer available (3)

42

ACROSS

6. Subdued grumbling (6)
7. Taunt (4)
8. Attired (4)
9. Dangers (6)
10. Soak (5)
12. Sour substances (5)
15. Issue (6)
17. Invites (4)
19. Meagre (4)
20. Instruments (6)

DOWN

1. Copious (4)
2. Claggy stuff (6)
3. Juicy fruit (5)
4. Slightly open (4)
5. Sounded forth (6)
11. Meddle (6)
13. Accusation (6)
14. Criminal (5)
16. Preach noisily (4)
18. Monarch (4)

43

ACROSS

1. Drugged (5)
4. Powder (5)
7. Accuse publicly (7)
8. Illuminated (3)
9. Examined critically (6)
11. Violet-blue dye (4)
13. Plunder (4)
14. Prayer-book (6)
17. Attention (3)
18. Item (7)
20. Drain (5)
21. Garments (5)

DOWN

1. Preliminary sketch (5)
2. The norm (3)
3. Slaver (6)
4. Bark (4)
5. Hilly areas (7)
6. Glorify (5)
10. Bird (7)
12. Season (6)
13. Casts off (5)
15. English city (5)
16. Retreat (4)
19. Strong horse (3)

44

ACROSS

1. Short passage (9)
8. Make fragrant (7)
9. Solemn person (3)
10. Record (5)
12. Fragment of bread (5)
13. Temptress (5)
15. European (5)
16. Admit (3)
17. Marvel (7)
19. Contemplates (9)

DOWN

2. Drink (3)
3. Player (5)
4. Written in mystic symbols (5)
5. Extravagant (7)
6. A going up to heaven (9)
7. Severely criticised (9)
11. Canadian city (7)
14. Designates (5)
15. Fragment (5)
18. Automobile (3)

45

ACROSS
1. Vessel (3)
3. Hide (7)
7. Imagine (5)
8. Broad and slow (5)
9. Plain (6)
10. Part of a brake (4)
12. Smart (4)
14. Firework (6)
18. Dance music (5)
19. A pansy, for example (5)
20. Rejections (7)
21. Silent (3)

DOWN
1. Traitor (5)
2. Flash (5)
3. Taste (6)
4. Hermit's dwelling (4)
5. Animal's burrow (5)
6. Bolt (5)
11. Artist's material (6)
12. Trimmed (5)
13. Boy's name (5)
15. Despondency (5)
16. Domain (5)
17. Icelandic tale (4)

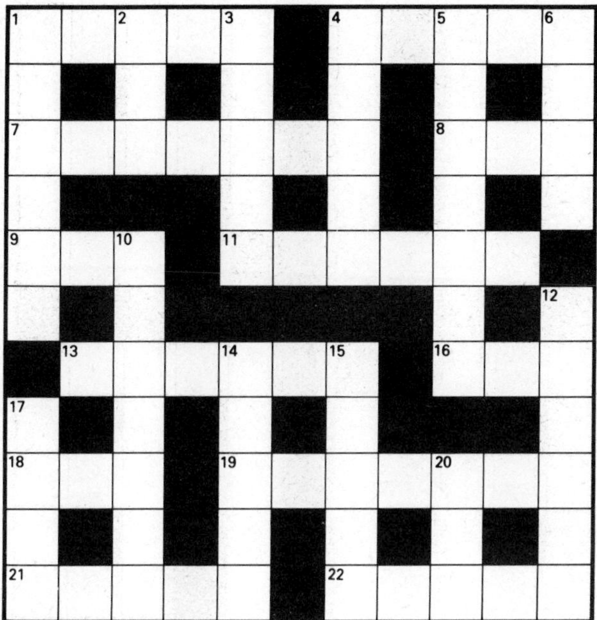

46

ACROSS
1. Coop (5)
4. Wild cat (5)
7. Marine shells (7)
8. Furious (3)
9. A handle (3)
11. Surviving (6)
13. Unfortunate condition (6)
16. English river (3)
18. Tint (3)
19. Confident (7)
21. Dance (5)
22. Indentation (5)

DOWN
1. Ply with embarrassing questions (6)
2. Muscular convulsion (3)
3. Split (5)
4. Beginning (5)
5. One appointed to stand (7)
6. Move round and round (4)
10. Large old vessel (7)
12. Draw (6)
14. Former film-star (5)
15. Bent nail (5)
17. Make keen (4)
20. Knack (3)

47

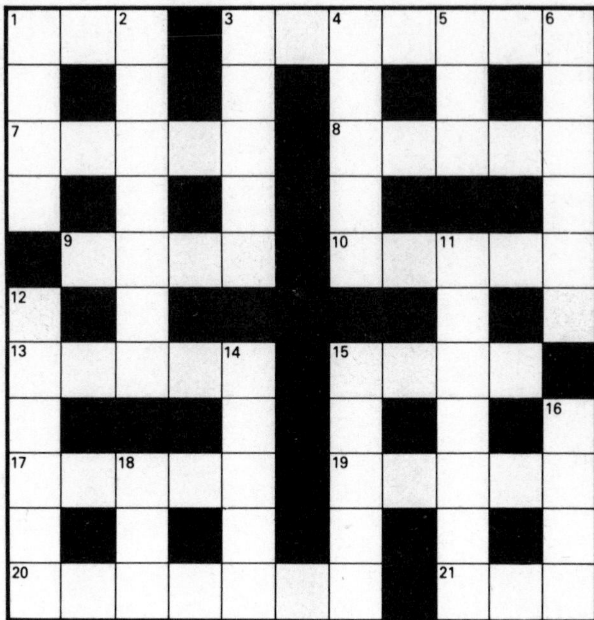

ACROSS

1. Ox with hump (3)
3. Flap in the air (7)
7. Holy book (5)
8. General rule (5)
9. Welfare (4)
10. Foreign currency unit (5)
13. Thrush (5)
15. Wear away (4)
17. Desert (5)
19. Open to view (5)
20. Rotted organic mixture (7)
21. Disseminate (3)

DOWN

1. Mark of slavery (4)
2. Nuclei (7)
3. Last (5)
4. Corrupting influence (5)
5. Beat (3)
6. Forest officer (6)
11. Members of team (7)
12. Pertaining to space travel (6)
14. Numbers game (5)
15. Obsolete silver coin (5)
16. Mental agitation (4)
18. Border (3)

48

ACROSS

1. The amount held (7)
5. Difficulty (3)
7. Reptile (5)
8. Carouse (5)
9. Classical poet (6)
11. Suburb of London (3)
13. Trophy (3)
14. Row gently (6)
17. Of pale complexion (5)
18. Cunning (5)
20. English or Scottish river (3)
21. First principle (7)

DOWN

1. Professional trainer (5)
2. Make a careless slip (3)
3. Enhance (6)
4. Elevated stretch of water (4)
5. Failed to follow suit (7)
6. Downstairs (5)
10. Repartee (7)
12. Anklet, for instance (6)
13. Dealt competently (5)
15. Bring to bear (5)
16. Cattle-shed (4)
19. Rage (3)

49

ACROSS
5. Dying away (6)
7. Appear dimly (4)
8. Foreign cheese (4)
9. Set down (6)
10. News agency (4)
12. Long coarse nap (4)
15. Fish (6)
17. Wounding remark (4)
18. State of the USA (4)
19. Willow-tree (6)

DOWN
1. Repeater (6)
2. Tall building (4)
3. Flinch (6)
4. Centre (4)
6. Dupe (4)
11. Lack of proper respect (6)
13. Boy's name (6)
14. Disorder (4)
16. Something long and thin (4)
17. Old battle-axe (4)

50

ACROSS

1. Predatory bird (7)
5. Brood (3)
7. European country (7)
8. Liable (3)
9. Distorted (4)
11. In due course (5)
14. Kind of bag-net (5)
15. Region (4)
17. Travel on snow (3)
18. Adorn (7)
20. Type of dog (3)
21. Disciplined (7)

DOWN

1. Material for base of road (7)
2. Vigour (3)
3. Woe is me! (4)
4. A snip (6)
5. Beginner (7)
6. Add up (3)
10. Interpreting (7)
12. Extended (7)
13. Frustrate (6)
16. Air (4)
17. Bribe (3)
19. Hostelry (3)

PART 2

SLIGHTLY CRYPTIC PUZZLES

51

ACROSS

1. Part of the leg (5)
4. One who wagers (7)
8. Umpire (7)
9. Australian dog – making noise disappear! (5)
10. An annoying child (4)
11. Lying next to (8)
13. Tentacle (6)
14. Saturated (6)
17. Altering (8)
19. Soft shapeless mass (4)
22. Dark brown colour – as pie (anag.) (5)
23. Adhesive label (7)
24. Perfumed (7)
25. Old doctor – a bloodsucker! (5)

DOWN

1. To pulsate (5)
2. To set ablaze (7)
3. A plucked instrument (4)
4. Angled (anag.) – getting a girl! (6)
5. A go-between (8)
6. Cavalryman's weapon (5)
7. Sat on a perch (7)
12. NCO – cloth worker! (8)
13. Adjusts lens (7)
15. Joint of the hand (7)
16. Still new (6)
18. Large enough – used in samples! (5)
20. Protection for doorway (5)
21. A testament – for Shakespeare? (4)

52

ACROSS

6. Ran mile (anag.) – for a soft drink! (7)
7. Head man (5)
8. Casual footwear (6)
9. Glass to see through (6)
10. Rehearsing (10)
12. Not frightened off (10)
16. Receive – cap, etc. (anag.) (6)
17. Human beings (6)
18. An outcast – drive back, back! (5)
19. Worrying over trifles (7)

DOWN

1. Kind of statistics – very important! (5)
2. To ridicule in a skit (4,2)
3. Legislative body – male, in part! (anag.) (10)
4. Articles (6)
5. Tell in detail – about a nobleman! (7)
9. Small tornado at sea (5-5)
11. Door-rapper (7)
13. Soccer or cricket team (6)
14. Sleepy (6)
15. Long flat piece of timber (5)

53

ACROSS

1. Newly enlisted servicemen (8)
5. Mark left by wound—in man's cartilage (4)
9. Painful muscular contraction (5)
10. Affect deeply (7)
11. Birds with long legs—stems, by the sound of it! (6)
12. Ancient Italian (5)
14. Trees—for senior members! (6)
16. To be adjacent to (6)
19. Projecting edge of roof (5)
21. Ask to come (6)
24. Propelling a ball (7)
25. Less wild (5)
26. Impolite—showed regret, we hear! (4)
27. Country folk (8)

DOWN

1. A grain—right on top of frozen water! (4)
2. Mapped (7)
3. Higher (5)
4. Desire for drink (6)
6. The best of the milk (5)
7. One rants (anag.)—resounding! (8)
8. Treated mercifully (6)
13. A month (8)
15. A vast country—USA, Sir? (anag.) (6)
17. Backless kind of sofa (7)
18. A thrill (6)
20. Five were in debt—gave a pledge (5)
22. Ballots (5)
23. Makes a mistake (4)

54

ACROSS

1. Large supporting beam (6)
5. Stared fiercely (6)
9. Tied with cord – grunts! (anag.) (6)
10. Like a picturesque landscape (6)
11. To jog (4)
12. Followed closely (8)
14. Smear (6)
16. Prepared for grass – as tennis stars are! (6)
19. Pestered (8)
21. Officer's assistant – in regalia, I'd expect (4)
22. Give pleasure to – Reginald, with beer! (6)
23. Expenditure (6)
24. Deviser of puzzles – the dog! (6)
25. Cruel pervert (6)

DOWN

2. Meanwhile – bury 'im! (7)
3. Hesitated to believe (7)
4. Lists of pupils – greet Sirs (anag.) (9)
6. Intermixed, in drinks (5)
7. Renovated (7)
8. Made mind up (7)
13. Diligent (9)
14. Globes (7)
15. Vertical (7)
17. Raised to a high position (7)
18. Makes beloved (7)
20. Loves (anag.) – to do crosswords! (5)

55

ACROSS

1. Polar regions – in cataract (anag.) (10)
7. Irish hockey – throwing violently! (7)
8. Debentures (5)
10. Communists (4)
11. A month (8)
13. Part of shirt (6)
15. Rural (6)
17. Inspected (8)
18. A continent (4)
21. Feature of flames in general – to scorch! (5)
22. Deliberately sink – a coal-vessel! (7)
23. Illegal intruder (10)

DOWN

1. Warmed and dried (5)
2. Labour (4)
3. Tattered – getting playfully teased! (6)
4. Roman Emperor (8)
5. Get in touch with – to study discretion! (7)
6. Letters of the alphabet – eccentric types! (10)
9. Very tall building (10)
12. Indolence (8)
14. An apprentice (7)
16. Expanse of water in the Middle East (3,3)
19. Greek woodland god – stray (anag.) (5)
20. Embraces (4)

56

ACROSS

1. Photograph books (6)
4. Iron and copper, for example (6)
8. An upland summit (7)
10. Hang in the air (5)
11. Regard with esteem (7)
12. A sweetmeat – little Andrew's after a hundred! (5)
13. Mercury (11)
18. Old Testament law-giver (5)
19. Tin-ores (anag.) – hoarded for future use! (2,5)
22. Parasitic insect (5)
23. Coining (7)
24. Manner, with Saint – chaste (6)
25. Trader – one who gives out cards! (6)

DOWN

1. On land – tree and mineral! (6)
2. Ringers – beauties, we hear! (5)
3. Bishop's head-dress (5)
5. Moral (7)
6. Go forward (7)
7. Sprinkles – small branches of blossom! (6)
9. An alkali metal (9)
14. Defective (7)
15. Jewellery-cases (7)
16. Badge (6)
17. Mendicant (6)
20. A feeling (5)
21. Type of window – for Oxford college! (5)

57

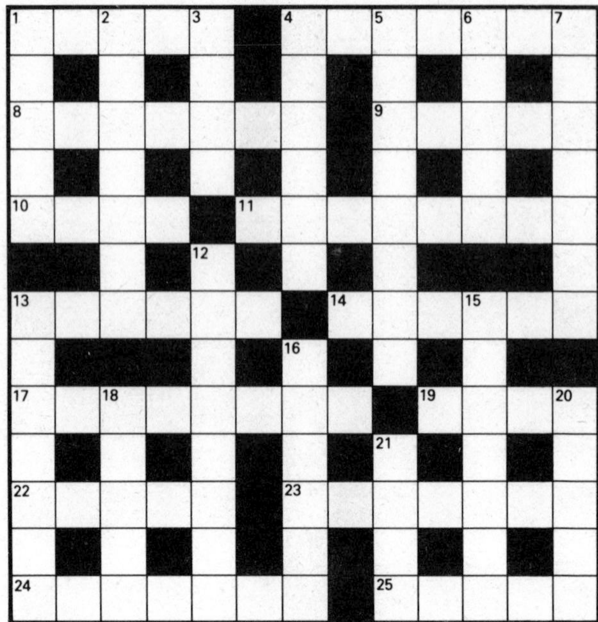

ACROSS

1. Brain's protective case (5)
4. Robbing with violence (7)
8. Cringed – one who lacks courage, by the sound of it! (7)
9. African country (5)
10. Despatched (4)
11. Casual trousers (8)
13. Body tissue – sounds like shellfish! (6)
14. Washes lightly (6)
17. Grip cans (anag.) – scratching (8)
19. A fellow – making a crack! (4)
22. Excessive (5)
23. Glowered (7)
24. Child acquired on marriage (7)
25. To harass (5)

DOWN

1. Religious groups (5)
2. Removes from reel (7)
3. Entice (4)
4. Interfere – getting an award, we hear! (6)
5. Enormous (8)
6. Fatuous (5)
7. Tumblers – giving spectacles! (7)
12. Old trading boats – cutters! (8)
13. Where antiques, etc., are displayed (7)
15. Student (7)
16. Complete agreement (6)
18. Crest of a hill – in Cambridgeshire! (5)
20. An Irishman (5)
21. The pair of them (4)

58

ACROSS

6. Rebuke—making travelling salesman roam! (7)
7. Fencer's weapon—used in crosswords! (5)
8. Type of bean—for a sprinter? (6)
9. Remove from high position (6)
10. Ali Baba's pass-word (4,6)
12. Eating place (6-4)
16. Small private room (6)
17. Rusted (anag.)—here's a cleaning cloth! (6)
18. Grind the teeth (5)
19. One taking part in contest (7)

DOWN

1. A planet—seen in heaven, usually! (5)
2. Horse not fully broken in (6)
3. Too heavy (10)
4. Steals—inferior beer! (6)
5. Tedious (7)
9. Dejected (10)
11. Ready and eager (7)
13. Maintain emphatically (6)
14. My rise (anag.)—bringing wretchedness! (6)
15. Swiss city (5)

59

ACROSS

1. Place for a soak (8)
5. A mountain-gap—overtake! (4)
9. Lower part of arm (5)
10. Duped (7)
11. Encourages—some breakfast, son? (4,2)
12. Use divining-rod—in meadow, searching (5)
14. Refined women (6)
16. I am Len (anag.)—a servant (6)
19. Pried (5)
21. Ill (6)
24. Lasted out (7)
25. Artless (5)
26. To sag (4)
27. Disclosed (8)

DOWN

1. Yell—sounds like a grand dance! (4)
2. Caught on (7)
3. Tries (anag.)—ceremonies (5)
4. An excursion (6)
6. Awry (5)
7. Duly ends (anag.)—abruptly! (8)
8. Conundrum (6)
13. Bed-clothes (8)
15. Ducks—they get you down! (6)
17. Malice (3-4)
18. Loose parcel (6)
20. Portable chair (5)
22. Flinch (5)
23. To fuse together (4)

60

ACROSS

1. Girl's name (6)
5. Very quick, in music (6)
9. Kind of attic (6)
10. Scribble (6)
11. A blunder–whichever way you look at it! (4)
12. Narcotic present in opium–or in hemp! (anag.) (8)
14. Agree–as despatched! (6)
16. Wantonly destructive person (6)
19. Strutting birds (8)
21. Edge of sleeve–blow! (4)
22. Irish county–worker at border! (6)
23. Unimpaired–in diplomacy! (6)
24. A short mission (6)
25. Lubricating substance (6)

DOWN

2. Warrior women (7)
3. Of lasting quality (7)
4. Kind of gun (9)
6. Go over main points again (5)
7. A gull, for instance–braised! (anag.) (3-4)
8. A gusher (3-4)
13. Stunningly attractive (9)
14. Pacify (7)
15. Smash–bit of a crash at terminus! (7)
17. Band round collar (7)
18. Influences (7)
20. Pungent vegetable (5)

61

ACROSS

1. Disguise—square Edam! (anag.) (10)
7. An atrocity (7)
8. A forward thrust (5)
10. Tax—for ring! (4)
11. Trader (8)
13. A cooking spice (6)
15. He keeps a fire burning (6)
17. Old Scandinavian (8)
18. Object of worship—lazy, one hears! (4)
21. A steam bath (5)
22. To mimic (7)
23. Allusions (10)

DOWN

1. Accommodation for motorists (5)
2. To bridge (4)
3. Irregular—that's odd! (6)
4. To put in a different place (8)
5. European country (7)
6. Great land-masses (10)
9. Herd, all ten (anag.)—captivated (10)
12. A chosen representative (8)
14. Torment (7)
16. Remain (anag.)—connected with the sea (6)
19. Tugs along—500 scraps! (5)
20. A metal (4)

62

ACROSS

1. Relatives by marriage (2-4)
4. Fights – for fragments! (6)
8. Girl's name (7)
10. Circus-ring (5)
11. Receive as successor (7)
12. Expel from home – some of the victims! (5)
13. Al cut capers (anag.) – sensational! (11)
18. Hasten (5)
19. Formal headwear (3-4)
22. Indicate with finger – or tip of pencil! (5)
23. Give birth to (7)
24. Dissolve in the stomach (6)
25. Ball of shot (6)

DOWN

1. Fruitlessly (2,4)
2. Execute without legal trial (5)
3. More sage (5)
5. French castle (7)
6. A continent (7)
7. What sailors sing – in a rough hut! (6)
9. Drawn by magnetism (9)
14. Going separate ways (7)
15. Prairie-dogs (7)
16. Fashioned (6)
17. Spirit – sprite! (anag.) (6)
20. To throb (5)
21. Blacksmith's block – found in E. Anglian village (5)

63

ACROSS

1. To incubate (5)
4. Reaping implements (7)
8. A sitting (7)
9. Take illegally—a girl takes ten! (5)
10. A loud cry (4)
11. Rip seeds (anag.)—to scatter! (8)
13. Mainly (6)
14. Bird with immense beak (6)
17. Apartment in a larger block (8)
19. Stuff—to study hastily! (4)
22. Tall flower (5)
23. To profess (7)
24. Lack of harmony—it's Diana's string! (7)
25. Tango, for example (5)

DOWN

1. Rashly quick (5)
2. Scuffles (7)
3. Greeting—it's chilly! (4)
4. Warmly illuminated (6)
5. I chop man! (anag.)—I'm the greatest! (8)
6. Ocean-going vessel (5)
7. A sweet age! (7)
12. Tropical bird—red-hot duck! (8)
13. Speckled (7)
15. Animated film (7)
16. Shot from cover (6)
18. Backs of necks (5)
20. A short distance—among the lime-trees (5)
21. A grating (4)

64

ACROSS

6. African animal (7)
7. Army officer (5)
8. Occasional (6)
9. Sell direct to customers (6)
10. Flower-bed with assorted stonework (4-6)
12. To manage – in 'ard times! (anag.) (10)
16. Gaol (6)
17. Hot gun (anag.) – it's nothing (6)
18. Cinema attendant (5)
19. Gliding on slippery surface (7)

DOWN

1. A giant – small bird on one! (5)
2. Assessor (6)
3. Great distress (10)
4. To stumble (6)
5. Fir-tree? – Fir-cone! (anag.) (7)
9. 90 degrees (5,5)
11. Speak to (7)
13. Part of the foot – good marchers keep it! (6)
14. Slices of toast (6)
15. Sing – some of church anthems! (5)

65

ACROSS

1. Large kettle (8)
5. Seize (4)
9. Dexterity (5)
10. Chiefs (7)
11. Up-to-date–RN follows fashion! (6)
12. Overturn–and distress! (5)
14. Man on guard (6)
16. Narrow-necked vessel (6)
19. Moral code of a group–those! (anag.) (5)
21. Smokes (6)
24. Floater on water (7)
25. A cereal (5)
26. Over-hasty–getting skin eruption! (4)
27. The new moon (8)

DOWN

1. A wine-vessel? A hundred enquire! (4)
2. Fabulous horned animal (7)
3. Dig deep (5)
4. A rectangular shape (6)
6. Gives off fumes–in creek, smouldering (5)
7. Infatuated (8)
8. Famous Italian tenor (6)
13. Property valuer (8)
15. A summary–start again! (6)
17. The white ant (7)
18. Recorder of runs–twenty? Right! (6)
20. Fibres on skin (5)
22. Sporting activities (5)
23. Period of fasting (4)

66

ACROSS

1. A rut (6)
5. A stiffening agent (6)
9. To obstruct (6)
10. Supporting column (6)
11. Lump of earth (4)
12. Grotesquely carved water-spout (8)
14. Part of horse's headgear (6)
16. Priggish people (6)
19. An example – in posture! (8)
21. Fruit-seeds – on officers' shoulders! (4)
22. Has being (6)
23. Kind of fir – very dapper! (6)
24. Guides – young oxen! (6)
25. Neglected condition (6)

DOWN

2. Rose – a hiker! (7)
3. I d-drove (anag.) – carried too far (7)
4. In leaf throughout the year (9)
6. Securing with rope – part of jetty in Galway (5)
7. Transmitted (7)
8. Gear of a draught horse (7)
13. Subdued – and flattened again! (9)
14. Those who corrupt with gifts (7)
15. Fill with enthusiasm (7)
17. Arbiters (7)
18. Anticipates (7)
20. Sacrificial table (5)

67

ACROSS

1. Deliberate attempt to mislead (3,7)
7. Jumping on one leg (7)
8. Toned down (5)
10. Team – breathed sadly, by the sound of it! (4)
11. Heightens (8)
13. Pantry (6)
15. Artist's work-room – Sid, out! (anag.) (6)
17. To teach (8)
18. A lure (4)
21. Zest – in August only (5)
22. Enthusiastic applause (7)
23. Son praises (anag.) – slanderous remarks! (10)

DOWN

1. Lassoed (5)
2. To trickle (4)
3. A machine (6)
4. Bits left over (8)
5. Espied (7)
6. Carving sculpture? That's cheating! (10)
9. Twisting out of shape (10)
12. See a form (anag.) – frightful! (8)
14. Stands up to (7)
16. Athwart (6)
19. Wrong – a young woman? (5)
20. Skirting-board (4)

ACROSS

1. Acceptors of bets – streak! (anag.) (6)
4. Herds of sheep (6)
8. Wireless inventor (7)
10. A load – making a vehicle run! (5)
11. Most protracted (7)
12. To strike (5)
13. Rural area – round SE city (anag.) (11)
18. Spaces under roofs (5)
19. Salad plants – from a friend I've several! (7)
22. Mediterranean island (5)
23. Sounded like a plucked string (7)
24. Revolve (6)
25. Safe harbours (6)

DOWN

1. Part of skull – in a place of worship! (6)
2. Girl's name (5)
3. French river (5)
5. Destructive insects (7)
6. Conveyed (7)
7. Slept noisily (6)
9. Seize in transit (9)
14. Unusual – not on strike! (7)
15. Just starting – ten cans! (anag.) (7)
16. Bacon-cutter, for instance (6)
17. Stage-whispers – a sporting team's! (6)
20. A play for the stage (5)
21. Prevailing fashion (5)

69

ACROSS

1. A stingy fellow – me, Sir? (anag.) (5)
4. Devilish (7)
8. Competitiveness (7)
9. To tinge deeply (5)
10. Ruth (anag.) – causing harm! (4)
11. Without stitched joins (8)
13. Ability (6)
14. Pieces of cutlery (6)
17. A Red lies (anag.) – that's understood! (8)
19. A flower – for a girl! (4)
22. Eskimo dwelling (5)
23. Occasion for a meal (3-4)
24. Outermost (7)
25. To chop finely (5)

DOWN

1. Soggy land (5)
2. Quite a few – cut Capone! (7)
3. Revolve – sounds like a stage-part! (4)
4. Designed for fashion (6)
5. Clipping into shape (8)
6. High-born (5)
7. Wrinkles (7)
12. Eat it, Don (anag.) – it will counteract poison! (8)
13. A rotary motor (7)
15. A translation (7)
16. The middle (6)
18. Apportion – everything 'eated! (5)
20. Eve is sent up – for a colander? (5)
21. Unruffled (4)

70

ACROSS

6. Eats roe (anag.) – pinkish in colour (7)
7. Killed (5)
8. Musical composition (6)
9. Medical officer got up – surly! (6)
10. A release from bondage (10)
12. Pale – and uninteresting! (10)
16. Part of a church steeple (6)
17. Change over (6)
18. Humorous (5)
19. Tape, Dad (anag.) – adjusted (7)

DOWN

1. A car (5)
2. Remember – to phone again! (6)
3. A fruit (10)
4. Red wine (6)
5. One's appointed work in life (7)
9. A NW county – see dry semi (anag.) (10)
11. Optimistic (7)
13. Transgress – where cigarette ash falls! (6)
14. Evasive (6)
15. Débris at foot of cliff (5)

71

ACROSS

1. Cut short—curt, neat! (anag.) (8)
5. Undergarment (4)
9. A bunch of yarn—or geese! (5)
10. Bitter regret—concerning code! (7)
11. Avoid (6)
12. Fools (5)
14. Appetising flavour (6)
16. Dazed condition (6)
19. Type of poplar—like an enclosure! (5)
21. An eraser (6)
24. Commit to safe-keeping (7)
25. Bulge out—that's great! (5)
26. Tender to the touch (4)
27. Apprehended (8)

DOWN

1. To hurl (4)
2. An implement (7)
3. A certainty (5)
4. Flings (6)
6. To enlist (5)
7. Wealth stored up (8)
8. Among (6)
13. Waves crashing on shore (8)
15. Wicked (6)
17. School pupil with authority (7)
18. Mouth of volcano (6)
20. A Saint—favourite with the Queen! (5)
22. Pour fat on when roasting (5)
23. Walk heavily—within cheap lodgings! (4)

72

ACROSS

1. Fitter (anag.) – for a hat! (6)
5. Frightened (6)
9. Prepared with aromatic herbs (6)
10. An armed encounter (6)
11. In addition (4)
12. Canadian police – some unit! (anag.) (8)
14. An individual – for each son! (6)
16. One who counterfeits (6)
19. Pledges (8)
21. A spice – it's carried in procession! (4)
22. Rubbish strewn about – little pigs! (6)
23. Please (anag.) – to pass (6)
24. Fame (6)
25. Pays out (6)

DOWN

2. Sup lime (anag.) – a sudden urge! (7)
3. Elements contributing to a result (7)
4. First principles (9)
6. Mountain range (5)
7. Deserting (7)
8. Kitchen sideboard (7)
13. Releases from clasps (9)
14. Liked by many (7)
15. Pro-Foot (anag.) – high point of the House! (4-3)
17. Rush about wildly (7)
18. Kept in a box (7)
20. Sluggish (5)

73

ACROSS

1. A branch of mathematics (10)
7. Oriental (7)
8. Stares open-mouthed (5)
10. Spaces (4)
11. Soft pads (8)
13. Accommodation for soldiers (6)
15. Jacket for gramophone record (6)
17. Fillet of sirloin – sell at a lower price! (8)
18. Southern shack – closed (4)
21. 'E nips back – or backbone! (5)
22. Encourage – to listen to X! (7)
23. Feelings (10)

DOWN

1. Teller of fables – as Poe (anag.) (5)
2. Notion (4)
3. Distinction (6)
4. Oval casing – for very thin china! (8)
5. Little devil, wander – and do better! (7)
6. The people next door (10)
9. Mistrusting (10)
12. Most jolly (8)
14. Old destroyer of machinery (7)
16. Northern cathedral city (6)
19. Loathes (5)
20. To pledge – a chess piece! (4)

74

ACROSS

1. To degrade (6)
4. Three-legged stand (6)
8. Short sword – to wound a girl! (7)
10. To sag (5)
11. Intrinsic nature (7)
12. Pen it (anag.) – fatuous (5)
13. Lake, N. Harris (anag.) – part of Scotland! (11)
18. Prisons (5)
19. Disinterred (7)
22. One who weeps (5)
23. Very grave (7)
24. Receptacle for refuse (3-3)
25. Invisible (6)

DOWN

1. Adorned (6)
2. Nocturnal insects (5)
3. A chief – with vigour! (5)
5. Somewhat scarlet – Russian course of food! (7)
6. One who's first in his field (7)
7. A stand-in (6)
9. Without a spot of dirt (9)
14. Mental agony (7)
15. European country (7)
16. Mimosa (6)
17. Inventor – upset no side! (6)
20. Wading-bird – or hen (anag.) (5)
21. American elk (5)

75

ACROSS

1. A marsh (5)
4. Self-important (7)
8. Try a lie? (anag.) – No, the truth! (7)
9. Respond to a stimulus – and perform again? (5)
10. Manner (4)
11. Slimmers count them (8)
13. First working day? (6)
14. Periodically – in a feeble way, they say! (6)
17. Rapidly (8)
19. Small fly (4)
22. Silly ass (5)
23. Made of pottery (7)
24. Conjectures (7)
25. A principle – either way! (5)

DOWN

1. Clear off! (5)
2. To forsake – unrestrained behaviour! (7)
3. A nip (anag.) – causing an ache! (4)
4. When wages are received (3-3)
5. Besides (8)
6. Kind of giraffe – seen in a book, a picture (5)
7. To supply fully (7)
12. Chap with fruit from the palm – getting orders! (8)
13. Failing to hit (7)
15. A relative (7)
16. Time-pieces (6)
18. To cut off a syllable (5)
20. Unspoken (5)
21. Courage (4)

76

ACROSS

6. Grins at (anag.) – looking fixedly (7)
7. Symbolic diagram (5)
8. Physical condition – feel TT? (anag.) (6)
9. Royal personage (6)
10. Pharmacy (10)
12. Bullets, shells, etc. (10)
16. Declare (6)
17. Pulled (6)
18. Cancel (5)
19. To feign (7)

DOWN

1. Alloy of iron and carbon – to pinch, as they say! (5)
2. Jarred (6)
3. Petticoat (10)
4. Tracks (6)
5. Person of refined tastes (7)
9. Time before records began (10)
11. Am employing – that's funny! (7)
13. The womb (6)
14. Get Ena (anag.) – to deny (6)
15. Not much money – for a girl! (5)

77

ACROSS

1. A split (8)
5. Thread laid lengthwise in a loom (4)
9. Slate (anag.) – to pilfer (5)
10. Eight-sided figure (7)
11. Be regretful about (6)
12. To make arid (5)
14. Edible tuber (6)
16. Heavy and dull (6)
19. Boy's name – message received! (5)
21. Cross-bred (6)
24. A moment (7)
25. Bears (anag.) – a sword (5)
26. Blast of wind (4)
27. Splendour (8)

DOWN

1. Snug (4)
2. High mountain – in severe storm (7)
3. Device controlling flow in one direction (5)
4. Picturesque cave (6)
6. To forebode (5)
7. Special inclination – to write a song! (8)
8. A paper fastener (6)
13. Ostentatiously wearing (8)
15. Eastern headwear (6)
17. Rib bled (anag.) – just a trickle! (7)
18. Paler (6)
20. Pants (5)
22. Kind of buffalo (5)
23. Burn – a prophet, by the sound of it! (4)

ACROSS

1. Shut (6)
5. Attics (anag.) – not moving! (6)
9. Head of convent (6)
10. District (6)
11. Ignore alteration, printer! (4)
12. A gamp (8)
14. Prickly shrubs – or pipes (6)
16. Kind of cement – it may explode! (6)
19. Water-falls (8)
21. Unconscious state (4)
22. Glossy coating for metal (6)
23. Extensive dominion (6)
24. Greet with a gesture (6)
25. They produce intense beams of light (6)

DOWN

2. Shellfish (7)
3. Respect (anag.) – a symbol of kingship! (7)
4. Given false appearance – I did guess! (anag.) (9)
6. Belonging to them (5)
7. Outing permitted – for one of a group of three! (7)
8. Mythical horse-man (7)
13. Shocking piece of news (9)
14. Pails (7)
15. Establish – in a stable! (7)
17. Cooking instructions – precise! (anag.) (7)
18. A suitor (7)
20. Watchful (5)

79

ACROSS

1. English county (10)
7. Some of the brides can talk—talk at length! (7)
8. A sudden jet (5)
10. Northern river—wet mud, we hear! (4)
11. Making a witty remark (8)
13. Drives on—simple! (anag.) (6)
15. Peg controlling a tap (6)
17. A parasite (6-2)
18. Type of singing voice (4)
21. A girl—in person I appear (5)
22. Syrup (7)
23. Pierced (10)

DOWN

1. Is defeated (5)
2. Tidy (4)
3. Crafty (6)
4. Water-carrier! (8)
5. Sour gin (anag.)—exciting! (7)
6. Rebukes (10)
9. Circus high wires (5-5)
12. To estrange—foreigner tucked in! (8)
14. Act of repentant sinner (7)
16. Strong beer—for luggage carrier! (6)
19. Very clear (5)
20. Saucy (4)

80

ACROSS

1. Strip of material (6)
4. Low joints! (6)
8. A bull-fighter (7)
10. Expanse of flat land – that's obvious! (5)
11. Stratified (7)
12. Small map printed in a corner – in a group! (5)
13. Made of transparent mineral (11)
18. A bedtime drink (5)
19. Stained (anag.) – as a substitute (7)
22. Fruit of oak – a hard growth! (5)
23. Recount (7)
24. Dwell (6)
25. Venerate (6)

DOWN

1. Sound of thunder (6)
2. Crazy – like a flying mammal! (5)
3. Command – to arrange neatly! (5)
5. Pertaining to marriage (7)
6. Co-operation between units (7)
7. Soundness of mind (6)
9. Emission of rays (9)
14. Clergymen (7)
15. Scrutinised (7)
16. Cream-filled cake (6)
17. To stick (6)
20. A binge (5)
21. Delete – part of answer, as entered (5)

3

BEAT THE CLOCK

81

ACROSS

1. To turn on a pin (5)
4. Elevated (5)
7. A box of cutlery (7)
8. A herb (3)
9. Official area of activity (6)
11. Courageous (4)
13. Long-necked bird (4)
14. An open air meal (6)
17. To fit out with sails (3)
18. Bounce back (7)
20. Forbearance (5)
21. Girl's name (5)

DOWN

1. An ancient people of Scotland (5)
2. Wine, in France (3)
3. Vibration (6)
4. To loan (4)
5. Wretched (7)
6. Cede (5)
10. A war-horse (7)
12. A strip of material (6)
13. A rugby formation (5)
15. Tea container (5)
16. What donkeys do (4)
19. Receptacle for ashes (3)

82

ACROSS

1. Money invested (7)
5. Droop (3)
7. Canal boat (5)
8. To swear (5)
9. To last (6)
11. To beat with a cane (3)
13. Hydrogen, for example (3)
14. Wealth (6)
17. A cosmetic (5)
18. Protrude (5)
20. River of SW England (3)
21. Merciful (7)

DOWN

1. Thick rope for hauling (5)
2. Standard (3)
3. Speculation (6)
4. Lake, as in Scotland (4)
5. A surface wound (7)
6. A colour (5)
10. Argument (7)
12. The 1 Across of Portugal (6)
13. A deep ravine (5)
15. Sugary (5)
16. The underpart of a ship (4)
19. Fib (3)

83

ACROSS

1. A sledge-dog (5)
4. Claptrap (5)
7. A painting (7)
8. Septic discharge (3)
9. Kind of fairy (3)
11. Blew violently (6)
13. Money chest (6)
16. Mass of water (3)
18. Girl's name (3)
19. Vague (7)
21. Gave one's support to (5)
22. Boy's name (5)

DOWN

1. Jumped on one leg (6)
2. Small bag-like structure (3)
3. Juvenile (5)
4. Braid of hair (5)
5. To fix deeply in the mind (7)
6. Orient (4)
10. Looked angry (7)
12. A collection of rabbit burrows (6)
14. Discovered (5)
15. Haystacks (5)
17. Church service (4)
20. Tree (3)

84

ACROSS

1. Caught out (7)
5. Settle a bill (3)
7. Harvester (7)
8. Rodent (3)
9. Grass (4)
11. Secures with metal spikes (5)
14. New (5)
15. A tiny insect (4)
17. Bituminous substance (3)
18. Container for writing liquid (7)
20. A long-eared animal (3)
21. Regional mode of speech (7)

DOWN

1. Make taut (7)
2. Eisenhower, familiarly (3)
3. Sort (4)
4. Fearless (6)
5. Having a preference for (7)
6. Still (3)
10. Turns back (7)
12. Young actress likely to make her mark (7)
13. In league with (6)
16. A predatory gull (4)
17. A drink (3)
19. Before (3)

85

ACROSS

1. A leg-guard (3)
3. A house on wheels (7)
7. Exterior (5)
8. Pertaining to sound (5)
9. To sweep along (4)
10. To climb (5)
13. Dares (5)
15. Playthings (4)
17. Forbidden (5)
19. Salt water (5)
20. A tower with a spire (7)
21. Take in food (3)

DOWN

1. Bed of soil (4)
2. Discerns (7)
3. Remedied (5)
4. Corrodes (5)
5. Commercial vehicle (3)
6. Notched (6)
11. Whatever the occasion (7)
12. Foams (6)
14. Bend down (5)
15. Board for food (5)
16. A great achievement (4)
18. Insect (3)

86

ACROSS

1. Disney's flying elephant (5)
4. Small tassels (5)
7. Confused (7)
8. A thick mat (3)
9. A season (6)
11. A refined woman (4)
13. Slim (4)
14. Not present (6)
17. A bone (3)
18. Possessed by ghosts (7)
20. Extinguish (5)
21. Humorous (5)

DOWN

1. Women (5)
2. Crazy (3)
3. A four-sided shape (6)
4. Neatly arranged (4)
5. A forge (7)
6. Sodden (5)
10. A spectral arc (7)
12. Ridiculous (6)
13. Weary (5)
15. Like movements of the sea (5)
16. Item of footwear (4)
19. A pair (3)

87

ACROSS

1. A book in the Bible (7)
5. Headwear (3)
7. To slacken (5)
8. A paddle-boat (5)
9. Scream (6)
11. Public house (3)
13. Item of crockery (3)
14. Joints on which doors swing (6)
17. Really (5)
18. Rubble at base of cliff (5)
20. A tint (3)
21. Status of a great actor (7)

DOWN

1. Disease carriers (5)
2. Nothing (3)
3. Group of six musicians (6)
4. Large cloth bag (4)
5. Lady's container for small articles (7)
6. Belonging to them (5)
10. A feeling of great joy (7)
12. Afternoon nap (6)
13. Capture (5)
15. Water vapour (5)
16. Extra runs (4)
19. To free oneself of (3)

ACROSS

1. Lukewarm (5)
4. Idiotic (5)
7. Trusting (7)
8. To entreat (3)
9. French lily (3)
11. Mistakes (6)
13. Ambassador (6)
16. Since (3)
18. A strong drink (3)
19. A marine creature (7)
21. Fortune-teller's card (5)
22. Pertaining to birth (5)

DOWN

1. Kind of tortoise (6)
2. Chum (3)
3. Male duck (5)
4. Supply with food (5)
5. Canadian province (7)
6. An ingredient of puddings (4)
10. Type of cooker (7)
12. Very small amount of food (6)
14. On high (5)
15. Devoured (5)
17. Annoying child (4)
20. Small lump of butter (3)

89

ACROSS

1. To stick out (7)
5. Witnessed (3)
7. Painters (7)
8. Japanese coin (3)
9. One's innermost being (4)
11. Iniquities (5)
14. Song (5)
15. A Greek letter (4)
17. Mist (3)
18. A sickness (7)
20. Damp (3)
21. Thin (7)

DOWN

1. Spoke highly of (7)
2. Unconscious (3)
3. Simple (4)
4. Ornamental tuft (6)
5. Breathe forth (7)
6. Gain a victory (3)
10. Nervously tense (7)
12. Strew about (7)
13. A route skirting a city (6)
16. Joy (4)
17. Not many (3)
19. Finale (3)

90

ACROSS

1. A preserve (3)
3. Coped with (7)
7. Leg-joints (5)
8. Moved by the wind (5)
9. Very small (4)
10. Delete (5)
13. Royal (5)
15. Chime of bells (4)
17. Danger signal (5)
19. A musical composition (5)
20. Reach out (7)
21. A weight (3)

DOWN

1. Funny story (4)
2. Gathering (7)
3. Cloudy (5)
4. Lordly (5)
5. Sticky substance (3)
6. A meal (6)
11. Versus (7)
12. Musical instruments (6)
14. Restrict (5)
15. A fish (5)
16. Presently (4)
18. A Scottish town (3)

91

ACROSS

1. Brag (5)
4. Damp-smelling (5)
7. Particular (7)
8. Meadowland (3)
9. Having a pale complexion (6)
11. Scottish garment (4)
13. Explosive sound (4)
14. A small conveyance (6)
17. Observe (3)
18. Type of dog (7)
20. Confection (5)
21. Humble (5)

DOWN

1. Sunbathes (5)
2. A drink (3)
3. A three-legged stand (6)
4. Thaw (4)
5. Warrior (7)
6. Substance used in brewing (5)
10. A kind of lamp (7)
12. Pertaining to the face (6)
13. Fundamental (5)
15. Amusing with words (5)
16. To oscillate (4)
19. Church bench (3)

92

ACROSS

1. Part of a circle (7)
5. A pig (3)
7. Tree (5)
8. Of the moon (5)
9. An organ of the body (6)
11. Climbing plant (3)
13. To spoil (3)
14. Seaman (6)
17. American state (5)
18. A pop-star's first name (5)
20. Tooth in a machine (3)
21. Pursues (7)

DOWN

1. A swindler (5)
2. Deity (3)
3. Merited (6)
4. High in stature (4)
5. Old-fashioned timepiece (7)
6. Anxiety (5)
10. Dearest beloved (7)
12. Package (6)
13. Imitate (5)
15. Cuts for harvesting (5)
16. Filthy lucre (4)
19. A card game (3)

93

ACROSS

1. Low in price (5)
4. A type of violin (5)
7. Chic (7)
8. Wet earth (3)
9. Fairy queen (3)
11. Old sixpenny piece (6)
13. Severe (6)
16. Source of light and heat (3)
18. Everybody (3)
19. Unyielding (7)
21. A body of lawmen (5)
22. Longed for (5)

DOWN

1. Of a pale yellow colour (6)
2. Organ of vision (3)
3. To place firmly (5)
4. A lustrous material (5)
5. Like unframed glasses (7)
6. Queen of ancient Carthage (4)
10. Liquid containers (7)
12. Married (6)
14. Nonsensical (5)
15. Vagrant (5)
17. A fresh-water fish (4)
20. A beard of barley (3)

94

ACROSS

1. Smoked herrings (7)
5. To shake to and fro (3)
7. The windflower (7)
8. Apply friction to (3)
9. Moose-like beasts (4)
11. Confound (5)
14. Young man (5)
15. Stylish (4)
17. Tibetan ox (3)
18. Endanger (7)
20. A baked dish (3)
21. Potters about (7)

DOWN

1. Dishonesty (7)
2. American author (3)
3. Roman name for York (4)
4. Move up and down (6)
5. Red Indian hostility (7)
6. To prattle (3)
10. Part of the hand (7)
12. Hair of a dog's neck (7)
13. A seaside plant (6)
16. To bridge (4)
17. Bark (3)
19. Type of grain (3)

95

ACROSS

1. An adhesive (3)
3. Regain one's health (7)
7. Regretful (5)
8. A liquid (5)
9. An animal (4)
10. Automaton (5)
13. Block of metal (5)
15. Small particle (4)
17. Woman's name (5)
19. Keen (5)
20. A spike in a heavy workshoe (7)
21. Vat (3)

DOWN

1. A convulsive breath (4)
2. Time of day (7)
3. A synthetic material (5)
4. Cringe (5)
5. A tax (3)
6. Uncommon quality (6)
11. Fetched (7)
12. A fraction (6)
14. Decorative head-piece (5)
15. Reside (5)
16. Shellfish (4)
18. A high ball, in tennis (3)

96

ACROSS

1. Refuse (5)
4. A line for holding a dog (5)
7. Burial service (7)
8. Groove (3)
9. Scenario (6)
11. Short measure (4)
13. Hollow place in rock (4)
14. Ripe (6)
17. Melody (3)
18. An abridgement (7)
20. Newspapers, generally (5)
21. A liquid measure (5)

DOWN

1. Floats on the wind (5)
2. A moral offence (3)
3. Continent (6)
4. A flower (4)
5. Beside the kidneys (7)
6. A snag (5)
10. The opposite (7)
12. Servile (6)
13. A fastener (5)
15. In which place? (5)
16. An optical device (4)
19. A type of grass (3)

97

ACROSS

1. Ogre (7)
5. Bundle of notes (3)
7. That which is owing (5)
8. To counterfeit (5)
9. Drives out (6)
11. A limb (3)
13. Enemy (3)
14. Protect (6)
17. Part of a church (5)
18. Vision (5)
20. Young goat (3)
21. A type of cathedral (7)

DOWN

1. Small fly (5)
2. A beak (3)
3. Iota (6)
4. A floating conveyance (4)
5. Open hostilities (7)
6. A distant hope (5)
10. Gratified (7)
12. An individual (6)
13. Plain-spoken (5)
15. Dissuade (5)
16. Ship's steering-wheel (4)
19. Intestine (3)

ACROSS

1. A mass of fog (5)
4. Blackboard support (5)
7. Communicating with (2,5)
8. Schoolmaster (3)
9. A bar (3)
11. European country (6)
13. A floor of a building (6)
16. Male cat (3)
18. Garden implement (3)
19. A strip of cloth (7)
21. GP's list of patients (5)
22. Stallion (5)

DOWN

1. Perky (6)
2. Choose (3)
3. Uncertainty of opinion (5)
4. An anaesthetic (5)
5. To mistrust (7)
6. Decoy (4)
10. Intermediate to (7)
12. To be about to happen (6)
14. Rise against authority (5)
15. Jerks (5)
17. Fellow (4)
20. Exist (3)

99

ACROSS

1. Deprived of contents (7)
5. Infant's bed (3)
7. A bird (7)
8. Drain (3)
9. A breach (4)
11. Lord, as in Scotland (5)
14. Middle Eastern country (5)
15. Hold tightly (4)
17. Early morning moisture (3)
18. Absence of sound (7)
20. Lad (3)
21. Companies of performers (7)

DOWN

1. Boards ship (7)
2. Favourite (3)
3. Caesar's fateful date (4)
4. Hang loosely (6)
5. To dismiss in disgrace (7)
6. Extremity (3)
10. Distant (7)
12. To dispirit (7)
13. Type of hound (6)
16. Muse of history (4)
17. Confer knighthood upon (3)
19. To pinch (3)

100

ACROSS

6. An English king (7)
7. Covered with powdered earth (5)
8. Plan (6)
9. Income from a tenant (6)
10. Of a person other than the insured and insurer (5-5)
12. One half of a geometrical figure (10)
16. Movement (6)
17. Frozen dribble of water (6)
18. A possession (5)
19. Made with needles (7)

DOWN

1. A mass of shaggy hair (5)
2. Zealous (6)
3. A mass medium (10)
4. Former coin (6)
5. Narrow passages by water (7)
9. Cuts (10)
11. Provide with a different dwelling (7)
13. Features of the eyes (6)
14. Turns out of home (6)
15. Wintry rain (5)

101

ACROSS

1. Mariner (6)
5. Walk like a duck (6)
8. One who puts something to a purpose (4)
9. Breeches (8)
10. One who tolls (4-6)
12. Airborne (6)
14. A Spanish coin (6)
15. Made spitting noises (10)
19. Commonsense (8)
20. Type of vaulted roof (4)
21. Conducts (6)
22. Goddess of dawn (6)

DOWN

2. A cold wind (8)
3. Ethical (5)
4. Nought (7)
5. Incorrect (5)
6. Abandons (7)
7. Cooking-fat (4)
11. A pennon (8)
13. Tasteless (7)
14. A flower (7)
16. Dens (5)
17. A soft-feathered bird (5)
18. A native of S. Africa (4)

102

ACROSS

1. A capital city (6)
5. Slumbering (6)
9. To reach by effort (6)
10. A manufacturer of headwear (6)
11. Lies (4)
12. Distinction (8)
14. To free from captivity (6)
16. The last of daylight (6)
19. Writer of music (8)
21. To choose at election time (4)
22. A lubricant container (6)
23. Girl's name (6)
24. Partition (6)
25. A Christian festival (6)

DOWN

2. External (7)
3. Any great literary work (7)
4. Ramblers (9)
6. A rustic person, poetically (5)
7. Prolongs (7)
8. Omen (7)
13. Financial safeguard (9)
14. Clergymen (7)
15. One who tries a small portion (7)
17. Beginners (7)
18. Girl's name (7)
20. Deliver a speech (5)

103

ACROSS

7. A Breton, for example (4)
8. Put to death by law (8)
9. Courteous (6)
10. One's vocation (6)
11. The sound a snake makes (4)
12. A place for ablutions (8)
15. Uncivilised (8)
17. Destiny (4)
18. Explosive noise (6)
21. An outfitter (6)
22. Affecting one's emotions (8)
23. Enclosure for hens (4)

DOWN

1. An ingredient of milk-puddings (8)
2. Undresses (6)
3. Call to mind (8)
4. Ray of light (4)
5. To flatter (6)
6. Venerable old historian (4)
13. Sound of a clock (4-4)
14. Conventional in doctrine (8)
16. Kiosks (6)
17. To shrink back (6)
19. A Biblical character (4)
20. Infants (4)

ACROSS

1. Nuisances (5)
4. Pertaining to the Greek Oracle (7)
8. The first Christian martyr (7)
9. Telegraphed (5)
10. A northern valley (4)
11. Goodbye (8)
13. The rest (6)
14. Means of entry (6)
17. Paternal (8)
19. A broach for roasting meat (4)
22. Language of Erin (5)
23. Varied (7)
24. Joins up as a soldier (7)
25. Wiles (5)

DOWN

1. Struck an attitude (5)
2. Furtiveness (7)
3. Part of London (4)
4. Refusal to admit (6)
5. T.E. ———, of Arabia (8)
6. A quadruped (5)
7. Pampers (7)
12. Trews (8)
13. Area to right of vehicle (7)
15. Goods traded abroad (7)
16. Girl's name (6)
18. A run of bird-song (5)
20. Long overland journeys (5)
21. Extra (4)

105

ACROSS

6. Adorn with garlands (7)
7. Frisk about – with headgear, before the Queen (5)
8. Whole (6)
9. Cruelty (6)
10. A drinking toast – fitness! (4,6)
12. Disastrous (10)
16. Plunging head first (6)
17. Shot forward – pointed weapon gets Edwin! (6)
18. Italian city (5)
19. Poison – CIA deny! (anag.) (7)

DOWN

1. Twilled-cotton garments – a girl's! (5)
2. Cord (6)
3. Premonition (10)
4. A girl – in a thousand, ravishing! (6)
5. Compactness (7)
9. Educational period of life (10)
11. An ocean – peaceful (7)
13. Any beast (6)
14. Oriental skirt – no rags! (anag.) (6)
15. Overrun by useless plants (5)

106

ACROSS

1. A coat (6)
5. Security (6)
8. A festive occasion – girl at one (4)
9. To water land by means of canals (8)
10. A diplomatic representative (10)
12. Excessively (6)
14. Swung off course (6)
15. Location for a meal – the noise gets fashionable newly-married man! (6-4)
19. Foot-rests for horsemen (8)
20. Bucket (4)
21. Fires – made with buds! (6)
22. One who approves of going naked? – I'd stun! (anag.) (6)

DOWN

2. Capone providing weapons – disconcerting! (8)
3. A kind of bear (5)
4. In need of a drink (7)
5. Fathered (5)
6. A fruit-bearing plant (3-4)
7. A London art gallery (4)
11. Tunes – some, idle (anag.) (8)
13. Suffer – short of pep! (7)
14. The flesh of deer (7)
16. Names of objects (5)
17. Lassoed (5)
18. Headgear, upper-class, tilted – in American state (4)

107

ACROSS

1. Disappear (6)
5. Fatigue resulting from long-distance flights (3,3)
9. Superintendent (6)
10. Regular trade – a convention (6)
11. A size of printing-type (4)
12. Like an emperor (8)
14. A spire (anag.) – in the country! (6)
16. Arranges – religious fraternities (6)
19. English county (8)
21. Doctors – for old soldiers! (4)
22. Show clearly – what Price (Vincent) is holding! (6)
23. Yearly (6)
24. Sweet (6)
25. Herons (6)

DOWN

2. Greed (7)
3. Natives of N. America (7)
4. Disadvantages? – Sounds like useful little explosives! (9)
6. To escape by trickery (5)
7. A network of laths (7)
8. Takes a chance (7)
13. Porter sat? (anag.) – Flat out! (9)
14. Annoys persistently (7)
15. Frolicking about (7)
17. Holy king – one who foresees (7)
18. Withdraw one's opinion – concerning a pamphlet (7)
20. Competitive runner (5)

108

ACROSS

7. A girl – among several (4)
8. Clothed (8)
9. Summon again – and repeat from memory (6)
10. Closer (6)
11. In a competent manner (4)
12. Meant 'dee' (anag.) – make correction (8)
15. Belief (8)
17. A fish (4)
18. Stiffly formal editor – briefed (6)
21. Bear witness – at cricket match (6)
22. Handel's 'Messiah', for instance (8)
23. An exam (4)

DOWN

1. A month (8)
2. One's kindred (6)
3. Almost a score (8)
4. One vehicle – for a tsar (4)
5. Place surrounded by water (6)
6. In this place (4)
13. Tea lover (anag.) – it might give one a lift! (8)
14. A division of the week (8)
16. Relegate (6)
17. Child's bed has weight – what's the material? (6)
19. Underdone – extraordinary! (4)
20. Filth (4)

109

ACROSS

1. A drinking-vessel (5)
4. A rich alcoholic drink (7)
8. Virginia has a visitor – most indistinct (7)
9. A river (5)
10. To skulk (4)
11. Brought back to former state (8)
13. Locations (6)
14. To pour in (6)
17. Art in USA (anag.) – European type (8)
19. High mass of land (4)
22. A note is heard – from this male singing voice! (5)
23. Small fish used in sauces (7)
24. An illustration – formerly copious (7)
25. One who fillets meat (5)

DOWN

1. A chairman's hammer (5)
2. Ail, rage (anag.) – in part of N. Africa (7)
3. Swing round – killed (4)
4. Recent (6)
5. Calms down (8)
6. A shrub (5)
7. Remainder (7)
12. Rip with fall – causing this sign of grief? (4-4)
13. Empty talk (7)
15. A mythical creature (7)
16. Accommodation for a car (6)
18. In person, I attracted – a girl (5)
20. Stratum (5)
21. Black-leg – locked in workers' cabin (4)

110

ACROSS

6. An Aztec (7)
7. A slant – in part of jamb, Eve, leaning (5)
8. Nomad – in Bude (anag.) (6)
9. Type of snake (6)
10. Preventives (10)
12. One's upbringing and previous experience (10)
16. Members of a treaty organisation (6)
17. Subscription charge – to overcome! (6)
18. Take a dip (5)
19. A periodical (7)

DOWN

1. A unit of length, do we hear? – Here's a measuring apparatus (5)
2. Water, for example (6)
3. Squalls (10)
4. Physical condition (6)
5. Expels undesirables (7)
9. Prose, in USA (anag.) – Jane Austen's novel (10)
11. Locomotive track (7)
13. Th' king (anag.) – chessman (6)
14. Socialite consumed – in discussion (6)
15. Flings (5)

ACROSS

1. Clever – and cheerful (6)
5. A place for a king – and a rook! (6)
8. Autocratic ruler – among Soviets, a royalist (4)
9. Trustworthy (8)
10. One who gives professional advice (10)
12. Fool has a letter – to evaluate (6)
14. Grief (6)
15. Type of bridge – cause of delay (10)
19. A month (8)
20. An aristocrat (4)
21. A key, perhaps (6)
22. Mythical spirits living in trees (6)

DOWN

2. Press one (anag.) – for a reply (8)
3. Lasses (5)
4. Excites (7)
5. Girl's name – Alice (anag.) (5)
6. First course of a meal (7)
7. A musical cadence (4)
11. Highly esteemed (8)
13. Oriental (7)
14. Pierced with a pointed weapon (7)
16. Thus live right – temperate (5)
17. An excursion – for little Sarah (5)
18. Circular band (4)

112

ACROSS

1. Propels with a short oar (6)
5. Hidden stores of provisions (6)
9. Born rascal – Irish accent! (6)
10. In tatters (6)
11. Sediment (4)
12. Ran motel (anag.) – in Canadian city (8)
14. Crush with the teeth (6)
16. Fractions (6)
19. A breakdown – colonel drinks, we hear (8)
21. Land measure (4)
22. Small cupboard (6)
23. A Middle Eastern language (6)
24. My sets (anag.) – in a scheme of classification (6)
25. A glossy surface on metal (6)

DOWN

2. A conveyance (7)
3. To make less burdensome (7)
4. Cooks joint – in a vessel! (9)
6. Aside – from a role on stage! (5)
7. Tallest (7)
8. Riders' seats (7)
13. Men read OT (anag.) – in a French cathedral (5-4)
14. Edible molluscs (7)
15. Unfastens one's shoes (7)
17. A king again, climbing – falls! (7)
18. Principal female figure in a story (7)
20. French girl's name – concealed by Madeleine (5)

113

ACROSS

7. Meat (4)
8. A gaming machine (8)
9. Press-chief – rioted (anag.) (6)
10. A farmhouse (6)
11. A burden – upon you and me (4)
12. An index of letters (8)
15. In favour of exams? – Objects! (8)
17. A close friend (4)
18. Fee (6)
21. Girl's name – in the diagram! (6)
22. Intended as a cure (8)
23. Cattle (4)

DOWN

1. A Cockney (8)
2. Fishes (6)
3. Highlanders' pouches (8)
4. Fire-arms turned up – in bar-parlour (4)
5. Type of cigar (6)
6. An ad – for cake of tobacco (4)
13. That may be done (8)
14. Tweed (in N) (anag.) – woven (8)
16. Sailor blushing – covered with pitch (6)
17. A grub (6)
19. Hastened – to conceal, by the sound of it (4)
20. N. African chieftain (4)

114

ACROSS

1. Orange-pink colour (5)
4. A room (7)
8. Stags' horns (7)
9. Parts of ears (5)
10. Cultivate (4)
11. Shaft of light (8)
13. A vegetable – spoil a line of them? (6)
14. Drooped (6)
17. A wired message (8)
19. Arm, for example (4)
22. Gorgeous eastern woman – time to meet one (5)
23. T' iguana (anag.) – in one of the W. Indies (7)
24. Christmas-tree decoration (7)
25. A flat hat (5)

DOWN

1. Religious song – from church worker! (5)
2. Kind of snake – an excellent specimen! (7)
3. Ogle (4)
4. Star – actors (anag.) (6)
5. An ocean (8)
6. A holy book (5)
7. Continued (7)
12. Clearing a ticklish throat (8)
13. Fits – fixtures! (7)
15. Feature of a gun (7)
16. Showy frontage – café 'ad (anag.) (6)
18. Girl's name (5)
20. Brute (5)
21. Cigarette end (4)

ACROSS

6. Hatchet – for a helicopter (7)
7. Tree – in a coppice, darkening (5)
8. Ill-feeling – shown by Mum with vermin (6)
9. Forks (6)
10. An aid to the partially deaf (3-7)
12. Cuts of beef (4-6)
16. A thread – maroon! (6)
17. Break out of captivity (6)
18. Cooked in fat (5)
19. An engraver's tool (7)

DOWN

1. Cut – almost vertical, we hear (5)
2. To unite in matrimony (6)
3. Entered? Apt (anag.) – pierced! (10)
4. Mend one's ways – concerning school class (6)
5. Bracelets (7)
9. Lasting quality (10)
11. A sauce for fruit-pie (7)
13. Supplication (6)
14. Gregarious (6)
15. Part of a group, perfect – and superior (5)

116

ACROSS

1. A strip of wood (6)
5. Stone used for smoothing (6)
8. In addition (4)
9. Rigs lens (anag.) – being short of metal circlets (8)
10. Row of bulbs illuminating a stage (10)
12. Crying like a gull (6)
14. Theatrical scenes – when following a wee drink! (6)
15. Needlework (10)
19. Models of perfection (8)
20. Stove, alight, contains – meat (4)
21. Fibrous tissue – take care of cricketer's leg! (6)
22. A metal (6)

DOWN

2. Kind of jersey (8)
3. Fashionable group – added detail (5)
4. Rotating (7)
5. Steal (5)
6. A girl – 'as smile (anag.) (7)
7. Truncheon (4)
11. A union (8)
13. Nice lad (anag.) – in northern country (7)
14. Nods off (7)
16. Tan-coloured (5)
17. Imp (5)
18. Fruit – 500 consumed (4)

ACROSS

1. One who picks off with a rifle (6)
5. OT tomb (anag.) – lowest part (6)
9. Stings (6)
10. Awards – for outsize automobiles (6)
11. Scheme (4)
12. A bleaching agent (8)
14. Decay of timber (3-3)
16. A humorous play (6)
19. Percolated (8)
21. Recognises, one hears – a physical feature (4)
22. Oil, see (anag.) – for a girl (6)
23. Little Helen (6)
24. SS sued (anag.) – thoroughly investigated (6)
25. Parts of ploughs – for allotments! (6)

DOWN

2. More agile (7)
3. A business associate (7)
4. Liquid distilled from a flower (4-5)
6. Attack – on stage scenery (5)
7. One under instruction – in a tree (anag.) (7)
8. Scrooge-like (7)
13. Happenings (9)
14. Disagrees (7)
15. Becomes jaundiced (7)
17. A cheroot – man poorly on one (7)
18. Regard with contempt (7)
20. Woman's name (5)

118

ACROSS

7. A barbarian (4)
8. Commanding (8)
9. Poet, from what we hear – banned (6)
10. Allot (6)
11. Caress with the lips (4)
12. Give a name to – name it, no? (anag.) (8)
15. Futile (8)
17. Public recreation ground – leave car (4)
18. Very drunk (6)
21. Sell to consumer (6)
22. A gift – from party, to the country (8)
23. Way out (4)

DOWN

1. Present an ethical view (8)
2. Pants – for strong drinks! (6)
3. Make more compact (8)
4. Ancient literature – dead (anag.) (4)
5. A prayer – from Boris, only (6)
6. Unexpected difficulty (4)
13. An error in the published word (8)
14. Fabulous! (8)
16. Type of knapsack (3-3)
17. Mess about idly (6)
19. See – card game with king (4)
20. Norse god (4)

119

ACROSS

1. Featureless (5)
4. Rugby Union craze – in European country (7)
8. Urges into action – in spectacles, from what we hear (7)
9. Second sea-bird – back end of boat (5)
10. A gas (4)
11. Charladies (8)
13. List of duties (6)
14. A vegetable (6)
17. Pertaining to a country (8)
19. Hare's tail (4)
22. Civvies (5)
23. An army officer (7)
24. Disperse (7)
25. Beast of burden – arrived with fifty! (5)

DOWN

1. Boy's name (5)
2. Stabilises (7)
3. Girl – involved in prank, a terror! (4)
4. Steal cattle (6)
5. In error (8)
6. A relative – from a French town, we hear (5)
7. A general pardon (7)
12. I con Vera (anag.) – and this girl, too! (8)
13. A mender (anag.) – given a different handle! (7)
15. Cry out (7)
16. Rank-smelling (6)
18. Gents (5)
20. Pertaining to quality of sound (5)
21. A tale of heroes (4)

120

ACROSS

6. Wild revelry, after tea – in state car (7)
7. Lady of rank (5)
8. Firm, Edward – abstained from food (6)
9. Raises one's spirits – for a toast! (6)
10. Confections (10)
12. A materialist (10)
16. Person of distinction (6)
17. High-pitched (6)
18. Recompense – a salesman? Yes (5)
19. Absence of restrictions – more fed! (anag.) (7)

DOWN

1. Cereal (5)
2. A book reviewer, for instance (6)
3. Marvellously (10)
4. Girl's name (6)
5. An obstacle (7)
9. Rector hiss? (anag.) – Must be the church singers! (10)
11. Seats (7)
13. Give power to Henry – deadly (6)
14. Small hole for lace (6)
15. Inundate (5)

121

ACROSS

1. Astonished (6)
5. Comes into flower (6)
8. Meat – for an essayist (4)
9. Vault over? – Flop, rage! (anag.) (4-4)
10. Arrange in good order (10)
12. Bring in from abroad? – I'm facing harbour (6)
14. Sword case (6)
15. A cleaning spirit (10)
19. A m-mother, say? – Obvious! (8)
20. Part of pear I devoured – very dry (4)
21. Emphasise (6)
22. Abhor (6)

DOWN

2. Occasion when one eats (4-4)
3. An animal (5)
4. Gratify (7)
5. Explosion (5)
6. Crime – of a receiver! (7)
7. Gloomy state of mind? – One's destiny's turned up! (4)
11. Sheets of wax on which letters are cut (8)
13. An atrocity – not in fashion! (7)
14. Perfumed (7)
16. Parts of sails (5)
17. Parch (5)
18. Spy – rising summits (4)

122

ACROSS

1. Priest has shivering fit – in a city (6)
5. Lethargic condition (6)
9. Taxes (6)
10. Arranged in rows (6)
11. Lend an ear to – a catalogue! (4)
12. Item of furniture (8)
14. Harsh – to cut with a point! (6)
16. A faint sound (6)
19. Thrives (8)
21. Towards (4)
22. A facial feature (6)
23. Of a sloping type (6)
24. Shoulder-bands (6)
25. Small number facing corpse? – None! (6)

DOWN

2. Massacre in East – unvarying course of action (7)
3. Cartilage (7)
4. In another place (9)
6. A fraction (5)
7. Act – on behalf of each class (7)
8. Stag (3-4)
13. Pardon (9)
14. Nickname of the Royal Engineers (7)
15. Flowers (7)
17. Garden-plant – a herb, we hear, with a thorn-like feature (7)
18. Inexperienced (7)
20. Cost (5)

123

ACROSS

7. Anatomical feature (4)
8. County (8)
9. Attract – everybody to the river (6)
10. Safe retreats (6)
11. £25 – for a horse! (4)
12. Ill-mannered (8)
15. Saint, one who roams about – an alien (8)
17. General information – provided by a fool (4)
18. Fuels (6)
21. Tradesman's distinctive garb – makes one irritable! (6)
22. Anonymous (8)
23. Oil container – for armed vehicle (4)

DOWN

1. An upright supporting a cross-bar (8)
2. A sheriff's subsidiary (6)
3. Coming into office – aircraftsman giving way (8)
4. A net-like fabric (4)
5. Implement – from second shed! (6)
6. Refuse of grain (4)
13. Render immobile (8)
14. Narrowing (8)
16. Joints (6)
17. To give up wholly to (6)
19. T' sheep – in public conveyance! (4)
20. Worried state – rising damps! (4)

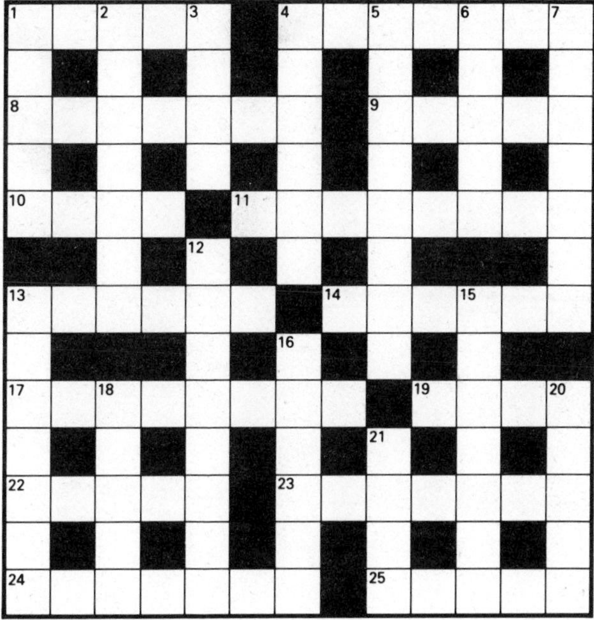

124

ACROSS

1. Show off – in fun! (5)
4. A Scottish town (7)
8. A unit of artillery (7)
9. Praise highly (5)
10. A deity – with wounded back! (4)
11. Money-lender's profit – enough to engage the mind! (8)
13. Symbols (6)
14. Funnels – loads of them! (6)
17. Urged (8)
19. A wintry feature (4)
22. Twisted loops in ropes (5)
23. Towers (7)
24. GT ready? (anag.) – What a terrible accident! (7)
25. Howls heard – in a Principality (5)

DOWN

1. Sword (5)
2. Prospect (7)
3. To pour forth abundantly (4)
4. Working steadily (6)
5. Ingredients of – the weather! (8)
6. Supple (5)
7. Takes one's hat off to – and addresses (7)
12. One to whom a cheque is assigned (8)
13. Ornament (7)
15. Hide – study a marine creature, we're told (7)
16. Brazenly (6)
18. An animal (5)
20. Western snakes – creatures that sting (5)
21. Ship's company (4)

4

THEMATIC PUZZLES

125

READY – STEADY – GO! In this puzzle (and in the next fourteen puzzles) the answers to clues in block capitals may be (a) synonyms of the clues; or (b) examples suggested by the clues; or (c) words which help the clues to form other expressions. For example, the answers to the clue BOOK could be (a) RESERVE/ENGAGE; or (b) BIBLE/KORAN; or (c) SHELF/MAKER. The other clues are straightforward definitions; or, occasionally, they are of the normal cryptic kind.

ACROSS

1. Morsel of bread (5)
4. READY (7)
8. Clothing, generally (7)
9. Mother – in a dilemma, terribly (5)
10. A recess (4)
11. READY (8)
13. Male domestic pet (3-3)
14. Strive for something high – a pointed church tower (6)
18. A vagrant (8)
20. Light military vehicle (4)
22. Circular (5)
23. STEADY (7)
24. Wide tidal part of a river (7)
25. To correct (5)

DOWN

1. A peer's crown (7)
2. STEADY (7)
3. S. African farmer (4)
4. Wishy-washy (6)
5. Pillar supporting a street-light (8)
6. Bury (5)
7. Gashed by a bull – blush! (5)
12. A country in the Far East (8)
15. Floating sheet of frozen water (3-4)
16. Breathed one's last (7)
17. GO (6)
18. GO (5)
19. Sound made by a pig (5)
21. A monster (4)

126

PALACE

ACROSS

1. A catastrophe – with Diana's flower (8)
5. Moved rapidly (4)
9. PAL (5)
10. Chicken quickly reared for the pot (7)
11. PAL (6)
12. Conductor's staff (5)
14. Made a start (6)
16. Urges (6)
19. Munch – having tea with MP (5)
21. Lacking sufficient strength (6)
24. Infuriated (7)
25. PAL (5)
26. Hut (4)
27. Disclosed in breach of trust (8)

DOWN

1. A common weed (4)
2. Cur goes (anag.) – must be the whip! (7)
3. Fashion (5)
4. Plants in soil (6)
6. ACE (5)
7. Absence of light (8)
8. Stockbroker (6)
13. ACE (3-5)
15. ACE (6)
17. In a logically sound way (7)
18. Small pool (6)
20. Corner (5)
22. Brownish yellow (5)
23. Tinted – but faded, we hear! (4)

127

BREAKFAST

ACROSS

1. BREAK (7)
5. Frolic (5)
8. A claimant to a throne – r-repented (anag.) (9)
9. Add up (3)
10. In a niggardly manner (8)
12. An impulse (4)
14. A gypsy (6)
15. BREAK (6)
17. An exam (4)
18. BREAK (4-4)
21. Hair-style's returned – that's the gist of it (3)
22. Completely involved (9)
24. To strain (5)
25. Landed properties (7)

DOWN

1. Cherished desires (5)
2. To rest (3)
3. Using a drag-net (8)
4. Sings like one in the Alps (6)
5. FAST (4)
6. Act as mediator (9)
7. Young cats (7)
11. FAST (9)
13. Promenade (3-5)
14. Retribution (7)
16. To bargain (6)
19. A king with ass's ears – is mad! (anag.) (5)
20. Subsequent (4)
23. FAST (3)

128

LEADING QUESTION

ACROSS
1. LEADING (5)
4. LEADING (7)
8. One's due (3)
9. LEADING (9)
10. Registers (7)
11. Steals – Nicholas's (5)
13. Threaten (6)
15. Written – and enclosed! (6)
18. A bit (5)
19. Encroach (7)
21. Defensive barriers made of stakes (9)
23. Fish-eggs (3)
24. Shorten – a span! (7)
25. A founder of Rome (5)

DOWN
1. Prop on which a lever moves (7)
2. Reserve (9)
3. Drunkard (5)
4. A minister (6)
5. To inflame with anger (7)
6. Mountain (3)
7. Shouts (5)
12. QUESTION (9)
14. Sounded like a grating hinge (7)
16. Becomes profound (7)
17. QUESTION (6)
18. An Italian dish – after one (5)
20. QUESTION (5)
22. Paddle (3)

129

COAT-COLLAR

ACROSS

1. Painful muscular contraction (5)
4. Offered oneself as candidate (7)
8. More sprightly (7)
9. COAT (5)
10. Unwrought metal (3)
11. The process of disbanding (9)
13. COAT (6)
15. COAT (6)
18. Dog's where? (anag.) – Borders of lane (9)
20. Letter (3)
21. Girl – among several in dance-hall (5)
23. Early English poet (7)
24. Trifled (7)
25. Danger (5)

DOWN

1. Line of altitude on a map (7)
2. COLLAR (9)
3. Showed impertinent curiosity – and haughtiness, we hear (5)
4. COLLAR (6)
5. A dressmaker's guide (7)
6. Electrically charged particle (3)
7. Of a duke (5)
12. American tram (9)
14. Globe of vision (3-4)
16. A bird (7)
17. Compelled (6)
18. Putted (5)
19. Rascal (5)
22. COLLAR (3)

130

BIGHEAD

ACROSS

1. A unit of weight (5)
4. Bitter (7)
8. BIG (7)
9. To treat over-indulgently (5)
10. Bird's bill (4)
11. BIG (8)
13. Tear in (anag.) – part of the eye (6)
14. Broken down cars (6)
18. Body of diplomatic etiquette (8)
20. BIG (4)
22. Foreign (5)
23. Conscripted, as in USA (7)
24. Genuine (7)
25. Senior member of a tribe (5)

DOWN

1. Ivy, for instance (7)
2. Batter and split – a fortification (7)
3. Fish – and a fruit, sent up (4)
4. Clergyman (6)
5. In a higher storey (8)
6. Freshwater fish (5)
7. A form of flatulence (5)
12. Declare (8)
15. Wooed (7)
16. One who pays out (7)
17. HEAD (6)
18. Dramatic works (5)
19. HEAD (5)
21. HEAD (4)

131

ROCK AND ROLL

ACROSS

1. Became overcast (8)
5. Employed (4)
9. Open sore – cruel (anag.) (5)
10. ROCK (7)
11. A measure of grain (6)
12. Writing-tables (5)
14. A charm (6)
16. Cowardly (6)
19. Not as young (5)
21. ROCK (6)
24. Late (7)
25. ROCK (5)
26. A small crisp cake (4)
27. Brought together again (8)

DOWN

1. ROLL (4)
2. Tell – about German nobleman (7)
3. Soil (5)
4. Swallow wholly (6)
6. ROLL (5)
7. Treating a wound (8)
8. Pantry (6)
13. ROLL (2,6)
15. Walk with long steps (6)
17. Heroic (7)
18. Unit of electricity (6)
20. Lees (5)
22. Rinse (anag.) – for an ingredient of plastics (5)
23. A metal – to conduct! (4)

132

TALL STORY

ACROSS

1. Unionist in American Civil War (7)
5. An Italian opera (5)
8. Kind of loaf (5-4)
9. Curved line – made with piece of charcoal (3)
10. TALL (8)
12. Archaic form of 'you' (4)
14. Observe (6)
15. No longer capable (4,2)
17. Hue (4)
18. TALL (8)
21. Middle Eastern name (3)
22. Bungler (9)
24. TALL (5)
25. Boy's name (7)

DOWN

1. STORY (5)
2. River (3)
3. A brilliant glow (8)
4. A boy – one ill (anag.) (6)
5. STORY (4)
6. An Italian food (9)
7. STORY (7)
11. An added piece (9)
13. Almanac (8)
14. A game (7)
16. Vigorous (6)
19. A moorland plant (5)
20. Do as one is told (4)
23. Take to one's heels (3)

133

THE GREAT DIVIDE

ACROSS

1. Festoons – parts of ships (5)
4. Gigantic (7)
8. I love (in Latin) (3)
9. THE GREAT (9)
10. Consume too much (7)
11. Electrical unit, to the French – is sufficient (5)
13. Seaweed – in confused mass (6)
15. THE GREAT (6)
18. THE GREAT (5)
19. Foes (7)
21. THE GREAT (9)
23. Frozen water (3)
24. Sirius (7)
25. Notes (anag.) – musical qualities (5)

DOWN

1. DIVIDE (4,3)
2. Kilts, once (anag.) – tightly woven (5-4)
3. DIVIDE (5)
4. Formal agreement between states (6)
5. Excessive toil (7)
6. Set up a study – for a small boy (3)
7. DIVIDE (5)
12. DIVIDE (9)
14. Most huge (7)
16. Drives away (7)
17. More advanced in years (6)
18. Walked with measured tread (5)
20. Throw out (5)
22. A tie-on label – in stage-coach (3)

134

DEVIL-MAY-CARE

ACROSS

1. Asks persistently – for plimsolls (5)
4. Walked in military manner (7)
8. Riled (7)
9. DEVIL (5)
10. DEVIL (3)
11. Run down? — GIs parade! (anag.) (9)
13. MAY (6)
15. Glasgow football team (6)
18. Warm winter coat (9)
20. Little Hannah (3)
21. Decorate a wall (5)
23. Form of syncopated music (7)
24. Types of hounds (7)
25. Material – with a narrow stripe, sent to North (5)

DOWN

1. The Pope (7)
2. Amplifier (9)
3. Hard and compact? – Well, the cover is (5)
4. Fashionable (6)
5. Emit rays of light (7)
6. MAY (3)
7. Duffer (5)
12. CARE (9)
14. Old-fashioned supermarkets (7)
16. CARE (7)
17. Borders – for garments! (6)
18. Shade of brown – ape is (anag.) (5)
19. Man's name (5)
22. Breed of dog – boxer! (3)

135

SECOND-SIGHT

ACROSS

1. SECOND (5)
4. Furrows (7)
8. To be victorious (7)
9. A publication – for children! (5)
10. SECOND (4)
11. The training of horses in deportment (8)
13. Girl has line – for string of beads! (6)
14. SECOND (6)
18. Morbidly preoccupied (8)
20. A leader – of the French Church (4)
22. SECOND (5)
23. Tombstone inscription (7)
24. Nullified (7)
25. Cries – with a little afterthought (5)

DOWN

1. A Roman god (7)
2. Strips one of money – and woollen coats (7)
3. Period of time (4)
4. Girl with metal – in abundance (6)
5. An item left out (8)
6. SIGHT (5)
7. SIGHT (5)
12. SIGHT (8)
15. Imitate – a bird, at close of day? (7)
16. Develops fangs (7)
17. Decapitate (6)
18. Characteristic of a cereal (5)
19. A catapult (5)
21. SIGHT (4)

136

MONEY-SPINNER

ACROSS

1. Imitators (4-4)
5. Boring instruments (4)
9. MONEY (5)
10. Feign – before nurse (7)
11. MONEY (6)
12. A young bird (5)
14. Prairie-wolf (6)
16. An inventor – with no false airs, on reflection! (6)
19. A Greek island (5)
21. MONEY (6)
24. Give a right to (7)
25. Fish with a dredging net (5)
26. MONEY (4)
27. Accompanied – listened courteously (8)

DOWN

1. Cover for the shoulders – and the head! (4)
2. Priggishness – pure, dry (anag.) (7)
3. Beg (5)
4. Formal headgear (3-3)
6. SPINNER (5)
7. Dates, gin (anag.) – medicinally calming (8)
8. SPINNER (6)
13. I cry out, very audibly – for a dessert! (3-5)
15. Honest (6)
17. Facing the ocean (7)
18. Most peculiar (6)
20. SPINNER (5)
22. SPINNER (5)
23. Lump of turf (4)

137

TRADE WINDS

ACROSS

1. TRADE (7)
5. Franz ———, composer of light operas (5)
8. Dying (9)
9. Local theatre company – getting through turns! (3)
10. TRADE (8)
12. Type of floor cover (4)
14. Sampled – t' dates (anag.) (6)
15. A combative sport (6)
17. Cycled, by the sound of it – making for highway! (4)
18. TRADE (8)
21. Help (3)
22. A reptile (9)
24. Excessively fat (5)
25. Hill with a fissure – must be the cataract! (7)

DOWN

1. Head in charge – providing subject for essay (5)
2. Atmosphere (3)
3. Rent safe (anag.) – a securing device (8)
4. Embrace (6)
5. Bulky pieces of wood – in the records (4)
6. WIND (9)
7. To censure (7)
11. Manage incompetently (9)
13. Shirk – with Mum, and loiter! (8)
14. WIND (7)
16. Young hen (6)
19. Traps (anag.) – for small fish (5)
20. WIND (4)
23. A limb (3)

138

SNAKE-CHARMER

ACROSS

1. A rice dish – with very good base! (5)
4. SNAKE (7)
8. Boy – left, with notice! (3)
9. SNAKE (4-5)
10. Purify (7)
11. Permeate (5)
13. Wanderers – small number, crazy, going South (6)
15. First appearances (6)
18. Continue beyond allotted time (3,2)
19. Sewer's protective device (7)
21. Male – as 'm' in clue! (anag.) (9)
23. SNAKE (3)
24. Jaunts (7)
25. SNAKE (5)

DOWN

1. Bird with huge bill (7)
2. CHARMER (6,3)
3. Rouse (5)
4. Vocalist (6)
5. Accept (7)
6. Withdraw like the tide (3)
7. Traffic – up eastern river (5)
12. CHARMER (9)
14. CHARMER (3,4)
16. Support for railway lines (7)
17. Blemishes? – Saints? (anag.) (6)
18. CHARMER (5)
20. Girl – from Cheshire (Nantwich) (5)
22. Heavy drinker? – Well, half TT! (3)

139

COUNTRYSIDE

ACROSS

1. COUNTRY (5)
4. COUNTRY (7)
8. A watch-dog – making an academic rigid! (7)
9. COUNTRY (5)
10. Poorly – in a state, in short! (3)
11. One who comes after (9)
13. COUNTRY (6)
15. Lend a hand (6)
18. A cascade (9)
20. COUNTRY (3, abbrev.)
21. Fortunate (5)
23. COUNTRY (7)
24. Reg, Stan (anag.) – odd (7)
25. The ocean's ebbing – with rapidity (5)

DOWN

1. Living under canvas (7)
2. Out of funds (9)
3. A young girl – out of order (5)
4. SIDE (6)
5. Books of the Bible (7)
6. Woman – in a homestead, abiding (3)
7. Spanish gentleman, or – the giving sort (5)
12. Specify (9)
14. Continue – to behave in unruly way (5,2)
16. SIDE (7)
17. SIDE (6)
18. SIDE (5)
19. SIDE (5)
22. SIDE (3)

140

TROUBLED WATERS Each clue in block capitals consists of the jumbled letters of a RIVER to be entered in the diagram at the number indicated.

ACROSS

1. Smallholdings (6)
4. Powerful (6)
8. EILOR (5)
9. AHNNNOS (7)
10. Letter (7)
11. A river plant (5)
12. AEEHPRSTU (9)
17. Rash (5)
19. Part of the gut (7)
21. Unmarried girls (7)
22. EHINR (5)
23. Detective (6)
24. EENRSV (6)

DOWN

1. RLDECA (6)
2. A mouth-like opening (7)
3. TTRNE (5)
5. Passage through (7)
6. Possessed (5)
7. SNGGEA (6)
9. A place on the Kentish coast (9)
13. Discharge of a debt (7)
14. Young pilchard (7)
15. TSMHEA (6)
16. Invisible (6)
18. SNIEE (5)
20. Spasm (5)

141

DIZZY HEIGHTS This time, the clues in block capitals are the jumbled letters of four MOUNTAINS and four MOUNTAIN RANGES.

ACROSS

1. ACGIMNORRS (10)
7. EEERSTV (7)
8. A type of cloth (5)
10. AENT (4)
11. Women's Lib supporter (8)
13. AAARRT (6)
15. Person granted tenure of property (6)
17. One who works a machine (8)
18. Cleanse with water (4)
21. Truth (5)
22. One who attacks another abusively (7)
23. Jollifications (10)

DOWN

1. Free from dirt (5)
2. A separate article in a list (4)
3. Caught, like a fish (6)
4. Past ages (3,5)
5. SPNMIED (7)
6. Apparatuses for producing gases, etc. (10)
9. TTRRONMHEA (10)
12. Long-distance race (8)
14. Inspiring wonder or fear (7)
16. URONME (6)
19. TSLAA (5)
20. Girl's name (4)

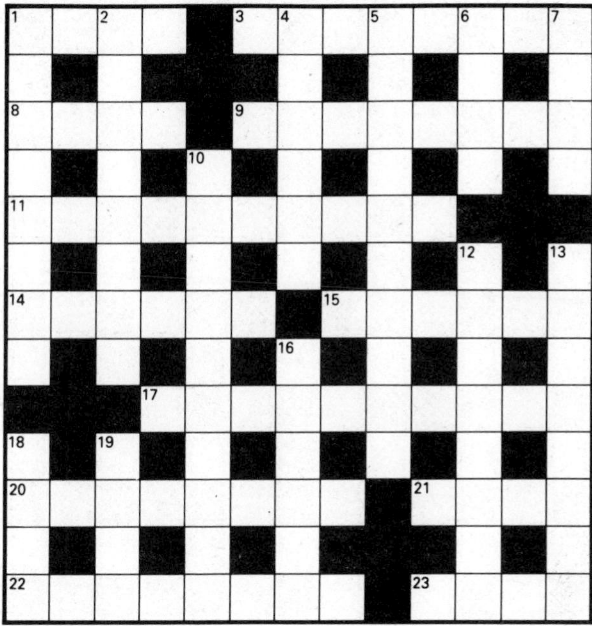

THE NAME OF THE GAME The diagram contains seven GAMES; each one is clued by a jumble of its letters, in block capitals.

ACROSS

1. Go about listlessly (4)
3. ABBCEGIR (8)
8. ANPS (4)
9. £1 notes (8)
11. The scientific study of alloys, etc. (10)
14. CCEORS (6)
15. Cigarettes, for example (6)
17. A type of bed (4-6)
20. A woman's name (8)
21. Thick slice of cake (4)
22. DEIMNOOS (8)
23. No longer new (4)

DOWN

1. Hotchpotch (8)
2. Application of a theory (8)
4. Hearsay (6)
5. AABCGKMMNO (10)
6. Declare (4)
7. Otherwise (4)
10. Former pupil of a public school (3,7)
12. EIKLSSTT (8)
13. Attributed (8)
16. BDEGIR (6)
18. Among (4)
19. Stalk (4)

143

RAINSTORM Four CATS and four DOGS appear in the diagram; each one is clued by a jumble of its letters, in block capitals. Two of these answers are in plural form.

ACROSS

7. AMPU (4)
8. Almond paste (8)
9. EERSTT (6)
10. EGIRST (6)
11. A cry to stop a horse (4)
13. ADELOPRS (8)
15. The act of giving out (8)
18. Certain (4)
19. DELOOP (6)
21. Farm animals (6)
23. With the hide removed (8)
24. Skin complaint (4)

DOWN

1. Stringed instrument (4)
2. Snares for trespassers (8)
3. Having no ethical basis (6)
4. A cave, poetically (6)
5. The side of a stage (4)
6. AABDLORR (8)
12. Beds for seamen (8)
14. AAAILNST (8)
16. People skilled in crossing frozen regions (6)
17. Most agreeable (6)
20. Humid (4)
22. XLNY (4)

144

MIXED FEELINGS Clues in block capitals are anagrams. In each case, the letters have to be rearranged to form the required answer – which is a FEELING or state of mind.

ACROSS

1. To incorporate (6)
4. Hangs cloth in folds (6)
8. Concise (5)
9. A travelling-bag (4-3)
10. Arrived at a total (5,2)
11. IN CAP (5)
12. MR. E. MINTER (9)
17. A writer of fables (5)
19. TOE-NAIL (7)
21. SEND ASS (7)
22. E.G. RED (5)
23. RON WED (6)
24. Soups (6)

DOWN

1. To snare (6)
2. BEDROOM (7)
3. ADDER (5)
5. Recurrence of illness (7)
6. Unadorned (5)
7. SCALE 'O' (6)
9. SNIP, SHAPE (9)
13. Full (7)
14. Three-pronged spear (7)
15. East European city (6)
16. Terminals of electrolytic cells (6)
18. Part of N. Africa (5)
20. RANGE (5)

145

SHIVER MY TIMBERS! Each type of TREE in the diagram is clued by a jumble of its letters, in block capitals.

ACROSS

7. Swindles (6)
8. Curls one's hair (6)
9. Ancient ship (4)
10. Splendid (8)
11. ACEMORSY (8)
13. Grind with the teeth (4)
14. Numerous (4)
16. Type of coffee-making machine (8)
18. AHHNORTW (8)
21. AEKT (4)
22. ALOPPR (6)
23. Bursts out (6)

DOWN

1. RCEHYR (6)
2. YONMHGAA (8)
3. A small wood, subject of a Welsh folk-song (3-5)
4. CERA (4)
5. PNIE (4)
6. USRPEC (6)
12. Consumed (8)
13. UTSNHECT (8)
15. King Arthur's resting-place (6)
17. Hare-brained (6)
19. A white mineral (4)
20. Belonging to us (4)

146

HANGAR The diagram accommodates six AIRCRAFT (one being a slang term); each is clued by a jumble of its letters, in block capitals.

ACROSS

1. Snug (4)
3. Complete forgetfulness (8)
8. No marines – as a rule (4)
9. Smearing (8)
11. To reach forth (10)
14. Not so shallow – river gets through! (6)
15. Footfall heard – in Asian plain (6)
17. CEEHILOPRT (10)
20. AEEJLNPT (3-5)
21. EIKT (4)
22. Salesman hiding the truth – in answering (8)
23. Little Elizabeth (4)

DOWN

1. ROONEDCC (8)
2. Walked in a self-important manner (8)
4. ROMEBB (6)
5. A mark (10)
6. Egyptian deity – found in the Thames (4)
7. Close by (4)
10. Heavenly (10)
12. TSRPIIFE (8)
13. Proximity (8)
16. Type of haddock – a Scandinavian one (6)
18. A container – open (4)
19. On the highest part (4)

147

HOPPING MAD! In this puzzle, the clues in block capitals are the jumbled letters of various DANCES.

ACROSS

7. Capital of Peru (4)
8. ONMLFECA (8)
9. A parish officer – giving ornament to the Parisian (6)
10. NNCCAA (6)
11. Humble, we hear – in one's bearing (4)
13. UUAAHHLL (4-4)
15. Confusion (8)
18. Travel on horseback (4)
19. YSMMIH (6)
21. South American ungulates (6)
23. Distribute (8)
24. A wharf – one high up, we're told! (4)

DOWN

1. EIJV (4)
2. AADFGNNO (8)
3. Newly (6)
4. Annul (6)
5. A woodland plant (4)
6. Saint moved slowly – then scribbled (8)
12. SGHIIIJR (5,3)
14. EHINOPPR (8)
16. Senior members of a profession – with Party yearnings! (6)
17. One who catches rodents (6)
20. Cleans up – bushy heads of hair (4)
22. ELRE (4)

148

SHIPWRECK In each case, the jumble of letters in block capitals represents the wreckage of a VESSEL. Two of them are in plural form.

ACROSS

1. ACEFHORRTV (10)
7. Military storehouse – an earl's (anag.) (7)
8. FFISK (5)
10. Try out – a match! (4)
11. What astronomers do (8)
13. Make use of – a measure, a dodge (6)
15. SERILN (6)
17. Pistols, for example (4-4)
18. Surface froth (4)
21. Religious, one number – for this instrument (5)
22. Malice (3-4)
23. YTSSRROEED (10)

DOWN

1. Dry, thin seed-cases (5)
2. See, in East – a climbing plant (4)
3. To connect (6)
4. Sappers, with force – take control (8)
5. RIATFEG (7)
6. LEPSTATBIH (10)
9. A commercial specimen costing nothing (4,6)
12. BLOGATON (8)
14. CANNPIE (7)
16. Coiner (anag.) – man from Sicily (6)
19. Mangers (5)
20. Small chimney (4)

149

PLAYING ONE'S PART The invented names in block capitals are anagrams. In each case, the letters must be rearranged to form the name of a SHAKESPEARIAN CHARACTER.

ACROSS

1. L. MEATH (6)
4. Sensitive plant (6)
8. Mother-of-pearl – from northern area (5)
9. Leaves off (7)
10. E. SALTER (7)
11. A native of the Middle East (5)
12. Women who succeed! (9)
17. A salad plant (5)
19. L.H. TOOLE (7)
21. ALI H. POE (7)
22. Constructed (5)
23. Regular income (6)
24. A help with women's service returns – in sports venues! (6)

DOWN

1. A name – to deal with! (6)
2. T. BECHAM (7)
3. Vote into power (5)
5. S.S. CAIUS (7)
6. A. SACC (5)
7. Attack – giving fool trouble (6)
9. A.M.E. SEDDON (9)
13. Cut off – in Urals (anag.) (7)
14. Soiled (7)
15. One peevish – on the other side (6)
16. O. PIART (6)
18. Girl's name (5)
20. It's the custom – this dress! (5)

150

BOUQUET The diagram contains eight kinds of FLOWERS (two of them plural). Each one is concealed in an *italic* expression, but with its letters jumbled. For example, DAHLIA is hidden in '*One hydrange*(A I HAD L)*opped*', at 7 Across. The other clues are normal definitions.

ACROSS

7. *One hydrangea I had lopped* (6)
8. *Snow in March hid crocus* (6)
9. Lake (4)
10. *Daisies are for making chains* (8)
11. Proprietor of a large guest-house (8)
13. Submissive (4)
14. Testament (4)
16. To produce (8)
18. *Sunflower must be old, if fading* (8)
21. In low spirits (4)
22. A ruler (6)
23. *Forget-me-not is pulled up* (6)

DOWN

1. Manage with inadequate means (4,2)
2. *A whorl bee'll buzz around* (8)
3. Bewildering (8)
4. *Fluorescent* (4)
5. High cards (4)
6. Enlarge (6)
12. Curls of hair (8)
13. *Flower-girl amid gorgeous blooms* (8)
15. Pictures (6)
17. Cards that take all others (6)
19. Limbs (4)
20. Be overfond (4)

TELESCOPIC SIGHTS Each *italic* expression contains the jumbled letters of a phenomenon found in OUTER SPACE. For example, VEGA is hidden in '*Libr*(A E.G., V)*isible*', at 1 Across.

ACROSS

1. *Libra e.g., visible* (4)
3. Enlivened (8)
8. *Solar year* (4)
9. Deserts (8)
11. Neutral in tone (10)
14. To increase vitality (4,2)
15. *Red, Aldebaran? Usually* (6)
17. Such an attack is meant to forestall the enemy (10)
20. Revenue from a business (8)
21. *A hole – black* (4)
22. Give confidence to (8)
23. To sell (4)

DOWN

1. Rate of motion (8)
2. Editing (8)
4. *Probe (lunar)* (6)
5. A hand-written document (10)
6. Sound made by a flute (4)
7. See 18
10. Glum (10)
12. To hint (8)
13. *Locate radio star* (8)
16. *Comet returning* (6)
18, 7. *Dr. Who trusts Tardis* (4-4)
19. Operatic song (4)

152

CHEESE AND WINE PARTY The diagram contains four CHEESES and four WINES; each appears somewhere in an *italic* expression, but with its letters jumbled. For example, EDAM occurs in '*Chees*(E, MAD)*am?*', at 2 Down.

ACROSS

1. Unrestricted utterance (4,6)
7. An enclosure (7)
8. A fish (5)
10. *Camembert, processed* (4)
11. Furnished (8)
13. A choice morsel (6)
15. *Full crate of wine* (6)
17. Retarded (8)
18. A sculpture of head and shoulders (4)
21. Boredom (5)
22. *Had Chianti, lots* (7)
23. *Cheese and fizz à gogo, Lorna!* (10)

DOWN

1. An affront (5)
2. *Cheese, madam?* (4)
3. *Wine (elderberry) shelved* (6)
4. Industrial area of Wales (4,4)
5. *Tasted a red cheese* (7)
6. To commit (10)
9. Contemplating (10)
12. *I sling red wine* (8)
14. Canadian city (7)
16. An extract from Scripture read during a service (6)
19. Prefix meaning 'excessively' (5)
20. Type of pen (4)

153

BIRD-WATCHING There are fourteen BIRDS in the diagram (one in plural form). Each may be seen, with letters jumbled, in one of the *italic* expressions. For example, LARK appears in '*Grebe nea*(R LAK)*e*', at 21 Across.

ACROSS

7. *Blackbirds sing – pie opened!* (6)
8. Rebellion (6)
9. Insect (4)
10. *Hovering dipper* (4-4)
11. *Hear willow-warbler sing late on* (8)
13. *Hen troubled with fowl-pest* (4)
14. Sour (4)
16. *Speckled US hawks* (8)
18. *Gulls in creek close by* (8)
21. *Grebe near lake* (4)
22. Butcher's pin (6)
23. *Cormorant, generally seen at sea* (6)

DOWN

1. *Eaglet in nest* (6)
2. Shackled (8)
3. Intestines (8)
4. *Toucan, we're told* (4)
5. Old Roman poet (4)
6. *Poultry may develop roup* (6)
12. *Egg-layers* (8)
13. Walking like an infant (8)
15. Sounds like a raven (6)
17. *Wakeful, crew like Chanticleer* (6)
19. *Gulls over Kontiki, wheeling* (4)
20. An Irish boy's name (4)

154

TRAFFIC-LIGHTS Six answers are clued by coloured lights in block capitals. Each answer is also hidden, with its letters jumbled, in the *italic* expression which follows the light.

ACROSS

7. Carry (4)
8. Surmount (8)
9. Cut into thin pieces (6)
10. GREEN: *Don't stop – run through* (6)
11. To scare birds away (4)
13. Late Victorian decade (8)
15. Oval (8)
18. Girl's name (4)
19. AMBER: *Slowly, easy does it* (6)
21. RED: *Halt, in saloon-car* (6)
23. One who provides dress patterns (8)
24. Title of a Mohammedan leader (4)

DOWN

1. Kind of duck (4)
2. GREEN: *Pass over diabolic crossroad* (8)
3. AMBER: *Old engine, slowing* (6)
4. A hold in wrestling (6)
5. Mark left by a wound (4)
6. Cheeky (8)
12. Greeks (8)
14. Tortoise (8)
16. Pulling (6)
17. RED: *Every car stopped* (6)
20. Put down (4)
22. Middle Eastern country (4)

5

DOUBLE TROUBLE

Each of the following crosswords numbered 155 to 164 consists of two puzzles. The two diagrams are identical, but the answers are different. The upper crossword is a plain one, with definition clues only, the lower one is fully cryptic.

PLAIN

ACROSS

7. Impetuous (4)
8. A boaster (8)
9. False (6)
10. Machine (6)
11. Not occupied (4)
13. A cooking vessel (8)
15. Precisely objective (8)
18. A cipher (4)
19. Scattered about (6)
21. Gaudy (6)
23. Impetus (8)
24. A board-game (4)

DOWN

1. Minor chess-piece (4)
2. Unlucky number (8)
3. Head of a religious establishment (6)
4. A fancy cake (6)
5. Eagerly excited (4)
6. A regular toper (8)
12. Process of thinning with water (8)
14. Surround (8)
16. Danish king of England (6)
17. A vegetable (6)
20. A water-jug (4)
22. Sodium carbonate (4)

CRYPTIC

ACROSS

7. Search for pole in shed (4)
8. A forged item, about deceased, flattered (8)
9. Meat for each in picnic basket (6)
10. A New Testament character, pious, departed (6)
11. Favour? Hoot disapprovingly at end of oration (4)
13. Close study shows mainly scrub, very small (8)
15. Rep's loan misread as one's own (8)
18. Skin from grape eliminated (4)
19. Igneous rock produced by a blast (6)
21. Girl from wooded valley meets DA (6)
23. This girl's a winner, coming before disheartened Ida (8)
24. Levi's designed bride's headwear (4)

DOWN

1. Instrument – lean against upright (4)
2. Dispatches (including gratuity) the salaries of church ministers (8)
3. Marine creature wauls crazily round top of reef (6)
4. A garment for an athlete (6)
5. Quite a blow, we hear, for the girl (4)
6. Condemn a grammatical expression (8)
12. Like musical dramas, with artist in strange poetic setting (8)
14. Have toy piano repaired – unbalanced in upper part (3-5)
16. Inborn character shows wild state (6)
17. Mum held by long ungainly woodcutter (3-3)
20. It's a blended Italian wine (4)
22. Lark, say, seen to rise – and drop! (4)

155

PLAIN

CRYPTIC

PLAIN

ACROSS

7. Rub gently (6)
8. A place where bees are kept (6)
9. A prejudice (4)
10. Beat up and cook eggs (8)
11. A dome-like canvas shelter (4-4)
13. A sly glimpse (4)
14. Clothed (4)
16. Kind of rodent (8)
18. Exceeded a limit (8)
21. Drag (4)
22. A loose-fitting garment (6)
23. German songs (6)

DOWN

1. To contend (6)
2. Comforted (8)
3. Support for a mattress (8)
4. Animal fibre (4)
5. A thin coating (4)
6. Young salmon (6)
12. Strangle (8)
13. One who helps actors to remember lines (8)
15. Beautiful (6)
17. A tray (6)
19. A disease afflicting poultry (4)
20. Part of the foot (4)

CRYPTIC

ACROSS

7. Sheep in Rome, running wild (6)
8. I, Ronald and Edward smoothed things out (6)
9. Mixture of spirits and water from river drunk by mythical giant (4)
10. Group of four lines? – Question, with a locomotive! (8)
11. Fetch help in for plaiting (8)
13. Woven thread taken from two, off-coloured (4)
14. To yearn is tedious? (4)
16. A proposal for opera's opening (8)
18. Nozzle is not spraying – throw away (8)
21. Mercenary writer, roughly cut up! (4)
22. A university fellow is a handsome man (6)
23. Light rain gets the Queen after display (6)

DOWN

1. Tom's first mistake, in panic (6)
2. Dance round pole with Heather, making bell-like sounds (8)
3. Medical Officer's left nothing for an insect carrying disease (8)
4. Location of leaning tower is snapped by father (4)
5. Obstinate, active type, we hear (4)
6. Doc, me? I could become a GP (6)
12. Sign of old age shown by English poet, we're told, on head! (8)
13. Child dipping into wad got disturbed – by this pet guard? (5-3)
15. Cook too much, on account of party (6)
17. Girl upset Charles, endlessly (6)
19. Casks – hundreds, from what we hear (4)
20. Very good? – Well, average! (2-2)

156

PLAIN

CRYPTIC

PLAIN

ACROSS

1. Of a European city (5)
4. Atones for (7)
8. Broken partially (7)
9. Lax (5)
10. German for 'and' (3)
11. To set ashore (9)
13. Enhance (6)
15. A void (6)
18. Impregnates with a curative drug (9)
20. Acted (3)
21. Remove headwear (5)
23. Pertaining to the Seven Seas (7)
24. Playhouse (7)
25. Unit of heat (5)

DOWN

1. Hermit (7)
2. Wandered (9)
3. Nude (5)
4. A root vegetable (6)
5. Quandary (7)
6. The self (3)
7. Smooth (5)
12. Amplitude (9)
14. Pilot's cabin (7)
16. A small quantity (7)
17. An optical instrument for studying rotating machinery (6)
18. To shed plumage (5)
19. Item of bed-linen (5)
22. Snooker-player's rod (3)

CRYPTIC

ACROSS

1. Rapid bird (5)
4. Spiced drinks causing fisticuffs (7)
8. Flowers, popular with the birds (7)
9. Chatter with the French film star (5)
10. Bit of a blow, Ernie, to be in debt (3)
11. A circus performer juggling with metal (iron) (4-5)
13. Something to cause vomiting? Call me back (6)
15. Secretary's t-tipsy, tipsy (6)
18. Such as sling stones and whip St. Paul badly (9)
20. Odd spirit (3)
21. Disturbed a snug Scotsman (5)
23. Letters to a celebrity – cool man, one hears (3,4)
24. Old hero rebuilt huts, see (7)
25. Files spars out of shape (5)

DOWN

1. Drink, over puzzle, then guess (7)
2. Mischievous child lent me faulty tool (9)
3. Case in Austria, legal (5)
4. Proceed with father's boy (4,2)
5. From sunset to dawn, the endless lying must change! (7)
6. Excerpt from Schubert, central part (3)
7. Contemptuous expression from prophet, about North (5)
12. Major traffic routes – or sea lanes? (4,5)
14. I'm on a free ticket, surmounting eastern deadlock (7)
16. Blue Mts., possible source of falls! (7)
17. Outspoken, sharper, initially – then deceives at cards (6)
18. When in small cottage, seashore can be seen (5)
19. Nears ruins not so cracked! (5)
22. Enthusiastic expression in letter (3)

PLAIN

CRYPTIC

PLAIN

ACROSS
1. Marvellous! (5)
4. Narrowly U-shaped (7)
8. Example of public transport (7)
9. Aptitude (5)
10. Joyful (4)
11. Discrepancy (8)
13. A group of Scouts (6)
14. A business establishment (6)
18. Retaliatory measure (8)
20. Stash away (4)
22. A device regulating flow (5)
23. Deep sleep (7)
24. Outburst of bad temper (7)
25. Beleaguered state (5)

DOWN
1. Temporary substitute (4-3)
2. A hanging ornament (7)
3. A precious stone (4)
4. Light cavalryman (6)
5. Violate a rule (8)
6. A shellfish (5)
7. A Scandinavian language (5)
12. To be overbearing (8)
15. Distinguished (7)
16. Plant yielding pliant timber (3-4)
17. A healing oily substance (6)
18. Heavy industrial bolt (5)
19. Support for power-cables (5)
21. Ado (4)

CRYPTIC

ACROSS
1. 100 departed, separated violently (5)
4. Pry clumsily in middle of Egyptian monument (7)
8. One coin I put in, very old (7)
9. Unrefined – could be cured (5)
10. Exhausted in defeat (4)
11. Calculator making Communist erupt wildly (8)
13. Cad, right, getting more 'eated (6)
14. Plot to strike is madness! (6)
18. Rear cute, playful animal (8)
20. Poet hailing from sheikdom, Araby (4)
22. Priest in river? Just the opposite – and cleaner! (5)
23. Okker, say, has a high ball returned in game (7)
24. She who betrayed Samson treated head ill! (7)
25. A metal, for example, reflected slight colouring (5)

DOWN
1. Climb awkwardly about on disorganised ramble (7)
2. Bewitch up NE with song (7)
3. Muscle, feature of most hewers (4)
4. Customer – an Irishman, Ronald (6)
5. Outdone again? – Went back over the main points (8)
6. Horse seen from hill (5)
7. Dull king embraced by beloved (5)
12. Breastplate – or plate designed to cover part of chest (8)
15. Satirical attack from a loon, confused about MP (7)
16. Spoil entrance in southern resort (7)
17. Person in a miserable state has to vomit, we're told (6)
18. Managed to nab Edward (5)
19. Flynn cast in swashbuckler roles (5)
21. Obscene talk, turning stomachs over (4)

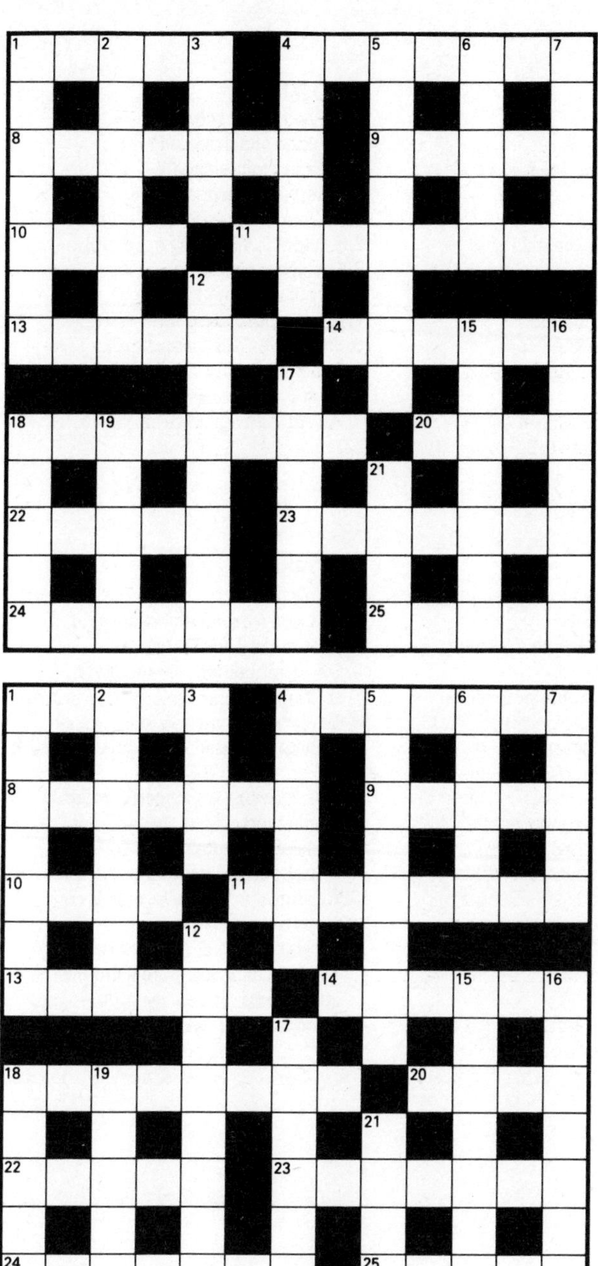

158

PLAIN

CRYPTIC

PLAIN

ACROSS

1. Sight (6)
4. Horrifies (6)
8. Receive punishment (3,2)
9. Forester (7)
10. Kind of syrup (7)
11. An ancient Greek dialect (5)
12. Declaration (9)
17. A senior monk (5)
19. To be unduly prominent (7)
21. To empty of air or gas (7)
22. William ———, an English king (5)
23. Artist's model (6)
24. Pincers (6)

DOWN

1. To leave empty (6)
2. Lacking vital juices (7)
3. Relating to the eye (5)
5. Side-view of a head (7)
6. People involved in commercials (2-3)
7. Ancient Roman playwright (6)
9. For what reason? (9)
13. To put into operation (7)
14. A rich chocolate confection (7)
15. Dr. Who's time-machine (6)
16. Tantalises (6)
18. To suit (5)
20. An Alpine region (5)

CRYPTIC

ACROSS

1. Dance with broken leg, move jerkily (6)
4. New atlas includes Pole obliquely (6)
8. Encourages grubs! (5)
9. Section of book in part of monastery (7)
10. Miles before vernal rugged town in English hills (7)
11. Drum wrapped in ribbon, golden (5)
12. Sid's back, treated, swelled! (9)
17. Spirit in strange level! (5)
19. Busts, scattered round isle, manage to survive (7)
21. First of girls lived in lodgings, kept tidy (7)
22. Sow's initial inclination is for hog-wash (5)
23. Rounded bar gripping cask (6)
24. Reduce exercise, we're told (6)

DOWN

1. Man's name, Jew, short on capital (6)
2. Old, grew crotchety, grumbled (7)
3. Yarn woven in Ellis (5)
5. SW sailor on bed, cleaned with cotton-wool (7)
6. To stern, on the river (5)
7. Fish for odd trout round head of brook (6)
9. Talked with a trickster, thoroughly acquainted (9)
13. Biblical king alone, over a day (7)
14. Newspapers provided by cleaners (7)
15. Aircraft shed made from hillside wood, it's said (6)
16. Nicked from NE, many turned up (6)
18. Old coin showing animal around king's head (5)
20. Beat, and drop fat on (5)

159

PLAIN

CRYPTIC

PLAIN

ACROSS

1. Bubbles in paint-work (8)
5. A set piece of work (4)
9. Clenched hands (5)
10. A blue-flowering herb (7)
11. Stupefied with horror (6)
12. To pinch sharply (5)
14. A rising movement (6)
16. Flung (6)
19. Ancient Roman robes (5)
21. A governing assembly (6)
24. A tableland (7)
25. Kind of spice (5)
26. Part of an egg (4)
27. Systematic investigation (8)

DOWN

1. A shade of yellow (4)
2. Perception (7)
3. Little Teresa (5)
4. Just claims (6)
6. To remain (5)
7. Giant gorilla (4,4)
8. Grab (6)
13. Increase the number of (8)
15. Slice of bacon (6)
17. Open-air (7)
18. Presuppose (6)
20. Holy vessel sought by knights (5)
22. A shallow recess (5)
23. Girl's name (4)

CRYPTIC

ACROSS

1. Camping out includes a series of military operations (8)
5. We hear yeast's a soothing agent (4)
9. Ship's spar tilts over, about right (5)
10. Source of fruit – or fish, last of cod (7)
11. Messy peat hides copper vessel (6)
12. Turns loose little pigs (5)
14. Sully a fool with a lubricant (6)
16. Fit for consumption? Edgar gets bad bile (6)
19. See a relation boast (5)
21. E.g., Len's translated a political philosopher (6)
24. To dress takes time? Rubbish (7)
25. Contact with end of filament leading to cry of pain (5)
26. Fire and plunder! (4)
27. Forced bird to church with Ted (8)

DOWN

1. Shed for all the players! (4)
2. Injures about ten animals (7)
3. Mexican 'olds, we hear, an investigator (5)
4. Sets – heartless grown-ups (6)
6. A win, once more (5)
7. Di's draped in tiny things, for fashion designers (8)
8. Got a point and scratched a line! (6)
13. Recovers pound grabbed by uncivilised types (8)
15. Container for mail requiring attention – untidy tin, Raymond (2-4)
17. Hear brute make dash for water plant (7)
18. 'E never changes face (6)
20. A German in beautiful Richmond (5)
22. Be successful – e.g., lifting weight (3,2)
23. Child I'd rebuked (4)

160

PLAIN

CRYPTIC

PLAIN

ACROSS

1. Humid and sticky (6)
4. Elevated terrain (6)
8. Right-hand page (5)
9. A faction in the Wars of the Roses (7)
10. Complaining (7)
11. ——— Welles, Hollywood personality (5)
12. Fastener for securing documents (5-4)
17. River in SW England (5)
19. A chemical element (7)
21. Careful examination (7)
22. Impecunious (5)
23. Lethal (6)
24. A recess in a room (6)

DOWN

1. A metallic compound (6)
2. A source of light (3-4)
3. Native of New Zealand (5)
5. Cook slightly in simmering water (7)
6. A sign of the zodiac (5)
7. Reckoning the age of (6)
9. The universal ash-tree of Norse mythology (9)
13. A sunshade (7)
14. Musical instrument (7)
15. Idiotic (6)
16. Violent expiration through the nose (6)
18. Girl's name (5)
20. False accusation (5)

CRYPTIC

ACROSS

1. Hesitate? 'E's modest (6)
4. Necks of sheep, last of carcasses, near high rocks (6)
8. Wireless disturbed road about one (5)
9. Get stuck with spies around one Caribbean island (7)
10. Girl needs a large drink, we hear (7)
11. Smuggle one hundred of those ancient symbols (5)
12. A story, loud, with insubstantial end part, they say (5,4)
17. Second instrument for cutting! (5)
19. Subtly induce fifty to enter, and enclose (7)
21. Academic part of London (N) is Hampstead (7)
22. Arrest old boy, wealthy man in India (5)
23. Dishes found by a youth in Sunday School (6)
24. Christmas? No, spring! (6)

DOWN

1. Girl grabs hour up in cathedral city (6)
2. Hoisted t-tree with dark part of trunk! (7)
3. Greek letter 'ad turned up for a girl (5)
5. Carbon and barium distributed in part of NW England (7)
6. A carriage includes one of the birds (5)
7. Spiritualists' sitting could create a scene (6)
9. Marine creature, fleshy, Jill almost crushed (9)
13. Insinuated one MP fibbed (7)
14. Eastern queen, skilful, level-headed (7)
15. Stage-whispers from amateur sets of players! (6)
16. Desert rat fractured leg, rib (6)
18. Invalidate part of plan, nullify (5)
20. Study a turn in a river (5)

161

PLAIN

CRYPTIC

PLAIN

ACROSS

7. Location of a Napoleonic victory (4)
8. Innate (8)
9. Of the mind (6)
10. Confirm (6)
11. Kind of carp (4)
13. Unexpected good fortune (8)
15. Type of footwear reaching above the knee (8)
18. Open-air swimming-pool (4)
19. Falsely incriminated (6)
21. One confined to an institution (6)
23. Playing for time (8)
24. Unacceptable in high society (3-1)

DOWN

1. Source of parental characteristics (4)
2. About seven days ago (4,4)
3. Kind of cushion (6)
4. Girl's name (6)
5. A young herring (4)
6. Purloined (8)
12. Briskness (8)
14. A thread (8)
16. Admit to holy orders (6)
17. A momentary sharp pain (6)
20. A Scottish isle (4)
22. Theatre's equivalent of an Oscar (4)

CRYPTIC

ACROSS

7. Mad dog bites a Spaniard (4)
8. Noel rang? That could be the name (8)
9. Chaste, good man tucking into meat (6)
10. Intend changes – print further in from the margin (6)
11. News agency in Soviet assembly (4)
13. Steam-engine inventor's caught rare, wild creature (5-3)
15. A girl round North, with funny hat – David's friend (8)
18. Buffalo Bill, shy about leader of Daltons (4)
19. Hissing bird making red horse back (6)
21. Pious, and very loud, the French? Nonsense! (6)
23. A weather signal makes turn, once, blown about! (4-4)
24. Clumsy boor left unconscious (4)

DOWN

1. Pale, evening's beginning to lose brightness (4)
2. A great deal of water makes up Earth, son (5,3)
3. Inexperienced, from California, and depressed (6)
4. I get so mad with self-centred type (6)
5. Poke pig's head with stick (4)
6. A small growth left Dan puzzled in agricultural area (8)
12. Actor, I am, outrageously spicy! (8)
14. Stagger loudly over all the scree (4-4)
16. A rake for the garden in a public school! (6)
17. Quietly he interrupts young relative (6)
20. Phoney eastern dandy (4)
22. Praise a nobleman, audibly (4)

162

PLAIN

CRYPTIC

PLAIN

ACROSS

1. A hybrid mythical creature (7)
5. A savoury meat-jelly (5)
8. Produces effects on one another (9)
9. Utter (3)
10. A marsupial (8)
12. Avoid (4)
14. Countrified (6)
15. Pure (6)
17. Summit (4)
18. Lanky quality (8)
21. Drag heavily (3)
22. Stubborn (9)
24. Old Venetian coin (5)
25. Replies (7)

DOWN

1. Muscular spasm in the neck (5)
2. A negative expression (3)
3. A European sea (8)
4. American animal (6)
5. Besides (4)
6. With all speed (4-5)
7. Kind of pepper (7)
11. Longing sentimentally for past times (9)
13. Shetland ponies (8)
14. Made slight waves (7)
16. Coarse kind of cinnamon (6)
19. Toboggans (5)
20. A spell, as of sickness (4)
23. Hail! (3)

CRYPTIC

ACROSS

1. Angels, half seen with harps askew (7)
5. Hint of grub in hair, dog's complaint (5)
8. Routes Tom miscalculated, being farthest away (9)
9. Boy making sound of insect (3)
10. Flattery will make Clare and Joy giddy (8)
12. River cutting into city – Newcastle (4)
14. OT note in junior's notebook (6)
15. Fragment of cloth? Not in stew! (6)
17. Not a complex alliance (4)
18. Wild parrot around Ed – bird of prey? (8)
21. Pour out endless letter (3)
22. Company member soon introduced one associate (9)
24. Right occasion to make return and send money (5)
25. Immortal eastern bird at a lake (7)

DOWN

1. Cost I worked out for old Greek philosopher (5)
2. Rubbish, to right, tipped up (3)
3. Corresponding with a line showing latitude! (8)
4. Scrubs second stage in meal, almost (6)
5. Great energy, we hear, for one so little (4)
6. An animal grandma acquired about first of April (5-4)
7. Beg something from Centre – a touch (7)
11. Very high winds demolished t-trees in crush (3-6)
13. Manufactured by a servant, it's said (4-4)
14. Caretaker sorted out a joint, right? (7)
16. Weight written in diagram, metrical (6)
19. Factual about a point pertaining to the kidneys (5)
20. Novelist, we hear, one from Edinburgh? (4)
23. Fashionable northern tavern (3)

163

PLAIN

CRYPTIC

PLAIN

ACROSS

7. Spiritual leader of Islam (6)
8. Repeat performance (6)
9. A Wimbledon champion (4)
10. Domesticated state (8)
11. Starved (8)
13. A thin strand (4)
14. Sullen (4)
16. Piece of camping equipment (4-4)
18. Unblemished (8)
21. The uterus (4)
22. System of government (6)
23. Open with a key (6)

DOWN

1. Oriental temple (6)
2. Militant patriotism (8)
3. Glowing with extreme heat (5-3)
4. A hair-do (4)
5. Examine all parts systematically (4)
6. Emergency (6)
12. Prehistoric monster (8)
13. Horrific creature of legend (8)
15. Contrivance for flattening roads (6)
17. Crushed apples for cider-making (6)
19. A legal document (4)
20. Letters (4)

CRYPTIC

ACROSS

7. Hostility in letter? Take precautions (6)
8. Wild cat, could be Leo, caught in October (6)
9. No score in most of tardy game (4)
10. Some of the good old rum sinks, in calm areas of the ocean (8)
11. Bette ill, possibly – run down! (8)
13. Regret about Left government (4)
14. Cause dullness in green stone (4)
16. Organised diet, not a cure for venom? (8)
18. Song from accountant perplexed client (8)
21. A towing boat carrying hot ruffian (4)
22. Blab about one sea-robber (6)
23. Pet ran amok, in ecstasy (6)

DOWN

1. Formerly ahead of (6)
2. Nameless one's in Church of England, to enrol as saint (8)
3. Blood-feud at end – vet made up (8)
4. Implement from sack up-ended! (4)
5. Wire tangled in river dam (4)
6. Methodical class, one with 50 (6)
12. Verges, formerly, with timbers – about 1000 (8)
13. Bird giving Commie a sudden fright (8)
15. Clara and I misread a name (6)
17. So grabs MP and pummels (6)
19. A pitfall for a horse-drawn carriage (4)
20. Cook for heartless principal (4)

164

PLAIN

CRYPTIC

In this puzzle (and in the following six puzzles) the clues are of the definition kind and are given in pairs. Solvers have to decide where the two answers belong – one in the upper and one in the lower diagram. In each puzzle, the answers to two pairs of clues are given as starters.

ACROSS

1. Stems of trees (6)
Tremble, as with cold (6)
5. A casual walk (6)
To steal (6)
8. A granular substance (4)
Profit (4)
9. The ant-bear of South Africa (8)
Flying about, like a moth (8)
10. Any carnivorous creature (5-5)
Fizz (10)
12. Works flour into dough (6)
Demented (6)
14. Native of the western Pyrenees (6)
Make restless movements (6)
15. Division into degrees (10)
Hindered (10)
19. Deceived (8)
Physical power (8)
20. Midday (4)
Two-masted type of vessel (4)
21. A colouring pencil (6)
A fragrant evergreen shrub (6)
22. Stylish in attire (6)
Method (6)

DOWN

2. A promontory (8)
To ratify a second time (8)
3. A gentle shove with the elbow (5)
Goddess of love (5)
4. Perished from hunger (7)
Beams supporting a roof (7)
5. Penniless (5)
Small sailing ships (5)
6. Critical appreciations of books, films, etc. (7)
Went into seclusion (7)
7. Heather (4)
Traditional learning (4)
11. Having power to poison (8)
The Christmas season (8)
13. The science of animal life (7)
To increase (7)
14. Tedium (7)
Red-faced (7)
16. A drawing-room (5)
Little Agnes (5)
17. Nervously strained (5)
A railway signal-box (5)
18. Remain (4)
To be dressed in (4)

165

1 2 3 4 5 6 7

8 9 F L I T T I N G

10 11

12 13 14

15 16 17

18

19 S T R E N G T H 20

21 22

1 2 3 4 5 6 7

8 9 A A R D V A R K

10 11

12 13 14

15 16 17

18

19 B E F O O L E D 20

21 22

ACROSS

1. Old kingdom of Spain (6)
   Ply with embarrassing questions (6)
5. Shrewd (6)
   Finely chopped (6)
9. Fisherman (6)
   A mowing implement (6)
10. Pertaining to minute particles (6)
    Register of inhabitants (6)
11. Shrub (4)
    Deep affection (4)
12. Protector (8)
    Piece of furniture on which headwear may be hung (8)
14. Quickly (6)
    Posture (6)
16. Sound of a goose (6)
    Those who are beaten in competitions (6)
19. Rotary engines (8)
    Displaced persons seeking asylum (8)
21. Run with long strides (4)
    An agreement (4)
22. Small ornamental case (6)
    The opposite of transparent (6)
23. A gas (6)
    To get the better of in a race (6)
24. Soundness of mind (6)
    At the present time (2,4)
25. Most advanced in years (6)
    Barked (6)

DOWN

2. Cover with a hard coating (7)
   Ill-feeling (7)
3. Place where food is cooked (7)
   Old sailing ship (7)
4. One end of the earth's axis (5,4)
   Ivy, for instance (9)
6. Mere jots (5)
   Precipitous (5)
7. Represent as similar (7)
   To free from adhesive (7)
8. Innermost distinctive quality (7)
   Makes up one's mind (7)
13. An optical instrument (9)
    A secondary item of equipment (9)
14. Alights (7)
    To convey meaning (7)
15. Impromptu (7)
    Native of a continent (7)
17. Spread outwards (7)
    Old Roman temple of Jupiter (7)
18. An academic discourse (7)
    To keep under, by force (7)
20. Irrelevant and futile (5)
    Haggard (5)

166

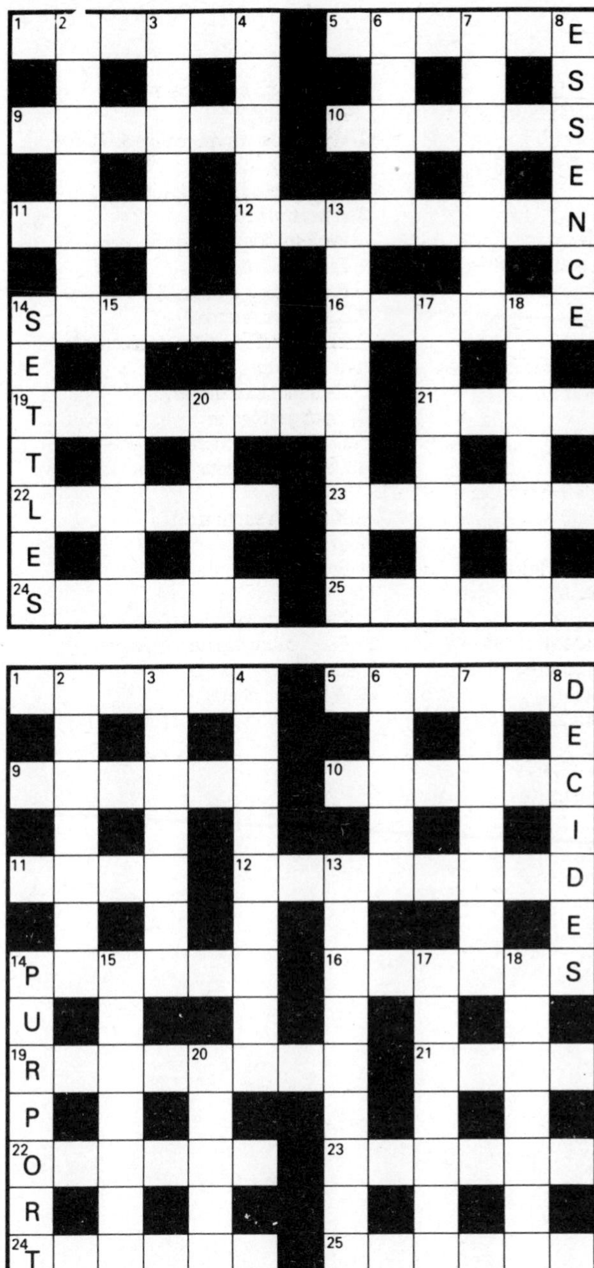

ACROSS

7. Shape (4)
Musical instrument (4)

8. One of our forebears (8)
A person who mends things (8)

9. Ladles (6)
A support (6)

10. Comparatively tidy (6)
Descends with a sweeping rush (6)

11. Deep male singing voice (4)
Bloodied (4)

12. A boy's name (8)
Amounted to (8)

15. Comprehended fully (8)
Postpones (8)

17. A dance movement (4)
To worry (4)

18. A preacher (6)
Brownish crimson (6)

21. Mischievous (6)
Small breed of poultry (6)

22. Part of a passenger ship with the lowest fares (8)
One who conveys passengers over water (8)

23. Respiratory organ (4)
A soldier in the Indian army (4)

DOWN

1. A sea-fish like the herring (8)
A quartet (8)

2. Workshop where metals are forged (6)
One-masted vessels (6)

3. A person in captivity (8)
Well-trodden routes (8)

4. French silver coins (4)
Rotate (4)

5. An armed guard (6)
The end of an opera, for example (6)

6. To deal out (4)
Ceremonious display (4)

13. Errands (8)
Obliged by something received (8)

14. Cold applications for feverish brows (8)
A church service (8)

16. Whipped (6)
Smells (6)

17. Lithe (6)
Most exquisite (6)

19. Short cough to draw attention (4)
Creative crafts (4)

20. A Biblical character (4)
Lacking the power of sensation (4)

167

ACROSS

1. A fragrant Mediterranean shrub (8)
   Ornamental wall cover (8)
5. Fitted with footwear (4)
   Sleeping (4)
9. Tricky (5)
   A dish prepared with mixed spices (5)
10. The art of clipping trees into imitative shapes (7)
    Quarrelled noisily (7)
11. Dormant (6)
    A military standard (6)
12. A railway carriage in which meals are served (5)
    Faithful (5)
14. Shaving foam (6)
    A European language (6)
16. Girl's name (6)
    Demonstrated as truth (6)
19. Full of irregular bulges (5)
    The full extent of anything (5)
21. A second transaction involving a purchased article (6)
    A kind of hare (6)
24. The fruit of a palm-tree (7)
    A French town (7)
25. Walk with a heavy tread (5)
    Splendour (5)
26. At another time (4)
    Type of bean (4)
27. Scampers along (8)
    A heavy fall of rain (8)

DOWN

1. Sway to and fro (4)
   A fuss (2-2)
2. A tool (7)
   A domestic (7)
3. Perhaps (5)
   To observe secretly (3,2)
4. Turning like a wheel (6)
   Refutes (6)
6. Muscular strength (5)
   An evergreen (5)
7. Cheating (8)
   Dawn (8)
8. Paleness of complexion (6)
   Web-spinner (6)
13. Distresses grievously (8)
    Outrageous (8)
15. Still in existence (6)
    Shedding tears (6)
17. Injurious to health (7)
    An eruptive mountain (7)
18. Famous Hollywood star of 'The Godfather' (6)
    Amorous (6)
20. Dirty (5)
    A staple cereal in USA (5)
22. One blindly devoted to a creed (5)
    Girl's name (5)
23. A goading instrument on a rider's heel (4)
    Positive votes (4)

168

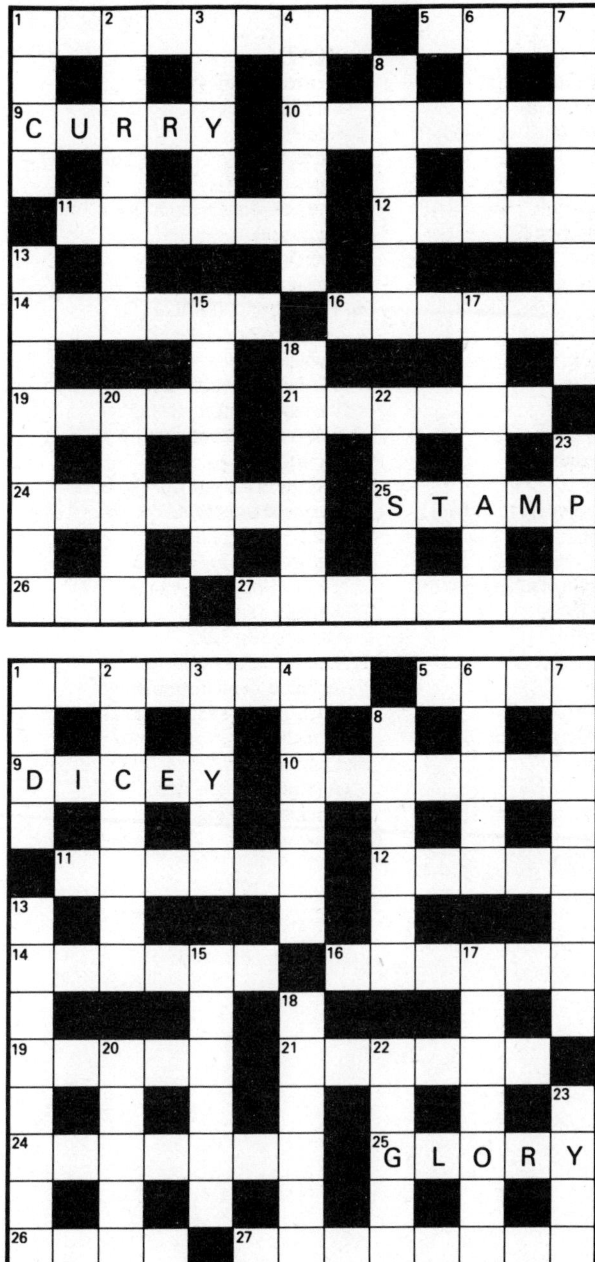

ACROSS

1. To contract into wrinkles (7)
Ferociously attacked (7)

5. Make a surly noise with bared teeth (5)
Charred (5)

8. Perfectly healthy (2,3,4)
A source of illumination (9)

9. French for 'sea' (3)
Short name for a breed of dog (3)

10. A Cornish headland associated with King Arthur (8)
A fragrant plant (8)

12. A haul of herrings (4)
Renown (4)

14. Makes trifling objections (6)
Act in a clumsy manner (6)

15. Sprees (6)
A cotton cloth originating in India (6)

17. Well ventilated (4)
Pouches (4)

18. Continuous showers of projectiles (8)
Of a prehistoric era (8)

21. Diminutive Robert (3)
Aflame (3)

22. A fruit-seed (6-3)
That can be borne (9)

24. Eats specially selected foods (5)
Town in N. Ireland (5)

25. Asserted without proof (7)
A small liquid medication for a pupil, perhaps (3-4)

DOWN

1. To overflow (5)
Rend asunder (5)

2. Edge (3)
Large tank for fermentation (3)

3. A plant-louse (8)
The heavenly home for slain Teutonic heroes (8)

4. Fell behind (6)
Nonsense (6)

5. The one and the other (4)
Japanese rice-beer (4)

6. Genus of plants whose shoots are used as a table delicacy (9)
Rushing about wildly (9)

7. Self-propelled submarine weapon (7)
Mourns (7)

11. Worthy of reverence, like Bede (9)
One who directs the course of a ship (9)

13. A part-song (8)
To be at variance with (8)

14. Repaired shoes (7)
Divulged secrets (7)

16. Coagulate, like milk (6)
A dance-band instrument (6)

19. Having a distinctive taste (5)
The chirp of a young bird (5)

20. Famous golfer (4)
A person's whole frame (4)

23. Prickly seed-case (3)
A beast (3)

SNARL
DIETS

BURNT
DERRY

ACROSS

1. Hunting-dog (5)
   Chew (5)
4. Rigorously austere (7)
   A N. American Indian (7)
8. Scrap of cloth (3)
   Opponent of a 'Rocker' (3)
9. Tobacco rolled in thin paper (9)
   Forceful and impetuous manner (9)
10. Instructed (7)
    An extract (7)
11. Female cat (5)
    An aromatic plant whose seeds are used in making cordials (5)
13. Stupefy (6)
    To numb (6)
15. Place of worship (6)
    Angular recess (6)
18. A city of Spain (5)
    The tuft on a bird's head (5)
19. Pair of rhyming lines (7)
    Mischievous children (7)
21. Childish (9)
    Wandering in mind, feverishly (9)
23. Hill (3)
    Jewish man's name (3)
24. Fundamental (7)
    To utter (7)
25. A bird-note (5)
    Weird (5)

DOWN

1. Deserved (7)
   In his real character (7)
2. Bad dream (9)
   Uncertain (9)
3. Stage scenery (5)
   Hang in the air (5)
4. Insects that attack plants (6)
   Powerful (6)
5. Man's name (7)
   A close companion (7)
6. A round figure (3)
   Kind of whip (3)
7. Very poor (5)
   NW town and railway junction (5)
12. Acting upon sudden inclination (9)
    Famous miler (9)
14. A small sweetmeat, sometimes medicated (7)
    Kind of fever affecting the intestines (7)
16. Reticence (7)
    A registered competitor (7)
17. A roll of parchment (6)
    Small birds of the partridge family (6)
18. Felony (5)
    Drink made from apples (5)
20. Rubber fabric (5)
    Distressed (5)
22. Pan cover (3)
    A dandy (3)

170

ANISE

CREST

TABBY

CADIZ

ACROSS

1. A hag (5)
   Angry (5)
4. Resembling (7)
   An American insect akin to the grasshopper (7)
8. One able to float in water (7)
   Struggle confusedly (7)
9. Early Soviet leader (5)
   Silly person (5)
10. A call for attention in a law-court (4)
    A dissolute type (4)
11. Paraffin-oil (8)
    Danger (8)
13. A written communication (6)
    Useless (6)
14. One's rank or standing in a group (6)
    Pertaining to stars (6)
18. Characteristic of a pungent chemical compound (8)
    Riding-breeches in India (8)
20. A disparaging remark (4)
    Bitter fluid secreted by the liver (4)
22. Like terriers, spaniels, etc. (5)
    Doctrine (5)
23. Fretful (7)
    Of an English county (7)
24. A line that touches a curve (7)
    Long seats with backs (7)
25. Turned a sickly colour (5)
    A high waterproof boot (5)

DOWN

1. Anything thrown aside (4-3)
   A profligate (7)
2. A dense clump of trees (7)
   Very wealthy (7)
3. To sieve (4)
   One's dwelling-place (4)
4. A Scandinavian country (6)
   Edible part of a nut (6)
5. Indian animal of the civet family (8)
   One capable of mental communication (8)
6. Ancient Arab gold coin (5)
   Long pointed weapon (5)
7. The chime of words in verse (5)
   Dim-coloured (5)
12. A present to remind one of the giver (8)
    An area of North America (8)
15. Revived (7)
    Paltry (7)
16. Boiled (7)
    A cross-breed of greyhound and collie (7)
17. Parcel (6)
    A Cambridge honours examination (6)
18. A betrayer (5)
    To examine accounts (5)
19. A finger (5)
    Welsh girl's name (5)
21. To bite with a scraping movement (4)
    A coarse fibre (4)

171

1		2		3	■	4		5		6 D		7
	■		■		■		■		■	I	■	
8							■	9		N		
	■		■		■		■		■	A	■	
10				■	11					R		
	■		■	12	■		■		■	■	■	■
13						■	14			15		16
■	■	■	■		■	17	■		■		■	
18		19 D						■	20			
	■	I	■		■		■	21	■		■	
22		G			■	23						
	■	I	■		■		■		■		■	
24		T					■	25				

1		2		3	■	4		5		6 L		7
	■		■		■		■		■	A	■	
8							■	9		N		
	■		■		■		■		■	C	■	
10				■	11					E		
	■		■	12	■		■		■	■	■	■
13						■	14			15		16
■	■	■	■		■	17	■		■		■	
18		19 M						■	20			
	■	E	■		■		■	21	■		■	
22		G			■	23						
	■	A	■		■		■		■		■	
24		N					■	25				

6

BARS NOT BLANKS

172

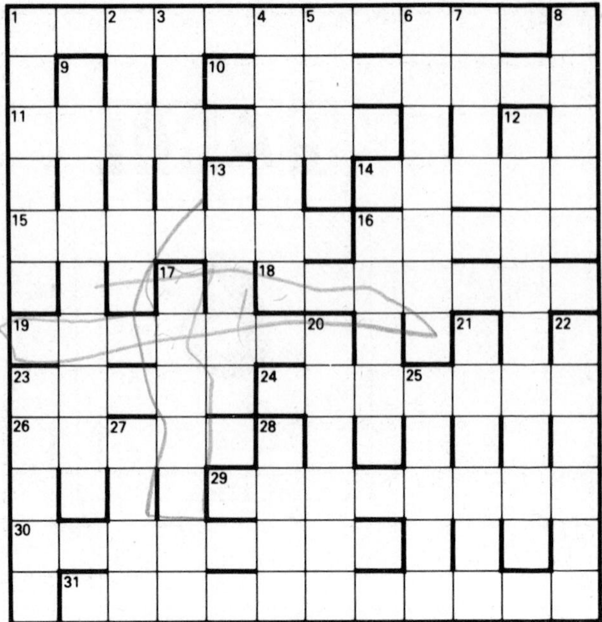

ACROSS

1. Sausage free? True, cooked and eaten by father (11)
10. Spicy additive – sailor has scrap in advance (8)
11. Scaremonger causing marital upset about Sunday (8)
14. Bird, say, and insect round about (5)
15. Edward, after a service, collected a great deal (7)
16. Burns prophets, from what we hear (5)
18. Go berserk? Rugby Union chap's spun around, OK! (3,4)
19. A moral offence in East is stupid (7)
23. Guide an ox (5)
24. Search for former penny, look about (7)
26. Girl from NE repelled fool (5)
29. Flowers for bereavement crushed by unruly mobs (8)
30. Where patients wait? Near to MO, possibly (8)
31. Dried spices copper sprinkled right among swans (11)

DOWN

1. One in neckwear raised uproar (6)
2. Arab, a dancer, will show you a town in Iran (6)
3. Annoys police informers (5)
4. Clearer, more impartial (6)
5. Bear contained by four savages (4)
6. List a 'U' picture (7)
7. Little Margaret's topless and covered with yolk? (4)
8. So Ern's crooked? Lies! (5)
9. Aged teacher and great artist (3,6)
12. Rode wildly into a city for airport (9)
13. Busy atmosphere about street (5)
16. Clip eastern bird (5)
17. Jazzy notes on disc for dance (7)
20. Former lodging up in part of Devon (6)
21. Commanding officer with scowl causes blush (6)
22. Severs badly written stanzas (6)
23. Snake might make you skulk (5)
25. Rope, look, round an animal (5)
27. Seconds consumed, to satisfy fully (4)
28. Blackthorn fruit's late, we hear (4)

173

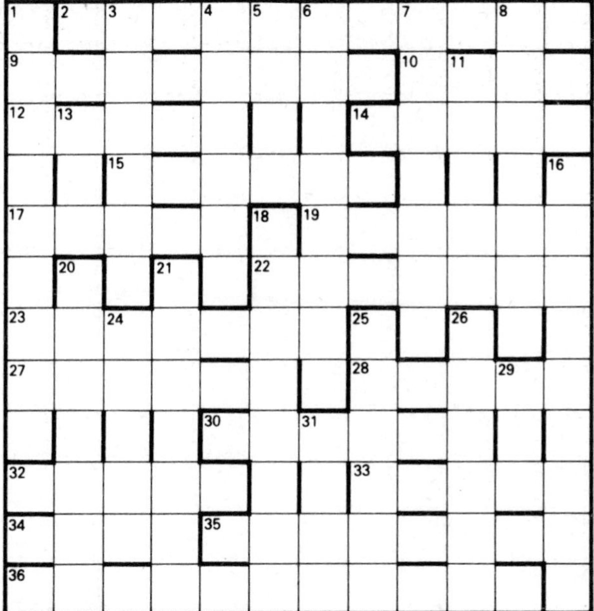

ACROSS

2. All led by sin, dissipated, will discover dead-ends (5-6)
9. One word about a railway book containing daily services! (8)
10. Boy needs drink, drop of cider (4)
12. A c-convulsion in upper storey (5)
14. Slur from Esme, a renegade (5)
15. Since changes, face of colliery is picturesque (6)
17. Biblical priest 'as Hebrew name (5)
19. Southern birds catching eastern gleams (6)
22. Gnarled teak or English timber (3-4)
23. Always negative backs in FA team! (7)
27. Made home for saint in want (6)
28. Odd heron in river (5)
30. B-binge breaking up, declining (6)
32. High-pitched signal – Bill's first to jump, we hear (5)
33. Twinges, onset of gripes, in depressions! (5)
34. Fishy features – Scandinavian's, it's said (4)
35. Drag length of ship for fish in a hulk, wrecked (8)
36. Peter's since developed tenacity (11)

DOWN

1. Degradation in a low place (9)
3. Admits it's Len at fault (4,2)
4. French town – street most attractive (6)
5. Bird on pole in early light (4)
6. People committed to a faction, with no head for workers (8)
7. Strike girl in part of London (7)
8. Longed for time, Edward? (7)
11. Stagger up, about five, for bar! (5)
13. Arab hill at heart of waste land (3)
16. Inferior yules chopped up outside, in futile way (9)
18. Farewells from worthy extras (8)
20. Stay abed too long, or live loosely, round East (7)
21. Callous? Not he – without guile (7)
24. Sense changes in German city (5)
25. Threefold rubbish round lake (6)
26. Brandy can leave 100 upset (6)
29. A drink with no gravity (3)
31. Insect on top of tall plant (4)

174

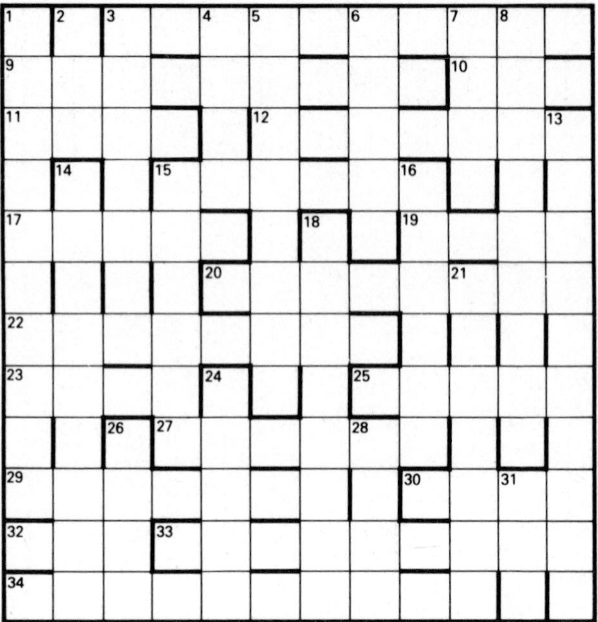

ACROSS

3. The crib, pal, gets rocked where one's born (5-5)
9. In love, a girl grieved – missing North (9)
10. Fellow turned to make slight bow (3)
11. Buns, crumbly in central parts (4)
12. Splitting object in arena! (7)
15. Cancel, including one year-book (6)
17. Aluminium's in iron? Untrue (5)
19. 'E cut skin with a sword (4)
20. Males about to arrive outside and begin (8)
22. Eton chap's elaborate memorial (8)
23. Musical piece in part riotous (4)
25. Old giant has Monsieur excited (5)
27. Smear tar round Roderick, in a burlesque (6)
29. Hugo shuffled, in line approximately (7)
30. Almost the scaffold for a brute (4)
32. Canny little creature (3)
33. Promote sales? Hostile about it, on reflection (9)
34. Inspect eel, as possible source of widespread disease (10)

DOWN

1. Patron has been puzzled over a significant item (10)
2. Sound of strange animal (3)
3. Infant, not quite isolated in a Biblical city (7)
4. Right to possess, we hear, a horse (4)
5. Count rat fickle, a renegade (8)
6. Punitive ring about hint of noose! (5)
7. Blue dye in Indian illustrations (4)
8. Link in company rent 'con' is well disguised (9)
13. Fruits, vegetables – round measure, we're told! (10)
14. Consumed river in entirety, and desert spring (5-4)
15. Like to work, crouching? (6)
16. Ground lost? A General has method (6)
18. Mope? Eye's wandering round lake for a worker (8)
21. Bed-gown, near neckwear (7)
24. I'd meat sent up for great leader (5)
26. Fellows with tent-ropes (4)
28. Embroider part of calendar neatly (4)
31. A quiet wood (3)

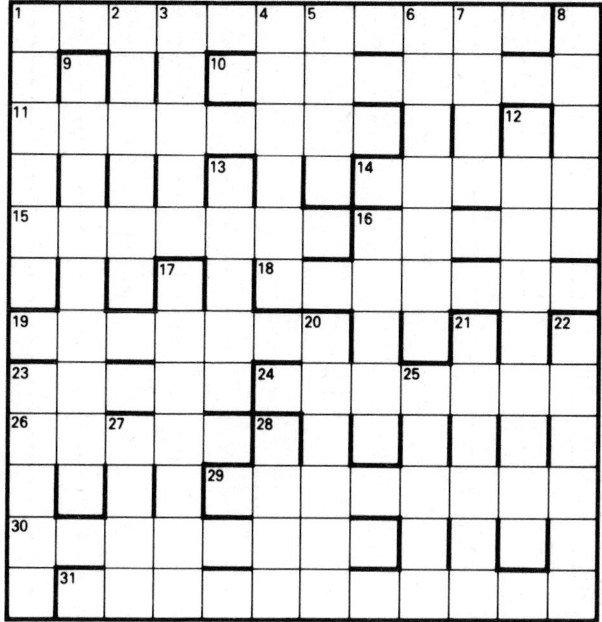

175

ACROSS

1. Bad player is not in character (11)
10. 'E has leg trapped in hoop, fretting (8)
11. Dull sounding match? The finest (8)
14. Did exam again – 'A' among others (5)
15. For instance, sick steed threw out food (7)
16. GI in drink becomes nimble (5)
18. Bad vice, in a letter, to mislead (7)
19. Mum's facing hectic trial of married life (7)
23. Ghastly English soot (5)
24. Smashed meter up for change! (7)
26. Yearned for a child, Edward (5)
29. One in charge – presiding over Norsemen, in part (8)
30. Exploits about river, making non-news items (8)
31. Loud quarrel with 'arsh Head shows perversity! (11)

DOWN

1. Young boar twisted leg in mine (6)
2. The Spanish in tall grass staggered (6)
3. Kills bodyguards grabbing deposit (5)
4. Compressed, we hear, as required (6)
5. Recess for primate about Sunday! (4)
6. A number get rein tangled (7)
7. Tilts extremities (4)
8. A stone from an entrance (5)
9. Carry a drunken prisoner out of vault, and put in part of gaol (4-5)
12. Redemption avails not? That's odd (9)
13. Declare a condition (5)
16. A growth producing fruit (5)
17. Pepper pot, mine, fancy (7)
20. One in bar, one on way out! (6)
21. One of five, this French fruit (6)
22. Suit requiring male crafts! (6)
23. Drudging schoolboy lifting iron makes blunder (5)
25. Gaze vacantly? That's about right, for a simpleton (5)
27. Zero in endless hard frost (4)
28. Girl propped up a bar! (4)

176

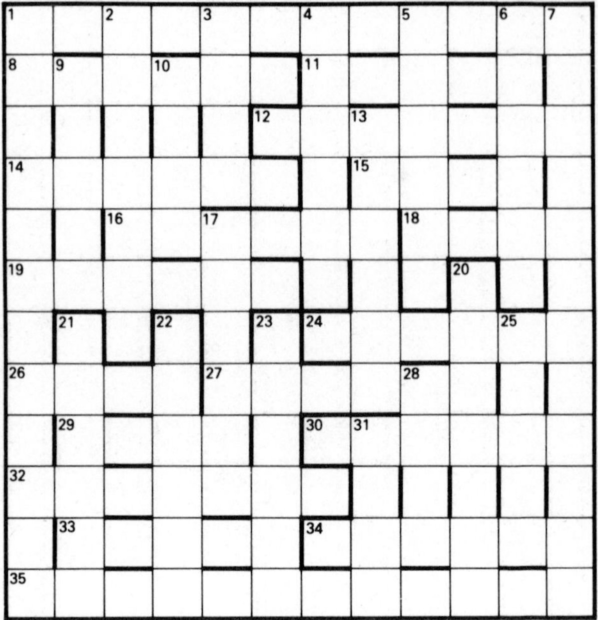

ACROSS

1. Hundred heckle at TUC, wildly, to stop useless talk (3,3,6)
8. A taxi's back with US counting device (6)
11. Place for drop of cha, if athirst (5)
12. Others with skill begin again (7)
14. Excise permit for meat! (6)
15. 'E's off colour? Sound as a bell! (4)
16. Dress one finally bought to wear out? (6)
18. Girl, northern, in uniform (4)
19. It's preached from Rome, possibly, among Poles! (6)
24. Against revolver's use? Partly (6)
26. Blast shattered a leg (4)
27. Awning – reproduce round one (6)
29. A mineral Micawber half spilt (4)
30. Plaster adhered, we hear, to nothing (6)
32. Sadly, it ain't a fairy queen (7)
33. Material, feature of many longbows (5)
34. A drive gets 'rough', went off course! (6)
35. Break down? I collapse left long out, shivering (4,2,6)

DOWN

1. Notice? – A tricky problem, with this fog swirling (5,5,2)
2. Hooligans, from craft, among Jacks (7)
3. Outsize garment's first in dye (4)
4. Guevara on rye, drunk, merry (6)
5. Large towns with names including capital of Iran (6)
6. More expansive with drink when last in decanter's swallowed (6)
7. Retract – make up for faults in English blades (3,4,5)
9. Second-class road, we're told – a beast! (5)
10. A fad, to reduce about a pound! (4)
13. Record player 'e put in store, out of order (6)
17. Break out with jail bird! (6)
20. Crafty spy, stylish, having ESP (7)
21. Boar, for instance, served up in plate! (6)
22. Remember to phone again? (6)
23. Where you can see a vice displayed in company (6)
25. Dirty article removed for relative (5)
28. A murmur from 'Hotspur' reader (4)
31. An Asian hat I crumpled (4)

177

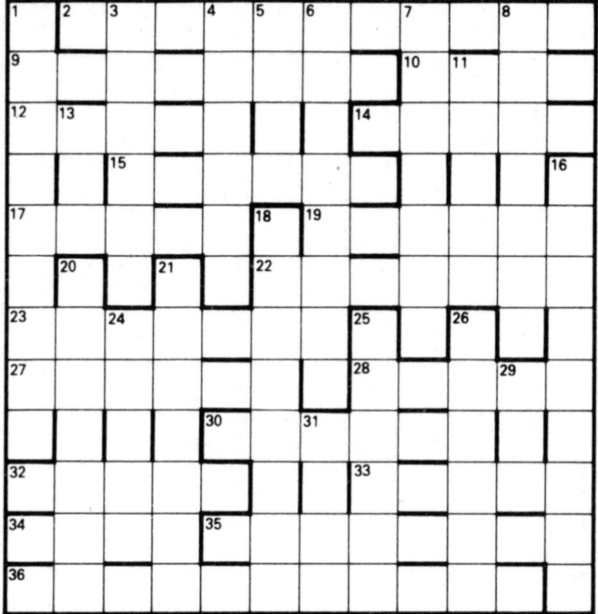

ACROSS

2. UK packs, if rioting round America, cause a stir (4,2,1,4)
9. Carry on, study metal – they say you must finish (8)
10. Raymond, about 100, is spirited (4)
12. A welcome haven in Samoa, sister (5)
14. Prohibition, Capone, is commonplace (5)
15. A drum and two big bells (3-3)
17. When one interrupts the beak, there's a row (5)
19. Hint of treachery in simple aborigine (6)
22. Controlled parasites in pea shell (7)
23. Old pals' meeting arranged in Rouen (7)
27. This could be the start of life, or be my undoing! (6)
28. A single state? Wedlock! (5)
30. Quick drinks, kinds including last of gin (6)
32. Put on play, part of series (5)
33. Additional minor film part (5)
34. Holiday time included in wage (4)
35. Unit (atom) involved in change (8)
36. Unsuspectingly? Closure duly disturbed (11)

DOWN

1. Cad's false counsel takes in doctor (9)
3. Pour into part of gin stillery (6)
4. Bad mistake ignoring one's destiny (6)
5. One out of condition, losing heart (4)
6. 'One up'? Not wrong to take advantage of a person? (3,2,3)
7. Frenzied French caper (7)
8. Neckwear cut up in steamer! (7)
11. Frolic with worker in charge (5)
13. A party in trouble (3)
16. Communist and German worker no longer employable (9)
18. 'Pools' fun? Could make a small amount (8)
20. Ill-humour round Satan's heart – that's the Devil for you! (7)
21. Angered frightfully? Yes! (7)
24. Submarine about, at sea (1-4)
25. Fop about old city office (6)
26. Part of flower I split clumsily (6)
29. Blade from middle of boat on river (3)
31. *Bismarck* in a spot, torpedoed! (4)

178

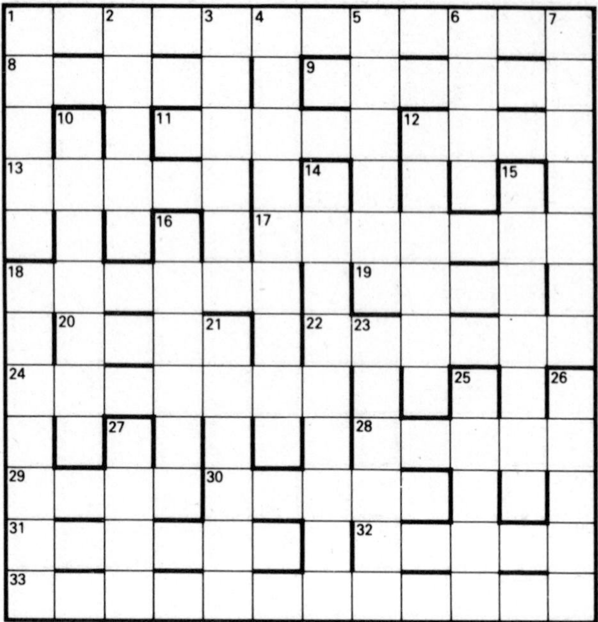

ACROSS

1. I order prawns, in cocktail, for an officer accustomed to porridge! (6,6)
8. Motorist defaced flower! (5)
9. Extol maid dancing about (6)
11. Shot full of enthusiasm (5)
12. Book edge – margin (4)
13. Gravity shown in dreadful song of mourning (5)
17. One who might harass a speaker? He upset clerk (7)
18. Mate, high tea shows sense of taste (6)
19. Work in the fields – there's usually money in it (4)
20. Girl with afterthought takes cursory look (4)
22. Touch of rheumatism getting joint will make you feel sore (6)
24. Storm encountered on way back – a nuisance (7)
28. Heathen utensil with silver lining (5)
29. Over river, cutting bend to North (4)
30. Order always arrives first (5)
31. Dog devoured vicar's assistant (6)
32. Part of poem, part of epic, Antony (5)
33. Infant school class painting in slapdash green? (12)

DOWN

1. Quiet journey on horse – a fall could follow it (5)
2. Girl has gold filling for tooth (5)
3. Tin-ore processed in East (6)
4. Heart's not broken, this way (5-4)
5. Bit of a fad, Dictaphones – for the devotee (6)
6. Muck I'd swept up – right? (4)
7. Regret about code (7)
10. Strange dialect in fortress (7)
12. Coral island beach-wear (6)
14. Hug rather playfully – here, in front of the fire (6-3)
15. Town-crier or campanologist? (7)
16. Chance to fall out (6)
18. Strip bird – 'eated inside, makes meal for unexpected guests (3-4)
21. Seen at riotous political assembly (6)
23. A hat the French turned up – woollen stuff (6)
25. One toff's a spy (5)
26. Man's name, perplexing to Ann (5)
27. Impaired by time, as clothing usually is (4)

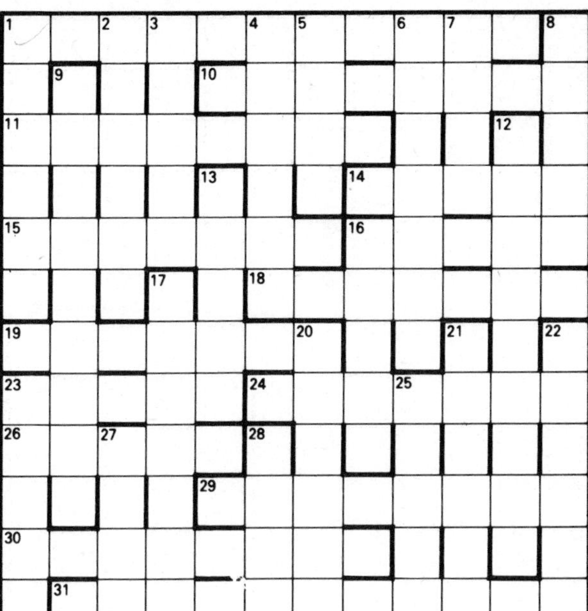

ACROSS

1. Visit White City, for example, and be ruined (2,2,3,4)
10. Arrived carrying chunk of pine, timber for scouts' blaze (4-4)
11. Baby's found here, annoyed? (2,2,4)
14. Dwelling place, adobe possibly (5)
15. A 'musical' piece? Barber will give you one (7)
16. Start to pray at home (5)
18. A strike's over, followed by cuts, it's said – apparent contradiction! (7)
19. Call-boy and worker make spectacle (7)
23. One wicket defeat! (5)
24. Small company, adequate for peer (7)
26. Goes sour in bouts (5)
29. Papist at hospital gripped by flatulence (8)
30. Bony lion amok in funny farm (5-3)
31. Witness at trial sounds oriental (11)

DOWN

1. Clumsy cowboy cut East (6)
2. Threesome reduced by way of trifles (6)
3. Proprietor to admit Her Majesty (5)
4. Impecunious – tough at university (4-2)
5. Girl upset me and mother (4)
6. Not on strike? Unusual! (7)
7. Put Irish in to work banking system (4)
8. Bird embraces me and virile types (2-3)
9. An Irishman hoards standard American equipment (9)
12. Fool holding degree in charge of dialect, say (9)
13. Fight for a morsel (5)
16. Rose-bush for coffin-stand holding king (5)
17. Something left over for bogus rentman (7)
20. Bird – cat has bit of trouble with it (6)
21. Atomic centres upset uncle and I (6)
22. Calf brought up on a bottle (6)
23. Saint with drink no longer fresh (5)
25. Ring left, round slice of onion! (5)
27. Revel in patriotism (4)
28. Fish experts (4)

180

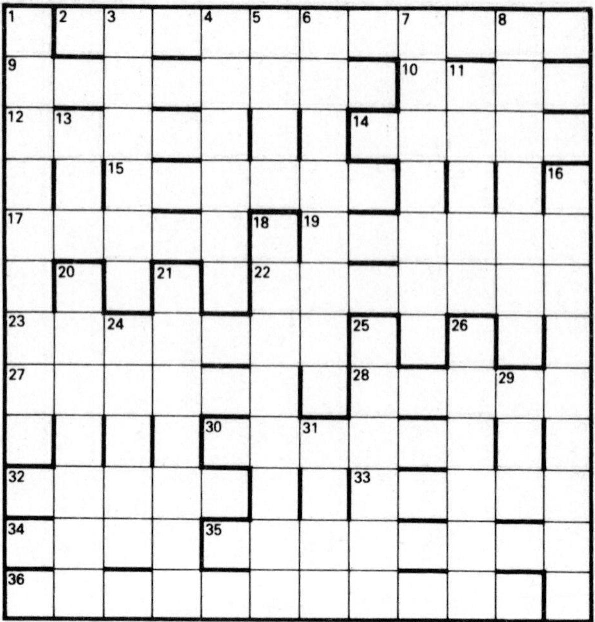

ACROSS

2. Record in minor, yet fanciful, diction (11)
9. Teutonic king, for example, turned crazy (8)
10. Greek god – one, with others, having no end (4)
12. Threads from stories (5)
14. Fruit, nameless one (5)
15. Bend, twitch, in icy region (6)
17. Dance has beat and vitality (5)
19. Dawdle, toiler? That's unusual (6)
22. Beast one's found in short index (7)
23. Fleets of ships – notice one ringed with weapons (7)
27. Neil's first, prompt – almost (6)
28. Begin again to renovate (5)
30. Chest, one seen in French port (6)
32. Seat money's returned (5)
33. County girl's short, fussy dog (5)
34. It takes a day, nothing more, to produce a disc (4)
35. Prophesy, favouring English archer (8)
36. A relative's term, almost, for a top-ranking chess player (11)

DOWN

1. Pet saying baffled N. Africans (9)
3. Wandering bombast – Queen's above it! (6)
4. Talisman, firm, stuck in pole (6)
5. This month isn't out! (4)
6. Odd hint, about the Italian isle, exposes one with no beliefs (8)
7. Falling to the ground from an upper level of a house (7)
8. Birds embracing no Italians (7)
11. Poke about audibly in the road (5)
13. Turkish commander lost in sea gale (3)
16. Wrist, heel, broken previously (9)
18. Where kids enjoy games – making Ma poorly? (8)
20. Maker about, busy in centre no end (7)
21. Instrument having nothing on a long barbed dart! (7)
24. Degree's advanced a stoneworker (5)
25. Detects vestiges (6)
26. Course goes among linden-trees (6)
29. Work unit, for instance, about right (3)
31. Last letter in time for this man (4)

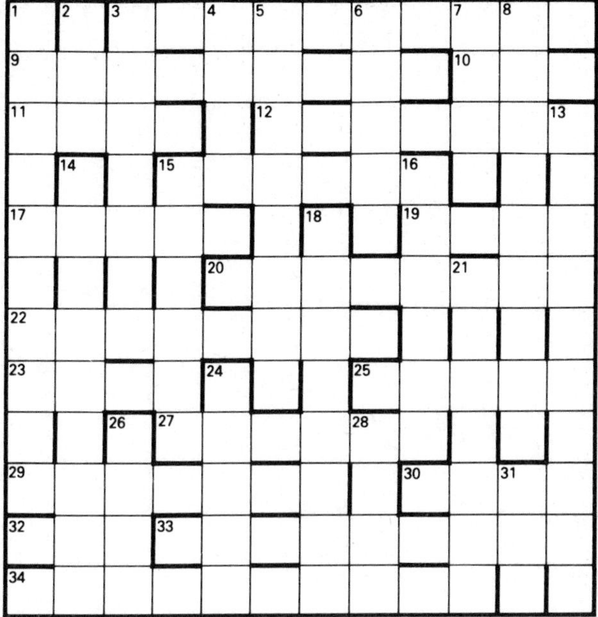

181

ACROSS

3. Sir, we hear, has smock for working hours (5-5)
9. Yeoman of the guard, no vegetarian (9)
10. Rent from disreputable person! (3)
11. Most of terrain round West is sward (4)
12. Crackpot can't sue, unfortunately (3-4)
15. A king with grim determination (6)
17. Single beadle possesses parish church estate (5)
19. Look back, taking in Welsh sheep (4)
20. An entry permit to be approved by the Left? (8)
22. Slow mover tires – too bad! (8)
23. Vain object of admiration, it's said (4)
25. Below uneven dune by river (5)
27. Take away most of Dee with tube (6)
29. Normal for an idiot (7)
30. A fairy in endless danger (4)
32. Filthy place – eye-sore, we're told (3)
33. Child (from what we hear) beaten, turned rather red? (3-6)
34. It controls temperature in highest degree, installed by shivering hatter (10)

DOWN

1. Old boy on diplomatic mission, they say – a duty (10)
2. Most of fruit and veg (3)
3. Were any resolved at this time? (3,4)
4. See in scrimmage a rugby tackle! (4)
5. Banister makes worker scoff (8)
6. Begin career in fixed situation (3,2)
7. One smuggled in a country (4)
8. Lead in film is with her males, such as casting involves! (9)
13. Dieters eat at random in this festive period (10)
14. Dandy at a spa in massacre (5-4)
15. A bad debt restricting one grew less (6)
16. Regret being shut up again? (6)
18. A seaman's audible attacks (8)
21. Queer fellows on time for scrap (7)
24. Kentish spirit, a watery liquid (5)
26. Tumour in nasty eyelid (4)
28. Bird's familiar conversation (4)
31. Communist rag's first editor (3)

182

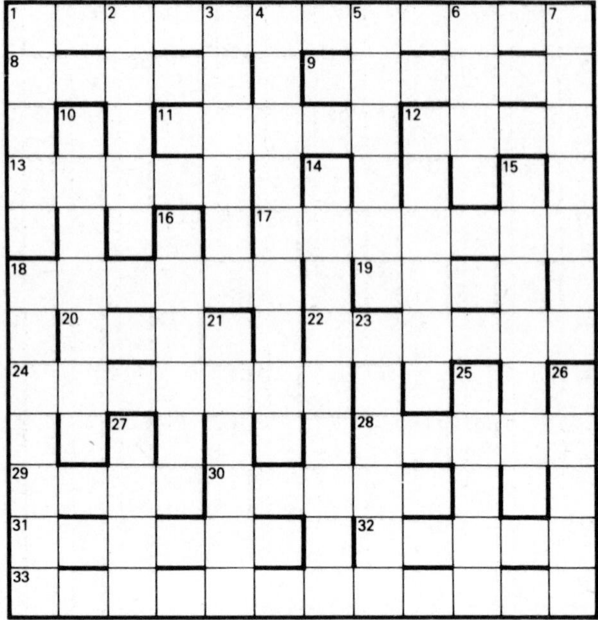

ACROSS

1. Drugs bestowed on brave GIs? (6,6)
8. Anger gets north-eastern girl (5)
9. Fabricate cosmetics (4,2)
11. Aid for lowering a lifeboat, or six, in short time (5)
12. Coffin cover for a Saint, it's said (4)
13. Enter with gravity? Running! (5)
17. One refusing to work with a soccer forward? (7)
18. Ex-PM, Edward, set to fight (6)
19. Thus Lord was betrayed (4)
20. Sack for loose money (4)
22. Scold deserter in a letter (6)
24. An intoxicant, a litre, given to Henry in chill surroundings (7)
28. Oils spurt messily (5)
29. Fit in tea guest (4)
30. Live coal ruined beer mat's surface (5)
31. Nothing fresh – always proceeding in single direction (3-3)
32. Follow directions with a girl (5)
33. Lad may hike, or could become a tourist (7-5)

DOWN

1. Feast, orgy (not half) for the little runt (5)
2. Priest in Roman Catholic ruin (5)
3. Confederacy's former measure (6)
4. Spy on dope raves, in bad way (9)
5. People dining from 'ot plates? (6)
6. Genuine Spanish coin (4)
7. Boisterous display leaders of some political Leftists encourage (7)
10. Duck in meat dish, one for a primate (7)
12. Former abbey, ultimately a convent (6)
14. Groom, well-balanced at the side, full of love! (6-3)
15. Predate crazy bureaucratic routine (3-4)
16. Stage butt goes to flicks! (6)
18. Egyptian king broke harp with a cry (7)
21. Step around hot filament (6)
23. 'E's suitable, rising in estimation (6)
25. Active British venture (5)
26. Flower festival isn't opening (5)
27. Maybe coal impaired flue (4)

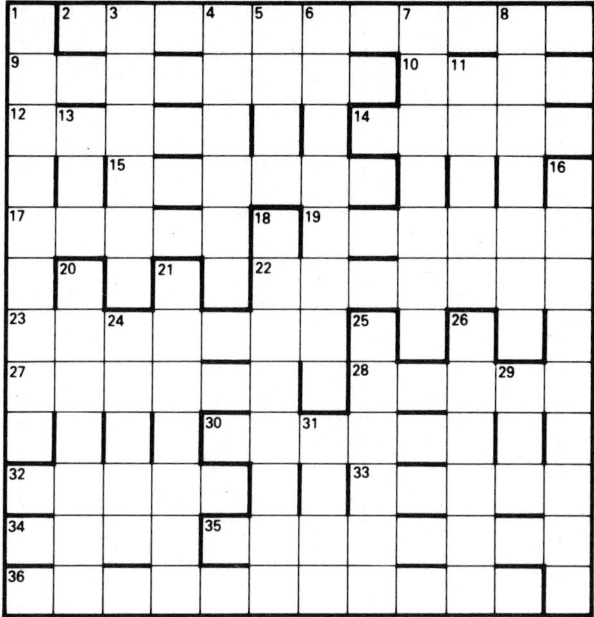

183

ACROSS

2. Worker has to grimace, with provision for only immediate needs (4,2,5)
9. Right, I'm seen among instruments that are blown, making glasses (8)
10. Dull poet rejected (4)
12. Artery, feature of great roadways winding about (5)
14. Fuss about love (5)
15. One member returned with a girl (6)
17. Kids' entertainment – Dad not bothered (5)
19. 'Times' editor made deletion! (6)
22. Sportsman allowed in heat, excited (7)
23. Hot guy collapsed, eating bit of rancid food (7)
27. Sin – and in a mission! (6)
28. 'Ow am I to produce a catcall? (5)
30. One that clings, flaccid, and French (6)
32. Saint, not well, inactive (5)
33. An excuse – a Liberal one (5)
34. Princess fled to part of India (4)
35. Malcolm's scoffing fat ducks (8)
36. First of church elders, alas, misrepresented a Methodist teacher (5-6)

DOWN

1. Instrument in odd seedy case? How observant (5-4)
3. Utter a right tirade! (6)
4. Fellow about to poke fun at mythical beast (6)
5. Roof piece – secure about 50 (4)
6. 'Ouse – rented, they say – provides an egg dish (8)
7. Eccentric's occasional dance (3-4)
8. Sailors about to gain objectives (7)
11. Stir up quarrels audibly (5)
13. Eggs from a duck, Virginia (3)
16. Alpine flower in weeds lies mangled (9)
18. Churchman, rum one in almost everything (8)
20. British Legion admits a sort reformed in a detention centre (7)
21. Drink tea – it's almost heaven! (7)
24. Smile, eating a cereal (5)
25. Almost transfix one antelope (6)
26. Invective literature modelled on anger (6)
29. Sphere or ball, initially (3)
31. Textile machine for obstinate type (4)

184

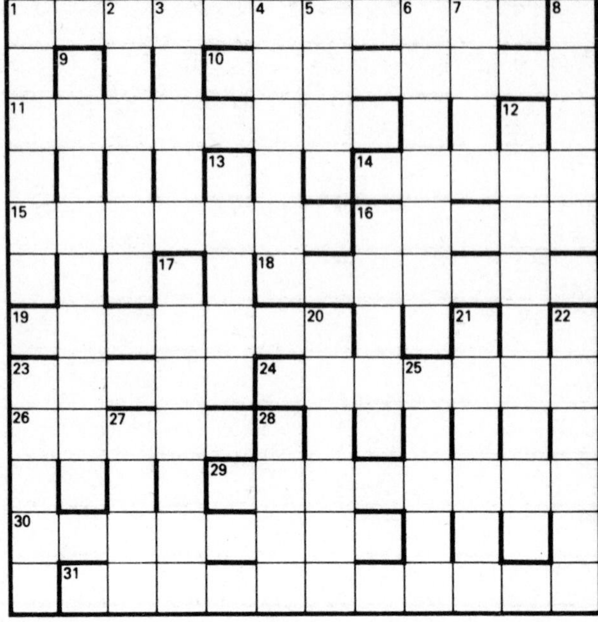

ACROSS

1. Did Duce rant, impromptu? Prepared in advance (3,3,5)
10. Recall wager after card game with king (4,4)
11. Professional note, letter, for female pupil (8)
14. Get Sappers in, and salute (5)
15. Producing leather for flogging! (7)
16. Colander is given back to girl (5)
18. One who muses, gloomy, about me (7)
19. Yearbook possessed by local man, a calendar (7)
23. Quantity of milk in pan – it's simmering (5)
24. Medicine gives room offensive smell (7)
26. Perform? 'E can't, being injured (5)
29. Marine creature shows little power or balance (8)
30. I r-recoup, twisting roulette operator (8)
31. I am relevant? – Saucy! (11)

DOWN

1. US author about – odd poet (6)
2. Troublesome god – nay, heartless (6)
3. Follow instruction, keep playing? (3,2)
4. Cigarette butt's gone out, clutched by Doctor of Divinity (3-3)
5. Cooks rabbits, for instance (4)
6. A Russian topped a Spaniard (7)
7. Relax in chaise-longue, a settee (4)
8. Ray takes off (5)
9. Subsistence level raised, we hear, over limit (9)
12. To lay low bets, possibly, is the most one can do (5,4)
13. Girl, an assistant, getting rise (5)
16. Silly lapse – bit of a bloomer! (5)
17. Overtake and seize hastily (5,2)
20. Woman with last of port wine (6)
21. Reverend is beginning to examine and make corrections (6)
22. Bad frost grips eastern woodland (6)
23. Fruit – the best (5)
25. Caught vulgar point in buffoon (5)
27. A cat, a tiny thing (4)
28. Iron turned black in Bordeaux (4)

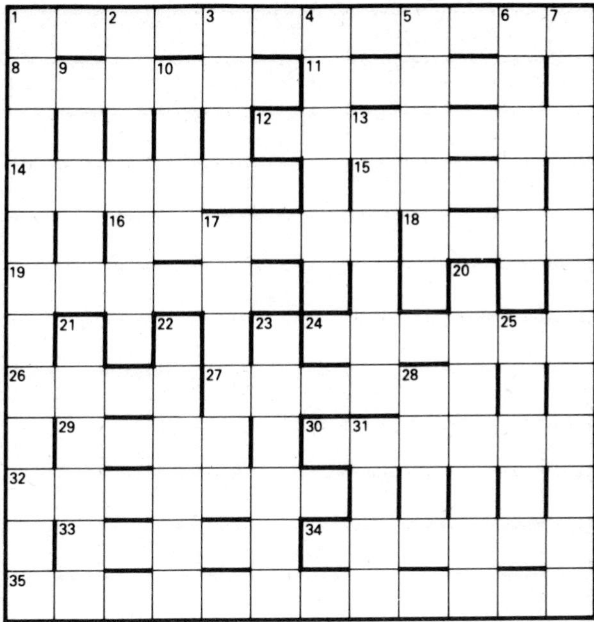

185

ACROSS

1. Seriously ill? Sad to hear Dot needs treatment (2,6,4)
8. Able to take in liquid, or soup, when cooked (6)
11. Antelope from eastern country (5)
12. Drink supplier forced, one hears, to follow Prohibition (7)
14. Officer returned, with a note, to find the place (6)
15. Bright ring from Henry, love (4)
16. Poles roaming round a Mexican town (2,4)
18. Stick first of earrings behind wrinkled lug (4)
19. Dashed along to beat Edward (6)
24. Boots I laced for musician (6)
26. Type of oven joint, right off (4)
27. Girl and chap skirting S. Am. city (6)
29. Rial converted into Roman money (4)
30. Circuitous route from Hyde to Urmston (6)
32. Wicked one in charge after a day (7)
33. Half familiar, possibly, with a criminal organisation (5)
34. Frontage mainly fixed by spies (6)
35. Men *and* women confused firm? (5,7)

DOWN

1. Tree bloom – hint of blight in maple's, so lop off! (5-7)
2. Torch-battery shows dull monastic room (3-4)
3. Worker hugging posh relation (4)
4. Listens to elegy's opening in funeral car (6)
5. Bank with time shows loss (6)
6. Offensive party upped the debts (6)
7. Special date – about D-day – having landlord installed (3-6,3)
9. Oxygen belt, part of atmosphere (5)
10. Love a little girl in part of Kennington (4)
13. Greek character with doctor – one providing lozenges (6)
17. Author, MA, in American state (6)
20. Junior goes on about an isle! (7)
21. Sausage? Alas, I'm made ill (6)
22. RAF set out to bombard (6)
23. Chap misled CIA, the lunatic! (6)
25. Country squandering US aid (5)
28. Regretful miss in spot, isolated (4)
31. Test former master set up (4)

186

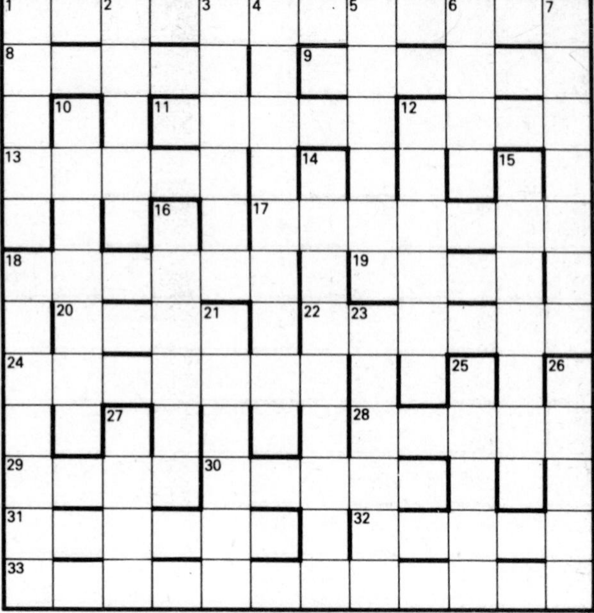

ACROSS

1. The art of gaining advantages makes Sue hoppin' mad about a male (3-9)
8. Left, a bird – right, a kind of monkey (5)
9. Signify a denial in a letter (6)
11. Nothing in the greatest to infatuate (5)
12. Short publisher's puff gives vague impression (4)
13. Esteem uranium found in valley (5)
17. Sappers go, we hear, to raise a siege (7)
18. Two parts of face swell, red (6)
19. Move sideways to get the advantage (4)
20. Rave with deserter about the North (4)
22. Old city man of good birth, needing immediate attention (6)
24. Instrument for measuring angles, Scott's first, still in existence (7)
28. Rock from part of Wales (5)
29. One month turned, became very cold (4)
30. Welshman, p-plump, backed last in Derby (5)
31. Author barging into poor Wells (6)
32. Boadicea's tribe shivering in ice (5)
33. Catch her with duke in lane, right – a Belgian? (12)

DOWN

1. Fruit girl (5)
2. Girl held up last of juicy fruit (5)
3. Arranges feathers, a swan's, round about (6)
4. Miner acts badly – vile wretch (9)
5. They say a trap will annoy (6)
6. Sacred evergreen with middle pruned (4)
7. Flawless piano, upright, with Fauré's initial inscribed (7)
10. Drew tea off, diluted (7)
12. Game bird's top crest! (6)
14. Fair one dipped into a fuel-tub, becoming messy (9)
15. Time for smoothing things out? (7)
16. Insinuated, at the back, hiding note (6)
18. Copper almost gleamed, enclosing one shock-absorber (7)
21. Lie about Tourist Trophy in idle gossip (6)
23. Affair's misread in palm! (6)
25. Rubbed off rising moisture round centre of pipe (5)
26. Fuss about a set of steps (5)
27. Pond creature, strange, with tadpole's head (4)

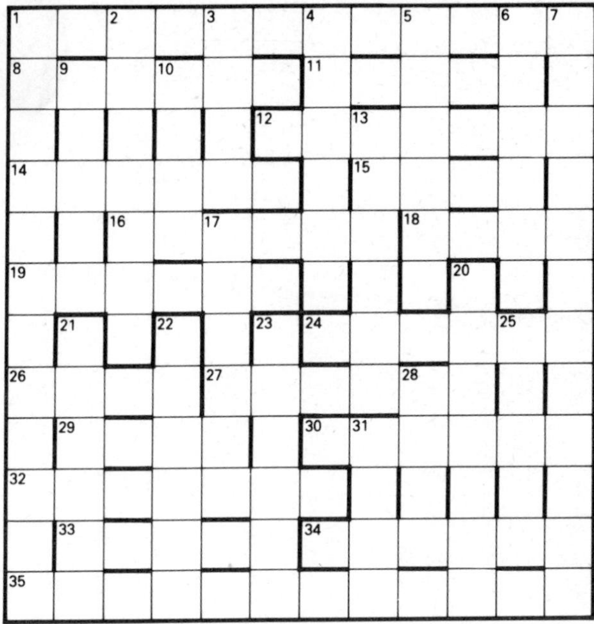

187

ACROSS

1. Flatter a northerner? Then child gets toffee (6-6)
8. Engineers fought, we hear, for payment that's merited (6)
11. Vehicle in recurring series (5)
12. Musical composition from jazzman in outrageous coat (7)
14. One Italian girl gets quinsy (6)
15. Glow from gold sun-god (4)
16. Great wild royal band! (6)
18. Dressing for fragment of shrapnel in thigh (4)
19. Note tree sawn-up for see-saw (6)
24. Carried to part of old island (6)
26. A deserter circling Scarlett O'Hara's home (4)
27. How a computer detects meanings (6)
29. Entice from lake to river (4)
30. Pitman's clipped dog (6)
32. Veteran sailor lost lad at sea (3,4)
33. Climber following others' lead, like sheep (5)
34. Astute with chopper, removing heart (6)
35. Gentleman struggling with net, in confused state (12)

DOWN

1. Swimming action might make Bert soak rest (12)
2. Touched round point, then understood! (7)
3. Queen in Ireland (4)
4. Sunday cornets and cakes (6)
5. Secret company set up a sect (6)
6. Ingredient of petroleum blasted most of canteen (6)
7. Candid US TV series, we're told (5-2-5)
9. Wise, making a computer? (5)
10. A land mass – among seas, I assume (4)
13. Spaniard, look, crushed by vehicles (6)
17. Wild reeds by a mass of water (3,3)
20. Subjugate Eastern European in endless trap (7)
21. Appeal to everyone in study (4,2)
22. Decorative inlay work is mounted in 26 Across (6)
23. Wooden limb, for instance, long, held by pin (3-3)
25. Banish from former French isle (5)
28. Two Continental articles in a Parisian periodical (4)
31. Gold on the French heraldic border (4)

188

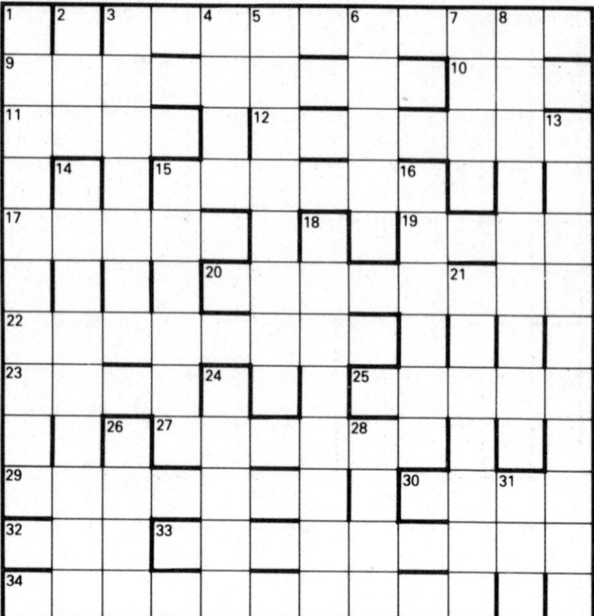

ACROSS

3. Blow dad's effort – you need a baker for this! (4-6)
9. Prepared for cooking, and done very unevenly about one (4-5)
10. Untrained for hostilities, retreated (3)
11. Opening charge (4)
12. Non-stop, but with no objective? (7)
15. Hour round verge for one who trims bushes (6)
17. One played out? Greek holds ace (5)
19. Skilful rounding an island (4)
20. Easy pace about one – Sevvy's first – caddy! (8)
22. Carbon Michael mixed in elemental compound (8)
23. Assistant in Jena I deployed (4)
25. Put on and/or off! (5)
27. Sad, no heart for Italian port (6)
29. Chic low dive to left could be his (7)
30. Ack-ack fragments almost form layers (4)
32. Hair-do cut through (3)
33. At ease! Roué, say, we agitated (2,3,4)
34. Now's the time for gifts? (7,3)

DOWN

1. Army headwear for a long time, with peak tucked in! (6-4)
2. Girl, not quite on the level (3)
3. One in the money makes act of contrition (7)
4. Cost's about right – gratis! (4)
5. Charged defender, in response (4-4)
6. Snake, in summer! (5)
7. Timber, note, round about (4)
8. Sign of disapproval for fruit (9)
13. Nude, Ken's first in streak and dances about! (5-5)
14. 2nd year student organised hop, with nurse around (9)
15. He braved about 50 in tin-hat (6)
16. Dwell in high rise on outskirts of Dieppe! (6)
18. Photograph footballer's opportunist effort? (8)
21. Truck still overturned, carrying a loaf (7)
24. What workers often want, to get up? (5)
26. Part of early recording instrument (4)
28. Beat so, endlessly on top of drum (4)
31. Bird headed for boat! (3)

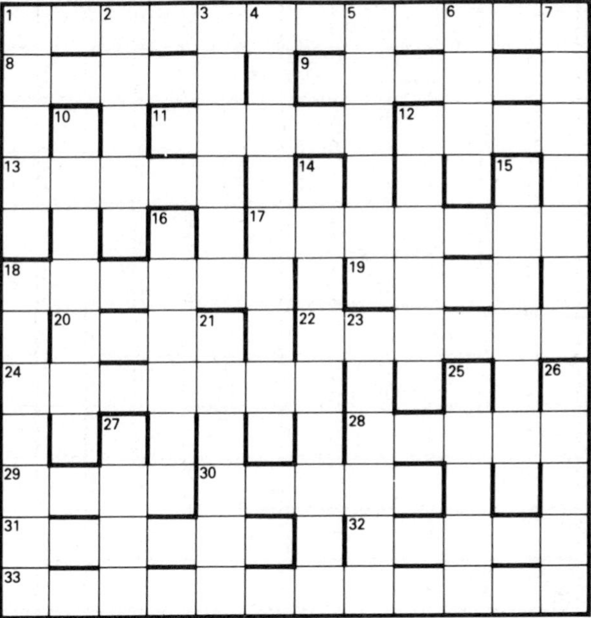

189

ACROSS

1. Oddly, the toff likes a mess (6,2,4)
8. A second-class cooker, not quite superior (5)
9. Neckwear includes fancy bib, for little Isabella (6)
11. Born with talent (by the sound of it) for utter confusion (5)
12. Girl provides a measure (4)
13. Brown pigment in river near 'ull! (5)
17. Pollution's certain, with oil in (7)
18. A number set out articles of faith (6)
19. A minute passage to study closely! (4)
20. Etna erupted before (4)
22. Force dispersed US Reds (6)
24. Groups of eight? One robe's unfinished after a month (7)
28. Partisan needs a drink, we hear (5)
29. Clique, round about 500 hooligans (4)
30. Neptune, perhaps, changed tide at start of year (5)
31. 'E bounded, ran off with lover (6)
32. Upright stake finally demolished, it's said (5)
33. Hurt gull hops badly, survives (5,7)

DOWN

1. Ruined king – one thrust (5)
2. Black cats around graves (5)
3. Discovered merit in lieutenant (6)
4. Bias seems unusual in diplomats' residences (9)
5. Boost from a Prince, say you? (6)
6. Bird nesting in Hibiscus (4)
7. Assistants from hospital treated lepers (7)
10. Arraign one MP? Every one (7)
12. Blood, about a litre, in abundance (6)
14. 18th Cent. author and metal-worker (9)
15. Forcibly extracted part of window, then had a breather (7)
16. Features of flowers, favourites, bordering a lake (6)
18. Roughly swept to the dance (3-4)
21. Eludes notice during times before festivals (6)
23. Shimmering lustre in Irish province (6)
25. Sounds like a proper goodbye (5)
26. Western seaman raised hot anger (5)
27. Look girl up, one that's worshipped (4)

190

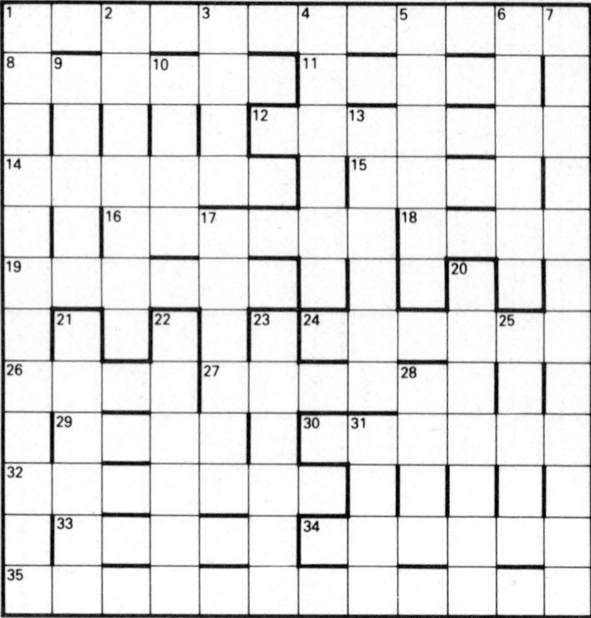

ACROSS

1. Author – no little one, on reflection – gripped by affairs (3,2,7)
8. A rendezvous in a boulevade (6)
11. Rent out meadow to SE (5)
12. Dizziness? I turn green first (7)
14. Cut off from cover in rolling river (6)
15. Priest with a writer of essays (4)
16. Piano, note, in fixed ensemble (6)
18. Throw out when gaol term's reversed (4)
19. Arab politician nears ruins round South (6)
24. River swallows others quickly (6)
26. School coterie, about 100 (4)
27. With peel half stripped, aunt cracked a dry fruit (6)
29. Danger-men initially live for a challenge (4)
30. Vapour enveloping river and beck (6)
32. An oiler modified a wing-flap (7)
33. Bit of camel fibre in seat (5)
34. Everything in marsh has sunk (6)
35. Going berserk, Yank licks ten tenacious fighters (8,4)

DOWN

1. Write 'X', to become rich and famous! (4,4,4)
2. Girl, like a vamp, turned up (7)
3. Head of match, in chopped material for fire, causes smoke (4)
4. Break-time for team? (6)
5. Rattle off a London journal (6)
6. Recover control around Georgia (6)
7. A breadline situation, kind absorbing House and Representatives (5,7)
9. Country house, ailing, in a state! (5)
10. Bare and dingy up to a point (4)
13. Give back profit (6)
17. Condiment very quietly bottled by a nobleman (6)
20. Discern, in rough sea, a girl (7)
21. Doc and I will produce a Florentine family name (6)
22. Dash, dash of relish, in meat! (6)
23. Spiritually refreshed – transported again, by the sound of it (6)
25. Old noble from North, an earl (5)
28. Russian river – large painting Monsieur's lost (4)
31. Shallow vessel for three, we hear (4)

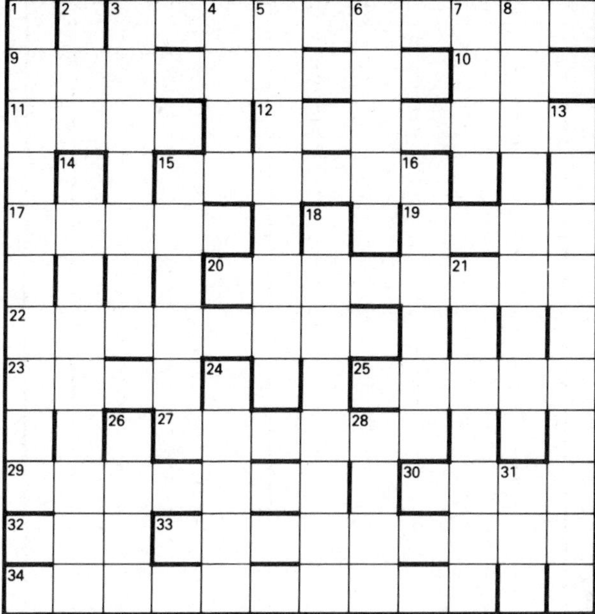

191

ACROSS

3. A Scot has loan, it's said, to settle inside (10)
9. To leave in the oven too long will ruin a rooster about five (9)
10. Cut former article, rejected (3)
11. French painter's short hair (4)
12. A victory that stirs up mirth (7)
15. Set up in office this month, with a bit of luck (6)
17. To be a candidate, you'll need a platform! (5)
19. Man has a key cut! (4)
20. Ex US politician round North makes for Southern sleepy state! (8)
22. Rise above grove, tangled and rank! (8)
23. Sounds close to the French river (4)
25. Father gets outsize skirting-boards (5)
27. Queen's after a timber merchant (6)
29. Sunday drink – then paint dottily! (7)
30. Last word from one facing soldiers (4)
32. Twitch when credit's reduced (3)
33. Sit in causes changes in educational establishments (9)
34. Learned saint gripped by colic has collapsed (10)

DOWN

1. Memorials a man placed over saint buried among relics (10)
2. Girl with adult carriage, almost! (3)
3. Bird with unusual bean, poisonous plant (7)
4. Smile, having king in card game (4)
5. Ardent incitements for a soccer team (8)
6. Like a Scot, one from the east (5)
7. Moisture mother found on piano (4)
8. 'E permed Xs in pool, in an outburst (9)
13. Plain nous – essential in picking winners at Ascot? (5,5)
14. Girl in upper room, having ancestral features (9)
15. Hardened to seasonal rude storms (6)
16. One in a ship, narrow with parallel sides (6)
18. Sell pots, crude, without design! (8)
21. Prevalent in pitchblende? Mica? (7)
24. The French writer up in Asian kingdom (5)
26. Highly decorated, deep in colour (4)
28. Revise a rising trend (4)
31. Wind in headless fish (3)

PART

FULLY CRYPTIC PUZZLES

192

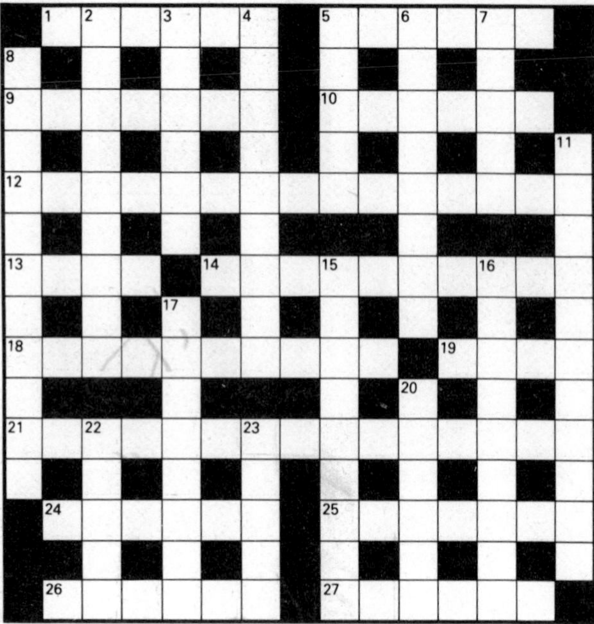

ACROSS

1. Drum for a couple of cats (3-3)
5. Bend a belt fastener (6)
9. Openings touts organised, admitting the French (7)
10. Boy from Standard One (6)
12. Support advertisers mistakenly – they give unwelcome advice (4-4,7)
13. A horse went quickly round the ring (4)
14. Communist with a fable that's similar (10)
18. Aunt is wrestling with lion, being cut off (10)
19. Cuts requiring fifty operations (4)
21. Cabinet minister's title – 'Another Glib Hour' – should be changed (5,10)
24. Cut off alongside northern river (6)
25. Bewitch with part of French anthem (7)
26. Leading player around you is one with stamina (6)
27. It's most certain the others will follow us about (6)

DOWN

2. Is caption blurred? See eye-specialists! (9)
3. The Saint embraces one believer in God (6)
4. Potter around in dining-hall before a boxing-match? (4,5)
5. 007 eats last bit of plaice, filleted (5)
6. Porters who transmit diseases? (8)
7. Grant to a tenant meadows, English (5)
8. NCOs in RA mobbed Sir, wildly (11)
11. Agrees about awful mess in valuations for tax (11)
15. They stage sporting events in favour of cars, we hear (9)
16. A dreadful waster, Bob bullies (9)
17. Smoother end to oratory – blarney (8)
20. Food supplier gets coarser, from what we hear (6)
22. Huge fireplace, by the sound of it (5)
23. Proprietor skulking in shadow, nervously (5)

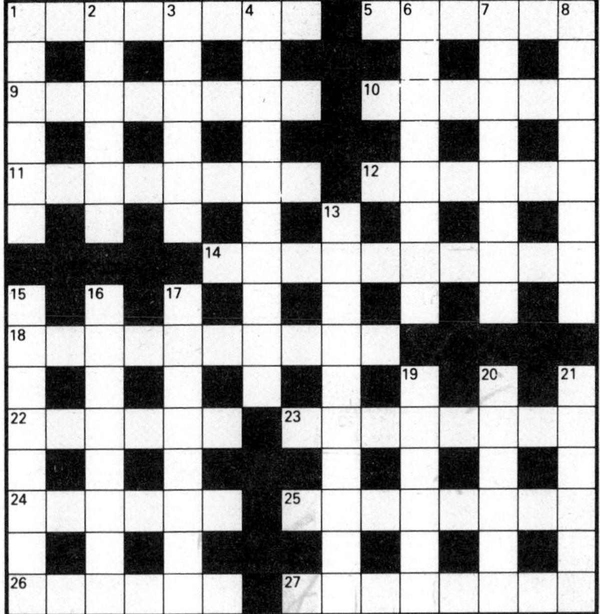

193

ACROSS

1,5. RAF pilot escort crashed in hot jungle (8,6)
9. Desmond, more ashen, turning over, suffered a setback (8)
10. Given assistance, he gets the record with Edward (6)
11. Member of family group calms Ann somehow (8)
12. Having got up, one needs rinse, possibly (6)
14. Arrivals round river are risky exploits (10)
18. Cinema reviewer has thin skin—very serious ignoring Capone! (4,6)
22. Lets down, and scowls (6)
23. Kitchen strainer for lard, once melted (8)
24. Amorous 'e-man with a twitch (6)
25. Most severe Saint, and sincere, by the sound of it (8)
26. Timothy in training finally using a stop-watch? (6)
27. Councillor's press-chief, one to whom money is owed (8)

DOWN

1. How often do we cheer the endless sort of pudding? (6)
2. Broken coal in a fuel-container (3-3)
3. I'm to sit for an artist, and put on something (6)
4. A Princess taken round one Egyptian city (10)
6. Estimate too highly on the subject of tax (8)
7. Showing one's body for a photo (8)
8. One row among disorderly sets shows neat condition (8)
13. Chopper scattered the police on the right (10)
15. A leader of France, smooth in speech, and well-off (8)
16. Luminous beetle makes owl grow excited—first sign of meal! (4-4)
17. Stinging creature has company in prison writhing (8)
19. Quietly made warm and dry, mated (6)
20. Part of wood destroyed—most strange (6)
21. Ceremony in W. Riding for author (6)

194

ACROSS

4. Long-winded talk he had cut severely (6)
6. Nice men circulating with eastern high-up (8)
9. A stubborn type beginning to trust a lucky charm (6)
10. I lied, tipsy with rum, causing wild excitement (8)
11. Green tint is vaguely intriguing (11)
15. Discover, after a search, some guru near Thailand (7)
17. Rather old tree, lofty—frequently cut! (7)
18. A throng sits, having the jitters, in these fairground rides! (5,6)
22. Old boy dipped into untidy drawer, a container for clothes (8)
23. Live, and yearn, to be a member (6)
24. Regular weekly occasions, says duet, for revision (8)
25. Rich globe-trotters, very dark and determined (3-3)

DOWN

1. Superficial show, never touring around the East (6)
2. I'm standing on a structure above the portico, causing an obstruction (10)
3. Deranged, I gunned at random around hospital (8)
4. My word, that's courteous! (8)
5. Illegal occupant composing jazzy quartets (8)
7. There's nothing holding a metal pin (4)
8. The girl with the Spanish mother (4)
12. Pupils anchored float, by the sound of it, among shoals of fish (10)
13. Betrayers, unruly rats, riot (8)
14. Visual faculty certainly needed in a rowing crew (8)
16. Clothing business, traditional, in fashion (3,5)
19. Cigarette found in midshipman's jacket (6)
20. Hit heavily amid tempestuous waters (4)
21. Genuine regret after end of fight (4)

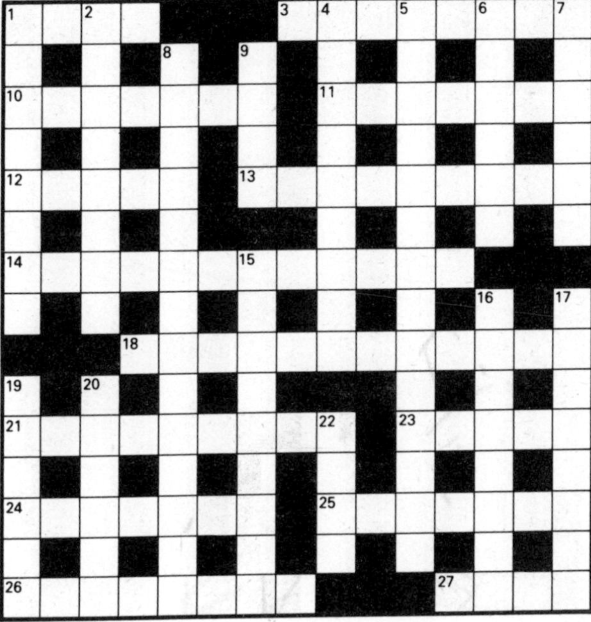

195

ACROSS

1. Brewing agent left soaking into rug (4)
3. Crazy parrot circling Edward – a bird of prey? (8)
10. Settle, and write a piece of music? (7)
11. Sounded like a goose? Clacked? Could be! (7)
12. A Scot is back in the desert (5)
13. The pound, and German currency, are a help to travellers (9)
14. Unable to be absorbed by stomach – it is bleeding badly (12)
18. Untenable belief Dennis corrected (12)
21. Places where paratroops land? They hang on (9)
23. The ones over there with t' watering-pipe (5)
24. Full up? Peer somehow gets allowed inside (7)
25. Wipe your feet here, or Mum's in a spot! (7)
26. Excessive medication can make dove sore (8)
27. Snow vehicle from South went ahead (4)

DOWN

1. Endlessly ridicule a fool in a soft shoe (8)
2. Noel made fizzy soft drink (8)
4. Relic once repaired, bring back to friendship (9)
5. O, I mislaid a cent, carelessly, in change to new currency (14)
6. Left in rows for roof-workers (6)
7. A vegetable gunners put on a platter (6)
8. Panicking – undergoing execution? (6,4,4)
9. Veg served up in lower part of ship (4)
15. Garden plants, small, used in various pastes (5,4)
16. Exceptional girl in reconstructed lab (8)
17. The Spanish provided in school 'e'd chosen (8)
19. Ducks drinking wine in a Portuguese town (6)
20. Threefold excursion with the Parisian (6)
22. Frothy water from potatoes quietly removed (4)

196

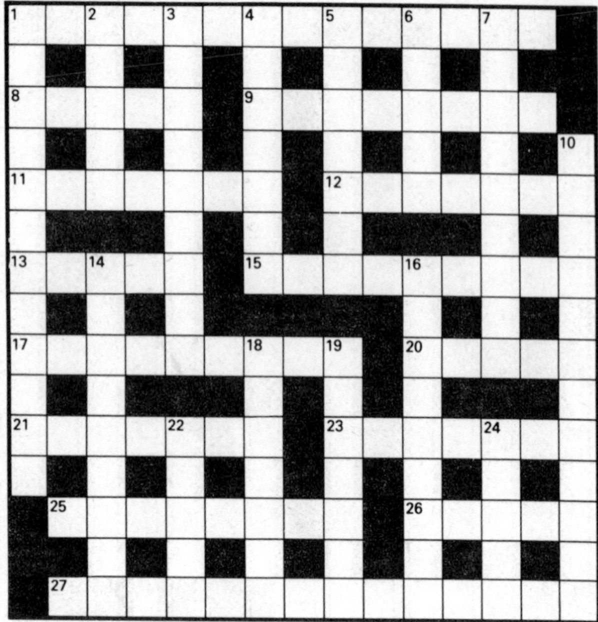

ACROSS

1. Very deeply involved at home with article – dithguthted with it! (2,3,5,2,2)
8. Cut the meat, showing anxiety, around five (5)
9. Praises record returns and examines accounts (8)
11. Came first, back in this place? Out of the running! (7)
12. Holiday island less important to Chartered Accountant (7)
13. Relax – the man with the stop-watch is back (5)
15. Rock, and, in the ship, musical sound (9)
17. Moulds made by volunteers back in places of worship (9)
20. It's worth having, when fixed (5)
21. Girl who's back among the smart-set tenants (7)
23. He, Clive, camouflaged a conveyance (7)
25. Higher up on the map, and not needing the Navy (8)
26. Famous otter found in stark area (5)
27. A fat lad is fed – is, oddly, in the best of health! (2,3,2,1,6)

DOWN

1. In the cinema, member of crew is burning (12)
2. Flung – from one end to the other, we hear (5)
3. Rudimentary eel, wriggling, crazy (9)
4. One very quietly comes among females and takes place (7)
5. Fuel suppliers in company nearly all males (7)
6. Look over a private retreat that's ancient (5)
7. Rioters in troubled inland areas (9)
10. Carries off the honours, and pinches the Madeira? (5,3,4)
14. Second ring must get us – it's very important (9)
16. Pasta – GP hates it badly cooked (9)
18. Over yonder's a girl (7)
19. Vehicle needed in S. African and N. American grassy plain (7)
22. Tut-tut! Timpanist is drowning all the players! (5)
24. Was anxious about a revolutionary (5)

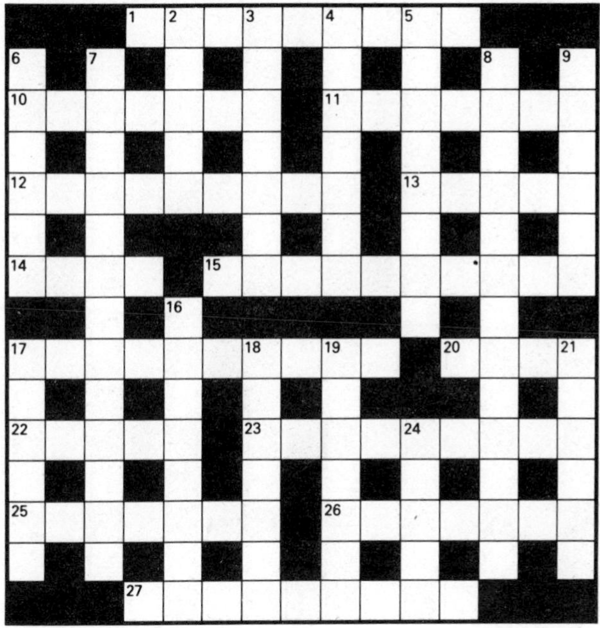

197

ACROSS

1. Messages the Spanish, for instance, carried in transports (9)
10. Like a Romantic poet of an earlier age – strange irony in that (7)
11. Detect nice uncertainty, by the sound of it (4,3)
12. Discredit the engineers in an argument (9)
13. Sculptor's staff at home (5)
14. US backs church of that kind (4)
15. Epidemic is let loose among coppers (10)
17. Owner in favour of report I revised (10)
20. Small portion of fried potato about a joint! (4)
22. Recesses are mistakes, with leader away (5)
23. About to get first-year student a cool drink (9)
25. Man found in bracken – Netherlander (7)
26. Greek letter that might make one lisp (7)
27. Wise politicians – US citizens? (9)

DOWN

2. Little boy from the North ducked in a lake (5)
3. Ninety in escape keep out (7)
4. Meditate, and turn back (7)
5. The chap to train a baboon (8)
6. Stays with military assistants around barracks, initially (6)
7. Christopher, we hear, going over like a trellis? (5-8)
8. Battered sausage – hold on, he ate it, surprisingly! (4-2-3-4)
9. Position assumed and held by earliest ancestors (6)
16. Wide view shows chance of success (8)
17. Practical jokes, played quietly on private soldiers (6)
18. Disturbed horse at listening distance (3-4)
19. Compensates slightly ill groups (7)
21. Mum, perhaps, or Dad, with a tear (6)
24. Follow Susan after north-eastern uprising (5)

198

ACROSS

7. Playful cat ruins draperies (8)
9. Summon me back for a nauseating medicine (6)
10. Counterfeit – that's almost a pity (4)
11. To protect, they say, straying hens, Edward makes an outhouse (6-4)
12. Rule with gravity over the North (6)
14. Violet, she gets embraced by youth, wasted (8)
15. Mutter, being an obstinate person, about the doctor (6)
17. In slumber, when cover's drawn back (6)
20. Buns brat ruined in lucky-dips (4-4)
22. Albert's after favourite floral features (6)
23. Nothing in Europe has changed this music theatre (5-5)
24. Eddie reversing feet is dexterous (4)
25. Cudgels frantically, losing head, in the mud (6)
26. Stylishness, for instance, noticeable in eastern weapon (8)

DOWN

1. Edible fungus, soft pulp found on rising heath (8)
2. Staunch good man raised me (4)
3. Chaste, having virtue – not half! – and strong spirit (6)
4. Is entitled to act as waiter, with Desmond around (8)
5. Tenacious, presents it anyhow (10)
6. Is trapped by simple call in solo whist (6)
8. Certainly sullen about first part of exams (6)
13. Girl who excites Red men? True (10)
16. Butchery, with decapitation, causing sound of amusement (8)
18. White man shows speed imbibing beer noisily (4-4)
19. Take for granted the fool will get the bird upset (6)
21. Reprobate, with 'elp brought up, gives a little wave (6)
22. Something of a dupe, Eve – deceived and irritated (6)
24. Cart in enclosure overturned (4)

199

ACROSS

1. Gate-arch specially designed for ancient N. African city (8)
5. Pal right in grip of demon (6)
9. Mules ran wild in numbers (8)
10. Odd tailless cat, causing uproar (6)
11. Without a match, like an empty House of Lords? (8)
12. Sherpa's strange expression (6)
14. Vocation of person is unusual (10)
18. Look fixedly, we hear, at suits in flights (10)
22. Some of the cast rallied – that's just like stars! (6)
23. Saint has irritations, and pricking pains (8)
24. Is choppy, initially, in bay – a famous one (6)
25. I defame a native of Skye, perhaps (8)
26. Beam above doorway, to allow nothing to fall back (6)
27. The lady 'e upset with passion (8)

DOWN

1. An awning, one in imitation (6)
2. Squeezed head off, battered (6)
3. King who had look upward – tough about that! (6)
4. RE flag must flutter in warm Atlantic current (4,6)
6. Most shaggy – ought to be clipped among the others! (8)
7. Remarkable impact, he stressed forcibly (8)
8. Observes little Ernest in the records (8)
13. Elaborate feast – treat – and the tang that remains (10)
15. Feature of Pakistan, Bulgaria, and Turkish city (8)
16. Quiet worker is an unreasoning adherent (8)
17. Faulty brake, with time, leads to a fracture (8)
19. Artist collapsed in narrow passage (6)
20. It's screened from light, notice, in the hut (6)
21. Off course, like a shallow vessel (6)

200

ACROSS

1. Pound to dine in the local when returning (4,2)
5. Creeps with twisted claws? That's about right (6)
9. An Italian, one not backward, I love (7)
10. Piquant morsel in small portion of goulash (6)
12. Battle squadron, not half getting about a London landmark (9,6)
13. Strikes occurring in Whitsuntide (4)
14. Some bitch, rabid, I injected, being a physiologist (10)
18. Trudging along to North London station (10)
19. A gun with catches retracted (4)
21. Pisces, for instance? Or dog-fish, Zoe? I can't sort it out! (4,2,3,6)
24. Gatherings of witches found in bays around the North (6)
25. A mother, a busy type, and unyielding (7)
26. A scallop – my, it's moist and sticky (6)
27. To reduce, exercise, they say! (6)

DOWN

2. Pulled out a pamphlet held by former editor (9)
3. Food container with brown colouring incorporated inside (3-3)
4. Tilling land that's sunk in deep lough in Galway (9)
5. Taxi about to turn over – toss it! (5)
6. Old collectors' items, awfully quaint, 'e's showing (8)
7. Notice love rising in a girl (5)
8. 'Pat's Pet' shot excitedly beyond the winning mark (4,3,4)
11. Saucy in a large town, showing obstinacy (11)
15. About to miss summons – a narrow escape! (5,4)
16. At home, endless attempts to catch the cat becoming complicated (9)
17. Mullion crumbling about English floor-covering (8)
20. Roams foolishly around southern marsh (6)
22. Small Greek bird makes rough throaty sound (5)
23. Exam taking year makes one irritable (5)

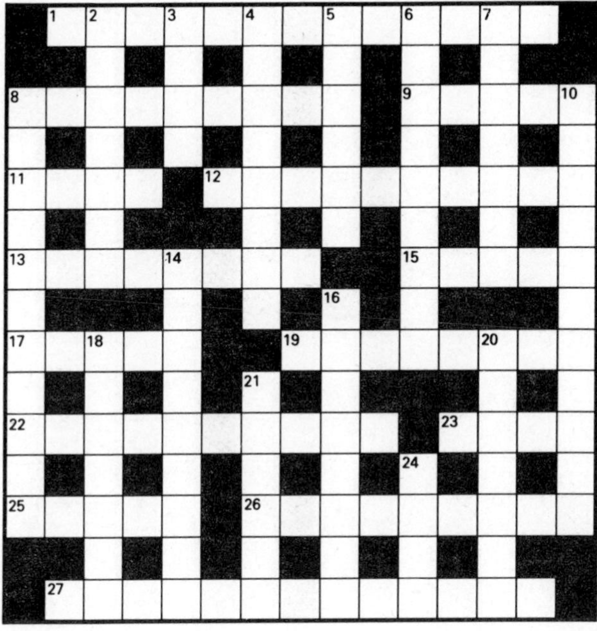

201

ACROSS

1. Flowers – odd end shorn or ragged (13)
8. Stock place where 'ero gets love in a tempest (9)
9. Musical sounds, with no backing group (5)
11. Sign name backwards – it's still a name (4)
12. Five in one bus, all entangled – impossible to unravel (10)
13. Bonding substance around a southern window-frame (8)
15. Temporary shelter round river – Midlands river (5)
17. Piano placed in narrow gap parted asunder (5)
19. Fir knocked over amid scattering choir – terrifying (8)
22. Intellectual, with flowing locks (4-6)
23. Ladle makes bachelor almost sick (4)
25. Strongly criticise part of roof (5)
26. In an artless way, of course! (9)
27. Recreational complex has unusual line – rest cure, eastern (7,6)

DOWN

2. Owls, perhaps, often heard on crowded roads (7)
3. Judge gets reward set up (4)
4. Submerging doctor, and confessing (8)
5. Hunter, nimble – not half – with stick! (6)
6. One who will repair crumbling nave or rising decay (9)
7. Eminent – but having no power, it seems! (7)
8. Salt ascends rickety, temporary edifices (4-7)
10. Celtic's play is haphazard – in a way that shows lack of belief (11)
14. Soccer fixture, minor? It's without equal (9)
16. Servant gets the Head to stay without limit (8)
18. A long time following the winding Nile, finding one's ancestry (7)
20. Iron round bar beginning to rust, becoming weaker (7)
21. West gets good shot on target – he's first in competition (6)
24. King, getting in the drink, gives broad smile (4)

202

ACROSS

1. Duke gets kick—having put his foot in it? (10-4)
9. Flies, for instance, in schools (7)
10. Pub beauty, we hear, demonstrates body-building apparatus (3-4)
11. Charge with gunpowder, chief (5)
12. Frame that buckled, and what happened later (9)
13. Reginald and the others, by the sound of it, went backwards (9)
14. Plant, tangled bush, about river (5)
15. Titled gentleman is heard in the darkness (5)
17. Glow from night sky has crazed loon in power (9)
20. University teacher baffled poor serfs (9)
22. Middle East detectives returned for student doctor (5)
23. Fencer's warning, necessary in open gardens (2,5)
24. Western lawman's sound, and warlike (7)
25. Comedy team with strange allure—also robust (6,3,5)

DOWN

1. Flogger's head boy, rather presumptuous (7-7)...
2. ...flogging convict about part of leg (7)
3. At home Attlee becomes severe (9)
4. Fuel controllers calling for openings around a street (3-4)
5. Circled, and rode madly around a little while (7)
6. Carrier, we're told, having less clothing on (5)
7. Outdoor work easterly rain spoilt (4-3)
8. A record rearranged by the CIA, all in order of initials (14)
14. Area flooded by sea halts rams, going astray (4-5)
16. First-class drink turns up around eastern American state (7)
17. Girl, we hear, ruined lead with faulty distribution of cards (7)
18. People having rows, causing trouble in San Remo (7)
19. US soldier and doctor, about to expire, getting dizzier (7)
21. Dread losing head, making a mistake (5)

203

ACROSS

4. Floor covering is needed for the vehicle, darling (6)
6. US politicians are not ill aboard ship (8)
9. Cause minor irritation to gee-gee, stuck in the river (6)
10. Tilt a can clumsily, producing a lot of water (8)
11. Put down loose coins to swap with each other (11)
15. Leave a ring on (7)
17. A whole number, for instance, found in Bury? (7)
18. Genealogies show first of forebears, possibly my earliest (6,5)
22. Everything Eric eats gets initially hypersensitive (8)
23. Cook sounds like an ass, we hear (6)
24. Georgia – in that place, five hundred assembled (8)
25. Scorches back for instance during transgressions (6)

DOWN

1. Bobby's potato-scraper? (6)
2. About Lent, Annie turned out for hundredth anniversary (10)
3. A garden tool pierces favourite bird (8)
4. Preserve – in lab, possibly – a man-eater (8)
5. A tar gets excited in boat-race meetings (8)
7. Swear-word coming from boat-house (4)
8. Smart losing a pound? Fed up! (4)
12. Female attendant disguised as a man, hidden (10)
13. Corresponding with a Hellene mostly in Greece's capital (8)
14. Salesman's on the upgrade among professionals, and flourishes (8)
16. Misshapen, from being maimed in action (8)
19. First sight of tropics, 'orrible – scorching (6)
20. Dance lacks nothing in taste (4)
21. Pose around lake's narrow opening (4)

204

ACROSS

1. Rebuffed, CO holds duel, foolishly, with Communist (4-10)
8. Priest with half zany girl (5)
9. One who sets tests – formerly a coalman (8)
11. Rebels' leader 'urried and whispered (7)
12. Show zeal for part of garden thus, ecstatically (7)
13. Bachelor's fashionable, a dish (5)
15. A holder of immoderate views, Tex merits reform (9)
17. Concession, giving leave to enter (9)
20. Female swan seen round about to trim feathers (5)
21. Laughs at the German before the fateful day (7)
23. A set, embracing Western Society, becomes adult (5,2)
25. Rambler has fitful rest, eating small loaf (8)
26. A Liberal, I will make a plea (5)
27. A very restrained remark Stan uttered, vaguely, about males (14)

DOWN

1. Liqueur and fruit on the railways – also a bit of yoghurt (6,6)
2. See, at home, Sunday joints (5)
3. Sailor has fish in the ship for birds (9)
4. Extra that ought to be paid, not yet arrived (7)
5. Most meagre, smallest around the North-East (7)
6. Civet's wild – remove forcibly (5)
7. Administrator put to death about four (9)
10. Where solids start to liquefy, Ming pot let in fluid (7–5)
14. Good helpful type finds Marie almost in Devil's grip (9)
16. In pose, disguised a long time, spying (9)
18. At home, sluts exchanged offensive remarks (7)
19. Elevated atmosphere, for example in African country (7)
22. Idle fellow's monotonous talk (5)
24. Ooze, spreading miles (5)

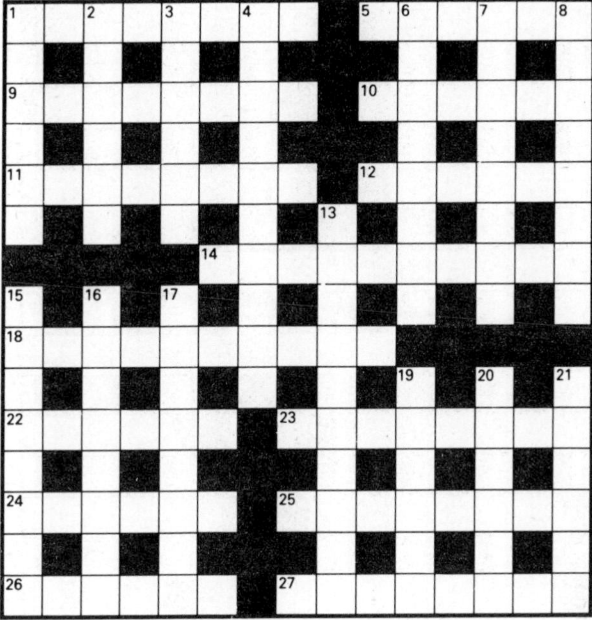

205

ACROSS

1. Does good to burst beef-tins (8)
5. Untidy fellow from S. Carolina, with a starched frill (6)
9. Muted ringer? It develops one's arm muscles! (4-4)
10. Corner by river for fisherman (6)
11. Formerly engaged in awful vice – imagine! (8)
12. Lift out of order in Kent area will make you suffocate (6)
14. Ten campers staggering about steep hillside (10)
18. RU, so we hope, may provide store of energy! (5-5)
22. Almost a nobleman in New York (6)
23. Spring of a nut broken at home (8)
24. Spies – toffs are following one (6)
25. Male almost cradling a bird like a mother (8)
26. Refrain from Preludes is terrific (6)
27. Gives special prominence to exploits around English river (8)

DOWN

1. I'd become shivery? Not me, in close-fitting garment! (6)
2. One upset Oriental pot, when christening? (6)
3. Mythical tales from bluff Able Seaman (6)
4. Household entertainment on set – I live for variety! (10)
6. A monument – Irishman has one raised in church (8)
7. Elated in revolt, getting pinched (8)
8. Stirs up people, and frets badly about it (8)
13. Overtake one, crashing at one, showing strong feeling (10)
15. A European from Paris, and unruly (8)
16. Thick jerseys will get more damp, we hear, in steamer (8)
17. Chatters about the Spanish priests (8)
19. In a hole, contrive something new (6)
20. Grand type of house, we hear, is the fashion (6)
21. Sounds of bells – Helen's, they say (6)

206

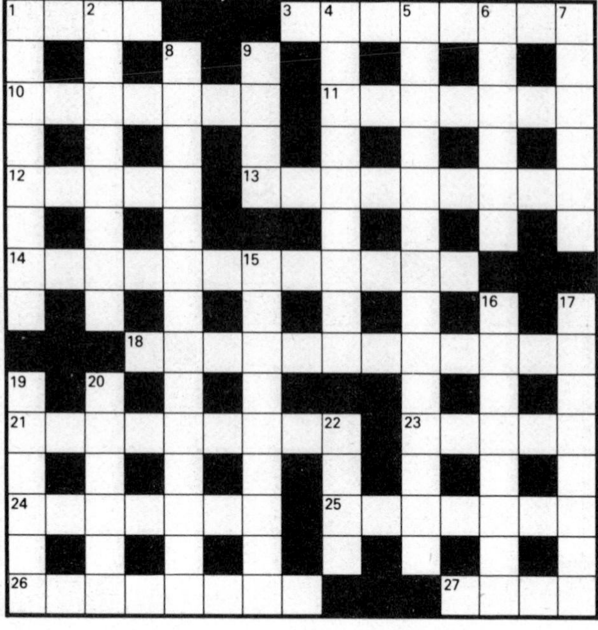

ACROSS

1. Take a seat, as they say, first in York, a large town (4)
3. Break in school session – left sadly with external injury (4-4)
10. We train bending metal articles (7)
11. Liquid measures from vessels 'e tipped out (7)
12. Catholic in CIA gets about (5)
13. Help by means of grant is grabbed by substitute team (9)
14. Theatrical artist has rug in tuneful surroundings (12)
18. Initially damning utterance, a public accusation (12)
21. Conservative girl I call almost Greek, perhaps, in form (9)
23. Suffer at home with wretched dog (5)
24. A TV station – in the groove! (7)
25. Hypocrisy at a choral work (7)
26. Eastern girl, a railway's secret agent (8)
27. One politician's mischievous children (4)

DOWN

1. Burial-place, where you see reserves come mostly in a taxi (8)
2. Climbers catch up on exercises, we hear (8)
4. I grab Alec, worried, concerned with mathematical symbols (9)
5. Forgeries stain officials badly (14)
6. Foreign former love has twitch (6)
7. Timber in the Mediterranean, beaten to pulp (6)
8. Putting clothes on among S. African youths – saucy things! (5,9)
9. Little Elizabeth's making wagers (4)
15. Just like uncle, making a van curl wildly round hairpin bend (9)
16. Renounce record before game, by the sound of it (8)
17. Begs for rent, naughtily, and has a meal (8)
19. A frozen trickle of water in the Arctic I cleared (6)
20. I'm unfortunately upset – it's the sausage (6)
22. Sound like a bird, topless, making fortune! (4)

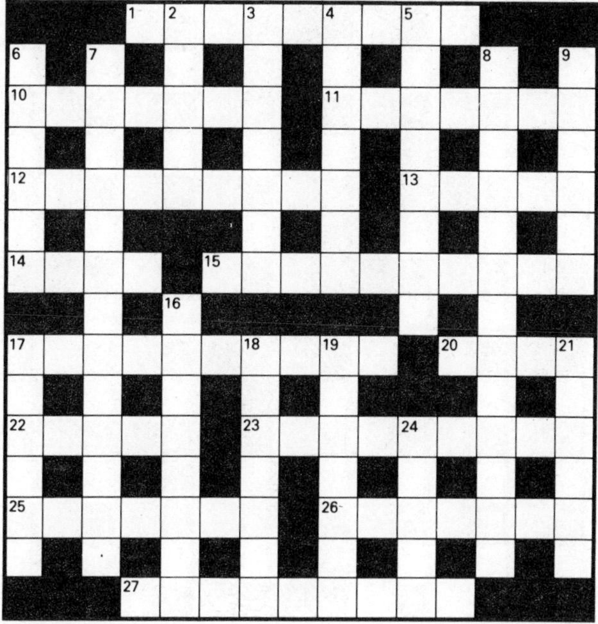

207

ACROSS

1. To relieve everyone, I've returned and dined (9)
10. Walked with unsteady tread around a member (7)
11. Leg all in one piece, we're told – just a tiny cavity (7)
12. Car-lights – lift with palms, somehow (4-5)
13. Tecs joining Queen for a drink (5)
14. Cheat gets a couple of pounds for a child's plaything (4)
15. Systematic – nice if it's organised by Conservative (10)
17. Team eats grilled livers and beef (10)
20. The old record gives a high-pitched sound (4)
22. Very little time to drag back a tycoon (5)
23. Fool once taking one in with sound correspondence (9)
25. People who harvest mostly red misshapen pears (7)
26. Warm and dry wine, where there are flighty passengers? (7)
27. Good man, before terribly sad fate, is unwavering (9)

DOWN

2. Feature of jacket that helps to make overlap elegant (5)
3. Put a stop to mice running riot in a particular area (7)
4. Dad's locked in semi, unfortunately – there's no way out of this! (7)
5. A large town, with X at the top showing stubbornness (8)
6. Leading journalist's boss gaped (6)
7. Roll a large map out, making a four-sided shape (13)
8. Greeting of dragon to one that's shaking (4,9)
9. A name, said Richard, for all to hear! (6)
16. A clanger, having explosive around eastern part of camp (4-4)
17. Around the railways one finds a few gloomy (6)
18. Graceful birds eat, mostly, in this Welsh city (7)
19. Spinning stick, I'd upset the people in the office (7)
21. Attractive, but trivial? That's about right! (6)
24. Annoys police informers (5)

208

ACROSS

7. Little members getting round Mother to produce love-apples (8)
9. Piece of cheap lint hiding base of statue (6)
10. Army entertainer (4)
11. Big city sent back bone china and salted meat (10)
12. Agile doctor dipped in the river (6)
14. If it bursts, one may get wet beard! (5-3)
15. Fibbed about starting price – and spoke with slight defect (6)
17. Reliable? There's corrosion in half the tyre (6)
20. Letting a ruined old castle in Cornwall (8)
22. Uninteresting rubbish, it causes damage in the House (3-3)
23. Company has a race on – a thousand poorly in textile factory (6-4)
24. Box, and treat mercifully, mostly (4)
25. Not admitted into the river – that's mean (6)
26. Those taking part in debate ask Peers for amendment (8)

DOWN

1. Settler shows depression, with a lion on the prowl (8)
2. Sweep along, having a bit of wake behind (4)
3. Be staggering with blow, and quiver (6)
4. Fast runner, Society person making an impression! (8)
5. Cry, sobbing dementedly for old crooner (4,6)
6. Bombard street, eastern, airmen diving in (6)
8. Lake twists northwards, spread all over the place (6)
13. I taunt boss madly in depot (3-7)
16. Arrange a locomotive to take on the Queen (8)
18. A body of farming gentry, you love to supply men for the railway (8)
19. Confederates – everyone that is southern (6)
21. I, Ronald and Ted got flat (6)
22. One in fight for honour, losing first of points, is less interesting (6)
24. Japanese liquor – has a keg, but some's missing (4)

209

ACROSS

1. Dominant chap, the spinner—follow closely (3,3)
5. Head fellow's sent the wrong way, led astray (6)
9. Like a big cat, wild one, in a row (7)
10. Outsize vehicles for Hollywood awards (6)
12. Famous sailor's teacher is a bird, holding foreign money (3,7,5)
13. Bar doesn't open at all times! (4)
14. Vulgar and expensive, we hear, to seize for military use (10)
18. Tool men trust in, oddly enough (10)
19. Form of wrestling that's fair—not half!—at a party (4)
21. County girls erect house with new design (15)
24. Ring again and cancel (6)
25. A seer, I yell to be heard (3-4)
26. Timber-cutter noticed the old bit of rot (6)
27. Teetotaller getting into a row causes a giggle (6)

DOWN

2. Having no smell? That's grim, with rotten soles about (9)
3. They extract water, making motorists lose heart (6)
4. Where actors rest, inexperienced Othello, perhaps, turns up (5-4)
5. Girl and I complain, being set up (5)
6. Translating ciphers needs a month—doing badly (8)
7. Girl in novel, forsaken one (5)
8. Bullying noises bring tussle that's nasty (11)
11. Good-for-nothings end sore troubled around spring (4-2-5)
15. Eastern mace mixed in garden herb for pie-filling (9)
16. Tortuous clue I, with time, clarify (9)
17. Pots, a hundred, found on stony flower-bed (8)
20. Piano, in a school, makes appearance (6)
22. A letter from Athens, and a precious stone on a ring, turned up (5)
23. Rise aloft, absorbing light, initially, of the sun (5)

210

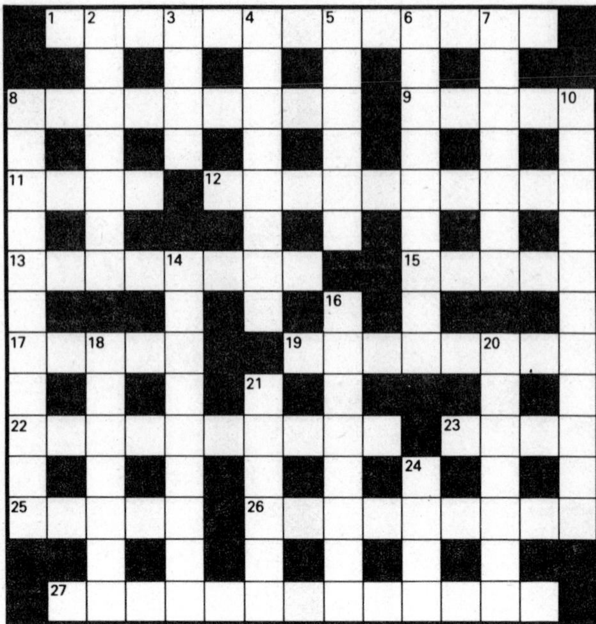

ACROSS

1. Mother's red pet, teased, is easily enraged (5-8)
8. Car manufacturer controlled by 'er, a bungler (9)
9. Bird with the French appellation of rank (5)
11. What bookies offer can cause scraps (4)
12. Occasion for meal in inn tired me out (6-4)
13. People who'll trick you with five hundred odd riddles (8)
15. Opera showing in Benvenuto's castle (5)
17. Commercial song for Robin (5)
19. Licentious, Edwin grew slack (8)
22. Portable lamp, right for use in Toc H – not heavy (5-5)
23. Female sheep in the trees, by the sound of it (4)
25. A clause added for a horseman (5)
26. Night's beginning and pot-holer's shivering in very cold spot (5,4)
27. Eve, left annoyed in the heather, finds passage over railway (5-8)

DOWN

2. Chased brick-carrier round windy dune (7)
3. Clears grates, with lid removed (4)
4. TA soldiers make slip in ranks (8)
5. Spanish sheep, in Rome for a change (6)
6. To begin, it is an internal inflammation (9)
7. Men on guard beheaded in narrow lanes (7)
8. Sower who's heard on radio (11)
10. Reels laid me out, in Ireland! (7,4)
14. Let archer loose in part of the forest? (5-4)
16. Gay seducer, unwilling to have a disturbance of the peace endlessly (8)
18. Shorten a card-game (7)
20. Just delivered from the North-East, and put on around baby, initially (3-4)
21. Aspic, nice to some extent for an open-air meal (6)
24. Huts collapsed in this way (4)

211

ACROSS

1. Sort of drinking-house, with alcohol, gets Ed keen to help everybody (6-8)
9. Entangle a ball in a tree, when thrown back (7)
10. Mum grips a rail shakily—it's the fever (7)
11. 'Ow am I to make a cat-call? (5)
12. Study rigorous contract (9)
13. Permissiveness makes Leo wild, in a dazed state (9)
14. Saint given a drink to play the guitar? (5)
15. Birds for the helmsman, we hear (5)
17. Member, stuck in taxi strike, wired message (9)
20. Becoming less dense, and awfully angry, fire! (9)
22. Warmth beginning in high tract of moorland (5)
23. The French prohibition includes no Middle-Eastern country (7)
24. One who harasses a cross-country runner (7)
25. Kind of myrtle—real cute US type, unusual (10-4)

DOWN

1. Training in inflation? That can bore very quickly (9,5)
2. Robert thanks the Italian, hair trimmed at the back (7)
3. Risk row on breaking up a smelting plant (9)
4. Element that's foolish, they say, to study (7)
5. Huge mines exploded around me (7)
6. Cove at home given permit (5)
7. Nobleman and I come upon the Queen sooner than expected (7)
8. Peter and Tom surprisingly hire some character in a Christmas show (9,5)
14. They tend flocks quietly with the girl in huts (9)
16. A cut of meat in half the course is deer (7)
17. Tailless ape longing to climb a sooty passage (7)
18. Confused both GIs and a VIP (3,4)
19. Lecturer embraces one prompter (7)
21. Film star, affectionate one (5)

212

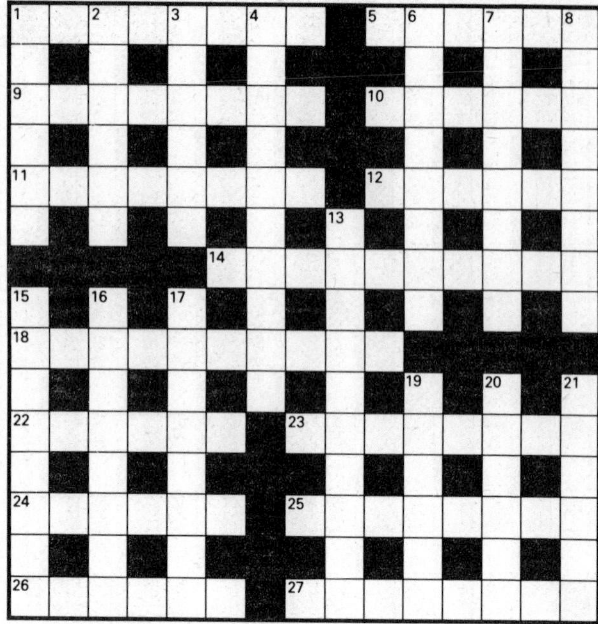

ACROSS

1. Sleigh with bag on got shaken about (8)
5. Rascal with one dish of large prawns (6)
9. Communist, among ancient Scots, makes prophecy (8)
10. Small dry fruit ape cracked with head! (6)
11. Former rioter, reformed, is outside (8)
12. Listens to condolence, finally, in funeral car (6)
14. PC Rooke we'd mistaken for a bird! (10)
18. A Post Office record – call reversed, expressing regret (10)
22. SW city, English, having cross by blasted tree (6)
23. Intentionally replete, and crafty about it (8)
24. A white vestment, with neck-piece reversed, though (6)
25. At home, Diana, saucy, reverses without fear (8)
26. Enticed to capture king, lay in wait (6)
27. Drama editor, out of bed, redoubled efforts (6,2)

DOWN

1. Upset, being given a gratuity? (6)
2. About to plunge in swimming-pool? You'll need a deep one! (6)
3. Swelling of throat, with clotted blood around it (6)
4. Zodiac expert consulted by superstitious people – or gloaters, possibly (10)
6. More ingenious Conservative, about to make merry after rising (8)
7. Male duck getting poisonous plant (8)
8. One has the alternative in New York, supposedly (2,6)
13. Notice, I do Latin, badly – extra needed! (10)
15. Vile yell is heard in US game (8)
16. Mob never riots in this month (8)
17. A headlong plunge – I do seven, stupidly (4-4)
19. A very noisy little boy in a brawl (6)
20. Old Bob ran with long strides and disappeared (6)
21. Bit of money Ed uppishly inspected (4,2)

ACROSS

4. Blonde initially irritating and spiteful (6)
6. Communication from a waggish person after an appointment (8)
9. Showy but worthless marble, uninteresting (6)
10. Narrow passage, we hear, without curve or bend (8)
11. Wild bear in a herd, running amok (4-7)
15. Calls the band to have a little drink (5,2)
17. Weed with soft beard gives hillbilly dance (7)
18. See man get in wrong locomotive (5-6)
22. Stagger the East with test for study of projectiles (8)
23. I never could be a covetous person (6)
24. Rickety pier and hut decayed (8)
25. Dramatically presented, for men only, by the editor (6)

DOWN

1. Young animal protecting the girl, a plump child (6)
2. Thin man got drunk in Midlands town (10)
3. Sit with legs apart, right up in rider's seat (8)
4. Nevertheless, weep about the man's slaughter (8)
5. Pulling along with Her Majesty inside – that's very elevated (8)
7. Jason's ship – and contents of hold, with the lid off (4)
8. A tax obligation (4)
12. Repel a pest that's damaged fruit plants (5-5)
13. Controlling by force Post Office letting, by the sound of it (8)
14. Went wrong after 'elpful tip, getting put down (8)
16. Uneasy uncertainty, a feeling gripping us quietly (8)
19. Fewer than a hundred I catch in New York (6)
20. Bobby holds right to show a whip (4)
21. Maple in Canada? Certainly (4)

214

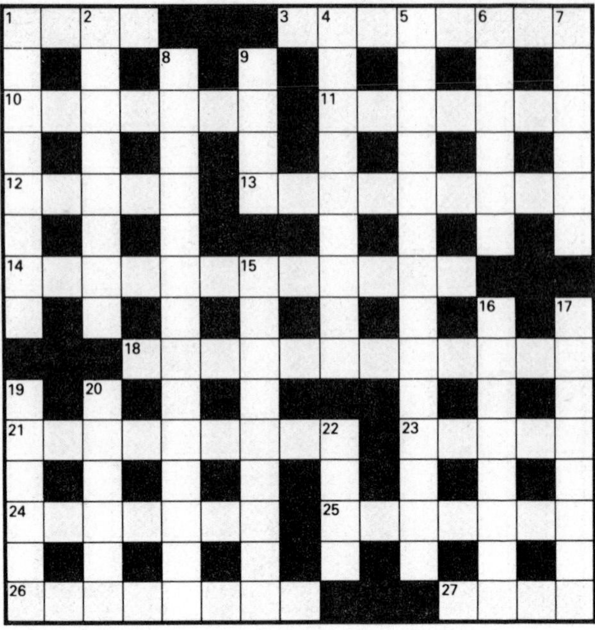

ACROSS

1. In crash, I nicked a leg-bone (4)
3. Relying on a bit of tin corroding (8)
10. A noisy promenade is an insult (7)
11. A letter-carrier – a man, we hear, to chatter on the way back (4-3)
12. Double edge of elastic thread (5)
13. King gets in a gambling machine – worth putting in the newspaper? (9)
14. Breathe with relief, perhaps, walking and playing without rehearsal (5-7)
18. Erasers bruised Brian, rather oddly (5-7)
21. Kernel, right inside cake, causing acrid feeling in the chest (9)
23. Farewell remark to the French, about to depart! (5)
24. I'm having a couple in the tavern initially, to impress (7)
25. Foreign car used by a high-up, an inspector of accounts (7)
26. Quiet and sturdy, showed indifference (8)
27. Sounds of cats in the stabling yard (4)

DOWN

1. Neatest, and most clever (8)
2. Violate fashionable border (8)
4. A jog to the memory about a part that's left (9)
5. Brisk rats doing wrong – they run round the walls (8-6)
6. Drink, in trim bib, elegantly (6)
7. Told jokes, getting silenced (6)
8. Wakes up needing love – turns out a failure (5,2,7)
9. A cooking vessel up on the summit (4)
15. Correct behaviour, awfully quiet – better without extremes (9)
16. Disparage one temperate person embraced by a beautiful woman (8)
17. Gentlemen, 'e's taking lots of paper (8)
19. Groups of singers – so rich, blending (6)
20. Poor person, genteel, getting into an organ of the press (6)
22. Ancient mariner getting no expression of sympathy? (4)

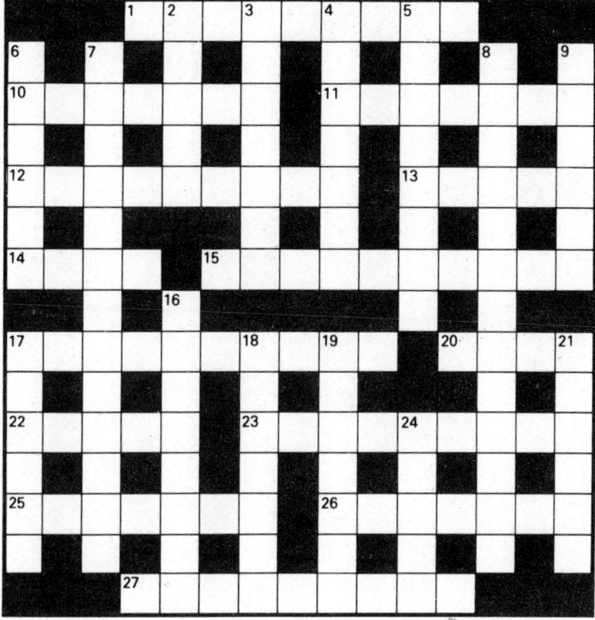

215

ACROSS

1. Weepy people stirred cabby's ire (3-6)
10. Second-class student, by the sound of it – one who raises dogs? (7)
11. Strongly criticises a state levy, we hear (7)
12. Forming a body of people, NCO's to make a speech (9)
13. Sound of bell brings him into church (5)
14. Take in through the lips some thick custard that's been brought back (4)
15. Observers near platforms set around the Queen (10)
17. Professional, one observed in oral, is notorious (10)
20. Irritation caused by Italian child (4)
22. Michael's heard about us making melodious sounds (5)
23. Eric's swallowed a piece of copper money – strange fellow! (9)
25. Prisoner has to deceive Victor, having no alternative (7)
26. Char holding your surgical instrument (7)
27. French policemen give General bad dreams (9)

DOWN

2. Wireless ad in S. American city (5)
3. In US Barry misused student's grant (7)
4. Most courageous, revealing two items of underwear! (7)
5. Ten whipped up cake-topping – it's tempting (8)
6. Old computer makes a graduate swear endlessly (6)
7. Zoe's car brings drunk where walkers have priority (5,8)
8. Liable to mishaps in stress, Di's knocked over, lying flat (8-5)
9. Daisies found during Easter Sunday (6)
16. Give account of editor, upset over writer (8)
17. Kind of stone, turned up, with vermin underneath (6)
18. How the lamb cried! Bet dale's stormy (7)
19. One who levels charges puts copper in an awful scare (7)
21. Back of knee, and eye, cut in ball-game (6)
24. Audacity's a feature of a planner, venturesome (5)

216

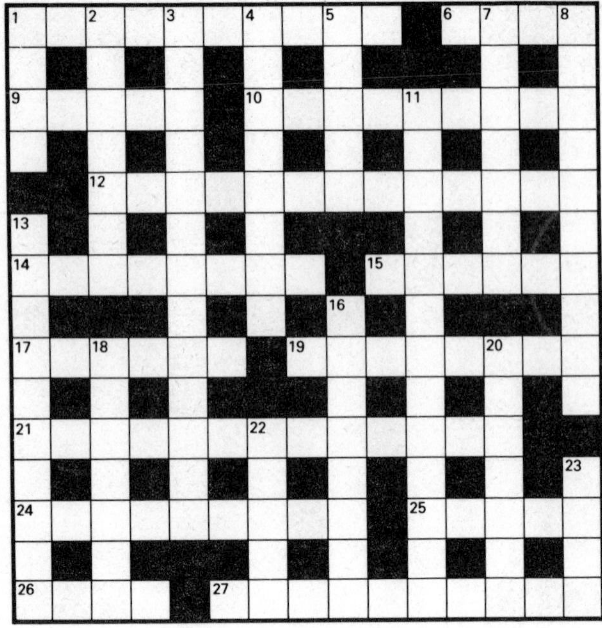

ACROSS

1. Very attractive people, at some drab dances! (10)
6. Second-class set, a disgrace (4)
9. A girl endlessly cooked (5)
10. A fool it's easy to name (9)
12. A bit rusty–like a retired GP? (3,2,8)
14. About to get handed food, being aloof (8)
15. Beware of our sailors in a deep hollow (6)
17. Nausea–not half!–grips idiot in capital of Bahamas (6)
19. One who departs in Civil Service choppers (8)
21. Pouts, entirely stupidly, in an affected manner (13)
24. Type of carpet, cut almost alongside cathedral (9)
25. Felony in church around the border (5)
26. Some of the colour slides belonging to us (4)
27. Casts around ridge of rocks endlessly for young birds (10)

DOWN

1. Five hundred behind–that's silly (4)
2. Newspaper chiefs swank about rubbish that's rejected (7)
3. Tired men near a stormy sea (13)
4. Turned into bone? If so, dies in agony (8)
5. Man with stop-watch gets leader in mile into a row (5)
7. Type of screen the French put round an upper room (7)
8. Offer the Head gentle feelings? (10)
11. To be without a platform I call almost listless (13)
13. Instrument makes Pa groan, din being awful (5,5)
16. Crimson-coloured penny-dreadful, revolutionary (5-3)
18. A ship's pressure-cooker? (7)
20. Heavenly Cambridgeshire town, one steeped in vice (7)
22. Drink a drop of liqueur? The lot! (5)
23. Critically examines doctors (4)

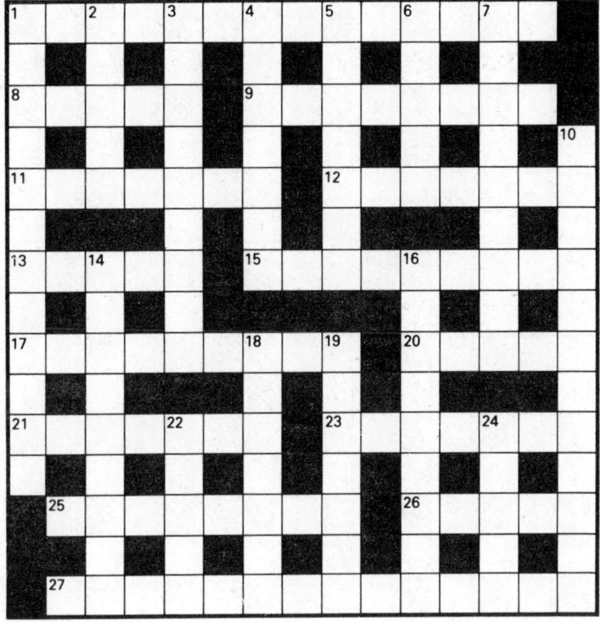

217

ACROSS

1. Country's first zoo lacks a hive—that's odd for an E. European country (14)
8. Rustic artist breaks the law endlessly (5)
9. Geometrical propositions unravelled in rest-home (8)
11. Relative with article that's dirty (7)
12. African spear stuck in grass again (7)
13. It's an epoch to a Muse (5)
15. Signal from a distance gives great help, in a way (9)
17. Head, after t' ceremony, shows hackneyed nature (9)
20. Strip of wood round about door fastener (5)
21. Clergyman conceals a source of nuclear energy (7)
23. Remarkable Alice, about a hundred and one, a Saint (7)
25. Balked, we hear, without a sign of hesitation, talked nonsense (8)
26. Perform—in Ibsen, actually (5)
27. Spontaneous NUPE matter died out (14)

DOWN

1. Engine parts from crate burst or disintegrated (12)
2. A boy cried convulsively (5)
3. He will drill around eastern plant (9)
4. Kind of thin silk for clique going about a vessel (7)
5. Protective garment—covering everything? (7)
6. See a bishop when hanging tapestry (5)
7. A settler from abroad, I'm on motorway, with permit (9)
10. Cheerful and bright, listen to Edward (5-7)
14. A tot? A gin? I may cause a disturbance (9)
16. Bird, having riches, beginning to crow over the others (9)
18. Part of an organ—one buried in hideous murder (7)
19. South-East yielded and withdrew (7)
22. Row around second-class foreign river (5)
24. Smallest shoemaker's model around the East (5)

218

ACROSS

7. Work location around a river—on the other side? (8)
9. A hound beginning to bark at a bird (6)
10. Wag pinching king's summons? (4)
11. Rejected, we hear, everywhere (10)
12. More humid, making returning salesman furious (6)
14. I excavated, hoarding silver, it's believed (8)
15. It's safer round western edge of Falmouth for one riding the waves (6)
17. Preceded the commercial—take notice about that (6)
20. The Italian sun-oil is spurious, a deception (8)
22. Top of hill outside ancient city provides hidden shelter (6)
23. Studies robbery at sea, making a plot (10)
24. What's superficially golden causes sinfulness, they say (4)
25. Fame derived from adventure now, normally (6)
26. Skin disease, grown out of control in the border (8)

DOWN

1. Knocks up and beats hardy fellows (8)
2. You may put your foot in it, getting sack (4)
3. One who assembles machines must be comparatively healthy (6)
4. Hard tube, a rod that's twisted (8)
5. A pioneer, an Irishman has to stop eating noisily (10)
6. Black parasitic insect seen in a feminine garment (6)...
8. ...I wager that could be a creepy-crawly insect (6)
13. Uses pain, or different inducement (10)
16. No Italian in team? That's shown up in newspaper issues (8)
18. Peer held up the French railway in jest (8)
19. Not just ugly? (6)
21. A man, one in a million, elected (6)
22. Purchasing extra, we hear—gin possibly (6)
24. Head of Government has to have an official robe (4)

219

ACROSS

1. Disastrous for GI in overturned wagon (6)
5. A Blue, one doing runs (6)
9. Bowmen, people who walk regularly without a leader (7)
10. Showed affection in the park—is seductive (6)
12. Man's track, or bird, vaguely seen in buildings (6,3,6)
13. Stumble right into a rubbish-heap (4)
14. Vessel beginning to dispense drink—you can beat it! (10)
18. Remedying, or treating wounds again (10)
19. I study a religious statue (4)
21. Imaginary figure, flickering in moment on heath (3,3,2,3,4)
24. Nocturnal creatures seen around the North for periods of the year (6)
25. Rave about Timothy's jazz music (7)
26. Save from horrible curse by miracle, ultimately (6)
27. Fodder is blown over by wild gale (6)

DOWN

2. Amended and certified anew (9)
3. Athenians, perhaps, responsible for start of gas fumes (6)
4. The actors one catches are usually clicking (9)
5. In drink, editor's covered with printing fluid! (5)
6. Find a record still remaining (8)
7. Receive, about to go inside, salute (5)
8. It's soporific in the pub, but I tear all over the place (11)
11. Remarkable men, so involved with Prince, they're outstanding (11)
15. Tinges metal cruets artfully (9)
16. Counting up—or guessing? (9)
17. Schoolmasterly deputy held up caper (8)
20. Mountain girl found in home of famous Lancers (6)
22. It's all right, in late part of day, to call out (5)
23. Offspring is a little girl (5)

220

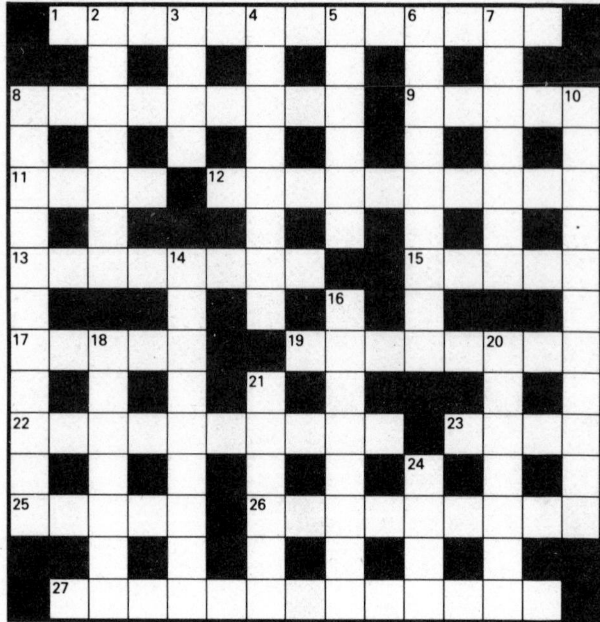

ACROSS

1. Reference book, clean copy, aide misused (13)
8. Works of art – gasps about one (9)
9. See doctor and primate hanging (5)
11. Principal source of electricity (4)
12. Howler, with changes, repaying the time spent on it (10)
13. Searches blindly round borders of Uruguay for tent-cords (3-5)
15. Boredom helps to make children nuisances (5)
17. Part of church where you'll hear, briefly, 'I will'! (5)
19. Father arranged strong melody for voices (4-4)
22. The air about us, polluting the prom and sea (10)
23. A blemish noticeable in western pictures, etc. (4)
25. Weird eastern lake (5)
26. Civil Service back seeker of revenge, one who cleans up the mess (9)
27. Sergeant slips badly with register of all on board (9-4)

DOWN

2. I'll enter in a prying manner, loudly (7)
3. Abominable snowman – there's still one to be seen! (4)
4. Solitary type embraces fellow capital dweller (8)
5. Foreign currency – Dad holds eastern collection (6)
6. Women tend, surprisingly, to make a bequest (9)
7. I raced with a Scot – and a Persian (7)
8. Orange MP messily consumed – it's full of pips (11)
10. Venus, usually, has smoothing, subtle arts (7,4)
14. Foremen rose, drunk, full of poetry (9)
16. Vehicle, automobile, one caught in storm (8)
18. Master's turned up with a song in charitable man's home (7)
20. Fruits wanted – there's nothing on mountain chains (7)
21. Selected from Groucho's entertainments (6)
24. Valerie's eating English meat (4)

221

ACROSS

1. Brass-hat is at one, having no backing for comprehensive statement (14)
9. 'E's getting into a reorganised Baltic state (7)
10. Horrific, endless speech given by Nelson? (7)
11. Former champion 'as an assumed name (5)
12. Fall in love, and become pessimistic? (4,5)
13. Swellings going into the flesh – girth's now in bad shape (9)
14. Country, fashionable, rejected help (5)
15. Stir up nonsense about you and me (5)
17. Pub and restaurant turned over by Ted – shameless! (4-5)
20. Punches one gets in superior joints (5-4)
22. Upper-class wise man creates custom (5)
23. The law catches four at head of trout stream (7)
24. Ship's capacity worries no agent (7)
25. Teacher cautioned, erratic with a register (14)

DOWN

1. Infantryman, camouflaged in red gear, getting protection (9,5)
2. Love making a written record about hospital (7)
3. Races, not tall, and becomes exhausted (4,5)
4. Small piece of foliage from meadow, left rotting (7)
5. Church is, in varying MSS, showing breaches in unity (7)
6. Light visible in transept or choir (5)
7. Away from port, unconscious, needing a hospital room (7)
8. Building material transforms permanent lot around D.C. (8,6)
14. In New Zealand one inhaling pipe gets respiratory ailment (9)
16. Smashed van up, 'e 'ad, without flagging (7)
17. Bird, and French, in badly built surroundings (4,3)
18. Drunkard in a disorderly riot gets a rice dish (7)
19. A fellow, at one, makes Indian bread (7)
21. Souvenir from priest held by RC (5)

222

ACROSS

4. Load makes Ned chafe back (6)
6. Fool, getting coppers to rent a gem (8)
9. Couple following motorway, reversing, causing damage (6)
10. Nevertheless, it's where the last runner comes in! (5,3)
11. 'Magic Art' MA revised, and left syntactical (11)
15. Destitute, requiring fund Lee organised (7)
17. Scrap of cloth fits eccentric fellows to a T (7)
18. Crushed, fool totters to right storey of building (6,5)
22. Loud site, strangely enough, is lonely place (8)
23. Catherine grips artist in Japanese combative sport (6)
24. Wrenches for bridges? (8)
25. Powerful short obtainable around the East – illicit whisky! (6)

DOWN

1. Gas causing bad smell around priest (6)
2. Obsolete coin making Henry scowl – about a cent (4-1-5)
3. Dad got up, rang, and made entreaty (8)
4. Small bangle, held by crooner, is fetching! (8)
5. Pete read badly – it must be done again (8)
7. Middle-Eastern country captured by fakir, a quack (4)
8. Fishes, almost glossy, hauled up (4)
12. Unreasonable demands Lords later adjusted (4,6)
13. Blow up public school during time of event (8)
14. Fish, small portion of trout, eaten by operator (8)
16. Scrapping fruit, a mushy thing (8)
19. Ensign on a drinking vessel (6)
20. Employs wiles, losing head (4)
21. An excuse, offered in a simple alibi (4)

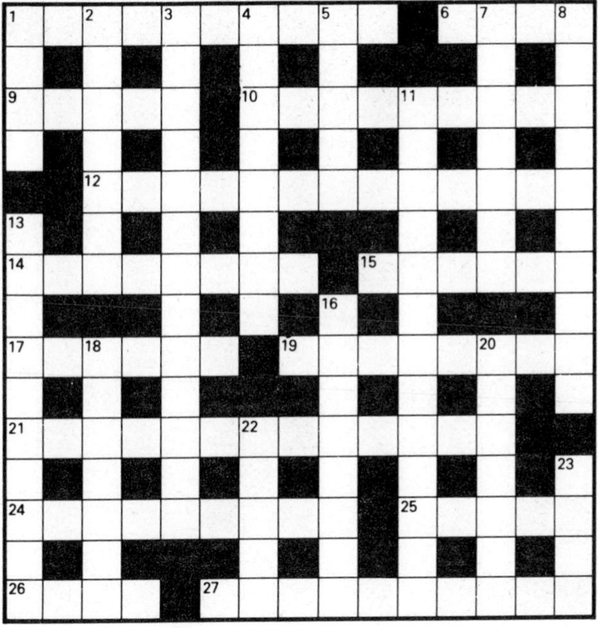

ACROSS

1. Biscuit that gives one spirit before break (6-4)
6. To squander makes one depressed (4)
9. Fright evident in rival armies (5)
10. Back-room taps making one grouse (9)
12. Anthems in church, with oranges, if poss., distributed (5,2,6)
14. Fans' favours went up in price – before test, curiously! (8)
15. A heavy object dislodged the wig (6)
17. Pillar, and almost everything relating to mail (6)
19. Coddled with presents initially, then 'indered (8)
21. Chopped up lions, striving to produce lots of cat-gut? (6,7)
24. Gossiping at ten, roughly, by phone (9)
25. Hat brought back, with eastern flower (5)
26. The kind that's looked for, one hears (4)
27. Intend to run naked? That shows an ignoble trait (4,6)

DOWN

1. Swine locks love in a pub (4)
2. Accumulates a thousand – estimate not quite complete (7)
3. Pointing out the devil's strange attire, including top of visor (13)
4. Sees term out – the academic term, that is (8)
5. A jumped-up idiot, stand-offish (5)
7. Not pulling weight, having no capital, being deficient (7)
8. Diner around the South has varied diet for festive season (10)
11. Letter writer has to agree to come in, dropping the Queen (13)
13. Even Pa rigs rickety bush telegraphs (10)
16. Something spicy makes sailor groan awfully (8)
18. One who quickly makes off with a two-wheeler? (7)
20. Telepathy in a ceremony brings relief (7)
22. Barb displayed by southern fish (5)
23. Cheering drink with king in wood (4)

224

ACROSS

1. A romantic set-up, ruined? Much ado about nothing (5,2,1,6)
8. Old golfer from Idaho, gangling (5)
9. In the South-East, a hospital room's facing the ocean (8)
11. A famous bishop, I'm brought in after a while (7)
12. Exceed the limit and take part in too many races? (7)
13. Harsh sounds made by river serpents (5)
15. Left one little pest embracing in the Rolls? (9)
17. What you have, looking back – high tension after awful shindig (9)
20. Unit of heat generated by the Royal Marines (5)
21. Clerics, nuisances about RI (7)
23. Letter's collector about – not heartless fellow (4-3)
25. A view that's wide – or confined by a straw-hat (8)
26. Smear front of book with publisher's puff (5)
27. Tipsy sot, very content, deliberately ignored by everyone (4,2,8)

DOWN

1. Rich? So splash out with academic awards (12)
2. Purchased without capital? Have the duty (5)
3. A small car teacher, going about the East, makes as light as possible (9)
4. Air-duct, unusual sort, with nothing round it (7)
5. Sort of café with rent the reverse of low (3-4)
6. An entrance made of stone (5)
7. Rude men, in dance, gradually weaken (9)
10. Endlessly military, Benn? That's quite wrong! (12)
14. Wicked city's a den for a group of businessmen (9)
16. Indefensible, without power to capture X (9)
18. Secret police travel carrying faked tapes (7)
19. To the Navy, trouble is a storm (7)
22. Beast's nose overturned wine-casks with nothing inside (5)
24. Climb a hill (5)

225

ACROSS

1. A mother – he didn't have one! (4)
3. Hides out-of-date remedies (8)
10. Priest's 'orrible blunder, one in search of prey (7)
11. I like this drink – it's an element in nuclear reactors (7)
12. Fine horses, in fear, absconded (5)
13. Bit of grey matter shown by feminine supporter in prison room (5-4)
14. Optimistic prospect excites virgins in 'Ell (6,6)
18. Study part about artist's act of dedication (12)
21. Printing device has sharp ends adjusted (4-5)
23. Provide food for puss before the Queen (5)
24. A conifer – get one right inside for nothing (3-4)
25. Engineers, in deluge, knocked to the ground (7)
26. Make a new estimate about a foolish woman? (8)
27. Standard river salmon (4)

DOWN

1. Article – very gently lift up, to value (8)
2. Lovable and talented, holding a stick up (8)
4. Crab in tin possibly British (9)
5. Nan among mob, a northern child, with gold for a dicing game (5,3,6)
6. Bird the editor swindled out of money (6)
7. Retails about a thousand scents (6)
8. Florist appears badly damaged – this will immobilise broken limbs (7,2,5)
9. Initially cracked a bone – that means bed (4)
15. Ears, perhaps, set twitching in passenger-ships (9)
16. Circulating air – it was for a plant (8)
17. 'Elpful suggestion given more unmannerly gatecrasher (8)
19. Beetle in tea – referee taken aback (6)
20. Girl appearing in a Freudian dream (6)
22. If seen in the highway, separate (4)

226

ACROSS

1. He's lasted remarkably, becoming immortal (9)
10. Disregards crude metal in fancy sign (7)
11. Beat swell that's touching line (7)
12. Simultaneous gunfire – first of bullets at the border of the highway (9)
13. One who adjusts pitch, concerned with the Head returning (5)
14. Sounds of rebuke from teachers having no alternative! (4)
15. Tray shaped with cunning, pretentious in style (4-6)
17. Nag has bled badly in eastern country (10)
20. Protective covering for a knock, we hear (4)
22. A caper gives one a convulsion (5)
23. Disappears after pinching king's shiny coats (9)
25. Fruit for a lady of the harem? (7)
26. Designer, one who shaves wood around a pole (7)
27. No one returns after vacation, causing decline in trade (9)

DOWN

2. Spiked like corn? Raised without top bit (5)
3. Examiner, around one, gets more ill-tempered (7)
4. A raffle? Let Tory organise it (7)
5. Hygienic, having stain treated on a railway (8)
6. Gallows, large, put up on stake (6)
7. One faulty turn is terrible, alas (13)
8. Penelope's distant object – an old bike (5-8)
9. Tempestuous tale grips a thousand (6)
16. Cut off group of houses needs help, we hear (8)
17. Impudent, sound like an ass around Sunday School (6)
18. I've turned up in time to digress (7)
19. Scenarios showing Saints encircling vault, by the sound of it (7)
21. Dad's effort, making doughy stuff (6)
24. In America, I had turned up with nothing (5)

227

ACROSS

7. Huge sum, or one fiddled (8)
9. Eat roughly, then steal the wherewithal for a drink (3-3)
10. Floated in the marsh endlessly (4)
11. A meat and potato dish – piece got at, tampered with (7,3)
12. Sixpence, once, for a leather worker (6)
14. State memorial containing a bar (8)
15. Gloss, an unexpected result (6)
17. Heavy lorries forming traffic, southern (6)
20. Flat-fish struggle violently (8)
22. Man on board is a prelate (6)
23. Eats out with the Queen, and urges seasonal confections (6,4)
24. Quaintly attractive copper given endless tea (4)
25. Cunningly lures about a thousand monkey-like creatures (6)
26. Team game gets ill-tempered with ale circulating about (8)

DOWN

1. Rapidly increase a type of missile common in Moscow? (8)
2. Lip of vessel, basin's top edge (4)
3. Rough score, about a hundred, in ball-game (6)
4. I'm tall and robust, and I administer corporal punishment! (8)
5. Soft-bound books a journal endorses (10)
6. Reserve soldiers strike one South Sea island (6)
8. A planet makes it go round (6)
13. Stir autumn's wild flower (10)
16. Those who treat the wounded, making Communist annoyed (3,5)
18. Glaswegian, perhaps, fuddled with drink around summit of Cairngorms (8)
19. RU flag repaired – that's economical (6)
21. Look after heartless idler (6)
22. Fragment's taken about a second to cut in two (6)
24. Bird's beginning to caw – an awful noise! (4)

228

ACROSS

1. Seaman, approaching rough seas, lowers (6)
5. Explosive sound about the harbour (6)
9. Wild glen as well as country (7)
10. Fearless loved one getting disheartened (6)
12. Discovered at one, about to sin badly—that's base, partly (10-5)
13. Fraudulently conducts oil-drilling plants (4)
14. Company representative, getting a hundred in fast time, is self-satisfied (10)
18. Imposer of burdens makes start awkwardly (10)
19. A mineral absorbed by formic acid (4)
21. State-ownership, anti-Italian, soon collapsed (15)
24. Another pipeful, perhaps, will make umpire poorly (6)
25. Treat with fast dye for English bad weather (7)
26. Only my reel is tangled (6)
27. Objective a sailor has to achieve (6)

DOWN

2. Envies Reg working in shifts! (9)
3. Bears? Remains still (6)
4. Is outside, rioting, undermining the state (9)
5. Had no horse, apparently, in cowboy circus! (5)
6. Frenchman is taken in by standard Scotsman (8)
7. Ronald has to perform a musical composition (5)
8. Bent pin, great for making holes (11)
11. Holding back—over-exerting again? (11)
15. Man at the top, one who lives quietly? Just the opposite! (9)
16. Remove odd-looking item in ale (9)
17. Rude little devil, to lie atrociously (8)
20. Where one may see aircraft hover above a surface of runway (6)
22. Topic—the Middle East (5)
23. Everyone's nearly always calm (5)

229

ACROSS

1. Upright pair go round ruined place, shattered (13)
8. Comprehending everything in having an Empire-builder around us (9)
9. Sheep around quiet slopes (5)
11. Biblical character 'e noticed, we're told (4)
12. Alan Baccas remade famous Bogart film (10)
13. Six balls, chum, bouncing? That's excessive! (8)
15. Flavour coming from ragout, a stew (5)
17. Graduate has Edward beaten at chess (5)
19. Principal gets student an electrical unit for front light (8)
22. Remembers – and assembles again? (10)
23. A girl, you'll find me back with Mother (4)
25. I'm the heroine of a Swiss novel and I hide playfully (5)
26. English fool, caught by coppers, shows remorse (9)
27. Regret pet hate, somehow, for a tsar (5,3,5)

DOWN

2. Enclosed area for 150 in eastern part of church (7)
3. Addition that's almost luxurious (4)
4. A pest might get cane in US (8)
5. One about to walk slowly up frozen summit (3-3)
6. UN gets told it's irrelevant (9)
7. A half-day among rough lads finding nuts (7)
8. Rich mad foes slily arranged for Caesar's last day (4,2,5)
10. Brandish long weapon over English dramatist (11)
14. A girl, Adèle, admitted into the pit (9)
16. Complete set of words forming legal judgment (8)
18. Cat up on part of roof, perceptible by touch (7)
20. Operatic song about people in a Soviet state (7)
21. Spouted vessel a potter left unfinished, stupidly (3-3)
24. Leading player from Costa Rica (4)

230

ACROSS

1. Upper part of building is excellent – cure strut that's rotten (14)
9. Fruit and eggs rejected, the bounder gets nothing (7)
10. Liverpool, for instance, are tops – fantastic! (7)
11. Former head of a religious house (5)
12. Mournful, with unadorned neckwear, about five (9)
13. The others – priests – will get periods of quiet convalescence (4-5)
14. Last steering device used by a novice (5)
15. Sounds of doves around quiet pens (5)
17. Pet CID spy is out of sorts, having indigestion (9)
20. One's in an eastern country, an eastern republic (9)
22. One of Caesar's assassins hiding in Francesca's castle (5)
23. Friendly relations – ten – twice embarrassed by Oriental (7)
24. Small bomb can get one enraged (7)
25. Lack of pals makes half-day interminable at the Cape (14)

DOWN

1. Shady dealings that keen GPs have? (5,9)
2. Gains made by forecasters, by the sound of it (7)
3. Cord areas off for long-distance runs (4-5)
4. Cavalryman is member of theatrical company, we hear (7)
5. Opens up US lanes after accident (7)
6. Mark Two (5)
7. Aegean islander had iron smelted (7)
8. Jumping horses Charles and the Queen kept in towers (14)
14. They make arrows – those that bring about a pound (9)
16. Elderly person invested in gold sterling (7)
17. Swell acted, gripping machine-gun (7)
18. Spy endlessly has fish in glittering plate (7)
19. After trial, tucked in with a will (7)
21. There's nobody round about, for the time being (5)

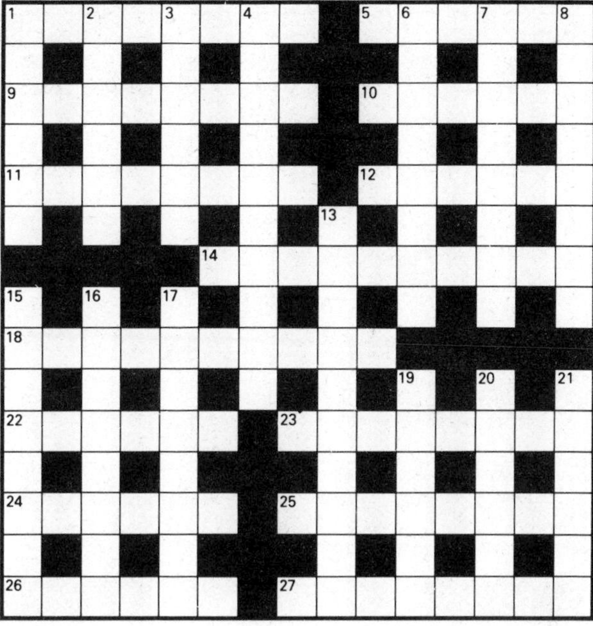

231

ACROSS

1. Very meagre pay – 'e can't tip, unfortunately! (8)
5. Fish seen about river and channel (6)
9. First of cast in leaving the stage is stirring (8)
10. Reply from a king full of bad news (6)
11. Queen, after having pepper, is comparatively cool (8)
12. To bribe or snub is wrong (6)
14. They carry wounded from street, and those who are sick (10)
18. I bend, Cyril, twisting in an unbelievable way (10)
22. A N. African pressman secured a boat (6)
23. Cunning, pinching car beside church? Hardly (8)
24. Not a railway official who certifies deeds (6)
25. Disarmed, perhaps, in duel? I'm blessed! (8)
26. Guy returning, carrying church vessels (6)
27. Relatives, a thousand, in the USA (5,3)

DOWN

1. Deliver a sermon, a real beauty, just about right (6)
2. A skilful device will get you, with diplomacy, in charge (6)
3. Hun held up by vandal? It tallies (6)
4. Agreement with Richard, we hear, having the same heart (10)
6. Disown cure, none having been suitably treated (8)
7. Recent arrival finds love among rough crew men (8)
8. Difficulty calls for firm Head (8)
13. Mirrored image results in contemplation (10)
15. Mine-pony, working, brings a bit extra for the wife (3-5)
16. A word-puzzle causing a bad-tempered moment, we hear (8)
17. Waterers disturbed a rodent (5-3)
19. Head of Bantus in court-case concerning large family group (6)
20. Wild revels in bars (6)
21. Agent's turned up covered in adhesive, an ingredient of plaster (6)

232

ACROSS

4. Stevedore – one who reduces earnings? (6)
6. Four lines of verse, oddly quaint, about the artist (8)
9. Firmly established, shouted encouragement (6)
10. Sharp pain gripping genteel MP is perplexing (8)
11. Bird's hours of darkness in strong wind (11)
15. Genuine Guards in ceremonials, to some extent (7)
17. At home, quiet primate's very fit (2,5)
18. Rotten sprig in Lent, breaking to pieces (11)
22. Once wept pathetically for a very small sum (8)
23. Oriental has to declare landed property (6)
24. Punish a writer, as lie gets broadcast (8)
25. Solitary Nelly's ill, having eaten nothing (6)

DOWN

1. Discern Teddy-boy overturning, smashing etc. (6)
2. A European holds a pound for one down under (10)
3. Speech defects shown by m-me among leading players! (8)
4. Gloom sends Ark off course (8)
5. A hundred recording, and choking (8)
7. Eager to have Violet in commercial (4)
8. A small number leave – in vain (2,2)
12. Housewife, perhaps, cleaned, see, frantically (6-4)
13. Mum gets a diner tipsy with pickle (8)
14. Only has silver in – and scantily (8)
16. Trees lay shattered in the wind (8)
19. Susan taken up to North London station (6)
20. Put a halt to street work (4)
21. A gift from a hobo, once (4)

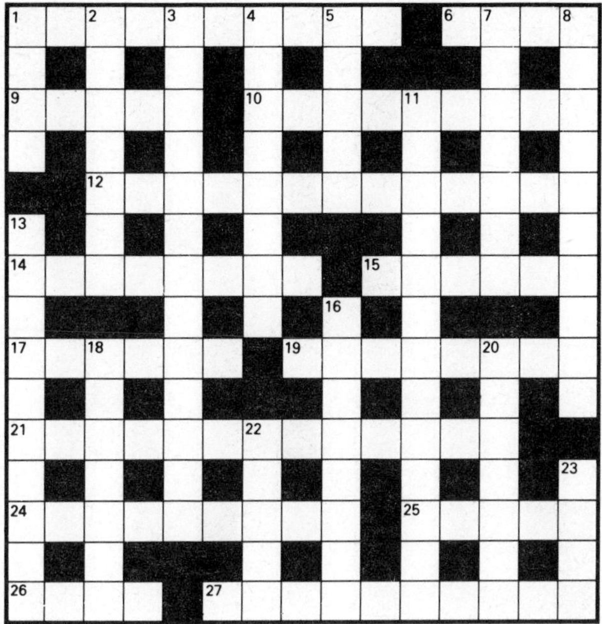

233

ACROSS

1. Sat struggling with rice pud for a sweet (7-3)
6. River goddess (4)
9. Wager about the Queen's flat cap (5)
10. Items overlooked start to outrage embassies (9)
12. Restitches arm that's lacerated, making spruce? (9,4)
14. A short sleep after retiring, then pastries, and egg dishes (8)
15. Wrote when confined (6)
17. Engineers with roll of wire draw back suddenly (6)
19. Battleship RAF woman redesigned (3-2-3)
21. Various parakeets etc., about a thousand, in trading vessel (6-7)
24. Show regret about incorrect May refund (9)
25. African creature – sounds like a river duck (5)
26. Building area – something ugly, from what one hears (4)
27. Good fellows holding cart back – they supply builders (10)

DOWN

1. Vehicles for accountant and surgeon (4)
2. Infidel, a breed captured by Poles (7)
3. On the other hand, change simply, without a bit of trouble (13)
4. Toe prods crumbling threshold (8)
5. I had the Isle of Man manner of speaking (5)
7. Apron's reshaped, about right for Highlander's pouch (7)
8. Supporters, those who lay out money around US (10)
11. The nun's upset in refectory, Miss (6,2,5)
13. Skill evident in sappers reshaping items for repair work (5,5)
16. Imposing master in charge grasps the joke (8)
18. Scene of blood-sport, where pilot's found? (7)
20. Fighter arrives in West Indies with gold (7)
22. Disdainful expression shown by prophet going around the North (5)
23. Doctor on steamer supplies green stuff (4)

234

ACROSS

1. A gambling device can make her woeful often (5,2,7)
8. Telling stories, stretched out in bed? (5)
9. At home, it's included in a money penalty, without limit (8)
11. Inn's short dram, a pound altogether (2,5)
12. Disease spoiled loch a long time (7)
13. Russian writer, having to depart twice, left (5)
15. Release Diana, seen struggling with gag (9)
17. Fancy patterns round southern parts of cathedrals (9)
20. Uncivilised, gripping middle of spear, to brandish (5)
21. Tea taken round other part of London (7)
23. Itch that is noticeable among blacklegs (7)
25. Sex-appeal by chap that almost gets the girl (8)
26. A girl I take out (5)
27. Henry, not fully lucid with people, having first of strange delusions (14)

DOWN

1. Cane Walt's kicking about (7-5)
2. Priest, Old Testament, was a famous poet (5)
3. Hate gills that get spilt—and lagers? (5,4)
4. Had food around brook that's ruffled (7)
5. No longer keen on sweets in business premises (7)
6. Smack love in dance (5)
7. Short letter about strange dream in famous cathedral (5,4)
10. Dealers in smallwares offering various bras, she heard (12)
14. Awfully U team in festivity in Central American state (9)
16. Where racehorses are often brought, young, to buy and sell (9)
18. To endure inside choose, by the sound of it, a modern material (7)
19. Support us in shame (7)
22. Shoulder-wear for modern dramatist on left (5)
24. Opening bars made of tin or plastic (5)

235

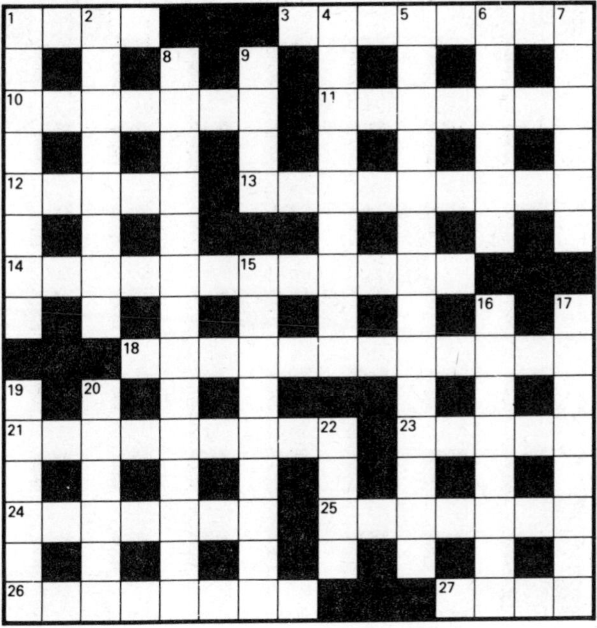

ACROSS

1. Child with eastern gambling-machine (4)
3. A blackleg poet that holds a sword? (8)
10. Full-time soldier's uniform (7)
11. Dance with mixed gin, tottering (7)
12. Breezy to the South back in Middle-Eastern country (5)
13. More than one house, perhaps, Gus upset with rattling bin-lid (9)
14. Give false impression of wretched miser with a gift (12)
18. Ali's boasting badly, displaying yachts, for instance (7-5)
21. Wage deductions for strikes? (9)
23. Pilferer, one caught by the force's leader (5)
24. A woman may wear this, with the air gusty around the North (4-3)
25. Eastern gull beside a lake, unchanging (7)
26. Stock-farmers organised cattle initially—the lady's (8)
27. Repudiate editor returning to New York (4)

DOWN

1. Rose wilts in time—that's vexing (8)
2. Like a wild cat strike about teacher, for example, rising (8)
4. Continues, and behaves unrestrainedly (7,2)
5. A branded wild goat, perhaps, will provide a livelihood (5,3,6)
6. Brings into a row, changing signal (6)
7. Assimilate joke heard after I'd turned up (6)
8. Excuses Edward when getting a drink, tickled pink (7,2,5)
9. Maggot found in food (4)
15. He refers to others for decision about one making a will (9)
16. Form of avarice seen about the North causes disagreement (8)
17. Sue changed completely, and advantageously (8)
19. A girl, she's among the bravest heroines (6)
20. A cosmetic liquid? A great deal I'll get on (6)
22. Fatty tissue, or extract of tissue, treated (4)

236

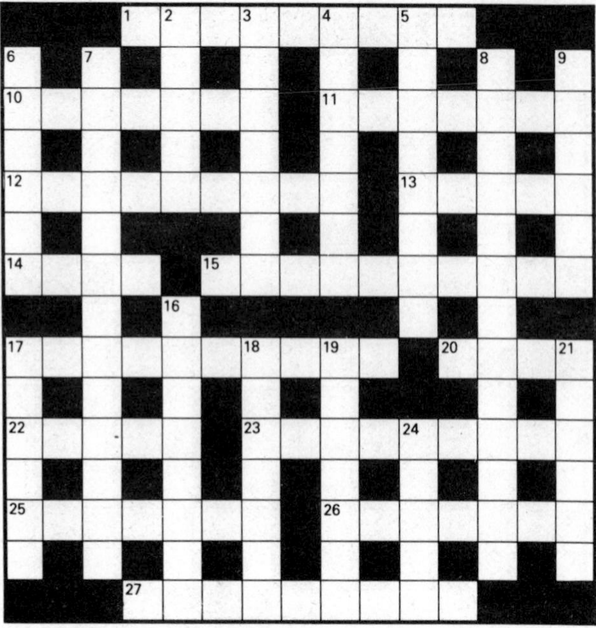

ACROSS

1. Plunderers with commands, we hear, to go after spoil (9)
10. An uncharged particle will possibly get none 'urt (7)
11. Body of attendants reunite in different order (7)
12. A sane age, shattered around eastern area encircling Greece (6,3)
13. Correct people should be used in commercial (5)
14. Former Persian ruler has fancy opening for harem (4)
15. Destroyer, for instance, second-class, that plies at sea (10)
17. Astronaut's vessel, beginning to soar with speed and skill (5-5)
20. Eve's son is talented, they say (4)
22. Some Senator at election is to make a speech (5)
23. Chaffing, or rating, Ben? It's not clear (9)
25. Drums give Timothy an awful pain (7)
26. A genteel Saint, before becoming stern (7)
27. Extinct beasts – one is encased by most excited fellows (9)

DOWN

2. Arterial trunk erected in great road-building (5)
3. Men wandering in the Continent – it's loss of memory (7)
4. Walked up carrying servant, sleeping (7)
5. Wagon, overturned in stiff grass, went over again (8)
6. Searches, one hears, around the North for tell-tales (6)
7. Precautions against intruders, or possibly rural alms grab! (7,6)
8. After dinner, losing head, he's embracing newlywed in Scottish Isles (5,8)
9. Males bathe in English hills (6)
16. Brown sugar fermenting in rare mead (8)
17. Irregular soldier initially crazy (6)
18. Spud, about fifty-one, turned up – erected a new home? (7)
19. Entrance to forest, away from coast, in northern country (7)
21. Boy, eating breakfast food up, dawdled (6)
24. German city shows unusual sense (5)

237

ACROSS

7. She's among a group of soldiers, crushed (8)
9. Married one in Paris has vermouth with editor (6)
10. A lecture in fundamental knowledge (4)
11. He spoke freely for each trader (10)
12. Fishes, about to be swallowed by tortured spies (6)
14. First of sailors cut off by the jetty gets more wet (8)
15. Church councils go wrong, taking chances, we hear (6)
17. Dilys artfully composed about fifty pastoral works (6)
20. A lucky charm corresponds, they say, with a servant (8)
22. Deigns, oddly enough, to plan (6)
23. Study the legal wrong by one on twisting (10)
24. Young animal – a stage of development that's intermediate (4)
25. One's taken in by weird scene in spiritualist session (6)
26. Dad's sole has disintegrated – it's a worthless thing (4,4)

DOWN

1. Constellation containing iodine and uranium, with quasar flying around (8)
2. Leave one's car in a recreation ground (4)
3. Article, 'Socialists' Capital', is a dissertation (6)
4. Avoid the river, and, losing head, a small lake with birds on it (4-4)
5. Long to have fruit, exotic fruit (10)
6. Calm, dry and almost fresh (6)
8. Complaint needing doctor and operations on youth's head (6)
13. Satisfied about half-sister being compatible (10)
16. Raised objections, getting murdered, unfortunately (8)
18. It shows the way to write one's name when getting a job (8)
19. Kid nun wickedly? That's cruel (6)
21. One foresees dwelling-places (6)
22. An impression, on aluminium, of teeth (6)
24. Quietly sick? This might help! (4)

238

ACROSS

1. A model Indian servant, he carries the banner (8-6)
9. College readers notable in intellect or stamina (7)
10. Price, for all to see, gets me dress (7)
11. One imprisoned by the ancient noble (5)
12. Evening out, say, while getting older (9)
13. Backing motorway design, Ted is firmly rooted (9)
14. Fairer person who imposes money penalty? (5)
15. Garbo's beginning – in a strange way, we hear – to become divine (5)
17. Ten operas rewritten in international language (9)
20. Commercial, likely to be successful around the South, to be recommended (9)
22. East wind ruffled Ned (5)
23. Organised a tribunal almost showing bitterness (7)
24. An ugly sight – a stye? (7)
25. Cost, in rupees, so varied for gems (8,6)

DOWN

1. Dividing fast runners, we hear, making fine distinctions (9,5)
2. One needs right sort of brace for a light (3-4)
3. A camel roamed at random in arid surroundings (9)
4. Remainder, with skill, begin again (7)
5. Laid bet about first of November – that's late autumn (4-3)
6. Sailing the ocean, confused? (2,3)
7. Act of evasion – sounds like a conjuror's trick! (7)
8. Reggie distributed small discs for radiation detectors (6,8)
14. Compel a thousand to consume seasoned stuffing (9)
16. Restaurant-car will hold four, he predicts (7)
17. Trade ban might make mob rage (7)
18. Look closely on eastern ship for noble lady (7)
19. Crescent should get no women excited (3,4)
21. Patient philosopher turns to ice, in part! (5)

239

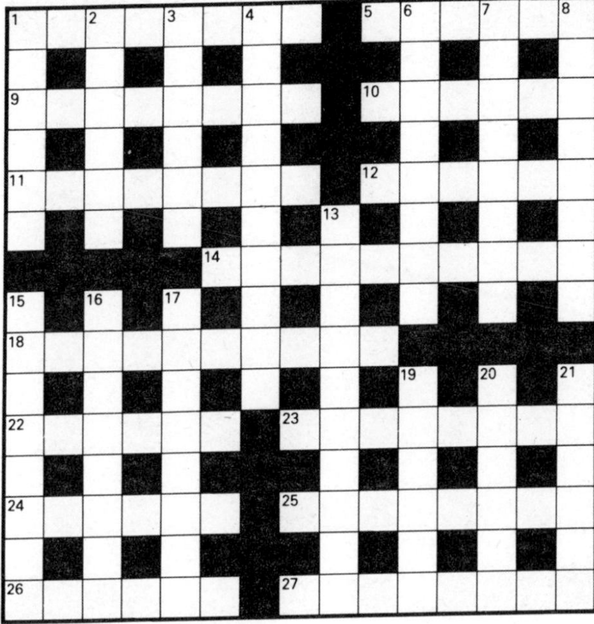

ACROSS

1. Church, fundamental one, entered by the Italian (8)
5. Endless ticking sound, when coming round in hospital (6)
9. Doing tedious work is jarring (8)
10. A girl, I'm offered love by General (6)
11. Missive to editor is literate (8)
12. Reaping implement, from S. Carolina, they smashed (6)
14. Charitable noble involved with event (10)
18. Very fat, I'll possibly make depression in earth's crust! (4,6)
22. Cover with a policy at home, certainly (6)
23. Move quickly to secure boat in part of Devon (8)
24. Work hard at an advertising catch-phrase (6)
25. Intellectuals, the endless users of ink (8)
26. Story about teetotaller is idle gossip (6)
27. Skating venues involving nice risk (3-5)

DOWN

1. Start with fright in marsh, having broken leg (6)
2. Change end of story—that's tricky (6)
3. Accounts book comes from shelf on right (6)
4. Pantomime heroine, awfully nice, all red (10)
6. Essayist and policeman eating hot cut of meat (4,4)
7. Bedtime garments close by, with bows (8)
8. Musical composition to study—a sure winner with the circle (8)
13. I help 'tec at unravelling, using ESP (10)
15. Domestic toy to exercise a group (5,3)
16. A branch, not on fire! (8)
17. Check for possible repairs above lobby, we're told (8)
19. In defeat, one realises, one makes amends (6)
20. Melons going rotten—that's serious (6)
21. Forces an opening, getting trophies, by the sound of it (6)

240

ACROSS

4. A drive, badly designed, gets altered (6)
6. Regrouped, and went (8)
9. Sweet boy follows us around (6)
10. Wayward rep rejected poetry (8)
11. Deputy leader, apt to be caught in immorality with murderer (4-7)
15. Red sun's shimmering – strip (7)
17. Sheet of frozen water makes one glide, we hear, around church (3-4)
18. Member of Royalty – men quote her inaccurately (5,6)
22. Those who try holding gunmen back – they dawdle (8)
23. Buy tea, well-blended, for a belle (6)
24. Japanese currency's held by nobody? Rubbish! (8)
25. Happened to live near a Cumbrian mountain (6)

DOWN

1. Rhythmical feature of some tricycles (6)
2. Plants, for instance, protected by doctor – Oriental, by the sound of it (10)
3. Persuade Conservative, once drinking French wine (8)
4. Four employ five when climbing US volcano (8)
5. Murder of a king puts Reginald on edge, we hear! (8)
7. Ripped roof off a shop? (4)
8. Animal that turns up in the tall grass (4)
12. Sterilise, making swirling endless steam rise up (10)
13. He's held up by a parasite in a tavern (3-5)
14. Wager Raymond a pound there'll be treachery (8)
16. A lot of papers, in the end, asked questions (8)
19. Frank, joining the Queen, will raise cap (6)
20. Name in a list – a nominee (4)
21. Paddy up North in Ireland! (4)

241

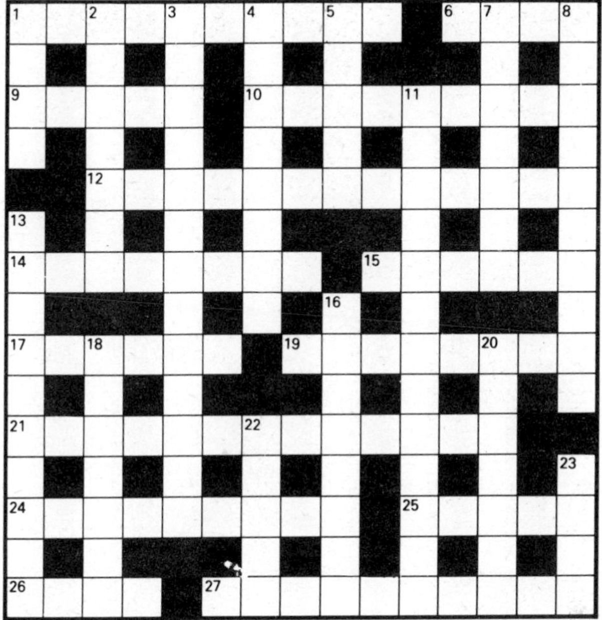

ACROSS

1. Commercial traveller has love tale about one store (10)
6. Put away some of the surplus towels (4)
9. Noisily bring up, we hear, comparatively unrestricted (5)
10. Defender paled, turning to retreat (4-5)
12. Where the air's fresher, look, Ms sneezes uncontrollably (9,4)
14. Rider's hunting instrument about same, only different! (8)
15. Use logical argument about a child (6)
17. Braided tresses, nearly all swept back in mines (6)
19. Activates severity, we hear, in returning Saint (8)
21. Changing shape, the crone erred, becoming triangular! (5-8)
24. It's polite to lean over for royal household expenses (5,4)
25. Sturdy novelist (5)
26. Sediment the Italian dumped in the highway (4)
27. Print piece, unusually discerning (10)

DOWN

1. Widespread fire out of control (4)
2. A flattening device for newspapers engineers set up (7)
3. Terrible poser perplexed founder of police-force (3,6,4)
4. A flap – twisted metal – on which a plate rests (5-3)
5. Regret about child's plaited frilling (5)
7. Edward, with promissory notes, is tiresome (7)
8. Wider lens roving over southern desert (10)
11. Circulate mixed greens with joint in holiday cruiser? (9-4)
13. Piece of pork, perhaps, stays fixed in these eating implements (10)
16. Feverish? Worry about north-easterly and endless ice (8)
18. A competitor, from what we hear, is coming (7)
20. Back the Derby runner that 'as finished last? (7)
22. Suppose there's work in the East (5)
23. Part of Nancy's thumb shows a morbid swelling (4)

CRYPTIC AND MORE CRYPTIC

242

ACROSS

1. Dead body (6)
4. This dish provides an especially good morsel (7)
9. Part of the British Isles (4,2,3)
10. Item of bric-a-brac, firm, split by Geller (5)
11. One who tends the sick (5)
12. Shires Ann trained – as working draught-horses usually are (2,7)
13. Put in quarantine? – One thus gets delayed (7)
15. A corset (4-2)
17. American General in most of mess brawls (6)
19. Feels pain (7)
22. Subject a person to systematic indoctrination (9)
24. Aquatic carnivore (5)
26. Send payment, for return of watch perhaps (5)
27. Smashed t' volley in – with excessive force (9)
28. Small rounded lumps (7)
29. Climb face of Cotopaxi in wild Andes (6)

DOWN

1. A wine from Tuscany (7)
2. A king, perhaps – one responsible for a line? (5)
3. Potter's product (9)
4. Stock-farmer managed head of cattle and reduced herd (7)
5. Come round again, about a dog (5)
6. Device for manoeuvring a river-craft (9)
7. A familiar term of endearment (6)
8. Arbitrator (6)
14. Cordially welcoming (4-5)
16. Remains bequeathed on Sunday (4-5)
18. Dies of hunger (7)
19. Bottom of class and indifferent, we hear, in the academy (6)
20. Saint beamed, then wandered off! (7)
21. Borneo's wild fairy-king (6)
23. S. African province (5)
25. Let it out, showing evidence of ownership (5)

243

ACROSS

1. Utterly crazy girl has turns during affair (3,2,1,6)
8. What judges do with a few, we hear, in court (3,2)
9. Progress gradually towards (4,2,2)
11. Stoppage? Proceed, after amber changes (7)
12. Well-boring plants (3-4)
13. Apply oneself in hot contest (3-2)
15. Chronometer (9)
17. Arouse a memory (4,1,4)
20. Musical composition for a fairly small ensemble (5)
21. A shindig (5-2)
23. A covered parking space about right? Left (7)
25. Revamped a score in film-script (8)
26. Maxim little Thomas returned to (5)
27. Instruments for testing horizontal surfaces (6-6)

DOWN

1. Stormer takes ruins in effective, well-timed coup (12)
2. Disband organized protest over book (5)
3. Exploding star (9)
4. Last offer! (4,3)
5. A place where one may drink and eat, possibly, on rolling heath (3-4)
6. Identical in quantity (5)
7. Grating a piece of Stilton with a fork (8)
10. Fond of self-display (12)
14. Inclination (8)
16. Feed the computer for me – enter a metric unit (9)
18. Ruler (7)
19. An industrial action which prevents employees from working (7)
22. Dawn (3-2)
24. Fantastic, way-out – revolutionary, in part (5)

244

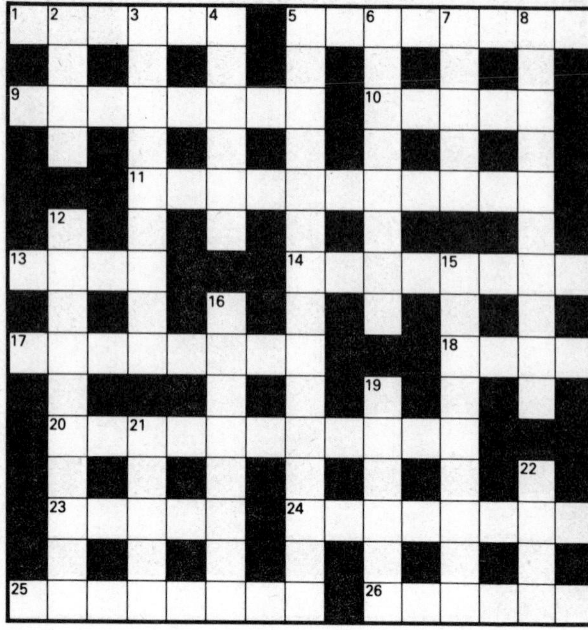

ACROSS

1. One of Tolkien's creatures (6)
5. An amorous adventurer (8)
9. A bottle for nectar Ed brewed (8)
10. Spice – almost split (5)
11. A decoy has point, goose being misled around lake (5-6)
13. Heracles half ignored the wife of Zeus (4)
14. Words of the same meaning (8)
17. Chinese vessel a wagon knocked over, in scrap-merchant's place (4-4)
18. Food for an offspring returning to hospital (4)
20. Devotion to sports (11)
23. A small insular place is rented out (5)
24. A shoe mounted on a blade (3-5)
25. The weaker party, insecurely grounded (8)
26. Whittling down to a point (6)

DOWN

2. Welcome news, concealing a portent (4)
3. A plant stem (9)
4. A military fête usually held at night (6)
5. What motorists *and* golfers should try to avoid? (8,7)
6. Divisions (8)
7. Quickly hoisted with end of rope – hangman's halter (5)
8. Oriental language makes native seem enigmatic (10)
12. Name (10)
15. Sort of railway carriage not meant for a puffer! (3-6)
16. Secured official protection for an invention (8)
19. A winning entry on the Pools will make you secure! (4,2)
21. Split in two (5)
22. Stupefy with second cask of wine (4)

245

ACROSS

1. Admit as a barrister – and invite one to drink on it? (4,2,3,3)
8. Kirk minister's house got by tortuous means (5)
9. A contagious febrile disease (8)
11. Lose oar, floundering in spray (7)
12. Extra-large piece of turkey, sumptuous bird (7)
13. Location of a Biblical witch (5)
15. Rugger formation gets little credit in the whole messy game (9)
17. Requisition sheet (5,4)
20. A girl for Lord Haw-Haw? (5)
21. Fence in (7)
23. American reindeer (7)
25. Dithering (8)
26. Due (5)
27. A support for a light, made from tin and considered, on reflection, more antiquated (6-6)

DOWN

1. Check one's findings against another's (7,5)
2. Individualist – an ace among Luftwaffe's first, right? (5)
3. A cashier (9)
4. Struggles (7)
5. A rum one? Eccentric enough to charm (7)
6. Distribute a large quantity, we're told (5)
7. Retired royalist affected by revolutionary changes (8)
10. See about grub up, during merriment, if you want an item of food (12)
14. Devote (8)
16. General steward responsible for rank bad mood! (5-4)
18. Make an unduly high bridge call (7)
19. Spiked war-club split by the crude Cuban knife (7)
22. A music drama (5)
24. Restrain about fifty drunk (5)

246

ACROSS

1. Maintenance (6)
5. Study German fish (6)
8. Illicitly distilled spirits, cause of gibberish (9)
9. Member of a mendicant religious order – and a cook, it's said (5)
11. Seaweed, caught in snorkel, peeves (4)
12. Representatives of the true character of an area (5-5)
13. Ready money (4,4)
15. A Greek character returned a precious stone and a fragment of onyx (5)
17. Concerning a spell (5)
19. Hog-wash (3-5)
22. A lookout (5-5)
23. Rigged vote, for Prohibition (4)
25. Lout (5)
26. Disunites primates, over taxes (9)
27. Mouth of a volcano (6)
28. Delicious drink, producing strange trance (6)

DOWN

2. Stealthy stalker (7)
3. They put on wartime shows in Aden, say (4)
4. Strait-laced girl produces flower (8)
5. A fold (6)
6. UFO is near, possibly evil (9)
7. Record one's poem for part of radio series? (7)
8. To progress (4,7)
10. This word meaning 'rogues' might help you to get all in, Across! (11)
14. Type of razor (3-6)
16. Makes one pay for word-play that's over-subtle (4-4)
18. Month (7)
20. Batting rate I made a hash of, showing inactivity (7)
21. One who sleeps where he can (6)
24. Name in a catalogue – Richard (4)

247

ACROSS

1. Drink contains very soft fruit (5)
4. Waylay (6)
9. Restricted (7)
10. A vertical post? Just! (7)
11. Edge (5)
12. Adequate space for freedom of movement (5-4)
13. As portion is doctored, it may get rid of vermin (3-6)
14. Pleasing sound (5)
15. Starter for high tea's prepared in hurry (5)
17. Eddy (9)
20. Leaves in a rush – the grouse-killing party's cancelled, apparently (6,3)
22. Violence, in spite of the Church of England (5)
23. Extend beyond the edge (7)
24. Wipe your shoes here – or mother's in a spot (7)
25. Ill (6)
26. One who adjusts musical pitch (5)

DOWN

1. Quite finished, the dance, about Sunday – so, dispersed (3,4,3,4)
2. Clean up ornamental network in old Yorkshire town (7)
3. A cut of steak (9)
4. Formal speech – notice the attire (7)
5. American whiskey (7)
6. Good man unprepared for trifle (5)
7. Dome-shaped dwellings (6)
8. Philatelist (5-9)
14. Type of delivery vehicle (4-5)
16. Did he provide fuel for the author of 'Dracula'? (6)
17. Very small round ring will produce a shout of delight (7)
18. One who rejects Christianity, etc. (7)
19. Terrible moaners – rowing types! (7)
21. Claw (5)

248

ACROSS

1. Dog needs help, by the sound of it – ointment for the hair (6)
4. Destined for trouble (2,3,2)
9. Submissively (3,2,4)
10. When with women, I'm at sea (5)
11. Move furtively (5)
12. Suddenly in unison (3,2,4)
13. Poster (7)
15. Former forward, a highly skilful one (6)
17. Impassive (6)
19. Show mercy on behalf of a creature (7)
22. Location of government offices (9)
24. 'Auls up roof projection (5)
26. Creature from source of Mississippi river (5)
27. Dense fog (3-6)
28. Ten-gallon hat (7)
29. Acid, in steamer, spurts (6)

DOWN

1. Stops crowds, on horseback (5,2)
2. Motor-cycle appeared blue? (5)
3. Palais de danse (5-4)
4. Pamper (7)
5. A banquet 'e's held in Lent (5)
6. Mountain-ash (5-4)
7. Moderate a fit of ill-humour (6)
8. A false rumour one joker put about (6)
14. A special characteristic, odd trait, but English (9)
16. Distribute in portions (6,3)
18. Expressionless (4-3)
19. Almost sated with meat in a London suburb (6)
20. Haunts (7)
21. Cloud of wasps, around Monsieur, overwhelms (6)
23. Quits! (5)
25. An adder makes it six for each! (5)

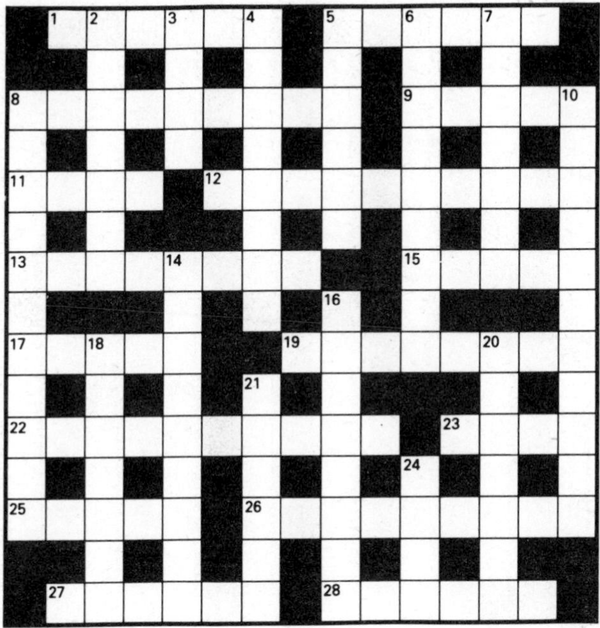

249

ACROSS

1. Red Indian (6)
5. Cricket, for example, is fashionable with a certain class of people! (6)
8. Weak alcoholic drink (5,4)
9. Commissioner in charge, an amusing person (5)
11. Swear-word (4)
12. Abroad with long-suffering one who might attend hospital (3-7)
13. Claptrap (5-3)
15. Employers and consumers (5)
17. General destruction (5)
19. Campaigner, comparatively vulgar about S. Africa (8)
22. Provocation (10)
23. A tailor provides a bargain (4)
25. Threefold examination (5)
26. Bestir yourself! (4,5)
27. A Derby winner, making girl very little (6)
28. Fruit in excess – little boy tucked in (6)

DOWN

2. Spectre (7)
3. Select? Copper will, shortly (4)
4. Trustee (8)
5. Burst in and trip clumsily, having drunk must of rum (6)
6. Pruning shears (9)
9. Firm favourite has me on the outside to contend with (7)
8. Summary treatment (5,6)
10. Disaster for star act: Hope ill (11)
14. Chay Blythe's initial cult, forming association of sailing enthusiasts (5-4)
16. Information from a computer (5-3)
18. Cowpox virus – one cc injected into wrong vein (7)
20. A type of surgeon (7)
21. One obstinate person has rabbit's foot – a charm (6)
24. Monsieur is above any intention to mutilate (4)

250

ACROSS

1. Nothing, nothing egg-shaped (5)
4. Beginning to bend, supple – sprightly (6)
9. Cross-beam, pole, well contained by public vehicle (7)
10. One breaking into a country house finds a flavouring substance (7)
11. Suppose (5)
12. Hoax? – Tipped as a winner, this novel (9)
13. Kitchen utensil can work – ne'er breaks (3-6)
14. To mature (5)
15. A Swiss mountain (5)
17. Gabriel, for example (9)
20. Clothier (9)
22. Crooner has love for housey-housey (5)
23. Nettles unnecessary – cut (7)
24. Pertaining to an imaginary ideal state (7)
25. Position adopted by diminutive boy at church (6)
26. Maintains parts of castles (5)

DOWN

1. Aiming to get German noble KO'd (3,3,3,5)
2. Speech (7)
3. Canine disease caused by paint (9)
4. Jolt family clown (7)
5. One who makes inroads (7)
6. This man lifted a girl's hair-dye (5)
7. First-class (4-2)
8. NEWS? (8,6)
14. An obstruction to vehicles – jam, after collapse of board (9)
16. Assemble (6)
17. Misguidedly train as a mechanic (7)
18. Indulge in a drinking-bout (7)
19. A non-Jew (7)
21. Bay (5)

251

ACROSS

1. Chief commodity tainted with infusion of phosphorus (6)
5. Ring back, twice, and express scorn (4-4)
9. An item of clothing that's bound to fit! (4,4)
10. Old German astrologer's quick, catching first sign of Uranus (5)
11. Piece of furniture (6-5)
13. In favour of Eastern Front? (4)
14. A guide for travellers (8)
17. Raging with love for a bird (8)
18. A country taken in by their explorations (4)
20. Made aware (11)
23. Stringed instrument (5)
24. A sobriquet (8)
25. A keenly fought stage in a tennis match (5,3)
26. Nurse a nun (6)

DOWN

2. Trip to an ancient city (4)
3. A fanciful hope (4-5)
4. Pertaining to horses – one of five in point-to-point? (6)
5. Commit a faux pas (3,4,4,2,2)
6. Fog fast obscures centre of set – invisible to the audience (3-5)
7. Sound fruit, it's said! (5)
8. Exceed in extent (10)
12. A beetle harmful to cotton, love, will be sprayed! (4-6)
15. Statements in a lawsuit (9)
16. Words formed from the letters of other words (8)
19. Caught in covers, lofting cricket strokes! (6)
21. Menacingly approaches weaving machines (5)
22. Type of duck, look, circling surface of mere (4)

252

ACROSS

1. Confusion in officers' quarters (4)
4. Item of wear for Punch? (4)
9. No rest in storm, with onset of raging gale (7)
10. A row about a youth, a pantomime hero (7)
12. A girl's date turns fiery, with 007 around (9)
13. Card found in the main part of a church, we hear (5)
14. Ending in gaol, individual gets solitary (4)
15. Photograph a monster flower (10)
17. Fling back and gather in long jet? (5-5)
20. A commotion in gaol (4)
22. Looking pale – when 'chicken'? (5)
23. Sea-bird causing almost all the racket near Scottish Isle (9)
25. Nothing in the 'box' but an animated film (7)
26. Indifferent gear? (7)
27. The drink's improved, but ignored by teetotaller (4)
28. A dog in a natty kennel (4)

DOWN

2. Register some of the recent errors (5)
3. Portion of stake, with egg on, for the army doctor (7)
4. Rise to one's feet, when dust-pan's upset (5,2)
5. They split open with a bang? Nuts? (8)
6. Girl lies wickedly, taking in sailor (6)
7. One who used to exhume dry bones, scattered around at church (4-8)
8. Seasonal spell, we hear, as boarder (6)
11. On which one can play games with army selection committee, it's said (12)
16. Fractured his neb? No, tibia (4-4)
17. Fish one caught in a particular locality (6)
18. Breadwinner, under fifty, becomes a student (7)
19. Taxi I catch for a group of ministers (7)
21. Outcome in troubled Ulster (6)
24. A wagon in traffic (5)

253

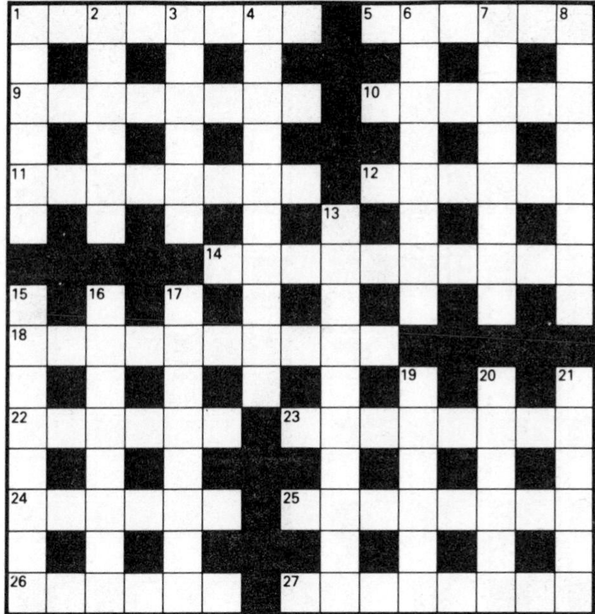

ACROSS

1. Strongly built, healthy servant girl, we hear (4-4)
5. Girl with a variety of medals (6)
9. Hinder obsolete vehicle almost, with part of toll-bar (8)
10. Light meal causes squabble at home (6)
11. Left Sidney, about one, making for a spot on the Suez Canal (4,4)
12. Sickness in Medina? Use antibiotics (6)
14. Like a footballer, on song? Tell about the penalty! (2,4,4)
18. A comfortable situation might make ye rest in the Orient (4,6)
22. Thief finds bit of a bundle in dress, on right (6)
23. Fully at home with a small body of GIs (2,6)
24. Banked on false statement when overdrawn? (6)
25. Displayed beer in part of Yorkshire (8)
26. Pass by the Spanish church recess (6)
27. 'E follows e.g. Laver, subtly playing advantage (8)

DOWN

1. Shouts from Welsh bands (6)
2. Polish, rambling in Ulster (6)
3. Gold, in large quantity, in marsh (6)
4. Wordbook for speech Ray broadcast (10)
6. Stirred up public feelings? One confined to school about it (8)
7. Affectionate feeling demonstrated by drunkard embracing feminine spy (4,4)
8. Wartime women farm workers arrive with Mary, well-trained (4-4)
13. Vehicle with boot over mechnical part! (4-6)
15. Repartee could be a fruitful thing (4-4)
16. Is one to ring a girl? (8)
17. Escort us in this place with bodyguards? (8)
19. Destroy permit in river (6)
20. Fruit – not quite nuts! (6)
21. Hippies ultimately go, we hear, for record cover (6)

254

ACROSS

7. Conscripted – everybody with Edward – and put aboard a vessel (6,2)
9. Flair shown by a copper with chess pieces (6)
10. Not quite nimble enough to escape (4)
11. I might teach at the theatre, but probably wouldn't arrive in one! (10)
12. Cut of meat at home for composer (6)
14. Spoon caught a flat, ribbon-shaped paste (8)
15. Flower, a feature of porch I decorated (6)
17. Artist's workshop for academic, not us (6)
20. Little whelper by chance reduced excess weight (5-3)
22. A padre involved in military display (6)
23. A Tchaikovsky 'Suite' may provide an opening for 4 Down! (10)
24. Short note from a child (4)
25. Decline to yield a second time? (6)
26. Sun airs various small things (8)

DOWN

1. Oh boy! All excited in a storm of publicity (8)
2. A sporting type from Oxford is livid (4)
3. Strange offspring, that's certain (4-2)
4. A fruit gets girl on the head (5-3)
5. Not functioning – in the wrong sequence? (3,2,5)
6. Drawing instrument for writer, one in class (6)
8. President managed this French caper (6)
13. Thief with a diamond, and pot! (4-6)
16. Find rare forms sensitive to radiation (5-3)
18. Sundial, one of long standing? (3-5)
19. Pales – because of cuts of meat, one hears (6)
21. Unaccustomed, being new (6)
22. Portion includes a measure for Mum or Dad (6)
24. Firm, about the centre (4)

255

ACROSS

1. A young animal circling a woman's chubby-faced child (6)
5. Bird, duck, near turbid Loire (6)
9. Hero's loved one, a chief around the North (7)
10. Mean figure found in poetic eastern country (6)
11. Accustomed from birth to be in line for noble estates, we hear (2,3,6,4)
13. An ex-PM's garden (4)
14. The tongue, apparently, is required for a harmonica (5-5)
18. To be good enough at sums, reps will have to be schooled (4,6)
19. A dab – a whopper! (4)
21. Hit nothing? Drunk in a car could make you crash! (2,2,4,3,4)
24. A drinking-vessel, note – and a copper beginning to pour (6)
25. Acute pain – ten sedatives contain it (7)
26. Drunk showing temper in S. Dakota (6)
27. A royal line's heraldic gold shrouded in thickening dust (6)

DOWN

2. A man, simple and callous (9)
3. Sailors, generally, admitting awful deed, blush (6)
4. Uncivilised girl, almost, has nothing on us (9)
5. The Head's often the cause of tears? (5)
6. Let pro in, to form a crime-fighting organisation (8)
7. Fast – nothing slow (5)
8. Hates, we hear, being in Communist Party – for instance, it keeps things on the line! (7-3)
12. Teetotaller, one with RN, intoxicated about the sea (3-7)
15. I can soothe the savage beast! (9)
16. Arms smuggler 'ung about, followed by a Bow Street officer (9)
17. Boy interrupts a fellow Yankee (8)
20. Teddie's novel, prepared for publication (6)
22. Negotiate for free entertainment (5)
23. The trophy I had, briefly, is a Roman god (5)

256

ACROSS

4. A challenge to attack – so, advance (4,2)
6. Expose to injury and death by fire? (8)
9. Boy meets girl with an affected manner (2-2-2)
10. Finish almost close to t' headland (8)
11. A slight quake might cause them terror, round edge of Etna (5-6)
15. Appeal to with a religious pamphlet, by the sound of it (7)
17. Devoted one, look, in God's embrace (7)
18. With pile-up, hire top co-op duplicator (11)
22. Like a crown? Right, on a king outwardly bashful (8)
23. Heavenly body posed with vase (6)
24. We're told to learn a bit about southern gulls, etc. (3-5)
25. Scribble, make poem about lover's face (6)

DOWN

1. Party had nothing raised, causing consternation (6)
2. An entracte from Ritz, Zoe, men improvised (10)
3. I ate crab, contaminated – such things cause food-poisoning, for instance (8)
4. Copper lingered at first, made prior investigation up blind-alley (3-2-3)
5. Form above standard? Average (8)
7. Low-down about Western girl (4)
8. Sally Reed! (4)
12. Degenerating? Retard gore, somehow (10)
13. Shaft of bird's feather found in bank of earth – almost extinct (8)
14. Alienate obnoxious sergeant (8)
16. A supplement – should be cut out if inflammatory! (8)
19. Public speaker – or one to recite, primarily (6)
20. Deeds – no head for data (4)
21. Girl with Irish Mum (4)

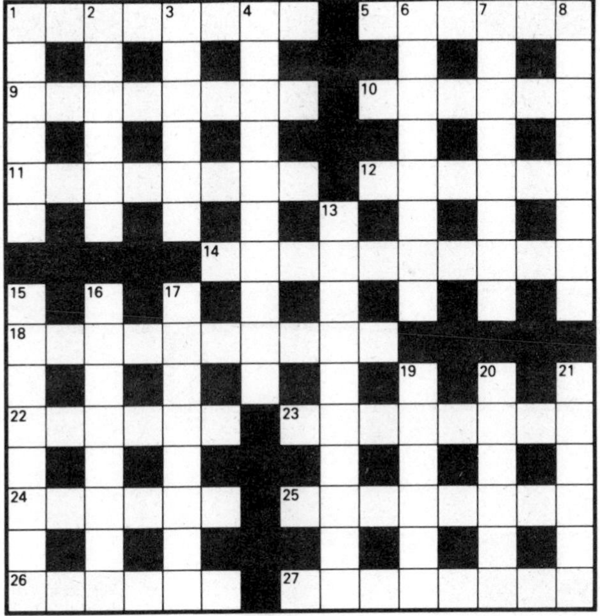

257

ACROSS

1. Girl pirouettes with Fred's last cane, possibly – Astaire's speciality (3-5)
5. B minus? Could be one sign of a storm brewing (6)
9. A cold dessert with a sprinkling of mace, Eric (3-5)
10. Arrived with painter – one that produces pictures (6)
11. In an emergency, a touch, a little measure, will do (2,1,5)
12. Satisfied about time, as specified (6)
14. Slice roasts, in night-clubs (4-6)
18. Sportsman's pale, poorly, unfortunately (4-6)
22. Expose one in binge (6)
23. Convict in bad shape, seen in mound of industrial waste (4-4)
24. A callow recruit – fleece one easily, at first (6)
25. One leading soldiers, competent and willing (6)
26. A whale, a bulge at sea (6)
27. Left helpless in street and in debt (8)

DOWN

1. Related to a clan, born in tribulation (6)
2. Rep's delirious over marvellous post-war bungalow quickly constructed (6)
3. Scared by a foe's first attack (6)
4. Neckwear includes tatty lace, found in basement? (4-6)
6. Idleness? Showing the opposite, it seems (8)
7. Fifty in a trouncing, grumbling (8)
8. Reckless couple of strikes? (4-4)
13. Re-planned simple diet, that drivers shouldn't exceed (5,5)
15. Piece of pork – Adam apparently had one! (5,3)
16. Cooking liquid – Popeye's favourite, we hear (5-3)
17. One in southern Chinese city, giving an address (8)
19. A General 'ad drawn up a list of items for discussion (6)
20. Early Channel-swimmer, Edward – having feet like a duck's! (6)
21. Add a very soft finish (6)

258

ACROSS

1. Game explorer (4)
4. Persistently question PM at college, on return (4)
9. RAF fuel's spluttering – alarming (7)
10. Overlooked nothing? Give a hand to the editor (7)
12. It blows in from the ocean, ruffling braes with gentle movement that's audible (3-6)
13. An Italian cuddled by Lulu, I gibed (5)
14. A road-tax – pound due on return journey (4)
15. What vampires do is unreliable (3-2-5)
17. Bet he'll act riskily, and take leading role in hazardous pursuit (4,3,3)
20. Horse-whip, cut short (4)
22. Range is 66 feet? (5)
23. Capital letters from superior odd character (5-4)
25. Faint chit (4,3)
26. A rugger player – very big, appropriately (7)
27. Leading actor deserts? Called back (4)
28. Gossip divulges an address? (4)

DOWN

2. Lid's lifted from money-box, for first advance (5)
3. Nothing? The Italian rightly supplies source of fuel (3-4)
4. Priest, in study of book, finds a saying (7)
5. Mum in a row with principal feature of BR (4,4)
6. Foil removed from collection! (6)
7. They'll never meet in pubs, but you can meet them in gyms (8,4)
8. I'd raft, breaking loose from moorings (6)
11. Descriptive of gunfighters? Doubtless Roy Rogers tried to keep ——— ———! (7-5)
16. Be proud – don't comply (5,3)
17. Seen in some lifts, stuck out on a limb? (6)
18. A torque designed as a belt (7)
19. Snake? Stop – it may be trodden on (7)
21. Submissions – wrestler's third – give delight (6)
24. Countrified part of Lower Urals (5)

259

ACROSS

4. Reverse, in second? (4,2)
6. One who seizes control of plane in transit – one knave, stowed aboard her (8)
9. Conway, perhaps, has first-class return for part of Europe (6)
10. The girl's eating cooked lamb, making a mess (8)
11. Quick-witted person seen at a bonfire, perhaps (6,5)
15. Catch, we hear, a deadly disease (7)
17. Sheep returned with Guide, we're told, making for tent (7)
18. Develop crack in water-pipe, say, around a washer – aluminium (6,1,4)
22. Recent arrival makes crew, men holding the lead for Oxford (8)
23. After fight, 'e shows an abrasion (6)
24. One giving a sermon before a church, with the Queen in attendance (8)
25. Formal US cooking equipment (6)

DOWN

1. Champ is boxing one in a German city! (6)
2. Robber drunk, with odd yawn, interrupted by Mum (10)
3. A heavy blow for a farmer, maybe (8)
4. An animal we're told to bet on – without a saddle? (8)
5. Rejected? A golf-club can make it hard (4-4)
7. Overcome king's-evil? (4)
8. Be at ease with others (4)
12. Head of research, during yesterday, got drunk – and out of touch with reality (6-4)
13. Half-hearted Saint has to contend with atheism, ultimately (8)
14. Freckles spreading, in part – must be rash! (8)
16. Settle snugly with gaol-bird in change of scene (8)
19. A combination of notes heard in harmony (6)
20. Break for a snack (4)
21. Quaint river – not Dee! (4)

260

ACROSS

1. Seer's sound gain (6)
5. Sailor gets nearly everything, the beast (6)
9. Satirical poem? Record one with little weight (7)
10. Counsellor – intended, we hear, as an alternative (6)
11. A communication from holiday-makers captured tropics unusually (7,8)
13. Bring up from the back (4)
14. Infant, bairn, beams – falling about (4,2,4)
18. Found record finished by a press-chief (10)
19. Repeat some of the pianoforte chords (4)
21. A little reserved – but of interest to the palmist? (9,2,4)
24. An attendant at a dance (6)
25. Virginia, drowned by reverberating din, makes attempt to escape (7)
26. Specify – about upper-class sculpture (6)
27. Untidy, drunk, in a state of undress (6)

DOWN

2. A car is not impaired in waterproof covers (9)
3. Intellectual, old Egyptian king – short, with Tutankhamen's face (3-3)
4. Moderate anger over a note (9)
5. A creature with a powerful jet! (5)
6. Studies one in race that's fixed (8)
7. A halo, oddly, signifies love in Hawaii (5)
8. The Dalton gang, say, dared posse recklessly (10)
12. Disheartened tyrant seen about northern retreat (10)
15. Ivy, perhaps, is always jealous (9)
16. Artist and spies on register, one filled with ethnic prejudices (9)
17. Support Labourite, and others (4-4)
20. Embedded in mug, upside-down (6)
22. Had in mind a composition of Manet's (5)
23. I scold, being irascible (5)

261

ACROSS

7. Quiet editor, busy one in charge, is precise (8)
9. Former tree chopped up in cathedral city (6)
10. The first man to make a reservoir (4)
11. Exposed landlord in correspondence intended for all to see (4,6)
12. Weak charge by British Legion at end of battle (6)
14. Advance made by prince towards a monstrous woman (8)
15. Beer-mugs to be taken round one Sunday (6)
17. Come back with a bottle (6)
20. Goes wild in wild go-go – for fruit (8)
22. With old shilling, writer returned for a spool (6)
23. What a judge should always be, as a precaution? (4,2,4)
24. Be effusive with us in outskirts of Greenwich (4)
25. Plucky tern half lost an egg-cell (6)
26. Run away from a spell? It's a lie, they say (4,4)

DOWN

1. Dull policeman's round, getting one exhausted (4-4)
2. Little girl grasps pound in hand (4)
3. In residence with a book about first of Hapsburgs (2,4)
4. Words of praise for how a steak may have been served? (4,4)
5. Explosive device scattered rebel mob, crushing sober type (6-4)
6. A form of rugger still seen aboard a steamship (6)
8. Boring people will produce an awful cringing sensation (6)
13. Child minder, or inexperienced model? (4-6)
16. Arrange for locomotive – about to turn up (8)
18. Aeroplane's spiral dive causes extreme agitation (4-4)
19. Horrified at hags cavorting about (6)
21. Jocularity – in part, visual (6)
22. Hazy, as a result of imbibing real rum! (6)
24. Entrance Georgia with a note (4)

262

ACROSS

4. Keeping out of sight, because of scolding – not about! (6)
6. Squander anything extra – then drift away (4,4)
9. Small drink, no s-spirit (6)
10. The clinging sort, in a pub, clean out! (8)
11. Suffice – that's what pelicans do with food? (4,3,4)
15. Judge about to cut loose round the East (7)
17. It gets the ball back into play, from a line outwardly narrow (5-2)
18. Money and t' chips combined to make stacks! (7-4)
22. In depression about part of London being obscene (8)
23. Damage – in a yacht station (6)
24. Rambler chewed up some rusk (4-4)
25. A catch-phrase to strike one (6)

DOWN

1. This month one's in demand (6)
2. Shabby felt – bet Ian changes (4-6)
3. Con-man wins? Led dummy King (8)
4. Wait for crone holding pole and sack (4,4)
5. Wretched existence for Fido – leg's broken (4,4)
7. A bad habit that has an irresistible hold? (4)
8. A river-plant requiring study, we hear (4)
12. It's 'Sweeney', in new format for the viewer (3-7)
13. Fainting quickly seizes women on gin cocktail (8)
14. A blot – it sank in and spread (3-5)
16. One vehicle in the road, in list of starters (4-4)
19. Annually, a nobleman appears in the outskirts of Yaratishky (6)
20. Movie from MGM – lifelike and rolling (4)
21. Poems – chaste, at heart (4)

263

ACROSS

7. Relaxation after winter sport? Ask Piers for new arrangement (5-3)
9. Emaciated, coming from tavern in a Scottish isle, and cut! (6)
10. Restore part of type in complete series (4)
11. Drunk, knocking back a short – this will thin out the dough! (7-3)
12. Ballerina cared desperately about Nureyev's lead (6)
14. Battle later got out of hand in court (8)
15. Wear kid! (4,2)
17. Road complex – it's masterful (6)
20. This kind of warfare has allure, GI being involved (8)
22. Car cut into a bird (6)
23. Gas-flame gets one and all in a predicament (5-5)
24. Fire in part of car (4)
25. Headwear displayed in German city – and French (6)
26. Adore car prepared for Grand Prix, perhaps (4,4)

DOWN

1. See about timber, with ready money (4,4)
2. Shower makes one hide (4)
3. Beau sure recoups, squeezing one who always takes interest (6)
4. Helped fool with a variety of diets (8)
5. Bit of a basin, covered with flowering patterns, in which you may clean your hands (6-4)
6. In excavation, part of opal shows blue (6)
8. Relations legally spliced, to begin with (2-4)
13. What people might do when explaining a fielding position? (5,5)
16. Too chill? Arrange for floor cover (8)
18. First-class upper-cut? (3-5)
19. Ragged, in tatters? Must be the knife (6)
21. Harmony's the height of success in marriage (6)
22. Goods thrown overboard from planes over America (6)
24. Store for bran, possibly (4)

264

ACROSS

1. Choice fruit (4)
4. Gaze vacantly at a satellite (4)
9. It's useful for a secretary – and poet, possibly (4-3)
10. Ground nut lies in a vessel (7)
12. Drink he hit, about litre, thoroughly (2,3,4)
13. Silent one, restricted by diplomacy (5)
14. German king displays a lump (4)
15. Compensate MD – namesake – at a loss (4,6)
17. Simple female rabbit with brood must be careful (4,4,2)
20. Returns to eat with a girl (4)
22. Sat awkwardly with a couple of pounds in booth (5)
23. One means of buttoning up Fleet Street boss? (5-4)
25. Put on different clothes, so as to 15 Across perhaps (7)
26. The last runner at 'Aydock to back (7)
27. Early English composer, by the way (4)
28. Crew one located in borders of Godalming (4)

DOWN

2. Drinks last of strychnine in error (5)
3. Wine produced, with regulated air (7)
4. Canadian cop, Monsieur, has nothing to solve (7)
5. Extra work? I've more, anyway, with Tuesday thrown in (8)
6. Pluck, producing fragment of song (6)
7. Part of New York, say – the North – is real estate (6,6)
8. Pieces of armour for heads, about fifty (6)
11. It's one's characteristic habit to back the Constitution? (6,6)
16. A sin that disturbs true lady (8)
17. Guarantee – when sûreté's carrying it? (6)
18. Revealed, once, and modelled (7)
19. In charge, bird rises – frigid type (7)
21. Shake dead stranger! (6)
24. Danes wrecked American car (5)

265

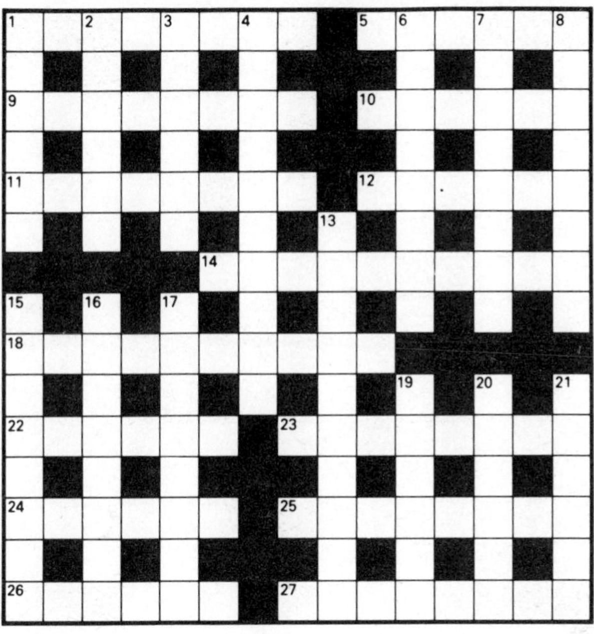

ACROSS

1. It takes a subordinate to provide an inadequate crew (8)
5. Filter the stock? (6)
9. Tranquillity – yet Siren's deceptive (8)
10. A squalid neighbourhood housing many, ultimately, as a place of refuge (6)
11. The audacity to streak, with a string of beads? (8)
12. Shops requiring deposits (6)
14. To diminish a really good man is to make a terrible mistake (4,1,5)
18. Odd types about, in very attractive scene (6-4)
22. He's dragged out of the turbulent Channel? (6)
23. One being embraced by her, twice, gives an exclamation of approval (4,4)
24. Spheres of action – regions around the North (6)
25. Diplomatic, etc. – Red is, for a change (8)
26. Painter, who uses a lathe? (6)
27. Restrain the little devil with fixed irons (8)

DOWN

1. Descriptive of unacclaimed lyricists? (6)
2. Outspoken Welshman ruined, from what we hear (6)
3. Name for a king, in addition to a lord (6)
4. Converted RC hit at sin, the great enemy of the Church (10)
6. Try the Underground – it's familiar to chemists (4-4)
7. Grace ill, delirious, hypersensitive (8)
8. English chap looks up account, for one with the same 'handle' (8)
13. Amusing transposition of initial letters will make no poems, sir (10)
15. Summarise sailor's treatise (8)
16. Wrecker tore a bus in pieces (8)
17. Food without relish, if rejected, will make you become lethargic (8)
19. This shopkeeper is comparatively coarse, we hear (6)
20. Alcove for a break from routine studies (6)
21. Moron gives some secret information (6)

9

NOVELTY PUZZLES

266

TRANSACROSTIC Write the answers to the clues in the diagram on this page. The letters of the first column, when read downwards, will spell the name of a writer and the title of one of his works.

CLUES

A Sudden puff of air (5)
B Coy (3)
C Blunder (5)
D Tavern (3)
E Plunder (4)
F Prickly seed-case (3)
G Officer of royal household (7)
H To value (4)
I Famous Tom (5)
J Excessively (3)
K Lofty (4)
L Locomotive (6)
M Large lizard (6)
N Extreme ring of target (5)
O Falls (7)
P Goddess of hunting (5)
Q Severe trial (6)
R Meadow (3)
S Badly (3)
T Equivalent (5)
U Rustic (5)
V Scatter seed (3)

A	21	78	11	61	52		
B	5	56	39				
C	77	89	59	62	22		
D	17	70	46				
E	34	48	92	79			
F	71	13	65				
G	68	42	97	23	30	10	93
H	37	57	15	98			
I	73	16	43	67	27		
J	3	81	38				
K	49	64	19	2			
L	44	83	7	76	54	31	
M	86	12	94	24	47	60	
N	1	33	25	45	91		
O	100	4	63	32	74	90	53
P	80	66	50	18	6		
Q	26	36	55	85	69	95	
R	58	99	35				
S	20	8	41				
T	28	96	72	40	88		
U	84	87	75	29	51		
V	14	9	82				

Now transfer all the letters on the opposite page to the diagram below, and an excerpt from the work will appear. The words are separated by the black squares.

1N	2K		3J	4O	5B		6P		7L	8S	9V	10G
11A	12M	13F	14V		15H	16I	17D	18P	19K		20S	
21A	22C	23G	24M		25N	26Q		27I	28T		29U	
30G	31L	32O	33N	34E	35R	36Q		37H	38J	39B	40T	41S
	42G	43I	44L	45N	46D		47M	48E		49K	50P	51U
52A		53O	54L	55Q		56B	57H	58R	59C		60M	61A
62C	63O	64K	65F		66P		67I	68G	69Q	70D		71F
72T	73I		74O		75U	76L	77C	78A	79E		80P	81J
82V	83L		84U	85Q	86M	87U	88T	89C	90O		91N	92E
93G	94M	95Q		96T	97G	98H	99R	100O				

267

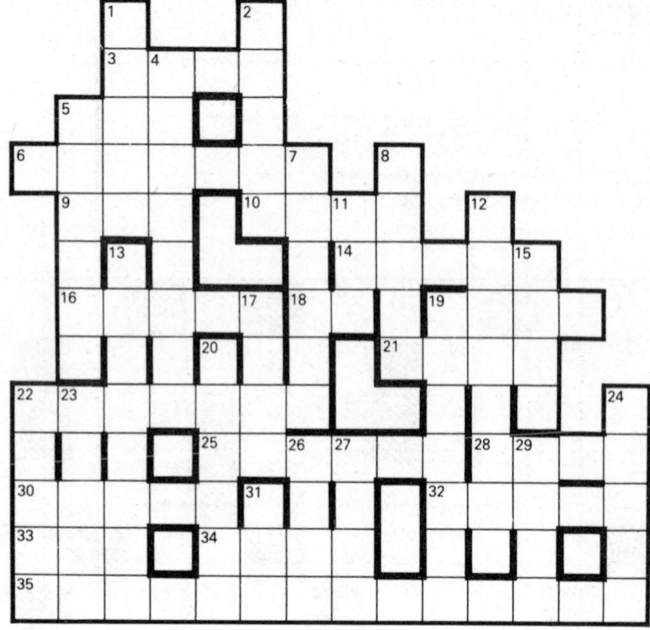

RUINED CASTLE In the completed diagram 6, 14, 18 and 35 Across spell out an appropriate phrase. They are unclued.

ACROSS
3. Jetty (4)
5. Offspring (3)
6. *See note above*
9. Entirely (3)
10. Skirting-board (4)
14. *See note above*
16. List of jurors (5)
18. *See note above*
19. Action (4)
21. Festive season (4)
22. Gauge (7)
25. Row gently (6)
28. Girl's name (4)
30. Military body (5)
32. Impel (5)
33. A hundred (3)
34. Mislay (4)
35. *See note above*

DOWN
1. Reel (5)
2. Cooked (5)
4. Tends (8)
5. Sharp and ill-tempered (6)
7. Potter (6)
8. Copper (5)
11. Period of time (3)
12. Fighters for honour (8)
13. Kind of pasta (8)
15. Pour (4)
17. Italian currency (4)
19. Noble rank (7)
20. Pliant (6)
22. Verse in a cracker (5)
23. Man's name (5)
24. Perfect (5)
26. Record (4)
27. Animal (4)
29. French town (4)
31. Because (3)

268

→	1			2			3			4
	14			15			16			
			25			26			17	
13	24			33			34	27 H		5
		32		38				E		
						39		R	18	
12	23		37				35	28 M		6
		31			36			I		
				30			29	T	19	
11	22			21			20			7
		10			9			8		

OVERLAP All answers are words of six letters. They should be entered in clockwise sequence from square 1 to the centre of the diagram. Each answer overlaps the next by *three* of its letters; for example, the answer to 27, which is given, consists of the last three letters of 26 and the first three letters of 28. The last three letters of 39 are the same as the first three letters of 1.

CLUES

1. Mode
2. Sensitive cords
3. Venus, the evening star
4. Allow
5. Headwear for bishops
6. Take offence at
7. Tempt
8. Toboggan slide (3-3)
9. Small brook
10. Famous admiral
11. Type of poem
12. Lower
13. Composed of aromatic plants
14. Song or narrative poem
15. Large spoons
16. Diminish
17. Spanish lady
18. A speech-maker
19. Scorching
20. Mounted, as a horse
21. Pertaining to teeth
22. Special aptitude
23. A course at dinner
24. Doped cigarette
25. Containing iron
26. More wealthy
27. A recluse
28. Type of glove
29. Gentle
30. Of the skin
31. Carpenter's tool
32. Deadly
33. Consecrate
34. Nearest the bottom
35. Girl's name
36. Messenger of the gods
37. Made of network
38. Trimmer of bushy fences
39. A European

269

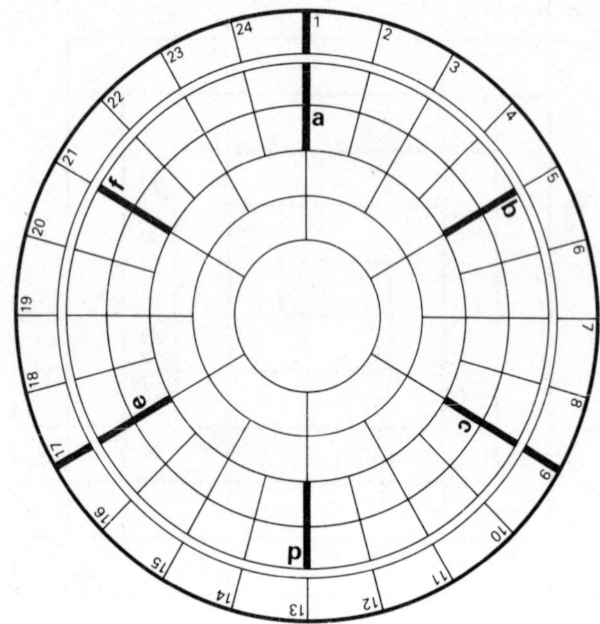

MAGIC CIRCLE There are 24 radial answers, each of five letters, which always read from their numbered spaces towards the centre; and 6 four-letter arcs, a-f. The outer arcs (1-8, 9-16, 17-24) spell out three suitable members of the Magic Circle.

RADIALS

1. Gathers
2. Exams
3. Amphibians
4. Jokes
5. Brown pigment
6. Sovereign
7. Willow
8. Make allusion
9. Mouldy
10. Relative
11. In a merry manner
12. Insinuate
13. Flogged
14. Annoyed
15. Intended
16. Cited
17. Elegant shop
18. A constellation
19. Italian
20. High type of heel
21. Mournful poem
22. Tall and slim
23. Girl's name
24. Answer

ARCS

a. Regulations
b. Contemplate
c. Cut
d. Operatic song
e. Member of body
f. Disabled

270

LEFT AND RIGHT Every answer is to be entered diagonally to the left or right, as indicated.

DIAGONALLY LEFT

2. A sphere (3)
3. Pull with sudden jerk (5)
4. Part of foot (3-4)
5. Bundle of notes (3)
6. A sweet (4,7)
7. Animal enclosure (3)
8. To subdue (5)
10. Vegetable (3)
13. Narrow cavity in head (5)
14. Tumbledown (11)
16. Originally named (3)
18. They deaden instruments' sound (5)
20. To put on (3)
23. Mounted bull-fighter (7)
25. Loop for hanging (3)
26. Part of flower (5)
29. Church dignitary (5)
31. Scarlet (3)
33. Youth (3)
35. Excavate (3)

DIAGONALLY RIGHT

1. Automatic weapon (4-3)
2. Be in debt (3)
3. Commotions (2-3)
4. Label (3)
5. Ambushed (7)
6. Horse (5)
7. Eat a late meal (3)
9. Animal noise (3)
11. Types (5)
12. Picture of attractive girl (3-2)
15. Hawaiian garland (3)
17. Deceived (5)
18. Affected by a mental illness (5)
19. Cut off (3)
21. Came in (7)
22. Colossal (7)
24. Confined within college bounds (5)
27. Drawing-room (5)
28. Ungentlemanly fellow (3)
30. Evil (3)
32. Sailor (3)
34. Follow closely (3)

271

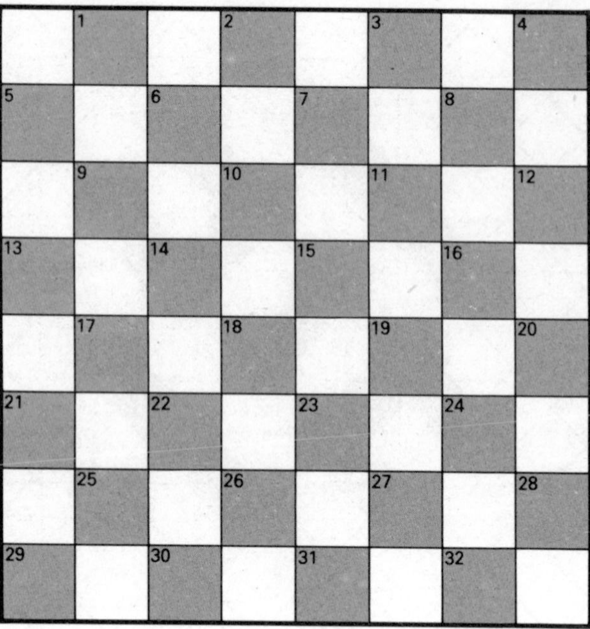

CROWNED MEN Eight answers, of eight letters each, are clued in random order; they are to be entered Across, one in each RANK. The other answers are entered diagonally, on the black squares, following the given numbers. The long white diagonal spells out an alternative title for this puzzle.

RANKS

Facing the Orient (8)
Flock minder (8)
Griddle cakes (8)
Half-suppressed laughs (8)
Eagerly desired (8)
Covers (8)
Unequalled (8)
Kitchen ware (8)

DIAGONAL MOVES

a. 32-27-31-26-22-18-23 – Curing (7)
b. 4-8-11-15-19-16-20 – Those who search (7)
c. 26-22-18-15-19-24-20 – Pan menders (7)
d. 9-14-17-22-18-23 – Sinking a putt (6)
e. 10-14-17-22-26-30 – Courteous (6)
f. 16-19-23-27-24-28 – Esteem (6)
g. 13-17-22-18-15 – Gaol (5)
h. 2-6-1-5-9 – Merriment (5)
i. 29-25-22-17-21 – Buckets (5)
j. 24-19-23-27-31 – Majestic (5)
k. 21-17-22-18-23 – Cast (5)
l. 5-1-6-2-7 – Clips (5)
m. 21-17-14-10-7 – Liquid refuse (5)
n. 5-9-14-18-23 – Strap (5)
o. 13-9-6-10 – A golf shot (4)
p. 16-11-8-12 – Rush (4)
q. 31-27-24-28 – Grease (4)
r. 7-3-8-12 – Pip (4)
s. 29-25-22-18 – Suffering (4)
t. 4-8-3-7 – Witnesses (4)
u. 32-27-23-19 – Herb (4)
v. 26-30-25-21 – Meals (4)

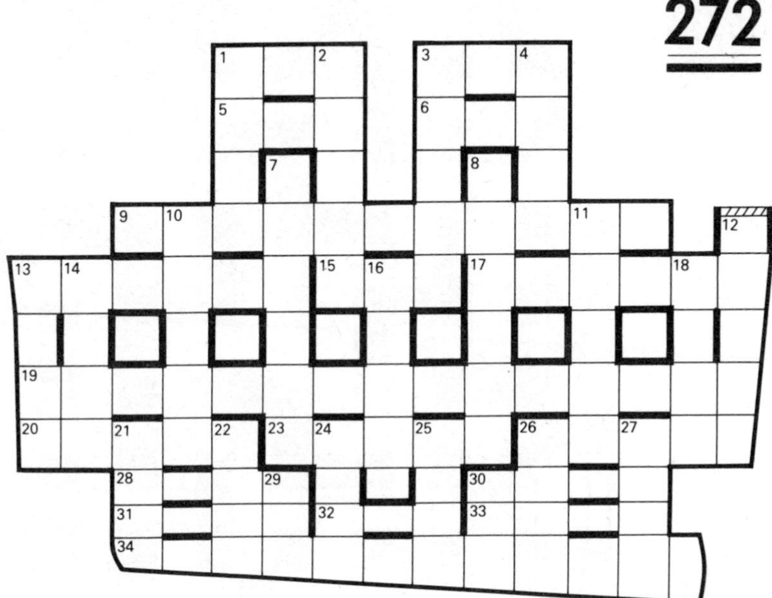

CRUISING The phrases at 19 and 34 Across, and the words at 12 and 13 Down, are all appropriate to the diagram. They are unclued.

ACROSS

1. Matter (3)
3. Taxi (3)
5. Timber (3)
6. Fish eggs (3)
9. Varieties (11)
13. To some extent (6)
15. Tidal movement (3)
17. Lasso (6)
19. *See note above*
20. Marine creature (5)
23. Bird (5)
26. Driven by the wind (5)
28. Hobble (4)
30. The high sea (4)
31. Domesticated (4)
32. Close (3)
33. Boy's name (4)
34. *See note above*

DOWN

1. Mates (4)
2. Coastal area (5)
3. Morsel (5)
4. Vegetable (4)
7. Journey (6)
8. Flood (6)
10. Purloin (5)
11. Lag behind (5)
12. *See note above*
13. *See note above*
14. Cunning (4)
16. Two-masted ships (5)
18. Again (4)
21. Singing voice (4)
22. Girl's name (4)
24. On the sheltered side (4)
25. Vein of ore (4)
26. Jib (4)
27. Formerly (4)
29. Swan (3)
30. Crew member (3)

273

CLUELESS This time, instead of clues, all the *answers* have been provided – but you have to discover where they fit in the diagram!

9-letter
DELINEATE
LIGATURES
RECTANGLE
VERTEBRAE

8-letter
ASBESTOS
FAREWELL
ROTATING
SMOULDER

7-letter
ECHELON
EXTINCT
HEEDFUL
PENDANT
SQUEEZE
UNEQUAL
WANGLED
WRESTLE

6-letter
CLOSES
FIDGET
REELED
TERROR

5-letter
CINCH
DIRGE
DUCAT
FIRST
NUDGE
RALPH
SKEIN
TACIT

4-letter
AVID
JEEP
LULL
WREN

3-letter
GAS
GUN
LEA
MAR

	10	11	28	29	46	47	64	65	82	83	100	101	118	119	
	9	12	27	30	45	48	63	66	81	84	99	102	117	120	
	8	13	26	31	44	49	62	67	80	85	98	103	116	121	
	7	14	25	32	43	50	61	68	79	86	97	104	115	122	
	6	15	24	33	42	51	60	69	78	87	96	105	114	123	
	5	16	23	34	41	52	59	70	77	88	95	106	113	124	
	4	17	22	35	40	53	58	71	76	89	94	107	112	125	
	3	18	21	36	39	54	57	72	75	90	93	108	111	126	
1	2	19	20	37	38	55	56	73	74	91	92	109	110	127	128

RADIATOR Write the letters of each answer in the appropriate numbered squares. When all have been completed, a personal message from the radiator will appear, reading in sequence from square 1 to square 128. The message has 29 words, two of them hyphenated.

CLUES

a. 1-86-54-125-75-42-68 – Original (7)
b. 3-46-100-126-30-94-82 – The least amount (7)
c. 9-96-60-90-106-36-33 – Having a coat of wool (7)
d. 122-84-117-78-98-29-25 – Robbers (7)
e. 34-2-120-59-69-72 – Server of food (6)
f. 61-8-105-85-67-23 – Realm (6)
g. 22-32-109-10-47-21 – Baby (6)
h. 114-73-15-102-110-79 – Handcart (6)
i. 48-99-118-24-12-81 – Vocalist (6)
j. 56-51-31-124-7 – Organ (5)
k. 18-44-64-77-39 – Former PM (5)
l. 41-93-108-58-37 – Female (5)
m. 27-38-49-11-88 – Adhere (5)
n. 119-20-28-57-70 – A liquid (5)
o 6-76-91-97-50 – Quick (5)
p. 115-104-107-112 – Plunder (4)
q. 35-40-53-17 – Part of the foot (4)
r. 4-66-103-45 – Poverty-stricken (4)
s. 5-52-128-13 – Last word (4)
t. 63-123-14-71 – Abominable snowman (4)
u. 65-89-121-43 – Curved (4)
v. 74-19-16-95 – Costly (4)
w. 127-116-83 – Encountered (3)
x. 62-113-92 – Type of window (3)
y. 87-111-26 – Parched (3)
z. 55-80-101 – Droop (3)

275

DOUBLE-DECKER These two diagrams are the same but the answers are different. The upper crossword is a plain one, with definition clues only. The lower one is fully cryptic.

PLAIN

ACROSS

1. Custom (5)
4. Planned (7)
8. Sorrowful (3)
9. Returning at intervals (9)
10. Divorcee's allowance (7)
11. To mean (5)
13. Marked with spots (6)
15. Next day (6)
18. Pertaining to the kidneys (5)
19. Indefinite number (7)
21. Conduct (9)
23. English river (3)
24. Tuft of hair (3-4)
25. Out of sorts (5)

DOWN

1. Spouse (7)
2. Game (9)
3. Trunk (5)
4. Lures (6)
5. Dizziness (7)
6. Notice (3)
7. Short song (5)
12. Persist (9)
14. Animate (7)
16. Cold and cheerless (7)
17. Expelled (3,3)
18. Automaton (5)
20. Ponders (5)
22. Joint (3)

CRYPTIC

ACROSS

1. Pile together in a heap for a service (5)
4. Bloke the Communist concealed (7)
8. Renegade gives sailor a turn (3)
9. Exasperates 'em with Angostura? (9)
10. Rome, for instance, is great! (7)
11. Sloppy – dear me! – going round American hospital (5)
13. After endless spiced drink, the French walk feebly (6)
15. A waterproof – artist fits into one all right (6)
18. Sheriff's men have to abandon ship (5)
19. A taxi I catch for a group of ministers (7)
21. Daily player, they say, is a personality (9)
23. Rest's responsible for falsehood (3)
24. Dawdles clumsily with bandage (7)
25. Swank's noticeable in sporting teams (5)

DOWN

1. Fruit, almost full-flavoured, kept in a jar (7)
2. Worker and I, dopes, wandering in New Zealand? (9)
3. Some bed linen put around male (5)
4. Deep-blue bed, with bachelor left in it (6)
5. A food factor – you'll find it in the morning in French wine (7)
6. Whisky will make you askew, we hear (3)
7. Study's in a mess, needing a clean-up (5)
12. Saint argued noisily, losing head, being throttled (9)
14. Haul fish up on the sheltered side (7)
16. Young animals Christopher has sent out (7)
17. Injure the girl, holding a whip (6)
18. Ancient Britons caught in mines (5)
20. Scottish poet is inflamed with passion (5)
22. A girl in a cravat (3)

PLAIN

CRYPTIC

276

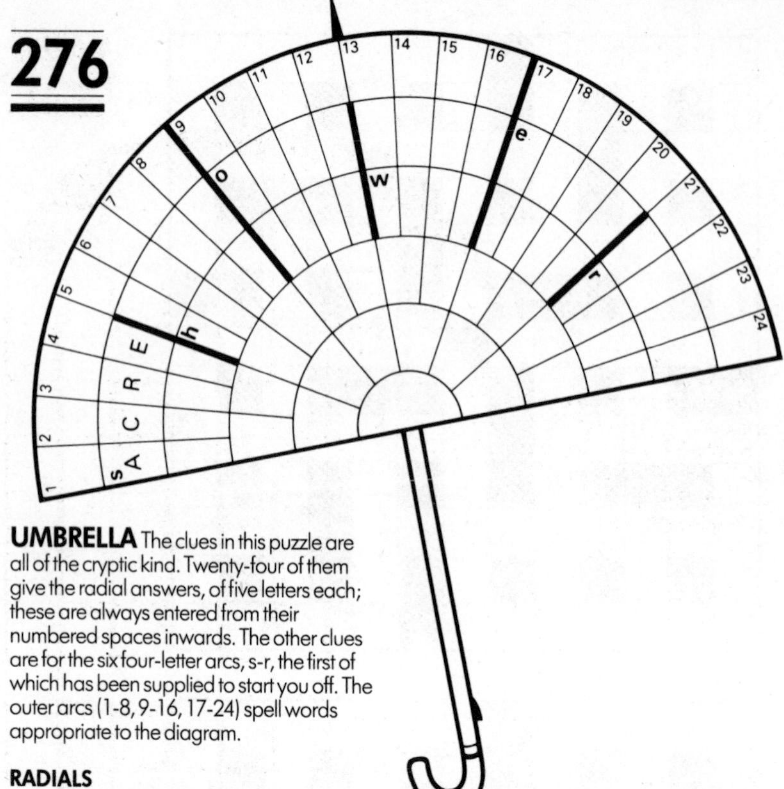

UMBRELLA The clues in this puzzle are all of the cryptic kind. Twenty-four of them give the radial answers, of five letters each; these are always entered from their numbered spaces inwards. The other clues are for the six four-letter arcs, s-r, the first of which has been supplied to start you off. The outer arcs (1-8, 9-16, 17-24) spell words appropriate to the diagram.

RADIALS

1. Birds missing northern storms
2. A game left unfinished from pains
3. Flattens with clubs
4. Lights – none twinkling on Sunday
5. Right in the mug! That's custard-pie comedy!
6. Girl, one attracting parasites
7. After a breather, 'e makes a sudden thrust
8. Book of accounts mainly for the shelf
9. A spot of rain in stamps evaporates
10. Very small amount of oats – sea's ruined fertile spots
11. Legal documents for posh hotel, we hear
12. Headland accommodates first of two snug homes
13. Casts votes for Heads
14. Mate appearing in extra large semi-precious stones
15. Swells, lacking capital, will get eggs
16. Conjuror finally employs tricks
17. Reserves on the range getting caught
18. Noel madly embracing western girl
19. A bird dressin'
20. Synthetic substance – used in fibres, incidentally
21. Get rid of king, and relax about it
22. Coming from Scandinavia, and not the Kentish area?
23. Article on the writer – something to discuss
24. False start to exercise – pity

ARCS

s. River seeping into one area of land
h. Bark from terrier in distress
o. Seldom seen underdone
w. More than one convict loiters
e. A shrub – one, look, from the Orient
r. Article about a region

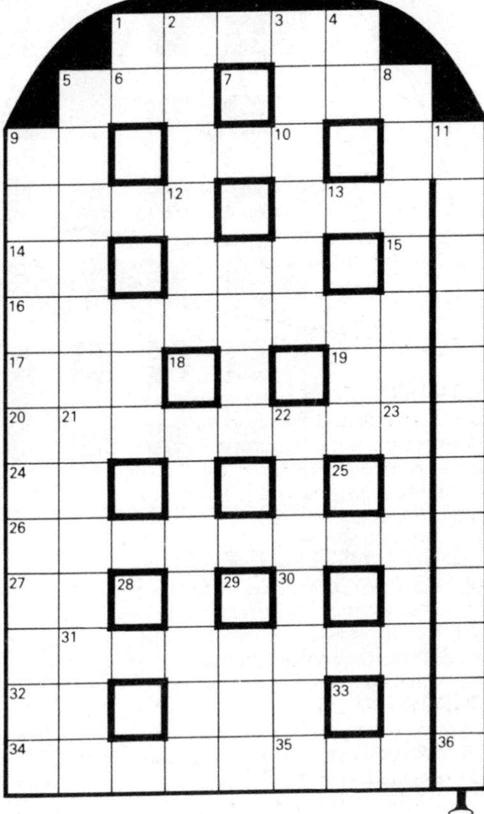

PIN-TABLE In the completed diagram the ball spells out a message along the following track: 36-11-8-4-3-7, followed by the remaining completely enclosed 'lights' travelling across the pin-table from top to bottom, and ending at 33. The message has seven words.

ACROSS

1. Cutter (5)
6. Long-serving prisoner (5)
9. Hew (4)
10. Portion of a surface (4)
12. Light footwear (6)
14. Host (4)
16. A show (9)
17. Chase (6)
19. Tree (3)
20. Encourage (5)
22. Unconscious state (4)
24. Objective (3)
25. Scold persistently (3)
26. Group of musicians (5,4)
27. Wager (3)
31. Spanish dance (8)
32. Part of the throat (6)
33. Tree (3)
34. Deer (4)
35. Ancient Icelandic poetry (4)

DOWN

1. Silly mistake (7)
2. Edges (4)
3. Cathedral dignitaries (5)
4. Go wrong (3)
5. Tart (5)
7. Breakages (9)
8. Affirmative (3)
9. Fastener (5)
13. Mussolini (4)
15. Poorly (3)
18. To mature (6)
20. Vegetable (7)
21. Engage for wages (4)
22. Small loaf (3)
23. Ran (7)
25. Domestic nurse (5)
28. Lecture (4)
29. Poems (4)
30. Speed (4)

278

ADDITIONS TO A THEME Two THEME-WORDS, A and B, may be said to describe the diagram; and each has a group of associated words, which can be added to it. These are all unclued.

ACROSS

1. Ranch hand (6)
4. Small coloured spots (8)
10. Clothing (7)
11. ADDITION TO A (7)
12. Searches for (5)
13. Assassins (9)
14. ADDITION TO A (9)
17. Monkey-like (5)
19. ADDITION TO A (5)
20. Swaps (9)
21. Blotches on the skin (9)
24. Systematic list of items (5)
26. Combining (7)
27. Organ of vision (3-4)
28. ADDITION TO B (8)
29. One who feeds a furnace (6)

DOWN

1. ADDITION TO B (9)
2. THEME-WORD B (5)
3. Be late in rising (9)
5. ADDITION TO B (5)
6. Sponge (5)
7. Dawdling (9)
8. Indications (5)
9. A panicking rush (8)
15. Scrutinise again (2-7)
16. Set back like an alcove (8)
17. A flat (9)
18. User of hikers' lodging, perhaps (9)
21. ADDITION TO B (5)
22. ADDITION TO A (5)
23. Musical instrument (5)
25. THEME-WORD A (5)

DROPPING AITCHES Answers to all clues in block capitals must drop their Hs before entry in the diagram. For example, the answer SHAVED would be entered as SAVED. All such entries are real words.

ACROSS

1. BRIEF DOWNPOUR (6)
4. INJURED (6)
7. DIVISION OF A COUNTY (6)
8. EXPRESSION OF GRATITUDE (6)
9. Disturbances of the peace (5)
10. Birds (5)
11. Duped (5,3,1,4)
15. TALKATIVE (6)
20. Describes falsely (13)
21. Tests (5)
23. Uttered (5)
24. CONTAINER (6)
25. FREQUENTS (6)
26. COUNTIES (6)
27. SCABBARDS (7)

DOWN

1. To part (8)
2. Male witches (8)
3. TALL GRASSES (6)
4. ROPE WITH NOOSE (6)
5. Stringed instrument (8)
6. Refrained (8)
12. Mother-of-pearl (5)
13. MORE FIERY (6)
14. Bottomless gulf (5)
16. Rulers (8)
17. Native of Skye, for instance (8)
18. Sleeplessness (8)
19. Values (8)
22. BEACHES (6)
23. CLIPPERS (6)

CIRCULAR SAW There are 24 radial answers, of five letters each, which always read from the numbered teeth towards the centre; and 6 arcs, a-f, of four letters each. The letters in the teeth, reading 1-24, spell out a phrase of four words, which describes the diagram.

RADIALS

1. Later
2. Niggard
3. Senior
4. Lid
5. Hang in the air
6. Fossil resin
7. At no time
8. Much colder
9. Pistols
10. Incites and helps
11. Musical instruments
12. Lassoes
13. Monsters
14. Contributions levied
15. Mountain range
16. Fatigues
17. European country
18. Recently
19. Splendour
20. Fruit
21. Expanses of water
22. Sign of the zodiac
23. Wipes over
24. Prepares for publication

ARCS

a. Poses
b. Textile machine
c. Loathsome
d. Eastern system of meditation
e. Pull
f. Dramatic king

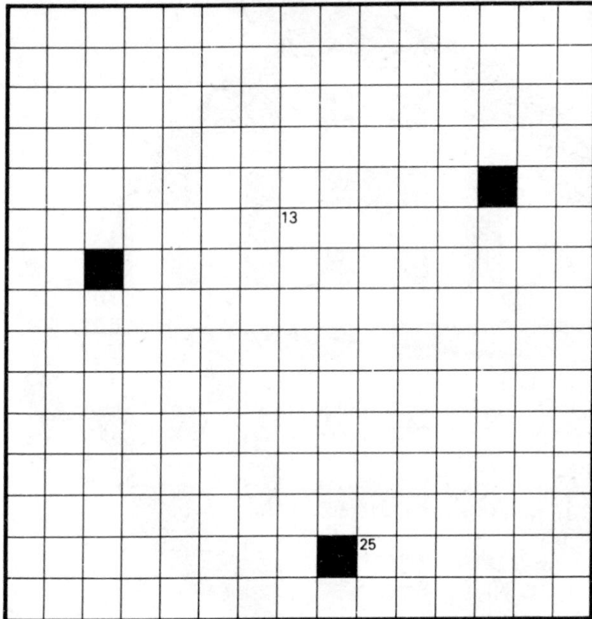

281

INK SHORTAGE The printer had only just enough ink to fill in three black squares and two numbers, so solvers will have to fill in the rest of the squares and numbers for themselves! The black squares should form a symmetrical pattern, which looks exactly the same whether the diagram is turned on its side or upside down.

ACROSS

6. I stick, as they say, in the White House
7. Introduction – for the record, we hear
9. Shouted 'Run!' wildly – and very loud
10. Beat a creature's hide
11. Right bird to show sorrow
13. 'Ots up too much, and acts the glutton?
14. True cinemas do somehow produce realistic films
17. Cultivated, by the sound of it, several – horrible!
20. Like a row? You'll have one in a passenger-ship
21. Terse, shortened? That's about right
22. A safeguard, possibly to cure pain
24. Most watery tavern in the street!
25. A girl the artist follows about Los Angeles

DOWN

1. Kept back in the wild, unfortunately, about an hour
2. Information about lake and wooded valley
3. One needs a short time – um – to create impetus
4. To employ about fifty is to get entangled
5. Pitmen cool off, finishing
7. I, for instance, Bond, will make a statement
8. A bed in Paris without illumination
12. Producing a new model, and kicking up a fuss again?
15. A call in troubled East for an association of countries
16. A lesson arranged about one, suitable to the time of year
18. Crude kind of frill, from what we hear
19. Bird, very large, hunted animal
23. Catch a horse-drawn vehicle

282

VERY FISHY! All Across answers are names of fishes. Each one is hidden in its clue, but with its letters jumbled. For example, the answer SARDINE could be hidden in the expression 'FlounDERS, IN Atlantic (7)'. Down clues are normal.

ACROSS

1. Roach netted easily (5)
4. On north bank congers wriggle (9)
6. Exotic dog-fish (3)
7. Beside the Humber, angling (5)
9. Grab dolphin by the tail (3)
11. Fish-cubes in batter (4)
12. Up the Rhine grilse spawn (7)
13. Angler back with a catch (4)
15. Like pilchards on toast? (4)
16. Useful bait, hook and sinker (7)
19. Shark heading for swimmer (4)
22. Elegant fish (3)
23. Record carp he caught (5)
24. Every range of sea-food (3)
25. Catch a crab, a rudd, etc. (9)
27. Fish and chips—take-away (5)

DOWN

1. Disturbance (7)
2. Woman in a convent (3)
3. Tribal chief (7)
4. Rise and fall of the sea (4)
5. Young goats (4)
6. Chortle (7)
8. Sooner (7)
10. Kind of ape (7)
11. Headwear (3)
14. Insect (3)
17. Desires earnestly (7)
18. Evict from a home (7)
20. Smooth-tongued (4)
21. Girl's name (4)
26. Former Turkish commander (3)

A 'CRYPTIC' TALE Every answer is a word or phrase which has been omitted from the narrative below. In each case, the answer has been replaced by its diagram number. (A = Across, D = Down)

You may not believe all you 10 in books, or all you hear; and what I'm about to relate may 8 an eyebrow or two. However, you can 28 on this: I am not 16D, but perfectly sane, and not liable to 4D with reality.

I well remember the 18D: it was 14 Year's Eve. The winter sun had 9, everything looked gloomy in the 18A twilight, and a wind was rising – all the 12, in fact, of a nasty night. I was about to drive home – to my 27 home beyond the city – when a stranger requested a lift in my pony and trap. I was willing enough, but I 33 uneasy, 6A. He was a 24, 21 man, thick-9, wearing a cloak of 32 tweed, 30 in colour. But there was an odd 31 about him. I 33 an evil, sinister presence, and soon 20 his company, though I could not explain my intense dislike.

A little 35, out in the country, as an owl hooted, and the 31 grew more gusty, the stranger suddenly broke the silence. He had once been a 11, he said, for Dr. Knox in Edinburgh, and had been familiar with that notorious pair, ID. One night, on his way to a graveyard, he had taken a 26 through a wood. 3 it was that he had come across a little mausoleum with an underground 25. This vault, he said, contained a 24 coffin of 30 stone, with a 21 lid, covered with a greenish 16A. Using his spade like a crow-bar, he had been able, with an effort, to 8 the lid. To his horror, he had found, not 23 or bones, but the body of 28 Dracula!

Then, at 29, I knew. My companion wasn't really 2 at all – just one of the living dead! It looked as if my trap had become a veritable 17! He turned his face towards me, baring his fangs like some wild 1A, his 4A curled with a sneer, and his 16D, piercing eyes devoid of all 5. My face was 15 with perspiration, and my jaw began to 19. My shot-22 was useless, I knew. How I wished for a wooden 7 with a sharpened 34 to drive through that monster's 6D – that 24 artery of the heart! I 33 faint with terror, and those approaching fangs were the 29 thing I remembered before passing out.

When I 13, some time 35, I was struck by an awful thought: what kind of vampire would *I* make, having only a 9 of false teeth!

284

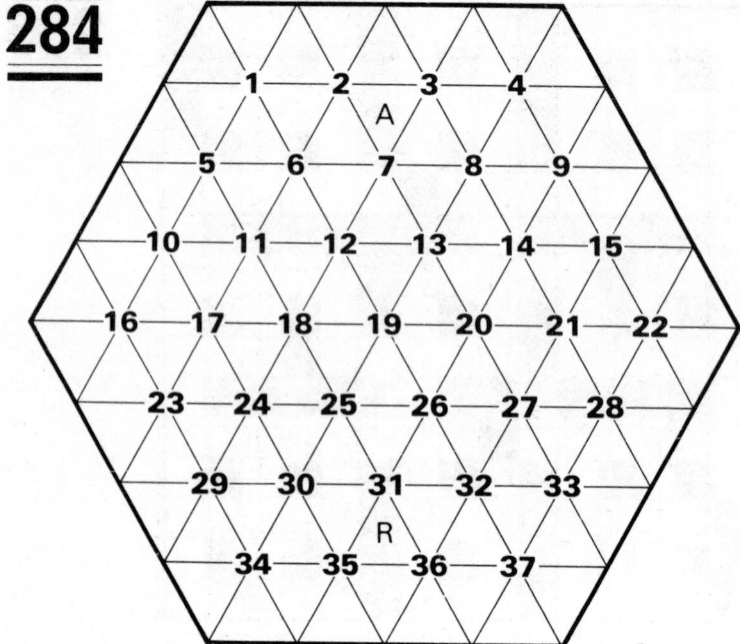

HEXAGON All answers are six-letter words (one hyphenated). Each answer may start in any of the spaces around its clue number, and must then continue either clockwise or anti-clockwise. Two letters have been entered in the diagram to give you a start.

CLUES

1. Grievously
2. Clergyman
3. Attack
4. A momentary look
5. Conditional release from prison
6. A condiment
7. Baby's napkin
8. Type of aircraft
9. A metal grating
10. To pester
11. Military engineer
12. Read carefully
13. Kill
14. Withdraw
15. Brood of young animals
16. Whipped
17. Hoarders of money
18. Calm
19. Begin again
20. More niggardly
21. Occupant
22. Habitual
23. Assessor
24. Seller
25. Make affectionate
26. Looking wide-eyed
27. Pineapple
28. A nine-day devotion
29. Wild excitement
30. Animal that gnaws
31. Tidier
32. Festival
33. Rested sideways
34. Reddish apple
35. Drink dispenser
36. Car suitable for long journeys
37. Bank employee

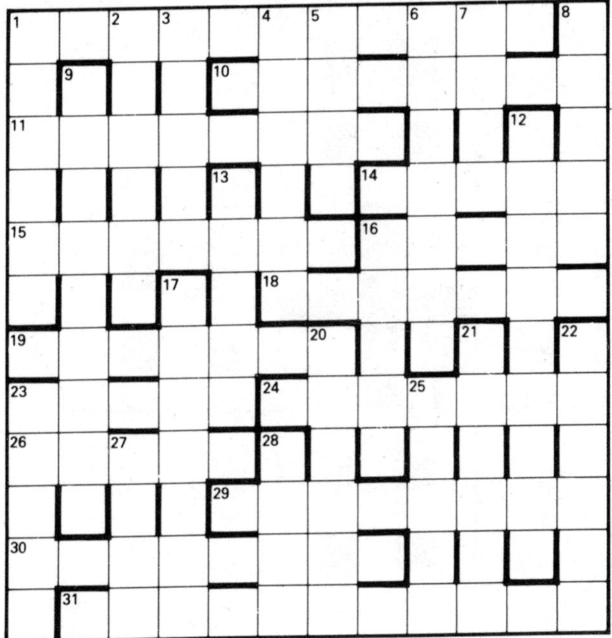

285

MISPRINTS Every Across clue contains a deliberate misprint of one letter. For example, the answer TABLE might be clued as 'BEARD (5)' – which is a misprinted form of BOARD. Down clues are normal.

ACROSS

1. A line from Spain (11)
10. Bores in front of joints (4-4)
11. Fund (8)
14. Right signal (5)
15. Furling (7)
16. Sluts (5)
18. Kind of padding (7)
19. A military change (7)
23. Name of a cook (5)
24. Tamper (7)
26. Old Peruvian rings (5)
29. Jewish yeast (8)
30. Brings (8)
31. Without pith (11)

DOWN

1. Examinations of accounts (6)
2. Preoccupy persistently (6)
3. Narrow parts of bottles (5)
4. Originate (6)
5. A vegetable (4)
6. Enthusiastic applause (7)
7. Facts given (4)
8. Remains of fire (5)
9. Large saloon-car (9)
12. Prevented (9)
13. Resentment (5)
16. Backbone (5)
17. Tropical fever (7)
20. Decorative tuft (6)
21. Longs for (6)
22. Ingratiating (6)
23. Exhausted (5)
25. Implements (5)
27. Dove-house (4)
28. Allurement (4)

286

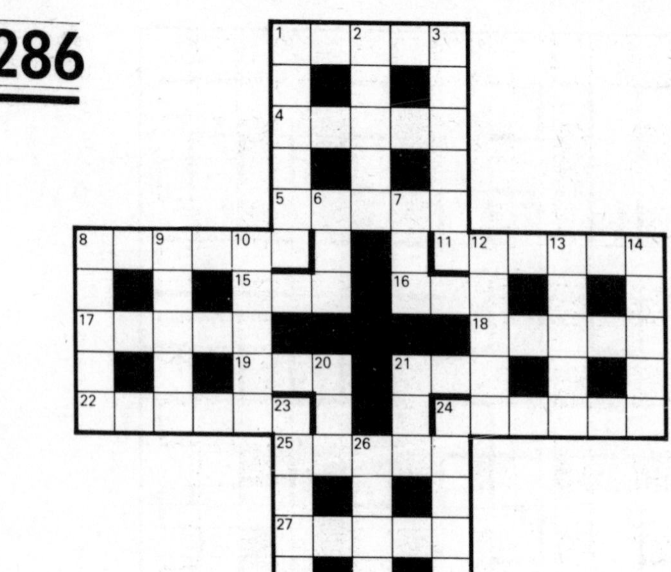

PLUS-SIGN Each clue in block capitals contains one added letter, without changing the order of the other letters. For example, the answer RACKET might be clued as 'BEAT (6)' – which is BAT plus E. The other clues are normal.

ACROSS

1. GRANGES, FOR EXAMPLE (5)
4. BREAD (5)
5. SUITE (5)
8. Wrinkle (6)
11. Ripe (6)
15. Strike gently (3)
16. Snake (3)
17. DRIVER (5)
18. DROVE (5)
19. Rubbish (3)
21. Tiny speck (3)
22. Scope (6)
24. Hunts (6)
25. TIRE (5)
27. SKEWER (5)
28. FACETS (5)

DOWN

1. Begin again (6)
2. SPARING (5)
3. Metrical beat (6)
6. Serpent (3)
7. Young animal (3)
8. BLEND (5)
9. BORDER (5)
10. DREAR (5)
12. GLAND (5)
13. CROWS (5)
14. HOPES (5)
20. Weight (3)
21. Stain (3)
23. Bicycle made for two (6)
24. Eccentrics (6)
26. DRANK (5)

ALPHABETICAL JIGSAW The letter in front of each clue is the first letter of its answer. When you have found all the answers, write them in the diagram wherever they will fit, in the manner of a jigsaw. To give you a start, one answer has already been filled in.

CLUES

A Worthy of love, so fair of face (8)
B One of an old Chaldean race (10)
C Produced by firing potter's clay (7)
D Clears windscreens with a rag or spray (7)
E Destroyed so that no-one may see (6)
F Show off quite ostentatiously (6)
G Proving a source of great delight (10)
H One's dwelling-place for day and night (10)
I Anthems intoned by those who pray (8)
J Rough-edged in an uneven way (6)
K Its donor's e'er in one's mind's eye (8)
L The pressure that one can apply (8)
M I act as go-between in strife (8)
N Promoting growth and healthy life (10)
O The path that suits a spacecraft well (7)
P What's roasted, in or out of shell? (6)
Q Is cowed in spirit, tends to flinch (6)
R Refusing to advance an inch (7)
S A curly line, quite hard to read (8)
T Warm draughts of air that gliders need (8)
U A tree that poisons all around (4)
V Those who no fixed abode have found (8)
W Through this you'll get both light and air (6)
To roam here, there and everywhere (6)
X Fork-tailed is this species of gull (4)
Photo that penetrates one's skull (1-3)
Y Told stories such as travellers' tales (6)
Z This god o'er all the rest prevails (4)

PART 10

JUMBOS

288

ACROSS

1. Jumbo, perhaps, flying near a Pole (9)
6. Trap a spiteful woman taking a small child (5)
9. Good man I found in abode that's dingy and unfriendly (7)
10. Liberal, in club with worker, is conspicuous (7)
11. Melons, for instance, in ancient city eaten by deities (6)
12. Professional model, one who makes toast? (8)
14. A theologian, I changed into something more (8)
16. Condemn to carry out an order (4)
19. Drag one back for a prize (5)
21. One caught in schemes by servant, a person on the level (9)
22. Trouble with breathing – English politician, Henry, has same upset (9)
23. Stagger, having seized Battalion's leader in revolt (5)
25. Obscure pieces, assorted, about fifty (7)
27. A witch's spell uses special jargon, followed by a tear (7)
29. Where an animal is normally found, a little hidden in cover (7)
32. I arrive, all excited, in holiday area (7)
33. Disgusting negative – I'll have a few! (7)
34. Assemble for a short prayer (7)
36. Kind of gamble that offers very little in the starting price (5)
38. Was silent, surprisingly, in an oblique way (9)
40. Cry, being in debt, turning a ghastly colour (9)
42. What a bishop often wears in a joint (5)
43. Terrified, initially, to embrace a ruffian (4)
44. Intimidating person no longer available to start the game (5,3)
48. Good-looking operative – therefore attracting me (8)
50. Here's the spinner – there'll be ducks again, on reflection (6)
53. Awfully bad rule, but it's permanent (7)
54. Former viceroy of Egypt back, finally, at male disreputable resort (7)
55. About to get into port, perhaps, start back (5)
56. Is dosing a devious result of examining patient's symptoms? (9)

DOWN

1. On a level with the view from a Jumbo, like corn in Oklahoma? (2,4,2,2,9,3)
2. About to get solid ring (7)
3. Journeyed back and forth quietly and told stories (5)
4. Declare a delirious person has lost his head (4)
5. Eastern doctor has an old ship to go aboard (6)
6. King, confined in temporary quarters, gets muscular contraction (5)
7. Convert rants wildly over class (9)
8. The girl's clutching at enemies (6)
13. Perfect lake to contend for a prize around (8)
15. Hot drink in yard Dorothy served up (5)
16. One who gives a fellow an alternative (5)
17. Bachelor, a light cavalryman, is an acrobat (8)
18. Shan't greet plane, even for change – such is a Jumbo's reputation! (2,8,5,7)
20. Horrify Dad, turning up with mate (5)
24. Conveyed tedious person around the North (5)
26. Courtyard an Irishman and I love (5)
28. Strange tale set down in print (5)
30. Cheese with nitrogen in it has a very salty taste (5)
31. Believing in God, he is accommodated by teetotaller in charge (8)
34. A stupid mistake, they say, making a loud noise (8)
35. Live way out around the South (5)
37. Spike's piano, not just heard (5)
39. In Calcutta, military language of the East (5)
41. See female show amusement in opera (9)
45. Makes a decree, or makes a row, about one (7)
46. Notice in exhibition you've to follow closely (6)
47. Threaten the little devil with death (6)
49. Bears unusual kind of sword (5)
51. Aged in vessel giving song of praise (5)
52. Large sea-bird that raises other sea-birds (4)

ACROSS

1. The Patron Saint of Wales (5)
4. An Indian dwelling (6)
9. The ridge between a nag's shoulder-bones wastes away (7)
10. The Elizabethan who introduced tobacco to Great Britain (7)
11. Peruvian Indians, in the event – not Eastern (5)
12. An earthwork running from the Wye near Monmouth to a point near Prestatyn (5,4)
13. To dumbfound (6-3)
14. Imposed a money penalty – fair old penny! (5)
15, 51. A German convoy route off the E. Anglian coast, during World War II (1-4,5)
17, 29 Down, 47. A pop singer – and many times unsuccessful parliamentary candidate (9,4,5)
20. Thoroughly (3-3-3)
22. Wild tract produced by a post-war Prime Minister (5)
24. Little child sheltering close at hand, this evening (7)
25. Roman sea-god, giving his name to a planet (7)
27. See 50
28. Wild mountain-goat (4)
33. Diffusion of liquids makes moss so sloppy about start of irrigations (7)
34. Uplift (7)
35. Greek character seen in mouth of river (5)
37. Exceed routine preparations for athletics – with public shower! (9)
38. Chews the cud? Muser ain't crazy! (9)
39. Banter (5)
40. Ability to s-slay (5)
42. A song featured in the film 'Breakfast at Tiffany's' (4,5)
45. Reformed sinner she instals in a hallowed place (9)
47. See 17 Across
48. One who makes an effort kennelling the Queen's dog (7)
49. Permanent dwelling? (7)
50, 27. Old music-hall song, a favourite of Barbers' Quartets (6,4)
51. See 15

DOWN

1. Miserable place where a dentist may work? (4,2,3,5)
2. Assemblage of Papal buildings (7)
3. Formal evening wear – for doctor, with letter, going to clubs, say (5-4)
4. A complete failure (4-3)
5. Long-necked animal (7)
6. Book of maps (5)
7. North African political party briefly raised a negative vote (6)
8. A collie, for example (5-3)
14. This telegraphed item of news is vulgar (5)
16. Belgian port (6)
17. Make a final effort – to emulate a crossbowman? (5,4,4)
18. The capacity to memorise (13)
19. Son of Daedalus, whose flight ended in the Aegean Sea (6)
21. With six-shooter cocked, grabs lumps of gold (7)
23. We're told the man *would* mind! (4)
26. Gift (7)
29. See 17 Across
30. Symbol (6)
31. Kind of hat – strongly criticise one on mother (6)
32. A begging request often heard in early November (5,3,3,3)
36. A girl left an entry in a chronicle (5)
38. See 39 Down
39, 38 Down. A 19th-century poetess whose works include 'In the bleak midwinter' (9,8)
41. To guarantee (6)
42. A dog of mixed breed (7)
43. An animal's in one, performing (2,5)
44. Concentrated sulphuric acid (7)
46. Erect beams, we're told (5)

289

ACROSS

1. Fabricates, including bit of a tale? Jumbo never does (7)
5. My, more changes! – But Jumbo can always rely on this (6)
8. Half rest limbs? Jumbo does (9)
9. Fleet vehicle's back – end of journey (4)
11. What could help to make you less reserved in manner? (4)
12. Dash out of hiding from thicket, audibly, reaching creek by river (5,5)
14. The plane's designed as a Jumbo (8)
15. Light timber, a thick slice, carried back (5)
17. Sheep's stomach provides for Rugby Union chaps (5)
19. Strenuous spell of work, with lading of fruits, in captain's record (5,3)
22. The *car* ain't crocked – it's the *fuel* (10)
23. Number turned to the Church, in the past (4)
25. Each one has a point, true (5)
27. Tight cord net, tangled (9)
29. Having made will, try brew of tea (7)
31. Conspirator from Left caught by a clay-worker (7)
32. Man glutted – swelling with vermouth – paused (9)
33. Cry over one French shipman (5)
35. Blue dye, last of indigo, in bundle (4)
36. Bad, the strike – unofficial (3,3,4)
39. Game bird in season, back around North (8)
41. Fellow in army squad, in poor shape (5)
43. Tremulous, like a swan (5)
45. Sportive? A few will go after lions, Jumbos, etc. (8)
48. Nark the narrator? (4-6)
50. Work produced by Poe, unfinished, about America (4)
52. Spike first of barrels behind pub (4)
53. Gather together again? Jumbos do (9)
55. Make a second visit? Jumbo's very likely to do so (6)
56. Men delirious in part of the Orient – but this never afflicts Jumbo (7)

DOWN

1. Tree giving warm cover, it's said (3)
2. Storm about and batter bell-boy (7)
3. Jane Austen's heroine is found among them, maybe (4)
4. Second trial, for fleecing sheep (8)
5. Unmarried girl has a pound for a prayer-book (6)
6. Feverishly elated, the chap needs a lot of ice (5)
7. See four in genuine recovery (7)
10. Thrice Jumbo-size, and plump, the lady's relatives! (5-5-12)
11. Others hear how a tent gets prepared – for a spectacle which surely includes a Jumbo or two? (3,8,4,2,5)
13. A cut of beef Sappers picked up, for a black eye (6)
15. Breakfast roll, or portion of cob, apparently (3)
16. Moisten, we're told, then sharpen a blade on the oil-stone (4)
18. Half a farthing's about right for this joint (5)
20. Most protracted part of Gospels absorbed by solitary saint (7)
21. Terrible easterly he cites, for the freeze-up over the whole region (3-5)
24. Bury cat in craggy ben (6)
26. A positive pig-house, full of froth (6)
28. Speed shown by pair revising song, we hear (8)
30. Support us in a spot (7)
34. Smell the soot on a wick (5)
37. Play 500, for the kitty (4)
38. Former dude, working, sweated (6)
40. Kind of double entendre implicit in quip? Unintended (3)
42. Northern secret agency under a girl (English) here in Spain (8)
44. An attendant at court hoards wicked loot (7)
46. Sea-birds, outsize victims (7)
47. More than one 'mate' includes pointless decoy? (6)
49. I snapped up a bone (5)
51. General's captured leader of Liberators in a valley (4)
54. Drink, for fresh-water duck, no end (3)

290

THE SOLUTIONS

Answers to cryptic clues are printed in an explanatory form, so as to correspond with the wording of their clues. They may be split into parts (e.g. disc-lose), show one word inside or outside another (e.g. s-at-in), or simply state whether an anagram (anag.), two meanings (two mngs.), a reversal (rev.), and so on, are involved.

PART 1

No.1
ACROSS: 1. slap 4. dash 8. niggard 9. ape 10. drill 12. eager 13. calls 15. purse 17. bee 18. candles 20. asps 21. Aden
DOWN: 2. leg 3. pearl 4. dodge 5. swagger 6. Enid 7. leer 11. illness 13. cube 14. sacks 15. panda 16. easy 19. lie

No.2
ACROSS: 6. kennel 7. rule 8. opal 9. bigger 10. flare 12. abuse 15. aghast 17. size 19. sofa 20. Indian
DOWN: 1. jeep 2. antler 3. globe 4. brag 5. fleets 11. legion 13. beside 14. stain 16. Alan 18. zeal

No.3
ACROSS: 1. mural 4. right 7. limited 8. rag 9. stable 11. cast 13. bear 14. hidden 17. boa 18. melting 20. exact 21. repel
DOWN: 1. mules 2. rum 3. little 4. rode 5. garland 6. tight 10. Alabama 12. killer 13. Bible 15. Nigel 16. smut 19. imp

No.4
ACROSS: 1. entertain 8. options 9. Eli 10. false 12. smash 13. digit 15. laden 16. nit 17. pebbles 19. tradesman
DOWN: 2. net 3. erode 4. tusks 5. Iceland 6. confident 7. dishonest 11. lighter 14. toped 15. lobes 18. lea

No.5
ACROSS: 1. tom 3. knights 7. urged 8. olive 9. batter 10. atom 12. gate 14. verger 18. aglow 19. drawn 20. expired 21. tie
DOWN: 1. thumb 2. might 3. kidded 4. iron 5. hoist 6. steam 11. mended 12. grave 13. tulip 15. grant 16. range 17. ewer

No.6
ACROSS: 1. cross 4. patch 7. preface 8. ark 9. end 11. prefer 13. groped 16. ere 18. Pan 19. extorts 21. reeds 22. spell
DOWN: 1. copper 2. one 3. sharp 4. piece 5. trapeze 6. hake 10. derange 12. vessel 14. press 15. dotes 17. spur 20. rye

No.7
ACROSS: 1. rap 3. shaking 7. icing 8. baker 9. stay 10. radii 13. horse 15. push 17. rivet 19. pause 20. sundaes 21. sly
DOWN: 1. raid 2. pointer 3. soggy 4. amber 5. ink 6. gerbil 11. discuss 12. chores 14. extra 15. pipes 16. very 18. van

No.8
ACROSS: 1. convent 5. ham 7. Colin 8. molar 9. excise 11. bay 13. ads 14. jutted 17. trice 18. Turin 20. hog 21. kingdom
DOWN: 1. cache 2. nil 3. Ernest 4. tomb 5. halibut 6. marry 10. casting 12. button 13. aitch 15. denim 16. jerk 19. rod

No.9
ACROSS: 5. repast 7. Cain 8. pale 9. opened 10. Nile 12. inch 15. palace 17. rump 18. lute 19. tureen
DOWN: 1. retain 2. gale 3. screen 4. lime 6. tool 11. leaped 13. Humber 14. pest 16. ague 17. rare

No.10
ACROSS: 1. penguin 5. rut 7. confine 8. map 9. lard 11. Laura 14. Devil 15. stye 17. tar 18. trident 20. Poe 21. haggled
DOWN: 1. pickled 2. nun 3. unit 4. needle 5. remount 6. top 10. reverse 12. abetted 13. flitch 16. ling 17. tap 19. ell

No.11
ACROSS: 1. gold 4. rush 8. Commons 9. pup 10. tease 12. skint 13. robot 15. regal 17. cur 18. raffled 20. halo 21. espy
DOWN: 2. ohm 3. drove 4. risks 5. sapping 6. scut 7. spit 11. Alberta 13. rick 14. torso 15. rifle 16. ludo 19. lap

No.12
ACROSS: 6. shrimp 7. oust 8. swan 9. mellow 10. stole 12. flute 15. ampere 17. nave 19. dear 20. veered
DOWN: 1. chow 2. Lionel 3. spume 4. foal 5. assort 11. timber 13. linger 14. leave 16. earl 18. vied

No. 13
ACROSS: 1. popes 4. shove 7. magical 8. fig 9. seemed 11. free 13. copy 14. wooden 17. bun 18. paragon 20. avert 21. windy
DOWN: 1. pumas 2. pig 3. sicken 4. sole 5. offered 6. eagle 10. expense 12. sorrow 13. cobra 15. nanny 16. spot 19. gin

No. 14
ACROSS: 1. strangled 8. luggage 9. ant 10. cabin 12. doing 13. pails 15. tenon 16. oft 17. annuals 19. protector
DOWN: 2. tug 3. again 4. greed 5. elation 6. Blackpool 7. staginess 11. blister 14. slant 15. tunic 18. ago.

No. 15
ACROSS: 1. jet 3. florist 7. mixed 8. expel 9. occult 10. byes 12. tiff 14. bandit 18. plume 19. liver 20. coddled 21. rue
DOWN: 1. jumbo 2. toxic 3. fiddle 4. oxen 5. imply 6. talks 11. ballad 12. topic 13. found 15. Dover 16. three 17. fell

No. 16
ACROSS: 1. gases 4. armed 7. blemish 8. tor 9. lad 11. tanker 13. gauged 16. sob 18. tun 19. askance 21. dated 22. sight
DOWN: 1. gobble 2. see 3. stint 4. ashen 5. matters 6. dire 10. drag-net 12. ablest 14. gland 15. dukes 17. stud 20. nag

No. 17
ACROSS: 1. bag 3. grumble 7. exile 8. dudes 9. vase 10. rotor 13. erect 15. ruin 17. elbow 19. bathe 20. dawdled 21. elk
DOWN: 1. beet 2. grimace 3. grebe 4. under 5. bud 6. ensure 11. thistle 12. legend 14. towel 15. rabid 16. peak 18. bow

No. 18
ACROSS: 1. cobbler 5. fog 7. donor 8. Beryl 9. Trojan 11. ivy 13. arc 14. tether 17. evade 18. knack 20. Ted 21. hurdles
DOWN: 1. cadet 2. bin 3. larvae 4. ruby 5. furnish 6. gully 10. orchard 12. beaker 13. adept 15. rakes 16. mesh 19. ail

No. 19
ACROSS: 5. carrot 7. tale 8. stub 9. rotten 10. damp 12. odes 15. basset 17. grip 18. file 19. gambol
DOWN: 1. lasted 2. crab 3. stated 4. flue 6. Tory 11. master 13. sailor 14. stag 16. arid 17. gamp

No. 20
ACROSS: 1. tombola 5. dip 7. obtrude 8. rig 9. Bude 11. David 14. erupt 15. Edna 17. jam 18. enslave 20. war 21. deepest
DOWN: 1. trouble 2. mat 3. opus 4. agenda 5. derived 6. peg 10. drummer 12. dearest 13. attend 16. isle 17. jaw 19. ace

No. 21
ACROSS: 1. coal 4. mine 8. intense 9. dam 10. tomes 12. swift 13. begin 15. lager 17. Dan 18. vaguely 20. mail 21. lift
DOWN: 2. oat 3. lungs 4. meets 5. nudging 6. pint 7. emit 11. magenta 13. Bede 14. novel 15. legal 16. rays 19. elf

No. 22
ACROSS: 6. panama 7. Edam 8. skid 9. mutton 10. thyme 12. geese 15. embers 17. soya 19. semi 20. raglan
DOWN: 1. yank 2. tandem 3. palms 4. Kent 5. barons 11. hamper 13. ensign 14. tsars 16. exit 18. year

No. 23
ACROSS: 1. quail 4. sprig 7. epitaph 8. cod 9. ragout 11. tidy 13. sand 14. weasel 17. ego 18. calls on 20. feast 21. witch
DOWN: 1. queer 2. Ali 3. league 4. Soho 5. Rockies 6. giddy 10. gondola 12. fellow 13. shelf 15. lunch 16. Scot 19. set

No. 24
ACROSS: 1. abundance 8. harbour 9. awe 10. tribe 12. logic 13. Ascot 15. burst 16. din 17. adulate 19. megaphone
DOWN: 2. bar 3. noose 4. aural 5. clanger 6. Shetlands 7. beech-tree 11. incense 14. tiara 15. blush 18. Ann

No. 25
ACROSS: 1. dog 3. monster 7. brown 8. reign 9. temper 10. etch 12. barn 14. barked 18. cover 19. exams 20. nonplus 21. ass
DOWN: 1. début 2. groom 3. manger 4. norm 5. twist 6. ranch 11. caress 12. bacon 13. raven 15. koala 16. desks 17. oral

No. 26
ACROSS: 1. Nesta 4. carat 7. tumbler 8. saw 9. rob 11. yellow 13. blocks 16. eye 18. yen 19. meander 21. event 22. frost
DOWN: 1. nature 2. sum 3. alloy 4. carol 5. restore 6. town 10. balance 12. ferret 14. comet 15. scarf 17. tyre 20. duo

No. 27
ACROSS: 1. jab 3. furrows 7. camel 8. bread 9. many 10. ingot 13. Hades 15. hark 17. razor 19. Malta 20. swelter 21. alp
DOWN: 1. jack 2. bombard 3. filly 4. rabbi 5. owe 6. sedate 11. gorilla 12. shires 14. sprat 15. Homer 16. carp 18. Zoe

No. 28
ACROSS: 1. pelican 5. pat 7. argue 8. octet 9. entire 11. elm 13. ban 14. crisis 17. irate 18. worse 20. fad 21. silvery
DOWN: 1. plane 2. lag 3. cherry 4. nook 5. potters 6. totem 10. tankard 12. trowel 13. brief 15. seedy 16. less 19. roe

No. 29
ACROSS: 5. chilli 7. roam 8. drug 9. anthem 10. same 12. snow 15. chance 17. pelt 18. fame 19. neuter
DOWN: 1. charms 2. flog 3. Briton 4. Tate 6. Ivan 11. monkey 13. wallet 14. mean 16. heat 17. plum

No. 30
ACROSS: 1. harvest 5. sot 7. tapioca 8. Amy 9. Hull

11. Cupid 14. tacks 15. Slav 17. foe 18. outlaws 20. pen 21. tangled
DOWN: 1. hatchet 2. rep 3. Eton 4. trance 5. scalpel 6. toy 10. lectern 12. devised 13. escort 16. stun 17. fop 19. awl

No. 31
ACROSS: 1. cold 4. maze 8. allowed 9. tag 10. tints 12. yield 13. alpha 15. posed 17. emu 18. guarded 20. fear 21. even
DOWN: 2. oil 3. dawns 4. muddy 5. zithers 6. cart 7. aged 11. Neptune 13. apex 14. anger 15. place 16. dodo 19. doe

No. 32
ACROSS: 6. jackal 7. help 8. zest 9. faggot 10. joust 12. house 15. active 17. task 19. hilt 20. linden
DOWN: 1. haze 2. skates 3. cliff 4. thug 5. blooms 11. orchid 13. Ostend 14. jelly 16. iota 18. seep

No. 33
ACROSS: 1. barge 4. Poles 7. lawyers 8. nib 9. enrage 11. cote 13. pact 14. bonnet 17. oar 18. blasted 20. fusty 21. newly
DOWN: 1. bulge 2. raw 3. energy 4. post 5. Lincoln 6. sable 10. records 12. domain 13. proof 15. toddy 16. obey 19. tow

No. 34
ACROSS: 1. imperfect 8. Margate 9. urn 10. rated 12. drake 13. verse 15. dwell 16. sun 17. excused 19. rectitude
DOWN: 2. mar 3. eland 4. fiend 5. crusade 6. improvise 7. interlude 11. Terence 14. elect 15. ducat 18. sod

No. 35
ACROSS: 1. boy 3. foresee 7. Andes 8. chess 9. sullen 10. wail 12. pork 14. wishes 18. apple 19. mange 20. minster 21. yet
DOWN: 1. brass 2. yodel 3. faster 4. rack 5. Sheba 6. easel 11. simmer 12. psalm 13. Ripon 15. honey 16. sleet 17. belt

No. 36
ACROSS: 1. bites 4. capon 7. fixture 8. rug 9. low 11. detain 13. dimmer 16. lax 18. rot 19. spindle 21. creed 22. eject
DOWN: 1. baffle 2. tax 3. sound 4. crest 5. partial 6. nigh 10. whistle 12. expert 14. mused 15. Rhine 17. Eric 20. die

No. 37
ACROSS: 1. bib 3. holster 7. after 8. banal 9. dean 10. yearn 13. fancy 15. bush 17. ether 19. tenor 20. treason 21. cut
DOWN: 1. bray 2. between 3. Huron 4. lobby 5. ton 6. relent 11. arsenic 12. effect 14. yards 15. baton 16. fret 18. hoe

No. 38
ACROSS: 1. javelin 5. bat 7. Latin 8. waist 9. Yankee 11. try 13. hat 14. scheme 17. Maria 18. usual 20. due 21. cistern
DOWN: 1. jolly 2. vat 3. linnet 4. newt 5. bristle 6. tatty 10. nut-tree 12. occurs 13. humid 15. Ellen 16. talc 19. Ure

No. 39
ACROSS: 5. quarts 7. boil 8. chum 9. scaled 10. lily 12. snub 15. summer 17. pent 18. adze 19. beaten
DOWN: 1. bushel 2. dram 3. obtain 4. wire 6. sash 11. lumber 13. banner 14. drab 16. Urdu 17. pray

No. 40
ACROSS: 1. Galileo 5. bog 7. altered 8. sad 9. envy 11. stiff 14. stove 15. ogre 17. ore 18. ravioli 20. bit 21. scratch
DOWN: 1. goatees 2. lot 3. lark 4. oldest 5. basking 6. god 10. violent 12. Flemish 13. beards 16. over 17. orb 19. out

No. 41
ACROSS: 1. slab 4. seek 8. tempest 9. pod 10. rigid 12. drain 13. peels 15. links 17. kin 18. respond 20. fray 21. soft
DOWN: 2. lam 3. blend 4. sated 5. explain 6. stir 7. Eden 11. gleaner 13. pike 14. surly 15. lists 16. soda 19. off

No. 42
ACROSS: 6. mutter 7. jeer 8. clad 9. perils 10. steep 12. acids 15. emerge 17. asks 19. lean 20. organs
DOWN: 1. full 2. stodge 3. grape 4. ajar 5. pealed 11. tamper 13. charge 14. felon 16. rant 18. king

No. 43
ACROSS: 1. doped 4. rouge 7. arraign 8. lit 9. tested 11. anil 13. swag 14. missal 17. ear 18. article 20. sewer 21. robes
DOWN: 1 draft 2. par 3. drivel 4. rind 5. uplands 6. extol 10. sparrow 12. winter 13. sheds 15. Leeds 16. lair 19. cob

No. 44
ACROSS: 1. paragraph 8. sweeten 9. owl 10. enter 12. crumb 13. siren 15. swede 16. own 17. miracle 19. considers
DOWN: 2. ale 3. actor 4. runic 5. profuse 6. ascension 7. clobbered 11. Toronto 14. names 15. shred 18. car

No. 45
ACROSS: 1. jug 3. secrete 7. dream 8. Largo 9. simple 10. shoe 12. posh 14. banger 18. rumba 19. viola 20. denials 21. mum
DOWN: 1. Judas 2. gleam 3. sample 4. cell 5. earth 6. elope 11. canvas 12. pared 13. Simon 15. gloom 16. realm 17. saga

No. 46
ACROSS: 1. hutch 4. ounce 7. cockles 8. mad 9. lug 11. extant 13. plight 16. Esk 18. hue 19. reliant 21. tango 22. notch
DOWN: 1. heckle 2. tic 3. halve 4. onset 5. nominee 6. eddy 10. galleon 12. sketch 14. Garbo 15. talon 17. whet 20. art

No. 47
ACROSS: 1. yak 3. flutter 7. Koran 8. canon 9. weal 10. rupee 13. ousel 15. gnaw 17. merit 19. overt 20. compost 21. sow
DOWN: 1. yoke 2. kernels 3. final 4. ulcer 5. tan 6. ranger 11. players 12. cosmic 14. lotto 15. groat 16. stew 18. rim

No. 48
ACROSS: 1. content 5. rub 7. adder 8. revel 9. Horace 11. Kew 13. cup 14. paddle 17. pasty 18. guile 20. Dee 21. element
DOWN: 1. coach 2. nod 3. enrich 4. tarn 5. revoked 6. below 10. riposte 12. bangle 13. coped 15. exert 16. byre 19. ire

No. 49
ACROSS: 5. fading 7. loom 8. Brie 9. landed 10. Tass 12. shag 15. plaice 17. barb 18. Utah 19. sallow
DOWN: 1. parrot 2. pile 3. blench 4. core 6. gull 11. slight 13. Gordon 14. mess 16. lath 17. bill

No. 50
ACROSS: 1. buzzard 5. sit 7. Lapland 8. apt 9. awry 11. later 14. trawl 15. area 17. ski 18. garnish 20. pug 21. trained
DOWN: 1. ballast 2. zip 3. alas 4. doddle 5. starter 6. tot 10. reading 12. reached 13. blight 16. aria 17. sop 19. inn

PART 2

No. 51
ACROSS: 1. thigh 4. gambler 8. referee 9. dingo (din-go) 10. brat 11. adjacent 13. feeler 14. soaked 17. changing 19. pulp 22. sepia 23. sticker 24. scented 25. leech (two mngs.)
DOWN: 1. throb 2. inflame 3. harp 4. Glenda 5. mediator 6. lance 7. roosted 12. sergeant (serge-ant) 13. focuses 15. knuckle 16. unused 18. ample (hidden in 'sAMPLEs') 20. porch 21. will (Will)

No. 52
ACROSS: 6. mineral 7. chief 8. sandal 9. window 10. practising 12. undeterred 16. accept 17. people 18. leper (rev. of repel) 19. fussing
DOWN: 1. vital (two mngs.) 2. send up 3. parliament 4. things 5. recount (re-count) 9. water-spout 11. knocker 13. eleven 14. drowsy 15. plank

No. 53
ACROSS: 1. recruits 5. scar (hidden in 'man'S CARtilage') 9. cramp 10. impress 11. storks (sound of stalks) 12. Roman 14. elders (two mngs.) 16. adjoin 19. eaves 21. invite 24. bowling 25. tamer 26. rude (sound of rued) 27. peasants
DOWN: 1. rice (R-ice) 2. charted 3. upper 4. thirst 6. cream 7. resonant 8. spared 13. December 15. Russia 17. ottoman 18. tingle 20. vowed (V-owed) 22. votes 23. errs

No. 54
ACROSS: 1. girder 5. glared 9. strung 10. scenic 11. trot 12. shadowed 14. smudge 16. seeded (two mngs.) 19. harassed 21. aide (hidden in 'regaliA, I'D Expect') 22. regale (Reg-ale) 23. outlay 24. setter (two mngs.) 25. sadist
DOWN: 2. interim (inter-'im) 3. doubted 4. registers 6. laced 7. renewed 8. decided 13. assiduous 14. spheres 15. upright 17. exalted 18. endears 20. solve.

No. 55
ACROSS: 1. Antarctica 7. hurling (two mngs.) 8. bonds 10. Reds 11. February 13. collar 15. rustic 17. examined 18. Asia 21. singe (hidden in 'flameS IN GEneral') 22. scuttle (two mngs.) 23. trespasser
DOWN: 1. aired 2. toil 3. ragged (two mngs.) 4. Tiberius 5. contact (con-tact) 6. characters (two mngs.) 9. skyscraper 12. laziness 14. learner 16. Red Sea 19. satyr 20. hugs

No. 56
ACROSS: 1. albums 4. metals 8. hilltop 10. hover 11. respect 12. candy (C-Andy) 13. quicksilver 18. Moses 19. in store 22. louse 23. minting 24. modest (mode-St.) 25. dealer (two mngs.)
DOWN: 1. ashore (ash-ore) 2. bells (sound of belles) 3. mitre 5. ethical 6. advance 7. sprays (two mngs.) 9. potassium 14. unsound 15. caskets 16. emblem 17. beggar 20. sense 21. oriel (Oriel)

No. 57
ACROSS: 1. skull 4. mugging 8. cowered (sound of coward) 9. Ghana 10. sent 11. flannels 13. muscle (sound of mussel) 14. rinses 17. scraping 19. chap (two mngs.) 22. undue 23. scowled 24. stepson 25. harry
DOWN: 1. sects 2. unwinds 3. lure 4. meddle (sound of medal) 5. gigantic 6. inane 7. glasses (two mngs.) 12. clippers (two mngs.) 13. museums 15. scholar 16. unison 18. ridge (hidden in 'CambRIDGEshire') 20. Paddy 21. both

No. 58
ACROSS: 6. reprove (rep-rove) 7. sword (hidden in 'crosSWORDs') 8. runner (two mngs.) 9. depose 10. Open Sesame 12. dining-room 16. closet 17. duster 18. gnash 19. entrant
DOWN: 1. Venus (hidden in 'heaVEN, USually') 2. bronco 3. overweight 4. swipes (two mngs.) 5. irksome 9. despondent 11. willing 13. insist 14. misery 15. Berne

No. 59
ACROSS: 1. bathroom 5. pass (two mngs.) 9. wrist 10. tricked 11. eggs on (egg-son) 12. dowse (hidden in 'meaDOW, SEarching') 14. ladies 16. menial 19. nosed 21. unwell 24. endured 25. naive 26. sink 27. revealed
DOWN: 1. bawl (sound of ball) 2. twigged 3. rites 4. outing 6. askew 7. suddenly 8. riddle 13. blankets 15. eiders (eider-down) 17. ill-will 18. bundle 20. sedan 22. wince 23. weld

No. 60
ACROSS: 1. Sandra 5. presto 9. garret 10. scrawl 11. boob (the same when reversed) 12. morphine 14. assent (as-sent) 16. vandal 19. peacocks 21. cuff 22. Antrim (ant-rim) 23. intact (in tact) 24. errand 25. grease
DOWN: 2. Amazons 3. durable 4. automatic 6. recap 7. sea-bird 8. oil-well 13. ravishing 14. appease 15. shatter (hidden in 'craSH AT TERminus') 17. necktie 18. affects 20. onion

No. 61
ACROSS: 1. masquerade 7. outrage 8. lunge 10. toll (two mngs.) 11. merchant 13. nutmeg 15. stoker 17. Norseman 18. idol (sound of idle) 21. sauna 22. imitate 23. references
DOWN: 1. motel 2. span 3. uneven 4. relocate 5. Denmark 6. continents 9. enthralled 12. delegate 14. torture 16. marine 19. drags (D-rags) 20. zinc

No. 62
ACROSS: 1. in-laws 4. scraps (two mngs.) 8. Vanessa 10. arena 11. inherit 12. evict (hidden in 'thEVICTims') 13. spectacular 18. hurry 19. top-hats 22. point (two mngs.) 23. deliver 24. digest 25. pellet
DOWN: 1. in vain 2. lynch 3. wiser 5. château 6. America 7. shanty (two mngs.) 9. attracted 14. parting 15. coyotes 16. shaped 17. esprit 20. pulse 21. anvil (hidden in 'E. AngliAN VILlage')

No. 63
ACROSS: 1. hatch 4. sickles 8. session 9. annex (Anne-X) 10. yell 11. disperse 13. mostly 14. toucan 17. tenement 19. cram (two mngs.) 22. lupin 23. purport 24. discord (Di's-cord) 25. dance
DOWN: 1. hasty 2. tussles 3. hail (two mngs.) 4. sunlit 5. champion 6. liner 7. sixteen 12. flamingo (flaming-O) 13. mottled 15. cartoon 16. sniped 18. napes 20. metre (hidden in 'liME-TREes') 21. grid

No. 64
ACROSS: 6. giraffe 7. major 8. casual 9. retail 10. rock-garden 12. administer 16. prison 17. nought 18. usher 19. sliding
DOWN: 1. Titan (tit-an) 2. valuer 3. affliction 4. falter 5. conifer 9. right angle 11. address 13. instep (in step) 14. rounds 15. chant (hidden in 'churCH ANThems')

No. 65
ACROSS: 1. cauldron 5. grab 9. skill 10. leaders 11. modern (mode-RN) 12. upset (two mngs.) 14. sentry 16. bottle 19. ethos 21. cigars 24. swimmer 25. maize 26. rash (two mngs.) 27. crescent
DOWN: 1. cask (C-ask) 2. unicorn 3. delve 4. oblong 6. reeks (hidden in 'cREEK, Smouldering') 7. besotted 8. Caruso 13. assessor 15. résumé (resume) 17. termite 18. scorer (score-R) 20. hairs 22. games 23. Lent

No. 66
ACROSS: 1. groove 5. starch 9. impede 10. pillar 11. clod 12. gargoyle 14. bridle 16. prudes 19. instance (in-stance) 21. pips (two mngs.) 22. exists 23. spruce (two mngs.) 24. steers (two mngs.) 25. disuse
DOWN: 2. rambler (two mngs.) 3. overdid 4. evergreen 6. tying (hidden in 'jetTY IN Galway') 7. relayed 8. harness 13. repressed (re-pressed) 14. bribers 15. inspire 17. umpires 18. expects 20. altar

No. 67
ACROSS: 1. red herring 7. hopping 8. muted 10. side (sound of sighed) 11. enhances 13. larder 15. studio 17. instruct 18. bait 21. gusto (hidden in 'AuGUST Only') 22. ovation 23. aspersions
DOWN: 1. roped 2. drip 3. engine 4. remnants 5. noticed 6. chiselling (two mngs.) 9. distorting 12. fearsome 14. resists 16. across 19. amiss (a-miss) 20. dado

No. 68
ACROSS: 1. takers 4. flocks 8. Marconi 10. cargo (car-go) 11. longest 12. smite 13. countryside 18. lofts 19. endives (hidden in 'friEND I'VE Several') 22. Crete 23. twanged 24. rotate 25. havens
DOWN: 1. temple (two mngs.) 2. Karen 3. Rhône 5. locusts 6. carried 7. snored 9. intercept 14. offbeat (off-beat) 15. nascent 16. slicer 17. asides (a-side's) 20. drama 21. vogue

No. 69
ACROSS: 1. miser 4. Satanic 8. rivalry 9. imbue 10. hurt 11. seamless 13. talent 14. knives 17. realised 19. iris (Iris) 22. igloo 23. tea-time 24. extreme 25. mince

No. 69 (continued)
DOWN: 1. marsh 2. several (sever-Al) 3. roll (sound of role) 4. styled 5. trimming 6. noble 7. creases 12. antidote 13. turbine 15. version 16. centre 18. allot (all-'ot) 20. sieve (rev. of Eve-is) 21. calm

No. 70
ACROSS: 6. roseate 7. slain 8. sonata 9. morose (MO-rose) 10. liberation 12. colourless (two mngs.) 16. belfry 17. switch 18. funny 19. adapted
DOWN: 1. motor 2. recall (re-call) 3. strawberry 4. claret 5. mission 9. Merseyside 11. hopeful 13. offend (off end) 14. slippy 15. scree

No. 71
ACROSS: 1. truncate 5. vest 9. skein (two mngs.) 10. remorse (re-Morse) 11. eschew 12. dolts 14. relish 16. stupor 19. aspen (as-pen) 21. rubber 24. entrust 25. swell (two mngs.) 26. sore 27. arrested
DOWN: 1. toss 2. utensil 3. cinch 4. throws 6. enrol 7. treasure 8. amidst 13. breakers 15. sinful 17. prefect 18. crater 20. Peter (pet-ER) 22. baste 23. plod (hidden in 'cheaP LODgings')

No. 72
ACROSS: 1. titfer 5. scared 9. spiced 10. battle 11. also 12. Mounties 14. person (per-son) 16. forger 19. promises 21. mace (two mngs.) 22. litter (two mngs.) 23. elapse 24. repute 25. spends
DOWN: 2. impulse 3. factors 4. rudiments 6. chain 7. ratting 8. dresser 13. unfastens 14. popular 15. roof-top 17. rampage 18. encased 20. inert

No. 73
ACROSS: 1. arithmetic 7. eastern 8. gapes 10. gaps 11. cushions 13. billet 15. sleeve 17. undercut (two mngs.) 18. shut (S.-hut) 21. spine (rev. of 'e-nips) 22. hearten (hear-ten) 23. sentiments
DOWN: 1. Aesop 2. idea 3. honour 4. eggshell (two mngs.) 5. improve (imp-rove) 6. neighbours 9. suspecting 12. merriest 14. Luddite 16. Durham 19. hates 20. pawn (two mngs.)

No. 74
ACROSS: 1. demean 4. tripod 8. cutlass (cut-lass) 10. droop 11. essence 12. inept 13. Lanarkshire 18. cages 19. exhumed 22. crier 23. serious 24. ash-can 25. unseen
DOWN: 1. decked 2. moths 3. amain (a-main) 5. reddish (Red-dish) 6. pioneer 7. deputy 9. speckless 14. anguish 15. Austria 16. acacia 17. Edison (rev. of no side) 20. heron 21. moose

No. 75
ACROSS: 1. swamp 4. pompous 8. reality 9. react (re-act) 10. mode 11. calories 13. Monday 14. weekly (sound of weakly) 17. speedily 19. gnat 22. idiot 23. ceramic 24. guesses 25. tenet (the same when reversed)
DOWN: 1. scram 2. abandon (two mngs.) 3. pain 4. pay-day 5. moreover 6. okapi (hidden in 'booK, A PIcture') 7. satisfy 12. mandates (man-dates) 13. missing 15. kinsman 16. clocks 18. elide 20. tacit 21. grit

No. 76
ACROSS: 6. staring 7. graph 8. fettle 9. prince 10. dispensary 12. ammunition 16. assert 17. tugged 18. annul 19. pretend
DOWN: 1. steel (sound of steal) 2. grated 3. underskirt 4. trails 5. epicure 9. prehistory 11. amusing (am-using) 13. uterus 14. negate 15. penny (Penny)

No. 77
ACROSS: 1. cleavage 5. warp 9. steal 10. octagon 11. repent 12. parch 14. potato 16. leaden 19. Roger (two mngs.) 21. hybrid 24. instant 25. sabre 26. gust 27. grandeur
DOWN: 1. cosy 2. Everest (hidden in 'sEVERE STorm') 3. valve 4. grotto 6. augur 7. penchant (pen-chant) 8. staple 13. sporting 15. turban 17. dribble 18. whiter 20. gasps 22. bison 23. sear (sound of seer)

No. 78
ACROSS: 1. closed 5. static 9. abbess 10. region 11. stet 12. umbrella 14. briers (two mngs.) 16. mortar (two mngs.) 19. cascades 21. coma 22. enamel 23. empire 24. salute 25. lasers
DOWN: 2. lobster 3. sceptre 4. disguised 6. their 7. triplet (trip-let) 8. centaur 13. bombshell 14. buckets 15. install (in-stall) 17. recipes 18. admirer 20. alert

No. 79
ACROSS: 1. Lancashire 7. descant (hidden in 'briDES CAN Talk') 8. spurt 10. Ouse (sound of ooze) 11. quipping 13. impels 15. spigot 17. hanger-on 18. alto 21. Sonia (hidden in 'perSON I Appear') 22. treacle 23. penetrated
DOWN: 1. loses 2. neat 3. artful 4. hosepipe 5. rousing 6. admonishes 9. tight-ropes 12. alienate (alien-ate) 14. penance 16. porter (two mngs.) 19. lucid 20. pert

No. 80
ACROSS: 1. ribbon 4. ankles 8. matador 10. plain (two mngs.) 11. layered 12. inset (in-set) 13. crystalline 18. cocoa 19. instead 22. acorn (a-corn) 23. narrate 24. reside 25. revere
DOWN: 1. rumble 2. batty (two mngs.) 3. order (two mngs.) 5. nuptial 6. liaison 7. sanity 9. radiation 14. rectors 15. scanned 16. éclair 17. adhere 20. spree 21. erase (hidden in 'answER, AS Entered')

PART 3

No. 81
ACROSS: 1. pivot 4. lofty 7. canteen 8. rue 9. sector 11. bold 13. swan 14. picnic 17. rig 18. rebound 20. mercy 21. Nancy
DOWN: 1. Picts 2. vin 3. tremor 4. lend 5. forlorn 6. yield 10. charger 12. ribbon 13. scrum 15. caddy 16. bray 19. urn

No. 82
ACROSS: 1. capital 5. sag 7. barge 8. curse 9. endure 11. tan 13. gas 14. riches 17. rouge 18. bulge 20. Exe 21. lenient
DOWN: 1. cable 2. par 3. theory 4. loch 5. scratch 6. green 10. dispute 12. Lisbon 13. gorge 15. sweet 16. keel 19. lie

No. 83
ACROSS: 1. husky 4. tripe 7. picture 8. pus 9. elf 11. gusted 13. coffer 16. sea 18. Ann 19. unclear 21. sided 22. Simon
DOWN: 1. hopped 2. sac 3. young 4. tress 5. impress 6. East 10. frowned 12. warren 14. found 15. ricks 17. mass 20. elm

No. 84
ACROSS: 1. tricked 5. pay 7. gleaner 8. rat 9. turf 11. nails 14. novel 15. flea 17. tar 18. inkwell 20. ass 21. dialect
DOWN: 1. tighten 2. Ike 3. kind 4. daring 5. partial 6. yet 10. reverts 12. starlet 13. allied 16. skua 17. tea 19. ere

No. 85
ACROSS: 1. pad 3. caravan 7. outer 8. sonic 9. scud 10. scale 13. risks 15. toys 17. taboo 19. brine 20. steeple 21. eat
DOWN: 1. plot 2. detects 3. cured 4. rusts 5. van 6. nicked 11. anytime 12. froths 14. stoop 15. table 16. feat 18. bee

No. 86
ACROSS: 1. Dumbo 4. tufts 7. muddled 8. rug 9. spring 11. lady 13. thin 14. absent 17. rib 18. haunted 20. dowse 21. droll
DOWN: 1. dames 2. mad 3. oblong 4. tidy 5. furnace 6. soggy 10. rainbow 12. absurd 13. tired 15. tidal 16. shoe 19. two

No. 87
ACROSS: 1. Genesis 5. hat 7. relax 8. canoe 9. shriek 11. bar 13. cup 14. hinges 17. truly 18. scree 20. hue 21. stardom
DOWN: 1. germs 2. nil 3. sextet 4. sack 5. handbag 6. their 10. rapture 12. siesta 13. catch 15. steam 16. byes 19. rid

No. 88
ACROSS: 1. tepid 4. crass 7. reliant 8. beg 9. lis 11. errors 13. legate 16. ago 18. rum 19. octopus 21. tarot 22. natal
DOWN: 1. turtle 2. pal 3. drake 4. cater 5. Alberta 6. sago 10. steamer 12. morsel 14. aloft 15. eaten 17. brat 20. pat

No. 89
ACROSS: 1. project 5. saw 7. artists 8. sen 9. soul 11. evils 14. ditty 15. beta 17. fog 18. ailment 20. wet 21. slender
DOWN: 1. praised 2. out 3. easy 4. tassel 5. suspire 6. win 10. uptight 12. scatter 13. bypass 16. glee 17. few 19. end

No. 90
ACROSS: 1. jam 3. managed 7. knees 8. blown 9. tiny 10. erase 13. regal 15. peal 17. alarm 19. rondo 20. stretch 21. ton
DOWN: 1. joke 2. meeting 3. misty 4. noble 5. goo 6. dinner 11. against 12. organs 14. limit 15. perch 16. soon 18. Ayr

No. 91
ACROSS: 1. boast 4. musty 7. special 8. lea 9. sallow 11. kilt 13. bang 14. barrow 17. see 18. whippet 20. candy 21. lowly
DOWN: 1. basks 2. ale 3. tripod 4. melt 5. soldier 6. yeast 10. lantern 12. facial 13. basic 15. witty 16. sway 19. pew

No. 92
ACROSS: 1. segment 5. sow 7. alder 8. lunar 9. kidney 11. ivy 13. mar 14. sailor 17. Maine 18. Cilla 20. cog 21. follows
DOWN: 1. shark 2. god 3. earned 4. tall 5. sundial 6. worry 10. darling 12. parcel 13. mimic 15. reaps 16. pelf 19. loo

No. 93
ACROSS: 1. cheap 4. strad 7. elegant 8. mud 9. Mab 11. tanner 13. strict 16. sun 18. all 19. adamant 21. posse 22. pined
DOWN: 1. creamy 2. eye 3. plant 4. satin 5. rimless 6. Dido 10. bottles 12. united 14. inane 15. tramp 17. carp 20. awn

No. 94
ACROSS: 1. kippers 5. wag 7. anemone 8. rub 9. elks 11. abash 14. youth 15. chic 17. yak 18. imperil 20. pie 21. tinkers
DOWN: 1. knavery 2. Poe 3. Ebor 4. seesaw 5. warpath 6. gab 10. knuckle 12. hackles 13. thrift 16. span 17. yap 19. rye

95-107/SOLUTIONS

No. 95

ACROSS: 1. gum 3. recover 7. sorry 8. water 9. lion 10. robot 13. ingot 15. drop 17. Hilda 19. eager 20. hobnail 21. tub
DOWN: 1. gasp 2. morning 3. rayon 4. cower 5. VAT 6. rarity 11. brought 12. eighth 14. tiara 15. dwell 16. crab 18. lob

No. 96

ACROSS: 1. waste 4. leash 7. funeral 8. rut 9. script 11. inch 13. cave 14. mellow 17. air 18. epitome 20. press 21. litre
DOWN: 1. wafts 2. sin 3. Europe 4. lily 5. adrenal 6. hitch 10. reverse 12. menial 13. clasp 15. where 16. lens 19. oat

No. 97

ACROSS: 1. monster 5. wad 7. debit 8. forge 9. expels 11. arm 13. foe 14. defend 17. aisle 18. sight 20. kid 21. minster
DOWN: 1. midge 2. neb 3. tittle 4. raft 5. warfare 6. dream 10. pleased 12. person 13. frank 15. deter 16. helm 19. gut

No. 98

ACROSS: 1. cloud 4. easel 7. in touch 8. sir 9. pub 11. Turkey 13. storey 16. tom 18. hoe 19. bandage 21. panel 22. steed
DOWN: 1. chirpy 2. opt 3. doubt 4. ether 5. suspect 6. lure 10. between 12. impend 14. rebel 15. yanks 17. chap 20. are

No. 99

ACROSS: 1. emptied 5. cot 7. bittern 8. sap 9. rift 11. laird 14. Syria 15. grip 17. dew 18. silence 20. boy 21. troupes
DOWN: 1. embarks 2. pet 3. Ides 4. dangle 5. cashier 6. tip 10. faraway 12. depress 13. basset 16. Clio 17. dub 19. nip

No. 100

ACROSS: 6. Charles 7. dusty 8. scheme 9. rental 10. third-party 12. semicircle 16. motion 17. icicle 18. asset 19. knitted
DOWN: 1. shock 2. ardent 3. television 4. guinea 5. straits 9. reductions 11. rehouse 13. irises 14. evicts 15. sleet

No. 101

ACROSS: 1. seaman 5. waddle 8. user 9. trousers 10. bell-ringer 12. flying 14. peseta 15. spluttered 19. gumption 20. dome 21. guides 22. Aurora
DOWN: 2. easterly 3. moral 4. nothing 5. wrong 6. deserts 7. lard 11. streamer 13. insipid 14. petunia 16. lairs 17. eider 18. Zulu

No. 102

ACROSS: 1. Moscow 5. asleep 9. attain 10. hatter 11. fibs 12. eminence 14. rescue 16. sunset 19. composer 21. vote 22. oilcan 23. Nicola 24. screen 25. Easter
DOWN: 2. outside 3. classic 4. wanderers 6. swain 7. extends 8. portent 13. insurance 14. rectors 15. sampler 17. novices 18. Estelle 20. orate

No. 103

ACROSS: 7. Celt 8. executed 9. polite 10. métier 11. hiss 12. bathroom 15. barbaric 17. fate 18. report 21. tailor 22. pathetic 23. coop
DOWN: 1. semolina 2. strips 3. remember 4. beam 5. butter 6. Bede 13. tick-tock 14. orthodox 16. booths. 17. flinch 19. Esau 20. tots

No. 104

ACROSS: 1. pests 4. Delphic 8. Stephen 9. wired 10. dale 11. farewell 13. others 14. access 17. fatherly 19. spit 22. Irish 23. diverse 24. enlists 25. ruses
DOWN: 1. posed 2. stealth 3. Soho 4. denial 5. Lawrence 6. horse 7. coddles 12. breeches 13. offside 15. exports 16. Gladys 18. trill 20. treks 21. over

No. 105

ACROSS: 6. festoon 7. caper (cap-ER) 8. entire 9. sadism 10. good health (two mngs.) 12. calamitous 16. diving 17. darted (dart-Ed) 18. Milan 19. cyanide
DOWN: 1. jeans (Jean's) 2. string 3. foreboding 4. Sandra (hidden in 'thouSAND, RAvishing') 5. density 9. schooldays 11. Pacific (two mngs.) 13. animal 14. sarong 15. weedy

No. 106

ACROSS: 1. jacket 5. safety 8. gala (gal-a) 9. irrigate 10. ambassador 12. unduly 14. veered 15. dining-room 19. stirrups 20. pail 21. shoots (two mngs.) 22. nudist
DOWN: 2. alarming (Al-arming) 3. koala 4. thirsty 5. sired 6. fig-tree 7. Tate 11. melodies 13. undergo (under-go) 14. venison 16. nouns 17. roped 18. Utah (rev. of hat-U)

No. 107

ACROSS: 1. vanish 5. jet lag 9. warden 10. custom (two mngs.) 11. pica 12. imperial 14. Persia 16. orders (two mngs.) 19. Somerset 21. vets (two mngs.) 22. evince (hidden in 'PricE (VINCEnt)') 23. annual 24. sugary 25. egrets

No. 107 (Contd)
DOWN: **2.** avarice **3.** Indians **4.** handicaps (sound of handy + caps) **6.** elude **7.** lattice **8.** gambles **13.** prostrate **14.** pesters **15.** romping **17.** diviner (divine-R) **18.** retract (re-tract) **20.** racer

No. 108
ACROSS: **7.** Vera (hidden in 'seVERAl') **8.** invested **9.** recite (i.e. re-cite) **10.** nearer **11.** ably **12.** emendate **15.** credence **17.** chub **18.** primed (prim-Ed.) **21.** attest (at-test) **22.** oratorio **23.** oral
DOWN: **1.** December **2.** family **3.** nineteen **4.** Ivan (I-van) **5.** island **6.** here **13.** elevator **14.** Thursday **16.** demote **17.** cotton (cot-ton) **19.** rare (two mngs.) **20.** dirt

No. 109
ACROSS: **1.** glass **4.** liqueur **8.** vaguest (Va.-guest) **9.** Indus **10.** lurk **11.** restored **13.** places **14.** infuse **17.** Austrian **19.** hill **22.** tenor (sound of tenner) **23.** anchovy **24.** example (ex-ample) **25.** boner
DOWN: **1.** gavel **2.** Algeria **3.** slew (two mngs.) **4.** latter **5.** quietens **6.** elder **7.** residue **12.** tear-drop (two mngs. of tear and drop) **13.** prattle **15.** unicorn **16.** garage **18.** Sonia (hidden in 'perSON, I Attracted') **20.** layer **21.** scab (hidden in 'workerS' CABin')

No. 110
ACROSS: **6.** Mexican **7.** bevel (hidden in 'jamB, EVE, Leaning') **8.** beduin **9.** python **10.** deterrents **12.** background **16.** allies **17.** subdue (sub-due) **18.** bathe **19.** monthly
DOWN: **1.** meter (sound of metre) **2.** liquid **3.** rainstorms **4.** fettle **5.** deports **9.** 'Persuasion' **11.** railway **13.** knight **14.** debate (deb-ate) **15.** hurls

No. 111
ACROSS: **1.** bright (two mngs.) **5.** castle (two mngs.) **8.** tsar (hidden in 'SovieTS, A Royalist') **9.** reliable **10.** consultant **12.** assess (ass-ess) **14.** sorrow **15.** suspension (two mngs.) **19.** November **20.** lord **21.** opener **22.** dryads
DOWN: **2.** response **3.** girls **4.** thrills **5.** Celia **6.** starter **7.** lilt **11.** honoured **13.** eastern **14.** speared **16.** sober (so-be-R.) **17.** Sally (two mngs.) **18.** hoop

No. 112
ACROSS: **1.** sculls **5.** caches **9.** brogue (b.-rogue) **10.** ragged **11.** silt **12.** Montreal **14.** crunch **16.** tenths **19.** collapse (Col. + sound of laps) **21.** acre **22.** locker **23.** Arabic **24.** system **25.** enamel
DOWN: **2.** carrier **3.** lighten **4.** steamship (steams-hip) **6.** apart (a-part) **7.** highest **8.** saddles **13.** Notre-Dame **14.** cockles **15.** unlaces **17.** Niagara (rev. of a-R-again) **18.** heroine **20.** Adèle (hidden in 'MADELEine')

No. 113
ACROSS: **7.** pork **8.** pintable **9.** editor **10.** grange **11.** onus (on-us) **12.** alphabet **15.** protests (pro-tests) **17.** mate **18.** charge **21.** Ingrid (in-grid) **22.** remedial **23.** oxen
DOWN: **1.** Londoner **2.** skates **3.** sporrans **4.** snug (rev. of guns) **5.** Havana **6.** plug (two mngs.) **13.** possible **14.** entwined **16.** tarred (tar-red) **17.** maggot **19.** hied (sound of hide) **20.** emir

No. 114
ACROSS: **1.** coral **4.** chamber **8.** antlers **9.** lobes **10.** till **11.** moonbeam **13.** marrow (mar-row) **14.** wilted **17.** telegram **19.** limb **22.** houri (hour-I) **23.** Antigua **24.** spangle **25.** beret
DOWN: **1.** chant (ch.-ant) **2.** rattler (two mngs.) **3.** leer **4.** Castor **5.** Atlantic **6.** Bible **7.** resumed **12.** coughing **13.** matches (two mngs.) **15.** trigger **16.** façade **18.** Laura **20.** beast **21.** stub

No. 115
ACROSS: **6.** chopper (two mngs.) **7.** cedar (hidden in 'coppiCE, DARkening') **8.** malice (Ma-lice) **9.** prongs **10.** ear-trumpet **12.** rump-steaks **16.** strand (two mngs.) **17.** escape **18.** fried **19.** scraper
DOWN: **1.** shear (sound of sheer) **2.** splice **3.** penetrated **4.** reform (re-form) **5.** bangles **9.** permanence **11.** custard **13.** prayer **14.** social **15.** upper (hidden in 'groUP, PERfect')

No. 116
ACROSS: **1.** splint **5.** pumice **8.** plus **9.** ringless **10.** footlights **12.** mewing **14.** dramas (dram-as) **15.** embroidery **19.** paragons **20.** veal (hidden in 'stoVE, ALight') **21.** tendon (tend-on) **22.** silver
DOWN: **2.** pullover **3.** inset (in-set) **4.** turning **5.** pinch **6.** Melissa **7.** cosh **11.** marriage **13.** Iceland **14.** drowses **16.** brown **17.** devil **18.** date (D-ate)

No. 117
ACROSS: **1.** sniper **5.** bottom **9.** smarts **10.** Oscars (OS-cars) **11.** plan **12.** whitener **14.** dry-rot **16.** comedy **19.** filtered **21.** nose (sound of knows) **22.** Eloise **23.** Nellie **24.** sussed **25.** shares (two mngs.)

DOWN: 2. nimbler 3. partner 4. rose-water 6. onset (on-set) 7. trainee 8. miserly 13. incidents 14. differs 15. yellows 17. manilla (man-ill-a) 18. despise 20. Elsie

No. 118

ACROSS: 7. Goth 8. ordering 9. barred (sound of bard) 10. assign 11. kiss 12. nominate 15. feckless 17. park (two mngs.) 18. blotto 21. retail 22. donation (do-nation) 23. exit
DOWN: 1. moralise 2. shorts (two mngs.) 3. condense 4. Edda 5. orison (hidden in 'BORIS, ONly') 6. snag 13. misprint 14. terrific 16. kit-bag 17. potter 19. look (loo-K) 20. Odin

No. 119

ACROSS: 1. blank 4. Rumania (RU-mania) 8. incites (in + sound of sights) 9. stern (s-tern) 10. neon 11. cleaners 13. roster 14. celery 17. national 19. scut 22. mufti 23. captain 24. disband 25. camel (came-L)
DOWN: 1. Brian 2. anchors 3. Kate (hidden in 'pranK, A TError') 4. rustle 5. mistaken 6. niece (sound of Nice) 7. amnesty 12. Veronica 13. renamed 15. exclaim 16. rancid 18. toffs 20. tonal 21. epic

No. 120

ACROSS: 6. chariot (cha-riot) 7. madam 8. fasted (fast-Ed) 9. cheers (two mngs.) 10. chocolates 12. Philistine 16. worthy 17. treble 18. repay (rep-ay) 19. freedom
DOWN: 1. wheat 2. critic 3. wondrously 4. Pamela 5. barrier 9. choristers 11. thrones 13. lethal (let-Hal) 14. eyelet 15. flood

No. 121

ACROSS: 1. amazed 5. blooms 8. lamb (two mngs.; Charles L.) 9. leap-frog 10. straighten 12. import (I'm-port) 14. sheath 15. turpentine 19. apparent (a + p-parent) 20. arid (hidden in 'PeAR I Devoured') 21. stress 22. detest
DOWN: 2. meal-time 3. zebra 4. delight 5. blast 6. offence (of-fence) 7. mood (rev. of doom) 11. stencils 13. outrage (out-rage) 14. scented 16. reefs 17. toast 18. spot (rev. of tops)

No. 122

ACROSS: 1. Prague (Pr.-ague) 5. stupor 9. duties 10. tiered 11. list (two mngs.) 12. wardrobe 14. severe (sever-E) 16. murmur 19. prospers 21. unto 22. eyelid 23. italic 24. sashes 25. nobody (No.-body)
DOWN: 2. routine (rout-in-E) 3. gristle 4. elsewhere 6. third 7. perform (per-form) 8. red-deer 13. remission 14. Sappers 15. violets 17. rhubarb (sound of rue + barb) 18. untried 20. price

No. 123

ACROSS: 7. bone 8. Cheshire 9. allure (all-Ure) 10. havens 11. pony (two mngs.) 12. impolite 15. stranger (St.-ranger) 17. dope (two mngs.) 18. stokes 21. livery (two mngs.) 22. nameless 23. tank (two mngs.)
DOWN: 1. goalpost 2. deputy 3. acceding (AC-ceding) 4. mesh 5. shovel (s-hovel) 6. bran 13. paralyse 14. tapering 16. ankles 17. devote 19. tram (t' ram) 20. stew (rev. of wets)

No. 124

ACROSS: 1. sport (two mngs.) 4. Peebles 8. battery 9. extol 10. Eros (rev. of sore) 11. interest (two mngs.) 13. tokens 14. stacks (two mngs.) 17. implored 19. snow 22. kinks 23. turrets 24. tragedy 25. Wales (sound of wails)
DOWN: 1. sabre 2. outlook 3. teem 4. plying 5. elements (two mngs.) 6. lithe 7. salutes (two mngs.) 12. endorsee 13. trinket 15. conceal (con + sound of seal) 16. pertly 18. panda 20. wasps (W.-asps) 21. crew

PART 4

No. 125

ACROSS: 1. crumb 4. WILLING 8. raiment 9. mater (hidden in 'dilemMA, TERribly') 10. nook 11. PREPARED 13. tom-cat 14. aspire (a-spire) 18. vagabond 20. jeep 22. round 23. REGULAR 24. estuary 25. emend
DOWN: 1. coronet 2. UNIFORM 3. boer 4. watery 5. lamppost 6. inter 7. gored (go red) 12. Cambodia 15. ice-floe 16. expired 17. ENERGY 18. VERVE 19. grunt 21. ogre

No. 126

ACROSS: 1. disaster (Di's-aster) 5. sped 9. CRONY 10. broiler 11. FRIEND 12. baton 14. opened 16. drives 19. champ (cha-MP) 21. unable 24. angered 25. BUDDY 26. shed 27. betrayed
DOWN: 1. dock 2. scourge 3. style 4. embeds 6. PILOT 7. darkness 8. jobber 13. TOP-CLASS 15. EXPERT 17. validly 18. puddle 20. angle 22. amber 23. dyed (sound of died)

No. 127

ACROSS: 1. HOLIDAY 5. frisk 8. pretender 9. tot 10. stingily 12. urge 14. romany 15. RECESS 17. viva 18. HALF-TERM 21. nub (rev. of bun) 22. engrossed 24. exert 25. estates

No. 127 (Contd)
DOWN: **1.** hopes **2.** lie **3.** dredging **4.** yodels **5.** FIRM **6.** intercede **7.** kittens **11.** IMMOVABLE **13.** sea-front **14.** revenge **16.** haggle **19.** Midas **20.** next **23.** SET

No. 128
ACROSS: **1.** FIRST **4.** PRIMARY **8.** lot **9.** PRINCIPAL **10.** records **11.** nicks (Nick's) **13.** menace **15.** penned (two mngs.) **18.** piece **19.** impinge **21.** stockades **23.** roe **24.** abridge (a-bridge) **25.** Remus
DOWN: **1.** fulcrum **2.** reticence **3.** toper **4.** priest **5.** incense **6.** alp **7.** yells **12.** CONUNDRUM **14.** creaked **16.** deepens **17.** RIDDLE **18.** pasta (past-a) **20.** POSER **22.** oar

No. 129
ACROSS: **1.** cramp **4.** applied **8.** nippier **9.** TUNIC **10.** ore **11.** dispersal **13.** REEFER **15.** ANORAK **18.** hedgerows **20.** ess **21.** Linda (hidden in 'severaL IN DAnce-hall') **23.** Chaucer **24.** dabbled **25.** peril
DOWN: **1.** contour **2.** APPREHEND **3.** pried (sound of pride) **4.** ARREST **5.** pattern **6.** ion **7.** ducal **12.** streetcar **14.** eye-ball **16.** kestrel **17.** forced **18.** holed **19.** scamp **22.** NAB

No. 130
ACROSS: **1.** carat **4.** caustic **8.** IMMENSE **9.** spoil **10.** beak **11.** GIGANTIC **13.** retina **14.** crocks **18.** protocol **20.** HUGE **22.** alien **23.** drafted **24.** sincere **25.** elder
DOWN: **1.** climber **2.** rampart (ram-part) **3.** tuna (rev. of a-nut) **4.** cleric **5.** upstairs **6.** trout **7.** colic **12.** announce **15.** courted **16.** spender **17.** NODDLE **18.** plays **19.** ONION **21.** PATE

No. 131
ACROSS: **1.** darkened **5.** used **9.** ulcer **10.** GRANITE **11.** bushel **12.** desks **14.** fetish **16.** craven **19.** older **21.** MARBLE **24.** overdue **25.** SLATE **26.** rusk **27.** reunited
DOWN: **1.** DRUM **2.** recount (re-count) **3.** earth **4.** engulf **6.** SWISS **7.** dressing **8.** larder **13.** OF HONOUR **15.** stride **17.** valiant **18.** ampere **20.** dregs **22.** resin **23.** lead (two mngs.)

No. 132
ACROSS: **1.** Federal **5.** Tosca **8.** bread-roll **9.** arc (hidden in 'chARCoal') **10.** ELEVATED **12.** thou **14.** notice **15.** past it **17.** tint **18.** TOWERING **21.** Ali **22.** blunderer **24.** LANKY **25.** Terence
DOWN: **1.** FABLE **2.** Dee **3.** radiance **4.** Lionel **5.** TALE **6.** spaghetti **7.** ACCOUNT **11.** extension **13.** calendar **14.** netball **16.** robust **19.** gorse **20.** obey **23.** run

No. 133
ACROSS: **1.** decks (two mngs.) **4.** titanic **8.** amo **9.** ALEXANDER **10.** overeat **11.** amp-le **13.** tangle (two mngs.) **15.** ALFRED **18.** PETER **19.** enemies **21.** CATHERINE **23.** ice **24.** Dogstar **25.** tones
DOWN: **1.** DEAL OUT **2.** close-knit **3.** SHARE **4.** treaty **5.** travail **6.** Ned (rev. of den) **7.** CARVE **12.** PARTITION **14.** largest **16.** dispels **17.** senior **18.** paced **20.** eject **22.** tag (hidden in 'sTAGe-coach')

No. 134
ACROSS: **1.** pumps (two mngs.) **4.** marched **8.** niggled **9.** DEMON **10.** IMP **11.** disparage **13.** -FLOWER **15.** Celtic **18.** sheepskin **20.** Nan **21.** paper **23.** ragtime **24.** Afghans **25.** linen (line-N)
DOWN: **1.** Pontiff **2.** megaphone **3.** solid (so-lid) **4.** modish **5.** radiate **6.** -HEM **7.** dunce **12.** ATTENTION **14.** emporia **16.** CONCERN **17.** skirts (two mngs.) **18.** sepia **19.** Nigel **22.** pug (two mngs.)

No. 135
ACROSS: **1.** JIFFY **4.** grooves **8.** prevail **9.** issue (two mngs.) **10.** TICK **11.** dressage **13.** rosary (Rosa-Ry) **14.** MOMENT **18.** obsessed **20.** duce (Du-CE) **22.** TRICE **23.** epitaph **24.** negated **25.** weeps (wee-PS)
DOWN: **1.** Jupiter **2.** fleeces (two mngs.) **3.** year **4.** galore (gal-ore) **5.** omission **6.** VISTA **7.** SCENE **12.** PROSPECT **15.** emulate (emu-late) **16.** teethes **17.** behead **18.** oaten **19.** sling **21.** VIEW

No. 136
ACROSS: **1.** copy-cats **5.** awls **9.** POUND **10.** pretend (pre-tend) **11.** PESETA **12.** owlet **14.** coyote **16.** Edison (rev. of no-side) **19.** Corfu **21.** DOLLAR **24.** entitle **25.** trawl **26.** MARK **27.** attended (two mngs.)
DOWN: **1.** cape (two mngs.) **2.** prudery **3.** cadge **4.** top-hat **6.** WHEEL **7.** sedating **8.** RECORD **13.** ice-cream (sound of I scream) **15.** trusty **17.** seaward **18.** oddest **20.** ROTOR **22.** LATHE **23.** clod

No. 137
ACROSS: **1.** TRAFFIC **5.** Lehár **8.** perishing **9.** rep (rev. of per) **10.** COMMERCE **12.** lino **14.** tasted **15.** karate **17.** road (sound of rode) **18.** BUSINESS **21.** aid **22.** alligator **24.** obese **25.** torrent (tor-rent)
DOWN: **1.** topic (top-i/c) **2.** air **3.** fastener **4.** clinch **5.** logs (two mngs.) **6.** HURRICANE **7.** reprove **11.** mishandle **13.** malinger (Ma-linger) **14.** TORNADO **16.** pullet **19.** sprat **20.** GALE **23.** toe

No. 138
ACROSS: **1.** pilow (pi-low) **4.** SERPENT **8.** lad (L-ad) **9.** KING-COBRA **10.** cleanse **11.** imbue **13.** nomads (No.-mad-S) **15.** débuts **18.** run on **19.** thimble **21.** masculine **23.** ASP **24.** outings **25.** ADDER
DOWN: **1.** pelican **2.** LADIES' MAN **3.** waken **4.** singer **5.** receive **6.** ebb **7.** trade (rev. of E.-Dart) **12.** BLUEBEARD **14.** DON JUAN **16.** sleeper **17.** stains **18.** ROMEO **20.** Irena (hidden in 'CheshIRE (NAntwich)') **22.** sot (so-T (T))

No. 139
ACROSS: **1.** CHINA **4.** ENGLAND **8.** mastiff (MA-stiff) **9.** SPAIN **10.** ill (Ill., short for Illinois) **11.** successor **13.** GREECE **15.** assist **18.** waterfall **20.** USA **21.** lucky **23.** DENMARK **24.** strange **25.** speed (rev. of deep's)
DOWN: **1.** camping **2.** insolvent **3.** amiss (a-Miss) **4.** -EFFECT **5.** Gospels **6.** Ada (hidden in 'homesteAD, Abiding') **7.** donor (Don-or) **12.** stipulate **14.** carry on (two mngs.) **16.** -TRACKED **17.** -SADDLE **18.** -WALKS **19.** -LINES **22.** -CAR

No. 140
ACROSS: **1.** crofts **4.** strong **8.** LOIRE **9.** SHANNON **10.** epistle **11.** sedge **12.** EUPHRATES **17.** hasty **19.** enteron **21.** maidens **22.** RHINE **23.** sleuth **24.** SEVERN
DOWN: **1.** CALDER **2.** orifice **3.** TRENT **5.** transit **6.** owned **7.** GANGES **9.** Sheerness **13.** payment **14.** sardine **15.** THAMES **16.** unseen **18.** SEINE **20.** throe

No. 141
ACROSS: **1.** CAIRNGORMS **7.** EVEREST **8.** denim **10.** ETNA **11.** feminist **13.** ARARAT **15.** lessee **17.** operator **18.** wash **21.** sooth **22.** reviler **23.** beanfeasts
DOWN: **1.** clean **2.** item **3.** netted **4.** old times **5.** MENDIPS **6.** generators **9.** MATTERHORN **12.** marathon **14.** awesome **16.** MOURNE **19.** ATLAS **20.** Avis

No. 142
ACROSS: **1.** mope **3.** CRIBBAGE **8.** SNAP **9.** smackers **11.** metallurgy **14.** SOCCER **15.** smokes **17.** four-poster **20.** Mathilda **21.** slab **22.** DOMINOES **23.** used
DOWN: **1.** mishmash **2.** practice **4.** rumour **5.** BACKGAMMON **6.** aver **7.** else **10.** old Etonian **12.** SKITTLES **13.** ascribed **16.** BRIDGE **18.** amid **19.** stem

No. 143
ACROSS: **7.** PUMA **8.** marzipan **9.** SETTER **10.** TIGERS **11.** whoa **13.** LEOPARDS **15.** emission **18.** sure **19.** POODLE **21.** cattle **23.** skinless **24.** acne
DOWN: **1.** lute **2.** mantraps **3.** amoral **4.** grotto **5.** wing **6.** LABRADOR **12.** hammocks **14.** ALSATIAN **16.** icemen **17.** nicest **20.** dank **22.** LYNX

No. 144
ACROSS: **1.** embody **4.** drapes **8.** terse **9.** hold-all **10.** added up **11.** PANIC **12.** MERRIMENT **17.** Aesop **19.** ELATION **21.** SADNESS **22.** GREED **23.** WONDER **24.** broths
DOWN: **1.** entrap **2.** BOREDOM **3.** DREAD **5.** relapse **6.** plain **7.** SOLACE **9.** HAPPINESS **13.** replete **14.** trident **15.** Warsaw **16.** anodes **18.** Sudan **20.** ANGER

No. 145
ACROSS: **7.** cheats **8.** crimps **9.** Argo **10.** gorgeous **11.** SYCAMORE **13.** chew **14.** many **16.** espresso **18.** HAWTHORN **21.** TEAK **22.** POPLAR **23.** erupts
DOWN: **1.** CHERRY **2.** MAHOGANY **3.** ash-grove **4.** ACER **5.** PINE **6.** SPRUCE **12.** expended **13.** CHESTNUT **15.** Avalon **17.** scatty **19.** talc **20.** ours

No. 146
ACROSS: **1.** cosy **3.** oblivion **8.** norm (no-RM) **9.** smudging **11.** outstretch **14.** deeper (Dee-per) **15.** steppe (sound of step) **17.** HELICOPTER **20.** JET-PLANE **21.** KITE **22.** replying (rep-lying) **23.** Bess
DOWN: **1.** CONCORDE **2.** strutted **4.** BOMBER **5.** indication **6.** Isis (two mngs.) **7.** nigh **10.** ethereally **12.** SPITFIRE **13.** nearness **16.** finnan (Finn-an) **18.** ajar (a-jar) **19.** atop

No. 147
ACROSS: **7.** Lima **8.** FLAMENCO **9.** beadle (bead-le) **10.** CANCAN **11.** mien (sound of mean) **13.** HULA-HULA **15.** disorder **18.** ride **19.** SHIMMY **21.** tapirs **23.** dispense **24.** pier (sound of peer)
DOWN: **1.** JIVE **2.** FANDANGO **3.** afresh **4.** cancel **5.** fern **6.** scrawled (S.-crawled) **12.** IRISH JIG **14.** HORNPIPE **16.** doyens (do-yens) **17.** ratter **20.** mops (two mngs.) **22.** REEL

No. 148
ACROSS: **1.** HOVERCRAFT **7.** arsenal **8.** SKIFF **10.** test (two mngs.) **11.** stargaze **13.** employ (em-ploy) **15.** LINERS **17.** hand-guns **18.** scum **21.** piano (pi-a-No.) **22.** ill-will **23.** DESTROYERS
DOWN: **1.** husks **2.** vine (v.-in-E) **3.** relate **4.** restrain (RE-strain) **5.** FRIGATE **6.** BATTLESHIP **9.** free sample **12.** LONGBOAT **14.** PINNACE **16.** Enrico **19.** cribs **20.** flue

No. 149
ACROSS: **1.** HAMLET **4.** acacia **8.** nacre (N.-acre) **9.** desists **10.** LAERTES **11.** Iraqi **12.** heiresses **17.** cress **19.** OTHELLO **21.** OPHELIA **22.** built **23.** salary **24.** stadia (rev. of aid-ATS)
DOWN: **1.** handle (two mngs.) **2.** MACBETH **3.** elect **5.** CASSIUS **6.** CASCA **7.** assail (ass-ail) **9.** DESDEMONA **13.** insular **14.** sullied **15.** across (a-cross) **16.** PORTIA **18.** Ethel **20.** habit (two mngs.)

No. 150
ACROSS: **7.** DAHLIA **8.** ORCHID **9.** mere **10.** FREESIAS **11.** hotelier **13.** meek **14.** will **16.** generate **18.** DAFFODIL **21.** glum **22.** regent **23.** TULIPS
DOWN: **1.** make do **2.** BLUEBELL **3.** baffling **4.** ROSE **5.** aces **6.** dilate **12.** ringlets **13.** MARIGOLD **15.** images **17.** trumps **19.** feet **20.** dote

No. 151
ACROSS: **1.** VEGA **3.** animated **8.** LYRA **9.** abandons **11.** colourless **14.** tone up **15.** URANUS **17.** preemptive **20.** turnover **21.** HALO **22.** reassure **23.** vend
DOWN: **1.** velocity **2.** garbling **4.** NEBULA **5.** manuscript **6.** toot **10.** lugubrious **12.** intimate **13.** ASTEROID **16.** METEOR **18,7.** STAR-DUST **19.** aria

No. 152
ACROSS: **1.** free speech **7.** enclave **8.** bream **10.** PORT **11.** provided **13.** titbit **15.** CLARET **17.** arrested **18.** bust **21.** ennui **22.** STILTON **23.** GORGONZOLA
DOWN: **1.** facer **2.** EDAM **3.** SHERRY **4.** Ebbw Vale **5.** CHEDDAR **6.** perpetrate **9.** meditating **12.** RIESLING **14.** Toronto **16.** lesson **19.** ultra **20.** biro

No. 153
ACROSS: **7.** PIGEON **8.** revolt **9.** gnat **10.** RING-DOVE **11.** STARLING **13.** TERN **14.** acid **16.** SHELDUCK **18.** COCKEREL **21.** LARK **22.** skewer **23.** GANNET
DOWN: **1.** LINNET **2.** fettered **3.** entrails **4.** WREN **5.** Ovid **6.** PLOVER **12.** GREYLAGS **13.** toddling **15.** croaks **17.** CURLEW **19.** KIWI **20.** Rory

No. 154
ACROSS: **7.** bear **8.** overcome **9.** sliced **10.** SPROUT **11.** shoo **13.** nineties **15.** elliptic **18.** Ruth **19.** YELLOW **21.** STALIN **23.** designer **24.** Imâm
DOWN: **1.** teal **2.** BROCCOLI **3.** GOLDEN **4.** nelson **5.** scar **6.** impudent **12.** Hellenes **14.** terrapin **16.** towing **17.** CASTRO **20.** laid **22.** Iran

PART 5

No. 155 PLAIN
ACROSS: **7.** rash **8.** braggart **9.** untrue **10.** engine **11.** idle **13.** saucepan **15.** clinical **18.** code **19.** strewn **21.** garish **23.** momentum **24.** ludo
DOWN: **1.** pawn **2.** thirteen **3.** abbess **4.** gâteau **5.** agog **6.** drunkard **12.** dilution **14.** encircle **16.** Canute **17.** legume **20.** ewer **22.** soda

No. 155 CRYPTIC
ACROSS: **7.** hu-N-t **8.** a + du-late-d **9.** ham-per **10.** Pi-late **11.** boo-(oratio)n **13.** scru(b)-tiny **15.** personal (anag.) **18.** peel (hidden) **19.** basalt (anag.) **21.** Glen-DA **23.** Victor-I(d)a **24.** veil (anag.)
DOWN: **1.** tuba (rev. of abut) **2.** s-tip-ends **3.** walrus (r(eef) in anag.) **4.** jumper (two mngs.) **5.** Gail (sound of gale) **6.** sentence (two mngs.) **12.** operatic (RA in anag.) **14.** top-heavy (anag.; piano = p) **16.** nature (two mngs.) **17.** log-man (Ma in anag.) **20.** Asti (anag.) **22.** drib (rev. of bird)

No. 156 PLAIN
ACROSS: **7.** stroke **8.** apiary **9.** bias **10.** scramble **11.** bell-tent **13.** peep **14.** clad **16.** dormouse **18.** overshot **21.** pull **22.** blouse **23.** lieder
DOWN: **1.** strive **2.** consoled **3.** bedstead **4.** hair **5.** film **6.** grilse **12.** throttle **13.** prompter **15.** lovely **17.** salver **19.** roup **20.** heel

No. 156 CRYPTIC
ACROSS: **7.** merino (anag.) **8.** I-Ron-Ed **9.** G-R.-og **10.** Qu.-a-train **11.** br-aid-ing **13.** woof (hidden) **14.** long (two mngs.) **16.** overture (two mngs.) **18.** jettison (jet + anag.) **21.** hack (two mngs.) **22.** A-don-is **23.** show-ER
DOWN: **1.** T(om)-error **2.** ji-N-g + ling **3.** MO's-quit-O **4.** P-is-a **5.** dour (sound of doer) **6.** medico (anag.) **12.** greyness (sound of Gray + ness) **13.** watch-dog (ch. in anag.) **15.** over-do **17.** Rachel (anag. of Charle(s)) **19.** tuns (sound of tons) **20.** so-so

No. 157 PLAIN
ACROSS: **1.** Roman **4.** redeems **8.** cracked **9.** loose **10.** und **11.** disembark **13.** enrich **15.** vacuum **18.** medicates **20.** did **21.** uncap **23.** oceanic **24.** theatre **25.** therm
DOWN: **1.** recluse **2.** meandered **3.** naked **4.** radish **5.** dilemma **6.** ego **7.** sleek **12.** abundance **14.** cockpit **16.** modicum **17.** strobe **18.** moult **19.** sheet **22.** cue

No. 157 CRYPTIC

ACROSS: 1. swift (two mngs.) **4.** punches (two mngs.) **8.** pop-pies **9.** Gab-le **10.** owe (hidden) **11.** lion-tamer (anag.) **13.** emetic (rev. of cite-me) **15.** typist (anag.) **18.** catapults (cat + anag.) **20.** rum (two mngs.) **21.** Angus (anag.) **23.** fan mail (fan + sound of male) **24.** Theseus (anag.) **25.** rasps (anag.)
DOWN: 1. sup-pose **2.** implement (imp + anag.) **3.** trial (hidden) **4.** pass on (i.e. Pa's son) **5.** nightly (anag. of th(e) lying) **6.** hub (hidden) **7.** s-N-eer **12.** main roads (two mngs. of main) **14.** I'm-pass-E. **16.** tumbles (anag.) **17.** bluff-s(harper) **18.** co-as-t **19.** saner (anag.) **22.** gee (two mngs.)

No. 158 PLAIN

ACROSS: 1. super **4.** hairpin **8.** omnibus **9.** flair **10.** glad **11.** variance **13.** patrol **14.** agency **18.** reprisal **20.** stow **22.** valve **23.** slumber **24.** tantrum **25.** siege
DOWN: 1. stop-gap **2.** pendant **3.** ruby **4.** hussar **5.** infringe **6.** prawn **7.** Norse **12.** domineer **15.** notable **16.** yew-tree **17.** balsam **18.** rivet **19.** pylon **21.** fuss

No. 158 CRYPTIC

ACROSS: 1. C-left **4.** pyramid (anag. + amid) **8.** ancient (an + c-I-ent) **9.** crude (anag.) **10.** beat (two mngs.) **11.** computer (Com. + anag.) **13.** R.-'otter **14.** bed-lam **18.** creature (anag.) **20.** Omar (hidden; O. Khayyam) **22.** purer (i.e. Ure in Pr.) **23.** tombola (Tom (Okker) + rev. of a-lob) **24.** Delilah (anag.) **25.** tinge (tin + rev. of e.g.)
DOWN: 1. clamber (c. + anag.) **2.** enchant (rev. of NE + chant) **3.** thew (hidden) **4.** Pat-Ron **5.** re-capped **6.** mount (two mngs.) **7.** d-R-ear **12.** pectoral (c(hest) in anag.) **15.** lampoon (MP in anag.) **16.** Mar-gate **17.** wretch (sound of retch) **18.** cop-Ed **19.** Errol (hidden) **21.** smut (rev. of tums)

No. 159 PLAIN

ACROSS: 1. vision **4.** appals **8.** cop it **9.** woodman **10.** treacle **11.** Ionic **12.** statement **17.** abbot **19.** obtrude **21.** deflate **22.** Rufus **23.** sitter **24.** pliers
DOWN: 1. vacate **2.** sapless **3.** optic **5.** profile **6.** ad-men **7.** Seneca **9.** wherefore **13.** actuate **14.** truffle **15.** Tardis **16.** teases **18.** befit **20.** Tyrol

No. 159 CRYPTIC

ACROSS: 1. jiggle (jig + anag.) **4.** aslant (N in anag.) **8.** roots (two mngs.) **9.** chapter (two mngs.) **10.** Malvern (m. + anag.) **11.** bongo (hidden) **12.** distended (rev. of Sid + tended) **17.** angel (hidden) **19.** subsist (Is. in anag.) **21.** g(irl)-roomed **22.** s(ow)-will **23.** ro-tun-d **24.** lessen (sound of lesson)
DOWN: 1. Je(w)-Rome **2.** growled (anag.) **3.** lisle (anag.) **5.** SW-AB-bed **6.** Aft-on **7.** turbot (b(rook) in anag.) **9.** con-versed **13.** Solo-Mon. **14.** dailies (two mngs.) **15.** hangar (sound of hanger) **16.** stolen (rev. of NE-lots) **18.** g-R-oat **20.** baste (two mngs.)

No. 160 PLAIN

ACROSS: 1. blisters **5.** task **9.** fists **10.** gentian **11.** aghast **12.** tweak **14.** upturn **16.** thrown **19.** togas **21.** senate **24.** plateau **25.** clove **26.** yolk **27.** research
DOWN: 1. buff **2.** insight **3.** Tessa **4.** rights **6.** abide **7.** King Kong **8.** snatch **13.** multiply **15.** rasher **17.** outdoor **18.** assume **20.** grail **22.** niche **23.** Beth

No. 160 CRYPTIC

ACROSS: 1. campaign (a in anag.) **5.** balm (sound of barm) **9.** sprit (R in rev. of tips) **10.** or-char-(co)d **11.** teacup (Cu in anag.) **12.** runts (anag.) **14.** ass-oil **16.** edible (Ed + anag.) **19.** v.-aunt **21.** Engels (anag.) **24.** garb-age **25.** (filamen)t-ouch! **26.** sack (two mngs.) **27.** wren-Ch.-Ed
DOWN: 1. cast (two mngs.) **2.** mar-ten-s **3.** Aztec (sound of 'as + tec) **4.** gro(wn-)ups **6.** a-gain **7.** mo-Di's-tes **8.** scored (two mngs.) **13.** sa-£-vages **15.** in-tray (anag. + Ray) **17.** bulrush (sound of bull + rush) **18.** veneer (anag.) **20.** Ulric (hidden) **22.** get on (rev. of e.g. + ton) **23.** ch.-I'd

No. 161 PLAIN

ACROSS: 1. clammy **4.** upland **8.** recto **9.** Yorkist **10.** moaning **11.** Orson **12.** paper-clip **17.** Tamar **19.** silicon **21.** perusal **22.** broke **23.** deadly **24.** alcove
DOWN: 1. chrome **2.** arc-lamp **3.** maori **5.** parboil **6.** Aries **7.** dating **9.** Yggdrasil **13.** parasol **14.** piccolo **15.** stupid **16.** sneeze **18.** Maria **20.** libel

No. 161 CRYPTIC

ACROSS: 1. demur-'e **4.** (carcasse)s-crags **8.** radio (I in anag.) **9.** Jamaica (jam + rev. of CIA + a) **10.** Abigail (a-big + sound of ale) **11.** run-I-C **12.** fairy tale (f-airy + sound of tail) **17.** s-harp **19.** include (L in anag.) **21.** donnish (hidden) **22.** nab-OB **23.** S-a-lad-S **24.** No-well
DOWN: 1. Durham (rev. of Ma-hr.-ud) **2.** midriff (rev. of f-fir-dim) **3.** Rhoda (rho + rev. of 'ad) **5.** Cumbria (C + anag.) **6.** a-v-I-an **7.** séance (anag.) **9.** jellyfish (anag. of fleshy Jil(l)) **13.** I-MP-lied **14.** E.-Qu.-able **15.** A-sides **16.** gerbil (anag.) **18.** annul (hidden) **20.** Con-go

No.162 PLAIN
ACROSS: **7.** Jena **8.** inherent **9.** mental **10.** ratify **11.** dace **13.** windfall **15.** jackboot **18.** lido **19.** framed **21.** inmate **23.** stalling **24.** non-U
DOWN: **1.** gene **2.** last week **3.** pillow **4.** Sharon **5.** brit **6.** snaffled **12.** alacrity **14.** filament **16.** ordain **17.** twinge **20.** Mull **22.** Tony

No. 162 CRYPTIC
ACROSS: **7.** dago (a in anag.) **8.** Algernon (anag.) **9.** ve-St.-al **10.** indent (anag.) **11.** Tass (hidden) **13.** water-rat (anag. in Watt) **15.** Jonathan (N + anag. in Joan) **18.** Co-D(altons)-y **19.** gander (rev. of red-nag) **21.** pi-ff-le **23.** wind-cone (wind + anag.) **24.** L-out
DOWN: **1.** wan-e(vening) **2.** North Sea (anag.) **3.** Cal.-low **4.** egoist (anag.) **5.** p(ig)-rod **6.** cornland (corn-L + anag.) **12.** aromatic (anag.) **14.** rock-f-all **16.** Harrow (two mngs.) **17.** nephew (p-he in new) **20.** dud-E. **22.** laud (sound of lord)

No.163 PLAIN
ACROSS: **1.** centaur **5.** aspic **8.** interacts **9.** say **10.** kangaroo **12.** shun **14.** rustic **15.** chaste **17.** peak **18.** tallness **21.** lug **22.** obstinate **24.** ducat **25.** answers
DOWN: **1.** crick **2.** not **3.** Adriatic **4.** racoon **5.** also **6.** post-haste **7.** cayenne **11.** nostalgic **13.** shelties **14.** rippled **16.** cassia **19.** sleds **20.** bout **23.** ave

No.163 CRYPTIC
ACROSS: **1.** seraphs (se(en) + anag.) **5.** man-g(rub)-e **8.** outermost (anag.) **9.** Nat (sound of gnat) **10.** cajolery (anag.) **12.** Tyne (hidden) **14.** jotter (OT-te in Jr.) **15.** rag-out **17.** NATO (anag.) **18.** predator (Ed in anag.) **21.** tee(m) **22.** companion (Co.-MP + I in anon) **24.** remit (R + rev. of time) **25.** E.-tern-a-L.
DOWN: **1.** Stoic (anag.) **2.** rot (rev. of to-R) **3.** parallel (two mngs.) **4.** s-cours(e) **5.** mite (sound of might) **6.** nanny-go-A(pril)-t **7.** entreat (hidden) **11.** jet-stream (anag. in jam) **13.** hand-made (sound of handmaid) **14.** janitor (anag. + R) **16.** gramme (hidden) **19.** re-N-al **20.** Scot (sound of Scott) **23.** in-N.

No. 164 PLAIN
ACROSS: **7.** caliph **8.** encore **9.** Borg **10.** tameness **11.** famished **13.** wisp **14.** grim **16.** tent-rope **18.** flawless **21.** womb **22.** régime **23.** unlock
DOWN: **1.** pagoda **2.** jingoism **3.** white-hot **4.** perm **5.** scan **6.** crisis **12.** dinosaur **13.** werewolf **15.** roller **17.** pomace **19.** writ **20.** exes

No.164 CRYPTIC
ACROSS: **7.** be-war-e **8.** ocelot (anag. in Oct.) **9.** s-O-lo(w) **10.** doldrums (hidden) **11.** belittle (anag.) **13.** ru-L-e **14.** jade (two mngs.) **16.** antidote (anag.) **18.** canticle (CA + anag.) **21.** t-H-ug **22.** p-I-rate **23.** enrapt (anag.)
DOWN: **1.** before (two mngs.) **2.** canonise (anon-I's in CE) **3.** vendetta (anag.) **4.** tool (rev. of loot) **5.** weir (anag.) **6.** form-a-L **12.** ex-tre-M-es **13.** Red-start **15.** Alaric (anag.) **17.** thu-MP-s **19.** trap (two mngs.) **20.** ch(i)ef

The following pairs of answers are given in the order of their respective clues.

No. 165
ACROSS: **1.** trunks/shiver **5.** stroll/burgle **8.** sand/gain **9.** aardvark/flitting **10.** flesh-eater/effervesce **12.** kneads/crazed **14.** Basque/fidget **15.** graduation/obstructed **19.** befooled/strength **20.** noon/brig **21.** crayon/myrtle **22.** dressy/manner
DOWN: **2.** headland/reaffirm **3.** nudge/Venus **4.** starved/rafters **5.** skint/barks **6.** reviews/retired **7.** ling/lore **11.** venomous/Yuletide **13.** zoology/augment **14.** boredom/flushed **16.** salon/Aggie **17.** tense/cabin **18.** stay/wear

No. 166
ACROSS: **1.** Aragon/heckle **5.** astute/minced **9.** angler/scythe **10.** atomic/census **11.** bush/love **12.** guardian/hatstand **14.** pronto/stance **16.** cackle/losers **19.** turbines/refugees **21.** lope/pact **22.** locket/opaque **23.** oxygen/outrun **24.** sanity/to date **25.** eldest/yelped
DOWN: **2.** encrust/rancour **3.** kitchen/galleon **4.** north pole/evergreen **6.** iotas/sheer **7.** compare/unstick **8.** essence/decides **13.** telescope/accessory **14.** settles/purport **15.** offhand/African **17.** splayed/Capitol **18.** lecture/repress **20.** inept/gaunt

No. 167
ACROSS: **7.** form/viol **8.** ancestor/repairer **9.** scoops/crutch **10.** neater/swoops **11.** bass/gory **12.** Alistair/numbered **15.** realised/adjourns **17.** step/fret **18.** parson/maroon **21.** impish/bantam **22.** steerage/ferryman **23.** lung/Sikh
DOWN: **1.** pilchard/foursome **2.** smithy/sloops **3.** prisoner/pathways **4.** écus/spin **5.** escort/finale **6.** mete/pomp **13.** missions/indebted **14.** icepacks/evensong **16.** lashed/odours **17.** supple/finest **19.** ahem/arts **20.** Noah/numb

No. 168
ACROSS: **1.** rosemary/tapestry **5.** shod/abed **9.** dicey/curry **10.** topiary/brawled **11.** latent/banner **12.** diner/loyal **14.** lather/French **16.** Brenda/proven **19.** lumpy/gamut **21.** resale/rabbit **24.** coconut/Avignon **25.** stamp/glory **26.** then/soya **27.** scutters/downpour

DOWN: **1.** rock/to-do **2.** pickaxe/servant **3.** maybe/spy on **4.** rotary/rebuts **6.** brawn/holly **7.** diddling/daybreak **8.** pallor/spider **13.** afflicts/flagrant **15.** extant/crying **17.** noisome/volcano **18.** Brando/erotic **20.** mucky/maize **22.** bigot/Susan **23.** spur/ayes

No. 169

ACROSS: **1.** shrivel/savaged **5.** snarl/burnt **8.** in the pink/lamplight **9.** mer/pom **10.** Tintagel/lavender **12.** cran/fame **14.** cavils/bungle **15.** binges/calico **17.** airy/bags **18.** barrages/Jurassic **21.** Bob/lit **22.** orange-pip/endurable **24.** diets/Derry **25.** alleged/eye-drop

DOWN: **1.** spill/split **2.** rim/vat **3.** greenfly/Valhalla **4.** lagged/drivel **5.** both/sake **6.** Asparagus/rampaging **7.** torpedo/laments **11.** venerable/navigator **13.** madrigal/disagree **14.** cobbled/blabbed **16.** curdle/maraca **19.** sapid/cheep **20.** Rees/body **23.** bur/pig

No. 170

ACROSS: **1.** hound/munch **4.** ascetic/Mohican **8.** rag/Mod **9.** cigarette/vehemence **10.** tutored/excerpt **11.** tabby/anise **13.** fuddle/deaden **15.** temple/corner **18.** Cadiz/crest **19.** couplet/urchins **21.** infantile/delirious **23.** tor/Ira **24.** radical/express **25.** tweet/eerie

DOWN: **1.** merited/himself **2.** nightmare/undecided **3.** décor/hover **4.** aphids/mighty **5.** Horatio/comrade **6.** ten/cat **7.** needy/Crewe **12.** impulsive/Bannister **14.** lozenge/enteric **16.** reserve/entrant **17.** scroll/quails **18.** crime/cider **20.** crêpe/upset **22.** lid/fop

No. 171

ACROSS: **1.** witch/cross **4.** similar/katydid **8.** swimmer/scuffle **9.** Lenin/ninny **10.** oyez/rake **11.** kerosene/jeopardy **13.** letter/futile **14.** status/astral **18.** ammoniac/jodhpurs **20.** slur/bile **22.** doggy/dogma **23.** peevish/Kentish **24.** tangent/settees **25.** paled/wader

DOWN: **1.** cast-off/wastrel **2.** thicket/opulent **3.** sift/home **4.** Sweden/kernel **5.** mongoose/telepath **6.** dinar/lance **7.** rhyme/dingy **12.** keepsake/Klondyke **15.** rallied/trivial **16.** seethed/lurcher **17.** packet/tripos **18.** Judas/audit **19.** digit/Megan **21.** gnaw/hemp

PART 6

No. 172

ACROSS: **1.** Frankfurter (frank + anag. in Fr.) **10.** tar-rag-on **11.** alarmist (S in anag.) **14.** flyer (fly + rev. of re) **15.** a-mass-Ed **16.** sears (sound of seers) **18.** run amok (RU + rev. of man + OK) **19.** a-sin-in-E **23.** steer (two mngs.) **24.** ex-p-lo-re **26.** Nessa (NE + rev. of ass) **29.** blossoms (loss in anag.) **30.** anteroom (anag.) **31.** peppercorns (anag. + R in pens)

DOWN: **1.** fracas (rev. of s-a-carf) **2.** Abadan (hidden) **3.** narks (two mngs.) **4.** fairer (two mngs.) **5.** Ursa (hidden) **6.** table-a-U **7.** (P)eggy **8.** oners (anag.) **9.** Old Master (two mngs.) **12.** aerodrome (anag. in a – Rome) **13.** a-St.-ir **16.** snip-E. **17.** onestep (anag. + EP) **20.** Exmoor (ex + rev. of room) **21.** CO-lour **22.** verses (anag.) **23.** sneak (anag.) **25.** l-ass-o **27.** s-ate **28.** sloe (sound of slow)

No. 173

ACROSS: **2.** blind-alleys (anag.) **9.** breviary (rev. of I-verb + a-Ry) **10.** Ale-c(ider) **12.** a-t-tic **14.** smear (hidden) **15.** scenic (anag. + c(olliery)) **17.** Eli-'as **19.** S.-he-E.-ns **22.** oak-tree (anag. + E) **23.** Everton (ever + rev. of not) **27.** ne-St.-ed **28.** Rhône (anag.) **30.** ebbing (anag.) **32.** bleep (B(ill) + sound of leap) **33.** pan-g(ripes)-s **34.** fins (sound of Finn's) **35.** keelhaul (eel in anag.) **36.** persistence (anag.)

DOWN: **1.** a-basement **3.** lets in (anag.) **4.** Nice-St. **5.** daw-N **6.** (p)artisans **7.** Lam-Beth **8.** year-Ned **11.** lever (V in rev. of reel) **13.** tel (hidden) **16.** uselessly (less in anag.) **18.** good-byes **20.** overlie (E in anag.) **21.** (he)artless **24.** Essen (anag.) **25.** trip-L.-e **26.** Cognac (rev. of can-go-C) **29.** no-g **31.** bee-t(all)

No. 174

ACROSS: **3.** birth-place (anag.) **9.** Ena-mour(N)ed **10.** nod (rev. of don) **11.** nubs (anag.) **12.** r-end-ing **15.** annu-a-l **17.** F-Al's-e **19.** épée ('e-pee(l)) **20.** commence (men-c. in come) **22.** cenotaph (anag.) **23.** trio (hidden) **25.** M.-agog **27.** pa-Rod-y **29.** roughly (anag. in Rly) **30.** stag(e) **32.** fly (two mngs.) **33.** advertise (rev. of it in adverse) **34.** pestilence (anag.)

DOWN: **1.** benefactor (anag. + factor) **2.** gnu (sound of new) **3.** Baby-lon(e) **4.** roan (R + sound of own) **5.** turncoat (anag.) **6.** pe-n(oose)-al **7.** anil (hidden) **8.** connector (Co. + anag.) **13.** greengages (sound of gauge in greens) **14.** water-hole (ate R. in whole) **15.** as-to-Op. **16.** Lee-way **18.** employee (L. in anag.) **21.** nigh-tie **24.** Mahdi (rev. of I'd ham) **26.** guys (two mngs.) **28.** darn (hidden) **31.** a-sh!

No. 175

ACROSS: **1.** personality (anag.) **10.** r-'e-pin-ing **11.** greatest (sound of grey + test) **14.** res-A-t **15.** egested (e.g. + anag.) **16.** a-GI-le **18.** deceive (anag. in dee) **19.** marital (Ma + anag.) **23.** grim-E **24.** permute (anag.) **26.** a-ch.-Ed **29.** governor (hidden) **30.** feat-Ure-s **31.** f-row-'ard-ness

No. 175 (Contd)
DOWN: **1.** piglet (anag. in pit) **2.** re-el-ed **3.** S-lay-S **4.** needed (sound of kneaded) **5.** ap-S-e **6.** integer (anag.) **7.** tips (two mngs.) **8.** a-gate **9.** frog-march (g(aol) in from-arch) **12.** salvation (anag.) **13.** state (two mngs.) **16.** a-corn **17.** pimento (anag.) **20.** le-a-ver **21.** quin-ce **22.** he-arts **23.** gaffe (rev. of fag + Fe) **25.** mo-R-on **27.** h-O-ar(d) **28.** Dora (rev. of a-rod)

No. 176
ACROSS: **1.** cut the cackle (C + anag.) **8.** abacus (a + rev. of cab + US) **11.** Haifa (hidden) **12.** rest-art **14.** cut-let **15.** ting(e) **16.** a-(bough)t-tire **18.** Eve-N. **19.** sermon (anag. in S-N) **24.** versus (hidden) **26.** gale (anag.) **27.** c-an-opy **29.** Mica(wber) **30.** stucco (sound of stuck + O) **32.** Titania (anag.; ref. Shakespeare's 'Midsummer Night's Dream') **33.** nylon (hidden) **34.** varied (anag.) **35.** fall to pieces (anag. of 'I collapse (l)eft')
DOWN: **1.** catch sight of (catch + anag.) **2.** T-art-ars **3.** hu-g(arment)-e **4.** cheery (Che +anag.) **5.** cit-I(ran)-es **6.** la-(decante)r-ger **7.** eat one's words (E-atone-swords) **9.** brute (B + sound of route) **10.** cu-£-t **13.** stereo (e in anag.) **17.** toucan (anag. + can (= gaol)) **20.** psychic (anag. + chic; ESP = extra-sensory perception) **21.** lamina (rev. of animal) **22.** recall (re-call) **23.** C-a-sin-o. **25.** uncle(an) **28.** purr (hidden) **31.** Thai (anag.)

No. 177
ACROSS: **2.** kick up a fuss (US in anag.) **9.** continue (con-tin + sound of you) **10.** Ra-C-y **12.** oasis (hidden) **14.** ban-Al **15.** tom-tom **17.** no-I-se **19.** na-t(reachery)-ive **22.** po-lice-d **23.** reunion (anag.) **27.** embryo (anag.) **28.** union (two mngs.) **30.** s-(gi)n-orts **32.** stage (two mngs.) **33.** extra (two mngs.) **34.** fête (fe-*t*-**e**) **35.** mutation (anag.) **36.** credulously (anag.)
DOWN: **1.** scoundrel (Dr. in anag.) **3.** instil (hidden) **4.** kismet (anag. of 'mist(a)ke') **5.** un(f)it **6.** put on one (anag.) **7.** Fr.-antic **8.** s.-carve-s. **11.** ant-i/c **13.** a-do **16.** red-und-ant **18.** spoonful (anag.) **20.** tempter ((Sa)t(an) in temper) **21.** enraged (anag.) **24.** U-boat (anag.) **25.** b-Ur-eau **26.** pistil (anag.) **29.** (b)oa(t)-R. **31.** Otto (hidden)

No. 178
ACROSS: **1.** prison warder (anag.; 'porridge' = time served in prison) **8.** (d)river **9.** admire (anag. + re) **11.** fired (two mngs.) **12.** b-rim **13.** dir-g-e **17.** heckler (he + anag.) **18.** palate (pal + anag.) **19.** till (two mngs.) **20.** Di-PS **22.** r(heumatism)-ankle **24.** tempest (rev. of met + pest) **28.** p-Ag-an **29.** U-Po-N **30.** arr.-ay **31.** cur-ate **32.** canto (hidden) **33.** kindergarten (kind + art in anag.)
DOWN: **1.** p-ride **2.** Iv-or-y **3.** Orient (anag.) **4.** north-east (anag.) **5.** addict (hidden) **6.** dirt (rev. of I'd + Rt.) **7.** re-Morse **10.** citadel (anag.) **12.** bikini (two mngs.) **14.** hearth-rug (anag.) **15.** bellman (two mngs.) **16.** happen (two mngs.) **18.** p-'ot-luck **21.** senate (anag.) **23.** alpaca (rev. of a-cap-la) **25.** a-gent **26.** Anton (anag.) **27.** worn (two mngs.)

No. 179
ACROSS: **1.** go to the dogs (two mngs.) **10.** camp-fire (p(ine)-fir in came) **11.** up in arms (two mngs.) **14.** abode (anag.) **15.** 'Hair'-cut **16.** beg-in **18.** paradox (rev. of a-rap + sound of docks) **19.** page-ant **23.** stump (two mngs.) **24.** Co.-equal **26.** turns (two mngs.) **29.** C-at-H-olic **30.** loony-bin (anag.) **31.** attestation (at-test + sound of Asian)
DOWN: **1.** gauch(o)-E **2.** tri(o)-via **3.** own-ER **4.** hard-up **5.** Emma (rev. of me + Ma) **6.** off-beat **7.** G-Ir.-o **8.** he-me-n **9.** a-P-par-at-US **12.** idio-MA-t-i/c **13.** scrap (two mngs.) **16.** b-R-ier **17.** remnant (anag.) **20.** tom-t(rouble)-it **21.** nuclei (anag. + I) **22.** flacon (rev. of calf + on) **23.** St.-ale **25.** qu-o(nion)-it **27.** riot (hidden) **28.** dabs (two mngs.)

No. 180
ACROSS: **2.** terminology (log in anag.) **9.** Germanic (rev. of R-e.g. + manic) **10.** A-res(t) **12.** yarns (two mngs.) **14.** Anon-a **15.** Arc-tic **17.** tan-go **19.** loiter (anag.) **22.** li-one's-s(t) **23.** arm-ad-a-s **27.** N(eil)-early **28.** renew (two mngs.) **30.** Bre-a-st **32.** stool (rev. of loot's) **33.** corgi (Co. + anag. of gir(l)) **34.** Mon.-O **35.** for-E-tell **36.** grandma's-ter(m)
DOWN: **1.** Egyptians (anag.) **3.** ER-rant **4.** mas-Co.-t **5.** inst (anag.) **6.** nihilist (il-Is. in anag.) **7.** landing (two mngs.) **8.** Ge-no-ese **11.** route (sound of root) **13.** aga (hidden) **16.** erstwhile (anag.) **18.** playroom (anag.) **20.** c-re-at-or(e) **21.** harp-O-on **24.** MA's-on **25.** traces (two mngs.) **26.** entrée (hidden) **29.** e.-R-g. **31.** E-z-ra

No. 181
ACROSS: **3.** night-shift (sound of knight + shift) **9.** beefeater (i.e. beef-eater) **10.** rip (two mngs.) **11.** la-W-n(d) **12.** nut-case (anag.) **15.** a-R-dour **17.** glebe (hidden) **19.** ewes (W in rev. of see) **20.** pass-port **22.** tortoise (anag.) **23.** idle (sound of idol) **25.** under (anag. + R.) **27.** De(e)-duct **29.** natural (two mngs.) **30.** peri(l) **32.** sty (sound of stye) **33.** sun-tanned (sound of son + tanned) **34.** thermostat (most in anag.)

DOWN: **1.** obligation (O.B. + sound of legation) **2.** pea(r) **3.** New Year (anag.) **4.** gear (hidden) **5.** hand-rail **6.** set up (set-up) **7.** I-ran **8.** f(ilm)-is-her-men (i.e. casting a line) **13.** Easter-tide (anag.) **14.** blood-Bath **15.** abated (a + a in anag.) **16.** repent (re-pent) **18.** assaults (sound of a-salt's) **21.** odd-men-*t* **24.** SE-rum **26.** stye (hidden) **28.** chat (two mngs.) **31.** r(ag)-Ed.

No. 182

ACROSS: **1.** purple hearts (two mngs.) **8.** Ire-NE **9.** make up (make-up) **11.** da-VI-t(e) **12.** pall (sound of Paul) **13.** go-in-g **17.** striker (two mngs.) **18.** Pitt-Ed **19.** so-Ld **20.** loot (two mngs.) **22.** be-rat-e **24.** a-l-co-H-ol **28.** turps (anag.) **29.** ague (hidden) **30.** ember (m(at) in anag.) **31.** one-way (O-new-ay) **32.** E-N-Sue **33.** holiday-maker (anag.)

DOWN: **1.** pig-(or)gy **2.** R-Eli-C **3.** league (two mngs.) **4.** eavesdrop (anag.) **5.** eaters (i.e. 'eaters) **6.** real (two mngs.) **7.** s(ome)-p(olitical)-L(eftists)-urge **10.** g-O-rill-a **12.** prior-(abbe)y **14.** stable-b-O-y **15.** red-tape (anag.) **16.** stooge (anag.) **18.** Pharaoh (anag. + a-oh!) **21.** t-H-read **23.** esteem ('e's + rev. of meet) **25.** B-risk **26.** (E)aster **27.** fuel (anag.)

No. 183

ACROSS: **2.** hand-to-mouth **9.** hornrims (R-I'm in horns) **10.** drab (rev. of bard) **12.** aorta (hidden, rev.) **14.** ado-re **15.** Angela (an + rev. of leg + a) **17.** panto (Pa + anag.) **19.** eras-Ed. **22.** athlete (let in anag.) **23.** yoghurt (r(ancid) in anag.) **27.** err-and **28.** miaow (anag.) **30.** limp-et **32.** St.-ill **33.** a-Lib-I **34.** ran-I(ndia) **35.** Mal-lard-'s **36.** class-leader (c(hurch) + anag.)

DOWN: **1.** sharp-eyed (harp in anag.) **3.** a-R-rant **4.** d-rag-on **5.** ti-L-e **6.** omelette ('ome + sound of let) **7.** odd-ball **8.** tar-get-s **11.** rouse (sound of rows) **13.** O-Va. **16.** edelweiss (anag.) **18.** card-in-al(l) **20.** Borstal (anag. in BL) **21.** Cha-blis(s) **24.** gr-a-in **25.** impal(e)-a **26.** sat-ire **29.** or-b(all) **31.** mule (two mngs.)

No. 184

ACROSS: **1.** cut and dried (anag.) **10.** loo-K-back **11.** protégée (pro-te-gee) **14.** g-RE-et **15.** tanning (two mngs.) **16.** sieve (rev. of is + Eve) **18.** drea-me-r **19.** almanac (hidden) **23.** pinta (anag.). **24.** place-B.O. **26.** enact (anag.) **29.** *P*-**or-poise** **30.** croupier (anag.) **31.** I'm-pertinent

DOWN: **1.** Capote (ca. + anag.; Truman C.) **2.** Thor-n(a)y **3.** act on (two mngs.) **4.** dog-end (anag. in DD) **5.** does (two mngs.) **6.** (S)Iberian **7.** ease (hidden) **8.** skate (anag.) **9.** breadline (sound of bred + line) **12.** level best (level + anag.) **13.** Diana (rev. of an-aid) **16.** sepal (anag.) **17.** catch up (two mngs.) **20.** Clare-(por)t **21.** Rev.-is-e(xamine) **22.** forest (E. in anag.) **23.** peach (two mngs.) **25.** C.-low-N **27.** a-tom **28.** noir (anag.; French)

No. 185

ACROSS: **1.** at death's door (anag.) **8.** porous (anag.) **11.** E.-land **12.** barmaid (bar + sound of made) **14.** locate (rev. of Col. + a-te) **15.** Hal-O **16.** El Paso (a in anag.) **18.** glue (anag. + e(arrings)) **19.** belt-Ed **24.** oboist (anag.) **26.** (R)oast **27.** Ma-Rio-n **29.** lira (anag.) **30.** detour (hidden) **32.** Sat.-an-i/c **33.** Mafia (anag. of fami(liar) + a) **34.** fas(t)-CIA **35.** mixed-company

DOWN: **1.** apple-blossom (b(light) in anag.) **2.** dry-cell **3.** a-U-nt **4.** hears-e(legy) **5.** dam-age **6.** odious (rev. of do + IOUs) **7.** red-letter day (letter (i.e. one who lets) in re D-day) **9.** O-zone **10.** O-Val **13.** rho-MB-I **17.** Pen-MA-n. **20.** Minor-ca. **21.** salami (anag.) **22.** strafe (anag.) **23.** maniac (man + anag.) **25.** Saudi (anag.) **28.** Otis (hidden; ref. 'Miss Otis regrets') **31.** exam (ex + rev. of MA)

No. 186

ACROSS: **1.** one-upmanship (man in anag.) **8.** L-emu-R **9.** de-not-e **11.** bes-O-t **12.** blur(b) **13.** val-U-e **17.** relieve (RE + sound of leave) **18.** (fa)ce-rise **19.** edge (two mngs.) **20.** ra-N-t **22.** Ur-gent **24.** S(cott)-extant **28.** flint (Flint) **29.** iced (I + rev. of Dec.) **30.** Taffy (rev. of f-fat + (Derb)y) **31.** Orwell (hidden; i.e. George O.) **32.** Iceni (anag.) **33.** Netherlander (net her + lan-d-e + R)

DOWN: **1.** olive (Olive) **2.** Emily (rev. of (juic)y-lime) **3.** p-re-en's **4.** miscreant (anag.) **5.** nettle (sound of net'll) **6.** ho(l)ly **7.** perfect (p + F(auré) in erect) **10.** watered (anag.) **12.** b(ird)-ridge **14.** beautiful (I in anag.) **15.** evening (two mngs.) **16.** hin-te-d **18.** Cu-sh-I-on(e) **21.** ta-TT-le **23.** raffia (anag.) **25.** wiped ((p)ip(e) in rev. of dew) **26.** st-a-ir **27.** new-t(adpole)

No. 187

ACROSS: **1.** butter-Scot-ch. **8.** reward (RE + sound of warred) **11.** cycle (two mngs.) **12.** toccata ('cat' in anag.) **14.** an-Gina **15.** Au-Ra **16.** garter (anag. + R) **18.** lint (hidden) **19.** teeter (te + anag.) **24.** Borne-o(ld) **26.** Tara (rev. of a-rat; ref. 'Gone With The Wind') **27.** senses (two mngs.) **29.** L.-Ure **30.** collie(r) **32.** old salt (anag.) **33.** o(thers)-vine **34.** cle(a)ver **35.** entanglement (anag. of gentleman/net)

No. 187 (Contd)

DOWN: **1.** breaststroke (anag.) **2.** t-W-igged **3.** ER-in **4.** S-cones **5.** occult (rev. of Co. + cult) **6.** cetane (anag. of cantee(n)) **7.** heart-to-heart (sound of 'Hart to Hart') **9.** Ernie (ERNIE; ref. Morecambe & Wise) **10.** Asia (hidden) **13.** Car-lo-s **17.** Red Sea (anag. + a) **20.** enslave (E. + Slav in ne(t)) **21.** call on (c-all-on) **22.** tarsia (rev. of is in Tara; see 26 Across) **23.** peg-leg (e.g.-L in peg) **25.** ex-île **28.** 'El-le' **31.** or-le

No. 188

ACROSS: **3.** puff-Pa's-try **9.** oven-ready (a in anag.) **10.** raw (rev. of war) **11.** rent (two mngs.) **12.** endless (two mngs.; i.e. less end) **15.** h-edge-r **17.** G-one-r. **19.** Elba (rev. of able) **20.** canister (I-S(evvy) in canter) **22.** chemical (C + anag.) **23.** aide (hidden) **25.** adorn (anag.) **27.** Tri(e)ste **29.** stylish (sty-L + anag.) **30.** flak(e) **32.** per(m) **33.** as you were (anag.) **34.** present day (two mngs.; i.e. present-giving day)

DOWN: **1.** forage-caps (cap in for-ages) **2.** Eve(n) **3.** pen-an-ce **4.** f-R-ee **5.** fee'd-back **6.** adder (two mngs.) **7.** t-re-e **8.** raspberry (two mngs.) **13.** stark-naked (K(en) in anag.) **14.** sophister (anag. in sister) **15.** he-L-met **16.** reside (anag. + D(iepp)e) **18.** snapshot (two mngs.) **21.** trolley (roll in rev. of yet) **24.** a-rise **26.** lyre (hidden) **28.** thu(s)-d(rum) **31.** (l)ark

No. 189

ACROSS: **1.** kettle of fish (anag.) **8.** a-B-ove(n) **9.** Tibbie (anag. in tie) **11.** Babel (b. + sound of able) **12.** Gill (gill) **13.** umber ((H)umber – i.e. river near (H)ull) **17.** s-oil-ure **18.** tenets (ten + anag.) **19.** pore (two mngs.) **20.** ante (anag.) **22.** duress (anag.) **24.** Oct.-a-ves(t) **28.** sider (sound of cider) **29.** Teds (D in rev. of set) **30.** deity (anag. + y(ear)) **31.** 'e-loped **32.** erect ((stak)e + sound of wrecked) **33.** pulls through (anag.)

DOWN: **1.** K-a-put **2.** tom-B-s **3.** L-earn-t. **4.** embassies (anag.) **5.** fillip (sound of Philip) **6.** ibis (hidden) **7.** helpers (H + anag.) **10.** I-MP-each **12.** g-a-l-ore **14.** Goldsmith (two mngs.; Oliver G.) **15.** w(indow)-rested **16.** pet-a-L.-s **18.** two-step (anag.) **21.** ev-ad-es **23.** Ulster (anag.) **25.** adieu (sound of a-due) **26.** wrath (W. + rev. of tar + H) **27.** idol (rev. of lo-Di)

No. 190

ACROSS: **1.** man of letters (no + rev. of elf in matters) **8.** a-venue **11.** lea-SE **12.** vert-I-go **14.** elided (lid in rev. of Dee) **15.** Eli-a (pen-name of Charles Lamb) **16.** se-p-te-t **18.** emit (rev. of time) **19.** Nasser (S in anag.) **24.** P-rest-o **26.** se-C-t **27.** peanut (pe(el) + anag.) **29.** d(anger-men)-are **30.** st-R.-eam **32.** aileron (anag.) **33.** c(amel)-hair **34.** f-all-en **35.** Kilkenny cats (anag.)

DOWN: **1.** make one's mark (two mngs.) **2.** Nerissa (rev. of as-siren) **3.** fu-m(atch)-e(l) **4.** eleven (two mngs.) **5.** 'Tatler' (anag.) **6.** re-Ga.-in **7.** short commons (s-H-ort + Commons) **9.** V-ill-a. **10.** nude (rev. of dun + E) **13.** return (two mngs.) **17.** pe-pp-er **20.** Estella (tell in anag.) **21.** Medic-I **22.** st-r(elish)-eak **23.** reborn (sound of re-borne) **25.** thane (hidden) **28.** (M.)Ural **31.** tray (sound of trey)

No. 191

ACROSS: **3.** Highlander (land in sound of hire) **9.** overroast (V in anag.) **10.** axe (rev. of ex-a) **11.** Mane(t) **12.** triumph (anag.) **15.** inst-a-l(uck) **17.** stand (two mngs.) **19.** Ivor(y) (i.e. piano-key) **20.** dullness (N in Dulles + S.; John Foster D.) **22.** overgrow (anag. + row) **23.** Nile (sound of nigh + le) **25.** Dad-OS **27.** deal-ER **29.** S-tipple **30.** a-men **32.** tic(k) **33.** var-sit-ies **34.** scholastic (St. in anag.)

DOWN: **1.** Tom-b-St.-ones **2.** A-va(n) **3.** henbane (hen + anag.) **4.** g-R-in **5.** Hot-spurs **6.** As-Ian **7.** dam-p **8.** explosion ('E + anag.) **13.** horse sense (two mngs.; i.e. knowledge of horses) **14.** at-Avis-tic **15.** inured (in + anag.) **16.** line-a-r **18.** plotless (anag.) **21.** endemic (hidden) **24.** Nepal (rev. of la-pen) **26.** rich (two mngs.) **28.** edit (rev. of tide) **31.** (r)eel

PART 7

No. 192
ACROSS: 1. tom-tom 5. buckle (two mngs.) 9. outlets (le in anag. of touts) 10. Norm-an 12. back-seat drivers (back + anag. of advertisers) 13. r-O-an 14. Com.-parable 18. insulation (anag.) 19. L-ops 21. Right Honourable (anag.) 24. Sever-N. 25. enchant (hidden) 26. sta-ye-r 27. surest (rev. of us + rest)
DOWN: 2. opticians (anag.) 3. the-I-St. 4. mess a-bout 5. Bon-(plaic)e-d (James B.) 6. carriers (two mngs.) 7. leas-E. 8. bombardiers (anag.) 11. assessments (anag. of mess in assents) 15. promoters (pro + sound of motors) 16. browbeats (anag.) 17. flatter-(orator)y 20. grocer (sound of grosser) 22. great (sound of grate) 23. owner (hidden)

No.193
ACROSS: 1,5. tropical forest (anag.) 9. relapsed (rev. of Des-paler) 10. he-LP-Ed 11. clansman (anag.) 12. arisen (a + anag. of rinse) 14. advent-Ure-s 18. film critic (film-critic(Al)) 22. lowers (two mngs.) 23. colander (anag.) 24. 'ero-tic 25. sternest (St. + sound of earnest) 26. timing (Tim-in-(trainin)g) 27. Cr.-editor
DOWN: 1. th(e)-rice 2. oil-can (anag.) 3. I'm-pose 4. Alexandr-I-a 6. over-rate 7. exposure (two mngs.) 8. tidiness (I-din in anag. of sets) 13. helicopter (anag. of the police + R) 15. affluent (a-F(rance)-fluent) 16. glow-worm (anag. of owl grow + m(eal)) 17. scorpion (Co. in anag. of prison) 19. p.-aired 20. oddest (hidden) 21. W-rite-R

No. 194
ACROSS: 4. gas-he'd 6. eminence (anag. of nice men + E.) 9. a-mule-t(rust) 10. delirium (anag.) 11. interesting (anag.) 15. unearth (hidden) 17. elder-l(oft)y 18. ghost trains (anag.) 22. wardrobe (OB in anag. of drawer) 23. be-long 24. Tuesdays (anag.) 25. jet-set
DOWN: 1. veneer (E in anag. of never) 2. I'm-pediment 3. unhinged (H in anag. of I gunned) 4. gracious (two mngs.) 5. squatter (anag.) 7. n-a-il 8. El-Ma 12. schoolboys (sound of buoy in schools) 13. traitors (anag.) 14. e-yes-ight 16. rag trade (trad in rage) 19. reefer (two mngs.) 20. swat (hidden) 21. (figh)t-rue

No. 195
ACROSS: 1. ma-L-t 3. predator (Ed in anag. of parrot) 10. compose (two mngs.) 11. cackled (anag.) 12. Sinai (rev. of Ian-is) 13. £-and-marks 14. indigestible (anag.) 18. indefensible (anag.) 21. parasites ('para' sites) 23. t' hose 24. replete (let in anag. of peer) 25. doormat (or-Ma in dot) 26. overdose (anag.) 27. S-led
DOWN: 1. moc(k)-ass-in 2. lemonade (anag.) 4. reconcile (anag.) 5. decimalisation (anag.) 6. ti-L-ers 7. RA-dish 8. losing one's head (two mngs.) 9. keel (rev. of leek) 15. sweet peas (wee in anag. of pastes) 16. abnormal (Norma in anag. of lab) 17. selected (el in sect-'e'd) 19. O-port-O 20. trip-le 22. s(p.)uds

No. 196
ACROSS: 1. in the thick of it (in-the + thick (i.e. sick) of it) 8. car-V-e 9. plaudits (rev. of LP + audits) 11. nowhere (rev. of won + here) 12. Minor-CA 13. remit (rev. of timer) 15. sandstone (s.-and-s. + tone) 17. templates (rev. of TA in temples) 20. as-set 21. Nanette (hidden, rev.) 23. vehicle (anag.) 25. nor-the-RN 26. Tarka (hidden; ref. Henry Williamson's novel) 27. as fit as a fiddle (anag.)
DOWN: 1. in-ciné-rating 2. threw (sound of through) 3. elemental (anag. of eel + mental) 4. happens (a-pp. in hens) 5. Co.-al(l)-men 6. olden (rev. of lo + den) 7. interiors (anag.) 10. takes the cake (two mngs.) 14. moment-O-us 16. spaghetti (anag.) 18. There's-a 19. savanna (SA-van-NA) 22. tutti (hidden) 24. c.-a-Red

No.197
ACROSS: 1. telegrams (el-e.g. in trams) 20. Byronic (anag. of irony in BC) 11. find out (sound of fine-doubt) 12. dis-RE-pute 13. Rod-in 14. such (rev. of US + ch.) 15. pestilence (anag. of is let in pence) 17. proprietor (pro + anag. of report I) 20. c.-hip 22. (l)apses 23. re-fresher 25. Kenneth (hidden) 26. epsilon (anag.) 27. States-men (i.e. US men)
DOWN: 2. Er-N-ie 3. e-XC-lude 4. reflect (two mngs.) 5. man-drill 6. a-b(arracks)-ides 7. criss-crossing (sound of Chris + crossing) 8. toad-in-the-hole (anag.) 9. stance (hidden) 16. prospect (two mngs.) 17. p.-ranks 18. ear-shot (anag.) 19. off-sets 21. Pa-rent 24. ensue (rev. of NE + Sue)

No. 198
ACROSS: 7. curtains (anag.) 9. emetic (rev. of cite-me) 10. sham(e) 11. garden-shed (sound of guard + anag. of hens + Ed) 12. g-over-N 14. lavished (Vi-she in lad) 15. mu-MB-le 17. asleep (as + rev. of peel) 20. bran-tubs (anag.) 22. pet-Al's 23. opera-house (O in anag. of Europe has) 24. deft (rev. of Ed + ft.) 25. sludge (anag. of (c)udgels) 26. elegance (e.g. in E.-lance)
DOWN: 1. mushroom (mush + rev. of moor) 2. stem (St. + rev. of me) 3. vir(tue)-gin 4. De-serve-s 5. persistent (anag.) 6. misère (m-is-ere) 8. sur-e(xams)-ly 13. Ermentrude (anag.) 16. (s)laughter 18. pale-face (ale-f. in pace) 19. assume (ass + rev. of emu) 21. ripple (rip + rev. of 'elp) 22. peeved (hidden) 24. dray (rev. of yard)

No. 199
ACROSS: 1. Carthage (anag.) 5. f-R-iend 9. numerals (anag.) 10. rum-pus(s) 11. peerless (two mngs.) 12. phrase (anag.) 14. profession (anag.) 18. staircases (sound of stare + cases) 22. astral (hidden) 23. St.-itches 24. Biscay (is-c(hoppy) in bay) 25. l-slander 26. lintel (rev. of let-nil) 27. heatedly (anag.)
DOWN: 1. c-an-opy 2. (c)rammed 3. Harold (rev. of lo in hard) 4. Gulf Stream (anag.) 6. r-ough(t)-est 7. emphatic (anag.) 8. disc-Ern-s 13. aftertaste (anag.) 15. Istanbul (hidden) 16. p.-artisan 17. breakage (anag. of brake + age) 19. strait (anag.) 20. shaded (ad in shed) 21. as-tray

No. 200
ACROSS: 1. beat up (eat in rev. of pub) 5. crawls (R in anag. of claws) 9. Antonio (an + rev. of not + I-O) 10. bit-in-g(oulash) 12. Trafalgar Squa(dron)-re 13. hits (hidden) 14. biochemist (I in anag. of some bitch) 18. Padding-to-N 19. Sten (rev. of nets) 21. sign of the zodiac (anag.) 24. cove-N-s 25. a-dam-ant 26. clam-my 27. lessen (sound of lesson)
DOWN: 2. ex-tract-Ed. 3. tin-can (t-Inc.-an) 4. ploughing (hidden) 5. caber (cab + rev. of re) 6. antiques (anag. of quaint + 'e's) 7. Linda (rev. of ad-nil) 8. past the post (anag.) 11. pert-in-a-city 15. c.-lose call 16. intricate (in + tri-cat-e(s)) 17. linoleum (E. in anag. of mullion) 20. morass (S. in anag. of roams) 22. Gr.-owl 23. test-y.

No. 201
ACROSS: 1. rhododendrons (anag.) 8. storeroom ('ero-O in storm) 9. notes (no + rev. of set) 11. Noël (rev. of Leo-n.) 12. unsolvable (V in anag. of one bus, all) 13. casement (a-S. in cement) 15. Trent (t-R.-ent) 17. s-p.-lit 19. horrific (rev. of fir in anag. of choir) 22. long-haired (two mngs.) 23. BA-il(l) 25. slate (two mngs.) 26. naturally (two mngs.) 27. leisure centre (anag. of line, rest cure + E.)
DOWN: 2. hooters (two mngs.) 3. deem (rev. of meed) 4. Dr.-owning 5. Nimrod (nim(ble)-rod) 6. renovator (anag. of nave or + rev. of rot) 7. notable (i.e. not able) 8. sand-castles (anag.) 10. sceptically (anag.) 14. match-less 16. dome-stic(k) 18. lineage (anag. of Nile + age) 20. frailer (rail in Fe + r(ust)) 21. W-inner 24. g-R.-in

No. 202
ACROSS: 1. Wellington-boot (two mngs.) 9. in-sects 10. bar-bell (bar + sound of belle) 11. prime (two mngs.) 12. aftermath (anag.) 13. regressed (Reg + sound of rest) 14. shrub (R. in anag. of bush) 15. night (sound of knight) 17. moonlight (anag. of loon in might) 20. professor (anag.) 22. medic (ME+ rev. of CID) 23. en garde (hidden) 24. martial (sound of marshal) 25. Laurel and Hardy (anag. of allure + and-hardy)
DOWN: 1. whipper-snapper (whipper's-napper) 2. la-shin-g 3. inclement (in-Clement) 4. gas-taps (g-a St.-aps) 5. orbited (bit in anag. of rode) 6. barer (sound of bearer) 7. open-air (op.-E. + anag. of rain) 8. alphabetically (a-LP + anag. of by the CIA, all) 14. salt-marsh (anag.) 16. Georgia (E. in rev. of A1-grog) 17. misdeal (sound of miss + anag. of lead) 18. oarsmen (anag.) 19. giddier (GI + D-die-r.) 21. (t)error

No. 203
ACROSS: 4. car-pet 6. senators (anag. of are not in s.s.) 9. Ni-GG-le 10. Atlantic (anag.) 11. inter-change 15. a-band-on 17. int-e.g.-er 18. family trees (f(orebears) + anag. of my earliest) 22. allergic (g(ets) in all-Eric) 23. braise (sound of brays) 24. Ga.-there-D 25. singes (rev. of e.g. in sins)
DOWN: 1. peeler (two mngs.) 2. centennial (c. + anag. of Lent, Annie) 3. parakeet (a rake in pet) 4. cannibal (can + anag. of in lab) 5. regattas (anag.) 7. oath (hidden) 8. s(£)ick 12. handmaiden (anag.) 13. a-Gree(k)-in-G(reece) 14. prospers (rev. of rep's in pros) 16. deformed (anag. of from in deed) 19. t(ropics)-'orrid 20. tang(O) 21. s-L.-it

No. 204
ACROSS: 1. cold-shouldered (CO + anag. of holds duel + Red) 8. Eli-za(ny) 9. ex-a-miner 11. r(ebels)-'ustled 12. enthuse (hidden) 13. BA's-in 15. extremist (anag.) 17. admission (two mngs.) 20. p-re-en 21. der-Ides 23. gro-W.-S.-up 25. stroller (roll in anag. of rest) 26. a-Lib.-l 27. understatement (men in anag. of Stan uttered)
DOWN: 1. cherry-BR-and-y(oghurt) 2. lo-in-S 3. starlings (tar-ling in s.s.) 4. over-due 5. lea-NE-st 6. evict (anag.) 7. execut-IV-e 10. melting-point (anag.) 14. Sa-Mari(e)-tan 16. espionage (anag. of in pose + age) 18. insults (in + anag. of sluts) 19. Nigeria (rev. of air-e.g.-in) 22. drone (two mngs.) 24. slime (anag.)

No. 205
ACROSS: 1. benefits (anag.) 5. SC-ruff 9. dumb-bell (two mngs.) 10. angle-R. 11. conceive (once in anag. of vice) 12. stifle (anag of lift in SE) 14. escarpment (anag.) 18. power-house (anag.) 22. N-earl-Y 23. fountain (anag. of of a nut + in) 24. a-gents 25. m-a tern-al(e) 26. desist (hidden) 27. feat-Ure-s
DOWN: 1. bodice (anag. of I'd beco(me)) 2. naming (rev. of an + Ming) 3. fables (hidden) 4. television (anag.) 6. cenotaph (rev. of Pat-one in ch.) 7. up-lifted 8. ferments (men in anag. of frets) 13. passionate (pass-I + anag. of at one) 15. Spaniard (anag.) 16. sweaters (sound of wetter in s.s.) 17. pr-el-ates 19. in-vent 20. manner (sound of manor) 21. knells (sound of Nell's)

No. 206
ACROSS: 1. city (sound of sit + Y(ork)) 3. half-term (anag. of left in harm) 10. tinware (anag.) 11. gall('e)ons 12. CI-RC-A 13. subsidise (is in sub-side) 14. melodramatic (RA-mat in melodic) 18. d(amning)-enunciation 21. C.-lass-I-cal(l) 23. in-cur 24. channel (two mngs.) 25. cant-at-a 26. E.-miss-a-ry. 27. I-MP's
DOWN: 1. catacomb (TA-com(e) in cab) 2. tendrils (rev. of net + sound of drills) 4. algebraic (anag.) 5. falsifications (anag.) 6. ex-O-tic 7. M-ash-ed. 8. salad dressings (dressing in SA-lads) 9. bets (Bet's) 15. avuncular (U in anag. of a van curl) 16. disclaim (disc + sound of lame) 17. entreats (anag. of rent + eats) 19. icicle (hidden) 20. salami (rev. of I'm-alas) 22. (c)luck

No. 207
ACROSS: 1. alleviate (all + rev. of I've + ate) 10. tramped (MP in anag. of tread) 11. pinhole (pin + sound of whole) 12. rear-lamps (rear + anag. of palms) 13. CID-ER 14. do-££ 15. scientific (anag. of nice if it's + C.) 17. silverside (anag. of livers in side) 20. ye-LP 22. mogul (mo + rev. of lug) 23. assonance (ass + an in once) 25. reapers (re(d) + anag. of pears) 26. air-port 27. steadfast (St. + anag. of sad fate)
DOWN: 2. lapel (hidden) 3. endemic (end + anag. of mice) 4. impasse (Pa's in anag. of semi) 5. ten-a-city 6. star-Ed. 7. parallelogram (anag.) 8. good afternoon (anag.) 9. Cedric (sound of said-Rick) 16. bell-tent (bell + T-E.-NT) 17. som-BR-e 18. Swans-ea(t) 19. distaff (rev. of I'd + staff) 21. p-R-etty 24. narks (two mngs.)

No. 208
ACROSS: 7. tomatoes (Ma-to in toes) 9. plinth (hidden) 10. host (two mngs.) 11. Birmingham (rev. of rib + Ming-ham) 12. Ni-MB-le 14. water-bed (anag.) 15. li-SP-ed 17. t-rust-y(re) 20. Tintagel (anag.) 22. dry-rot (two mngs.) 23. Co.-TT-on-M-ill 24. spar(e) 25. De-not-e 26. speakers (anag.)
DOWN: 1. colonial (col + anag. of a lion) 2. w(ake)-aft 3. wobble (anag.) 4. S.-printer 5. Bing Crosby (anag.) 6. St.-RAF-E. 8. sprawl (rev. of L.-warps) 13. bus-station (anag.) 16. engine-ER 18. ye-O-man-ry. 19. all-i.e.-S. 21. I-Ron-Ed 22. du(E)ller 24. sake (hidden)

No. 209
ACROSS: 1. top dog (two mngs.) 5. noddle (rev. of don + anag. of led) 9. leonine (anag. of one in line) 10. OS-cars 12. Sir Francis Drake (franc in Sir-is-drake) 13. (l)ever 14. commandeer (sound of common, dear) 18. instrument (anag.) 19. ju(st)-do 21. Gloucestershire (anag.) 24. repeal (re-peal) 25. eye-ball (sound of I bawl) 26. saw-ye-r(ot) 27. ti-TT-er
DOWN: 2. odourless (dour in anag. of soles) 3. dri(v)ers 4. green-room (green + rev. of Moor) 5. Naomi (rev. of I moan) 6. decoding (Dec. + anag. of doing) 7. Lorn-a (L. Doone) 8. blusterings (anag.) 11. ne'er-do-wells (well in anag. of end sore) 15. mincemeat (anag. of E. mace in mint) 16. elucidate (anag. of clue + I-date) 17. C-rockery 20. aspect (p. in a sect) 22. omega (rev. of a-gem-0) 23. so-l(ight)-ar

No. 210
ACROSS: 1. short-tempered (anag.) 8. blunderer (BL-under-'er) 9. tit-le 11. odds (two mngs.) 12. dinner-time (anag.) 13. diddlers (D + anag. of riddles) 15. Tosca (hidden) 17. Ad-air 19. loose-Ned 22. torch-light (R in Toc H + light) 23. ewes (sound of yews) 25. rider (two mngs.) 26. North Pole (n(ight) + anag. of pot-holer) 27. level-crossing (Eve-L-cross in ling)
DOWN: 2. hounded (anag. of dune in hod) 3. (g)rids 4. t-err-iers 5. merino (anag.) 6. enter-it-is 7. (s)entries 8. broadcaster (two mngs.) 10. Emerald Isle (anag.) 14. larch-tree (anag.) 16. Loth-a rio(t) 18. a-bridge 20. new-born (NE + b(aby) in worn) 21. picnic (hidden) 24. thus (anag.)

No. 211
ACROSS: 1. public(house)-spirit-Ed 9. embroil (rev. of li-orb-me) 10. malaria (anag. of a rail in Ma) 11. miaow (anag.) 12. con-strict 13. tolerance (anag. of Leo in trance) 14. St.-rum 15. cocks (sound of cox) 17. cab-leg-ram 20. rarefying (anag.) 22. heat-h(igh) 23. Lebanon (le + ba-no-n) 24. harrier (two mngs.) 25. eucalyptus-tree (anag.)
DOWN: 1. pneumatic drill (two mngs.) 2. Bob-ta-il 3. ironworks (anag.) 4. silicon (sound of silly + con) 5. immense (me in anag. of mines) 6. in-let 7. earl-I-ER 8. pantomime horse ((Peter)Pan-Tom + anag. of hire some) 14. shepherds (p.-her in sheds) 16. c-a rib-ou(rse) 17. chimney (chim(p) + rev. of yen) 18. big shot (anag.) 19. read-I-er 21. Fond-a (Jane F.)

No. 212
ACROSS: 1. toboggan (anag.) 5. scamp-I 9. P-Red-icts 10. peanut (anag. of ape + nut) 11. exterior (ex + anag. of rioter) 12. hears-(condolenc)e 14. woodpecker (anag.) 18. apologetic (a-PO-log + rev. of cite) 22. Exeter (E.-X + anag. of tree) 23. wil-full-y 24. albeit (alb + rev. of tie) 25. intrepid (in + rev. of Di-pert) 26. lur-K-ed 27. play-Ed. up
DOWN: 1. tipped (two mngs.) 2. b-re-ath 3. go-it-re 4. astrologer (anag.) 6. cleverer (C. + rev. of re-revel) 7. man-drake 8. in theory (I + the-or in NY) 13. additional (ad + anag. of I do Latin) 15. baseball (base + sound of bawl) 16. November (anag.) 17. nose-dive (anag.) 19. a-ff.-Ray 20. S.-loped 21. eyed up (hidden)

No. 213
ACROSS: 4. b(londe)-itchy 6. post-card 9. taw-dry 10. straight (sound of strait) 11. hare-brained (anag.) 15. rings up (ring-sup) 17. hoe-down 18. steam-engine (anag.) 22. rock-E-try 23. envier (anag.) 24. perished (anag. of pier + shed) 25. stag-Ed.
DOWN: 1. c-her-ub 2. Nottingham (anag.) 3. straddle (rev. of Rt. in saddle) 4. butchery (but + c-he-ry) 5. tow-ER-ing 7. (c)Argo 8. duty (two mngs.) 12. apple-trees (anag.) 13. policing (PO + sound of leasing; force = the police) 14. interred ('int-erred) 16. suspense (us-p. in sense) 19. ninety (I net in NY) 20. c-R-op 21. Acer (hidden)

No. 214
ACROSS: 1. shin (hidden) 3. t(in)-rusting 10. a-f.-front 11. mail-bag (sound of male + rev. of gab) 12. twin-e(lastic) 13. p-R.-in-table 14. sight-reading (sigh-treading) 18. india-rubbers (anag.) 21. heartburn (heart + bu-R-n) 23. a-die-u 24. I'm-pr.-in-t(avern) 25. Audi-tor 26. sh!-rugged 27. mews (two mngs.)
DOWN: 1. smartest (two mngs.) 2. in-fringe 4. rem-a-inder 5. skirting-boards (anag.) 6. imbibe (hidden) 7. gagged (two mngs.) 8. comes to nothing (comes to + nothing) 9. atop (a + rev. of pot) 15. etiquette (anag. of quiet + (b)ette(r)) 16. belittle (I-TT in belle) 17. 'e's-quires 19. choirs (anag.) 20. pa-U-per 22. No-ah!

No. 215
ACROSS: 1. cry-babies (anag.) 10. breeder (B + sound of reader) 11. attacks (sound of a tax) 12. Corp.-orate 13. C-him-E 14. suck (hidden, rev.) 15. bystanders (by + stand-ER-s) 17. proverbial (pro + I in verbal) 20. It-ch. 22. music (us in sound of Mick) 23. eccentric (c(opper)-cent in Eric) 25. con-Vict(or) 26. s-yr.-inge 27. gendarmes (Gen. + anag. of dreams)
DOWN: 2. R-ad-io 3. bursary (anag.) 4. bra-vest 5. enticing (anag. of ten + icing) 6. a-BA-cus(s) 7. zebra crossing (anag.) 8. accident-prone (rev. of Di in accent + prone) 9. asters (hidden) 16. describe (rev. of Ed. + scribe) 17. pumice (rev. of up + mice) 18. bleated (anag.) 19. accuser (Cu in anag. of scare) 21. hock-ey(e) 24. nerve (hidden)

No. 216
ACROSS: 1. dreamboats (anag.) 6. B-lot 9. Fried(a) 10. simple-to-n. 12. out of practice (two mngs.) 14. re-served 15. cave-RN 17. N-ass-au(sea) 19. C-leaver-S 21. pretentiously (anag.) 24. Ax(e)-minster 25. C-rim-E 26. ours (hidden) 27. f-ledg(e)-lings
DOWN: 1. D-aft 2. editors (s-rot-ide, all rev.) 3. Mediterranean (anag.) 4. ossified (anag.) 5. ti-m(ile)-er 7. l-attic-e 8. tender-ness 11. lack-a-dais-I-cal(l) 13. grand piano (anag.) 16. blood-red (two mngs.) 18. steamer (two mngs.) 20. Elysian (Ely + si-a-n) 22. tot-a-l(iqueur) 23. vets (two mngs.)

No. 217
ACROSS: 1. Czechoslovakia (C(ountry) + anag. of zoo lacks a hive) 8. ru-RA-l(e) 9. theorems (anag.) 11. uncle-an 12. assagai (hidden) 13. Era-to 15. telegraph (anag.) 17. t' rite-ness 20. lat-c.-h 21. re-a-ctor 23. Cecilia (Cl in anag. of Alice) 25. gibbered (er in sound of jibbed) 26. enact (hidden) 27. unpremeditated (anag.)
DOWN: 1. carburettors (anag.) 2. Edric (anag.) 3. he'll-E.-bore 4. s-a tin-et 5. overall (two mngs.) 6. a-RR-as 7. I'm-M1-grant 10. light-hear-Ted 14. agitation (anag.) 16. gold-c(row)-rest 18. eardrum (a in anag. of murder) 19. SE-ceded 22. Ti-B-er 24. I-E-ast

No. 218
ACROSS: 7. op.-Po-site 9. b(ark)-eagle 10. w-R.-it 11. throughout (sound of threw out) 12. damper (rev. of rep-mad) 14. imagined (Ag in I-mined) 15. sur-F(almouth)-er 17. he-ad-ed 20. illusion (il + anag. of sun-oil) 22. b-Ur-row 23. cons-piracy 24. gilt (sound of guilt) 25. renown (hidden) 26. ringworm (anag. of grown in rim)
DOWN: 1. Spartans (rev. of raps + tans) 2. boot (two mngs.) 3. fitter (two mngs.) 4. obdurate (anag.) 5. pathfinder (Pat + h-f.-inder) 6. B-louse 8. earwig (anag.) 13. persuasion (anag.) 16. editions (no It in side, all rev.) 18. drollery (rev. of lord + le-ry.) 19. unfair (two mngs.) 21. Lionel (hidden) 22. buying (sound of bye + anag. of gin) 24. G(overnment)-own

No. 219
ACROSS: 1. tragic (GI in rev. of cart) 5. indigo (I + anag. of doing) 9. (m)archers 10. kissed (hidden) 12. bricks and mortar (anag.) 13. t-R-ip 14. kettle-d(ispense)-rum 18. redressing (two mngs.) 19. I-con 21. the man in the moon (anag.) 24. mo-N-ths 25. rag-Tim-e 26. rescue (anag. of curse + (miracl)e) 27. silage (rev. of is + anag. of gale)
DOWN: 2. rectified (anag.) 3. G(as)-reeks 4. cast-a-nets 5. inked (hidden) 6. disc-over 7. g-re-et 8. barbiturate (bar + anag. of but I tear) 11. prominences (anag.) 15. tinctures (tin + anag. of cruets) 16. reckoning (two mngs.) 17. pedantic (rev. of dep. + antic) 20. Ben-gal (the B. Lancers) 22. ev-OK-e 23. is-Sue

No. 220
ACROSS: 1. encyclopaedia (anag.) 8. pa-I-ntings 9. Dr.-ape 11. main (two mngs.) 12. worthwhile (anag.) 13. guy-ropes (U(rugua)y in gropes) 15. ennui (hidden) 17. aisle (sound of I'll) 19. part-song (Pa + anag. of strong) 22. atmosphere (anag.) 23. W.-art 25. E.-Erie 26. scavenger (rev. of CS +

avenger) 27. passenger-list (anag.)
DOWN: 2. no-l-sily 3. yet-I 4. Lon-don-er 5. peseta (E.-set in Pa) 6. endowment (anag.) 7. I-ran-Ian 8. pomegranate (anag. of orange MP + ate) 10. evening star (evening (= making even) + anag. of arts) 14. overseers (verse in anag. of rose) 16. carriage (car + r-I-age) 18. Samaria (rev. of MA's + aria) 20. O-ranges 21. chosen (hidden) 24. V-E.-al

No. 221
ACROSS: 1. generalisation (general-is-at-I + rev. of no) 9. Estonia ('E's + anag. of into a) 10. H-oratio(n) 11. Ali-'as 12. lose heart (two mngs.) 13. ingrowths (anag.) 14. India (in + rev. of aid) 15. ro-us-t 17. bare-faced (bar + rev. of café + Ed) 20. upper-cuts (two mngs.) 22. U-sage 23. rivulet (IV in rule + t(rout)) 24. tonnage (anag.) 25. educationalist (anag. of cautioned + a list)
DOWN: 1. Grenadier Guard (anag. of in red gear + guard) 2. not-H-ing 3. runs short (two mngs.) 4. leaflet (lea + anag. of left) 5. schisms (ch.-is in anag. of MSS) 6. torch (hidden) 7. out-ward 8. Portland cement (D.C. in anag. of permanent lot) 14. influenza (flue in in-NZ-a) 16. unpaved (anag. of van up + 'e'd) 17. blue tit (et in anag. of built) 18. risotto (sot in anag. of riot) 19. chap-at-I 21. R-Eli-C

No. 222
ACROSS: 4. burden (rev. of Ned-rub) 6. sap-p-hire 9. impair (rev. of M1 + pair) 10. after all (two mngs.) 11. grammatical (anag. of Magic Art MA + L) 15. needful (anag.) 17. odd-men-T 18. ground floor (ground + anag. of fool + R) 22. solitude (anag.) 23. Ka-RA-te 24. spanners (two mngs.) 25. pot-E-en(t)
DOWN: 1. h-Eli-um 2. half-a-crown (Hal + f-a c.-rown) 3. appealed (rev. of Pa + pealed) 4. B-ring-ing 5. repeated (anag.) 7. Iraq (hidden) 8. eels (rev. of slee(k)) 12. tall orders (anag.) 13. d-Eton-ate 14. s-t(rout)-urgeon 16. fighting (fig + anag. of thing) 19. flag-on 20. (r)uses 21. plea (hidden)

No. 223
ACROSS: 1. brandy-snap 6. blue (two mngs.) 9. alarm (hidden) 10. moorcocks (rev. of room + cocks) 12. songs of praise (anag.) 14. rosettes (rose + anag. of test) 15. weight (anag.) 17. post-al(l) 19. p(resents)-'ampered 21. violin strings (anag.) 24. nattering (anag. of at ten + ring) 25. élite (rev. of tile + E.) 26. sort (sound of sought) 27. mean streak (two mngs.)
DOWN: 1. b-O-ar 2. a-M-asses(s) 3. demonstrative (demon's + v(isor) in anag. of attire) 4. semester (anag.) 5. aloof (a + rev. of fool) 7. (s)lacking 8. Eastertide (ea-S-ter + anag. of diet) 11. correspondent (correspond + ent(ER)) 13. grapevines (anag.) 16. tarragon (tar + anag. of groan) 18. scooter (two mngs.) 20. r-ESP-ite 22. S.-pike 23. tea-K

No. 224
ACROSS: 1. storm in a teacup (anag.) 8. Hogan (hidden; Ben H.) 9. SE-a-ward's 11. Lat-I'm-er 12. overrun (two mngs.) 13. R.-asps 15. limousine (L + in in I-mouse) 17. hindsight (anag. of shindig + HT) 20. the-RM 21. p-RI-ests 23. rent-man (re-n(o)t-man; letter = one who lets) 25. pan-or-ama 26. blur-b(ook) 27. sent to Coventry (anag.)
DOWN: 1. scholarships (anag.) 2. (b)ought 3. minimises (Mini + Mis-E-s) 4. nostril (anag. of sort in nil) 5. tea-room (tear + rev. of moo) 6. a-gate 7. undermine (anag.) 10. interminably (anag.) 14. syndicate (anag.) 16. un-ten-able 18. Gestapo (anag. of tapes in go) 19. to-RN-ado 22. snout (O in rev. of tuns) 24. mount (two mngs.)

No. 225
ACROSS: 1. A-dam 3. obs.-cures 10. Pr.-'owler 11. I-so-tope 12. Arabs (hidden) 13. bra-in-cell 14. silver lining (anag.) 18. consecration (RA in con-section) 21. hand-press (anag.) 23. cat-ER 24. fir-tree (I-Rt. in free) 25. floo-RE-d 26. re-assess (i.e. female ass) 27. par-R.
DOWN: 1. a-pp.-raise 2. adorable (rev. of a rod in able) 4. Britannic (anag.) 5. crown and anchor (crow-Nan-d + a-N.-ch.-or) 6. rook-Ed. 7. s-M-ells 8. plaster of Paris (anag.) 9. c(racked)-rib 15. listeners (anag. of set in liners) 16. wistaria (anag.) 17. 'int-ruder 19. chafer (cha + rev. of ref.) 20. Andrea (hidden) 22. S-if-t.

No. 226
ACROSS: 1. deathless (anag.) 10. ignores (ore in anag. of sign) 11. tan-gent 12. b(ullets)-roadside 13. tuner (rev. of re-nut) 14. tut(or)s 15. arty-crafty (anag. of tray + crafty) 17. Bangladesh (anag.) 20. wrap (sound of rap) 22. an-tic 23. va-R.-nishes 25. sultana (two mngs.) 26. plan-N-er 27. recession (recess + rev. of no-I)
DOWN: 2. (r)eared 3. test-I-er 4. lottery (anag.) 5. sanitary (anag. of stain + a ry.) 6. gibbet (rev. of big + bet) 7. unfortunately (anag.) 8. Penny-far-thing 9. stor-M-y 16. blockade (block + sound of aid) 17. bra-SS-y 18. deviate (rev. of I've in date) 19. scripts (sound of crypt in SS) 21. Pa's-try 24. Idaho (I + rev. of had + O)

No. 227
ACROSS: 7. enormous (anag.) 9. tea-bag (anag. of eat + bag) 10. swam(p) 11. cottage pie (anag.) 12. tanner (two mngs.) 14. re-pub-lic 15. lustre (anag.) 17. truck-S. 20. flounder (two mngs.) 22. bishop (two mngs.; chess-board) 23. Easter eggs (anag. of eats + ER-eggs) 24. Cu-te(a) 25. lemurs

No.227 (continued)
(M in anag. of lures) 26. lacrosse (cross in anag. of ale)
DOWN: 1. snowball (two mngs.) 2. b(asin)-rim 3. soccer (C in anag. of score) 4. strapper (two mngs.) 5. paper-backs 6. TA-hit-I 8. SA-turn (it = sex-appeal) 13. nasturtium (anag.) 16. Red Cross (two mngs.) 18. S-C(airngorms)-ottish 19. frugal (anag.) 21. lo-af(t)er 22. bi-sec.-t 24. c(aw)-row

No. 228
ACROSS: 1. abases (AB + anag. of seas) 5. re-port 9. England (anag. of glen + and) 10. dar(l)ing 12. foundation-stone (anag. of to sin in found-at-one) 13. rigs (two mngs.) 14. complacent (Co.-MP + a C in Lent) 18. taskmaster (anag.) 19. mica (hidden) 21. nationalisation (anag.) 24. ref.-ill 25. Eng.-rain 26. merely (anag.) 27. tar-get
DOWN: 2. begrudges (anag. of Reg in budges) 3. stands (two mngs.) 4. seditious (anag.) 5. rode-O (i.e. rode nothing) 6. Parisian (is in par-Ian) 7. Ron-do 8. perforating (anag.) 11. restraining (re-straining) 15. p.-resident (opposite of resident-p.) 16. eliminate (anag.) 17. impolite (imp + anag. of to lie) 20. hang-a-r(unway) 22. the-ME 23. all-ay(e)

No. 229
ACROSS: 1. perpendicular (anag. of ruined place in pr.) 8. inclusive (in + Cl-us-ive) 9. ram-p.-s 11. Esau ('e + sound of saw) 12. Casablanca (anag.) 13. overmuch (over + anag. of chum) 15. taste (hidden) 17. MA-Ted 19. head-L-amp 22. recollects (re-collects) 23. Emma (rev. of me + Ma) 25. Heidi (anag.) 26. penitence (E.-nit in pence) 27. Peter the Great (anag.)
DOWN: 2. enclave (CL in E.-nave) 3. plus(h) 4. nuisance (anag.) 5. ice-cap (I-c. + rev. of pace) 6. UN-related 7. almonds (Mon(day) in anag. of lads) 8. Ides of March (anag.) 10. Shake-spear-E. 14. Madeleine (Adèle in mine) 16. sentence (two mngs.) 18. tactile (rev. of cat + tile) 20. Ar-men-ia 21. tea-pot (anag. of a potte(r)) 24. star (hidden)

No. 230
ACROSS: 1. superstructure (super + anag. of cure strut) 9. avocado (rev. of ova + cad-O) 10. seaport (anag.) 11. prior (two mngs.) 12. plaintive (plain + ti-V-e) 13. rest-curés 14. fin-a-L 15. coo-p.-s 17. dyspeptic (anag.) 20. Ind-one's-ia 22. Casca (hidden) 23. entente (anag. of ten ten + E.) 24. grenade (anag.) 25. Fri(day)-endless-ness
DOWN: 1. sharp practices (two mngs.) 2. profits (sound of prophets) 3. road-races (anag.) 4. trooper (sound of trouper) 5. unseals (anag.) 6. twain (M. Twain) 7. Rhodian (anag.) 8. steeplechasers (Chas.-ER in steeples) 14. f-£-etchers 16. oldster (hidden) 17. di-Sten-d 18. sp(y)-angle 19. test-ate 21. non-c.-e

No. 231
ACROSS: 1. pittance (anag.) 5. t-R.-ench 9. ex-c(ast)-iting 10. answer (anag. of news in a-R.) 11. chilli-ER 12. suborn (anag.) 14. St.-retchers 18. incredibly (anag.) 22. Moor-Ed. 23. scarcely (car-CE in sly) 24. not-a-ry. 25. limbless (hidden) 26. yachts (ch. in rev. of stay) 27. Uncle Sam (uncles-a-M)
DOWN: 1. p-R-each 2. tact-i/c 3. Attila (hidden, rev.) 4. concentric (sound of consent-Rick) 6. renounce (anag.) 7. newcomer (O in anag. of crew men) 8. hard-ness 13. reflection (two mngs.) 15. pin-money (anag.) 16. acrostic (sound of a cross tick) 17. sewer-rat (anag.) 19. tri-B(antus)-al 20. levers (anag.) 21. gypsum (rev. of spy in gum)

No. 232
ACROSS: 4. docker (two mngs.) 6. quatrain (RA in anag. of quaint) 9. rooted (two mngs.) 10. stumping (U-MP in sting) 11. night-in-gale 15. sincere (hidden) 17. in sh!-ape 18. splintering (anag.) 22. twopence (anag.) 23. E.-state 24. penalise (pen + anag. of as lie) 25. lonely (O in anag. of Nelly)
DOWN: 1. detect (rev. of Ted + anag. of etc.) 2. Austr-a £-ian 3. stammers (m-me in stars) 4. darkness (anag.) 5. C-logging 7. a-Vi-d 8. no. go 12. needle-case (anag.) 13. marinade (Ma + anag. of a diner) 14. me-Ag-rely 16. easterly (anag.) 19. Euston (rev. of Sue + to-N) 20. St.-op. 21. boon (hidden)

No. 233
ACROSS: 1. custard-pie (anag. of sat rice pud) 6. Isis (two mngs.) 9. b-ER-et 10. o(utrage)-missions 12. Christmas tree (anag.) 14. pancakes (rev. of nap + cakes) 15. penned (two mngs.) 17. RE-coil 19. man-of-war (anag.) 21. packet-steamer (M in anag. of parakeets etc.) 24. repayment (anag. of May in repent) 25. rhino (sound of Rhine + O) 26. site (sound of sight) 27. brickyards (rev. of dray in bricks)
DOWN: 1. CA-BS 2. S-a race-N 3. alternatively (alter + t(rouble) in naively) 4. doorstep (anag.) 5. I'd-IOM 7. sporran (R in anag. of apron's) 8. s-US-penders 11. Sister of Mercy (anag.) 13. spare parts (art in anag. of sappers) 16. MA-jest-i/c 18. cockpit (two mngs.) 20. warrior (W-arr.-I + or) 22. s-N-eer 23. MO-s.s.

No. 234
ACROSS: 1. wheel of fortune (anag.) 8. lying (two mngs.) 9. infinite (in + it in fine) 11. in total (in(n) tot-a-£) 12. cholera (anag. of loch + era) 13. Go-go-L 15. disengage (Di + anag. of seen, gag) 17. transepts (S. in anag. of patterns) 20. wi-(sp)e(ar)-ld 21. Ch-else-a 23. scab-i.e.-s 25. SA-man-tha(t) 26. Katie (anag.) 27. hallucinations (Hal-luci(d)-nation-s(trange))

DOWN: 1. walking-stick (anag.) 2. Eli-OT 3. light ales (anag.) 4. f-rill-ed 5. off-ices 6. tang-O 7. Notre Dame (anag. of dream in note) 10. haberdashers (anag.) 14. Guatemala (anag. of U team in gala) 16. New-market 18. plastic (last in sound of pick) 19. s-us-tain 22. Shaw-L 24. intro (anag.)

No. 235
ACROSS: 1. tot-E. 3. scab-bard 10. regular (two mngs.) 11. reeling (reel + anag. of gin) 12. Syria (rev. of airy-S) 13. buildings (anag.) 14. misrepresent (anag. of miser + present) 18. sailing-boats (anag.) 21. stoppages (two mngs.) 23. thief (I in the-f(orce)) 24. hair-net (N in anag. of the air) 25. E.-tern-a-L. 26. ran-c(attle)-hers 27. deny (rev. of Ed. + NY)
DOWN: 1. tiresome (anag. of rose in time) 2. tigerish (Sir-e.g. in hit, all rev.) 4. carries on (two mngs.) 5. bread and butter (anag. of a branded + goat; butter = an animal that butts) 6. aligns (anag.) 7. digest (rev. of I'd + sound of jest) 8. pleas-Ed as Punch 9. grub (two mngs.) 15. re-legator 16. variance (N in anag. of avarice) 17. usefully (anag. of Sue + fully) 19. Esther (hidden) 20. lot-I-on 22. suet (hidden)

No. 236
ACROSS: 1. marauders (mar + sound of orders) 10. neutron (anag.) 11. retinue (anag.) 12. Aegean Sea (E. in anag. of a sane age) 13. a-men-d 14. shah (anag. of has + h(arem)) 15. battleship (B + (anag.) 7. digest (rev. of I'd + sound of jest) 8. (sound of able) 22. orate (hidden) 23. bantering (anag.) 25. timpani (Tim + anag. of pain) 26. a-U-St.-ere 27. mastodons (a in anag. of most + dons)
DOWN: 2. aorta (hidden, rev.) 3. amnesia (anag. of men in Asia) 4. dormant (man in rev. of trod) 5. retraced (rev. of cart in reed) 6. sneaks (N in sound of seeks) 7. burglar alarms (anag.) 8. Inner Hebrides ((d) inner + bride in he's) 9. Mendip (men-dip) 16. demerara (anag.) 17. s(oldier)-potty 18. rebuilt (rev. of t-LI-uber) 19. F(orest)-inland 21. lagged (rev. of egg in lad) 24. Essen (anag.)

No. 237
ACROSS: 7. squa-she-d 9. un-It-Ed. 10. talk (hidden) 11. shopkeeper (anag. of he spoke + per) 12. Pisces (c. in anag. of spies) 14. sloppier (s(ailors)-lop-pier) 15. synods (sound of sin-odds) 17. idylls (L in anag. of Dilys) 20. talisman (sound of tallies + man) 22. design (anag.) 23. contortion (con-tort-I-on) 24. pup-a 25. séance (a in anag. of scene) 26. dead loss (anag.)
DOWN: 1. Aquarius (I-U in anag. of quasar) 2. park (two mngs.) 3. the-S(ocialists)-is 4. duck-Po-(a)nd 5. pine-apples 6. sere-ne(w) 8. Dr.-ops-y(outh) 13. con-sis(ter)-tent 16. demurred (anag.) 18. sign-post 19. unkind (anag.) 21. a-bodes 22. dent-Al 24. p.-ill

No. 238
ACROSS: 1. standard-bearer (two mngs.) 9. lectors (hidden) 10. cost-U-me 11. th-an-e 12. aver-aging 13. implanted (rev. of M1 + plan-Ted) 14. finer (two mngs.) 15. godly (G(arbo) + sound of oddly) 17. Esperanto (anag.) 20. advisable (ad + vi-S-able) 22. Edwin (E + anag. of wind) 23. ran-cour(t) 24. eyesore (two mngs.) 25. precious stones (anag.)
DOWN: 1. splitting (= dividing) hairs (sound of hares) 2. arc-lamp (a-R-clamp) 3. dromedary (anag. of roamed in dry) 4. rest-art 5. back-end (backe-N(ovember)-d) 6. at sea (two mngs.) 7. elusion (sound of illusion) 8. Geiger counters (anag. of Reggie + counters) 14. force-M-eat 16. d-IV-iner 17. embargo (anag.) 18. peer-E.-s.s. 19. new moon (anag.) 21. Stoic (hidden)

No. 239
ACROSS: 1. basilica (il in basic-a) 5. cl-in-ic(k) 9. grinding (two mngs.) 10. I'm-O-Gen. 11. letter-Ed. 12. scythe (SC + anag. of they) 14. benevolent (anag.) 18. rift valley (anag.) 22. in-sure 23. Dart-moor 24. slog-an 25. th(e)-inkers 26. ta-TT-le 27. ice-rinks (anag.)
DOWN: 1. boggle (bog + anag. of leg) 2. shift-(stor)y 3. ledge-R 4. Cinderella (anag.) 6. lamb chop (Lamb + c-H-op) 7. nigh-ties 8. con-cert-O 13. telepathic (anag.) 15. train set (two mngs.) 16. off-shoot 17. overhaul (over + sound of hall) 19. atoner (hidden) 20. solemn (anag.) 21. prises (sound of prizes)

No. 240
ACROSS: 4. varied (anag.) 6. resorted (re-sorted) 9. sugary (rev. of us + Gary) 10. perverse (rev. of rep + verse) 11. vice-captain (apt in vice-Cain) 15. undress (anag.) 17. ice-floe (CE in I + sound of flow) 18. Queen Mother (anag.) 22. tarriers (rev. of RA in triers) 23. beauty (anag.) 24. non-sen's-e 25. be-fell
DOWN: 1. metric (hidden) 2. vegetation (v-e.g.-et + sound of Asian) 3. convince (C. + vin in once) 4. Vesuvius (rev. of IV-use-V + US) 5. regicide (sound of Reggie-side) 7. (s)tore 8. deer (rev. of reed) 12. pasteurise (anag. of stea(m) rise up) 13. ale-house (rev. of he in a louse) 14. bet-Ray-a-£ 16. en-quire-d 19. open-ER 20. Stan (hidden) 21. Erin (rev. of ire + N)

No. 241
ACROSS: 1. repository (rep + O + s-I-tory) 6. stow (hidden) 9. freer (f. + sound of rear) 10. back-pedal (back + anag. of paled) 12. smokeless zone (anag.) 14. horseman (anag. of same in horn) 15. re-a-son 17. plaits (rev. of al(l) in pits) 19. triggers

No. 241 (continued)
(sound of rigour in rev. of St.) 21. three-cornered (anag.) 24. civil list (two mngs.) 25. hardy ((Thomas) Hardy) 26. S-il-t. 27. percipient (anag.)
DOWN: 1. rife (anag.) 2. presser (press + rev. of RE) 3. Sir Robert Peel (anag.) 4. table-mat (tab + anag. of metal) 5. ru-ch.-e 7. Ted-IOUs 8. wilderness (anag. of wider lens + S.) 11. passenger-ship (pass + anag. of greens + hip) 13. chop-sticks 16. frenetic (NE in fret + ic(e)) 18. arrival (sound of a rival) 20. end-'orse 22. op.-in-E 23. cyst (hidden)

PART 8

No. 242
ACROSS: **1.** corpse **4.** rare-bit **9.** Isle of Man **10.** C-Uri-o. **11.** nurse **12.** in harness (anag.) **13.** I-so-late **15.** roll-on **17.** mêlées (Lee in mes(s)) **19.** suffers **22.** brainwash **24.** otter **26.** remit (rev. of timer) **27.** violently (anag.) **28.** nodules **29.** ascend (C(otopaxi) in anag.)
DOWN: **1.** Chianti **2.** ruler (two mngs.) **3.** stoneware **4.** ran-c(attle)-her(d) **5.** re-cur **6.** bargepole **7.** tootsy **8.** umpire **14.** open-armed **16.** left-over-S **18.** starves **19.** school ((clas)s + sound of cool) **20.** St.-rayed **21.** Oberon (anag.; ref. Shakespeare's 'Midsummer Night's Dream') **23.** Natal **25.** title (anag.)

No. 243
ACROSS: **1.** mad as a hatter (Ada + rev. of has in matter) **8.** sum up (sound of some + up) **9.** lead up to **11.** embargo (anag. + go) **12.** oil-rigs **13.** set-to (set to) **15.** timepiece **17.** ring a bell **20.** octet **21.** knees-up **23.** ca.-R-port **25.** scenario (anag.) **26.** motto (rev. of Tom + to) **27.** spirit-levels
DOWN: **1.** masterstroke (anag.) **2.** demo-b **3.** supernova **4.** hold out (two mngs.) **5.** tea-room (anag. + rev. of moor) **6.** equal **7.** S(tilton)-trident **10.** ostentatious **14.** tendency **16.** pro-gram-me **18.** emperor **19.** lockout **22.** sun-up **24.** outré (hidden)

No. 244
ACROSS: **1.** Hobbit (from e.g. 'The Hobbit' – J. R. R. Tolkien) **5.** Casanova **9.** decanter (anag.) **10.** clove(n) **11.** stool-pigeon (L. in anag.) **13.** Hera(cles) **14.** synonyms **17.** junk-yard (junk + rev. of dray) **18.** nosh (rev. of son + H) **20.** athleticism **23.** is-let **24.** ice-skate **25.** underdog (anag.) **26.** paring
DOWN: **2.** omen (hidden) **3.** beanstalk **4.** tattoo **5.** careless driving (two mngs.) **6.** sections **7.** noose (rev. of soon + (rop)e) **8.** Vietnamese (anag.) **12.** reputation **15.** non-smoker (two mngs. of puffer) **16.** patented **19.** line up (two mngs.) **21.** halve **22.** s-tun

No. 245
ACROSS: **1.** call to the bar (two mngs.) **8.** manse (anag.) **9.** smallpox **11.** aerosol (anag.) **12.** OS-t(urkey)-rich **13.** Endor **15.** scrummage (s-cr.-um + anag.) **17.** order form **20.** Joyce (cf. William J.) **21.** enclose **23.** caribou **25.** atremble **26.** owing **27.** candle-holder (tin + rev. of held + older)
DOWN: **1.** compare notes **2.** loner (one in L(uftwaffe)-R) **3.** treasurer **4.** tussles **5.** enamour (anag.) **6.** allot (sound of a lot) **7.** solitary (anag.) **10.** cheeseburger (rev. of grub in see, in cheer) **14.** dedicate **16.** major-domo (major + anag.) **18.** overbid **19.** machete (anag. in mace) **22.** opera **24.** b-L-ind

No. 246
ACROSS: **1.** upkeep **5.** con-Ger. **8.** moonshine (two mngs.) **9.** friar (sound of frier) **11.** kelp (hidden) **12.** grass-roots **13.** hard cash **15.** omega (rev. of a-gem-o(nyx)) **17.** a-bout **19.** pig-swill **22.** watch-tower **23.** veto (anag.) **25.** yobbo **26.** separates (rev. of apes + rates) **27.** crater **28.** nectar (anag.)
DOWN: **2.** prowler **3.** ENSA (hidden) **4.** prim-Rose **5.** crease **6.** nefarious (anag.) **7.** EP-I's-ode **8.** make headway **10.** rascallions (anag.) **14.** cut-throat **16.** fine-spun (fines-pun) **18.** October **20.** inertia (in + anag.) **21.** dosser **24.** Eric (hidden)

No. 247
ACROSS: **1.** a-pp-le **4.** ambush **9.** limited **10.** upright (two mngs.) **11.** verge **12.** elbow-room **13.** rat-poison (anag.) **14.** music **15.** haste (h(igh) + anag.) **17.** whirlpool **20.** shoots off (i.e. shoot's off) **22.** for-CE **23.** overlap **24.** do-or-Ma-t **25.** unwell **26.** tuner
DOWN: **1.** all over the shop (all over + the-S-hop) **2.** Pomfret (rev. of mop + fret; old form of Pontefract) **3.** entrecôte **4.** ad-dress **5.** bourbon **6.** St.-raw **7.** igloos **8.** stamp-collector **14.** milk-float **16.** stoker (two mngs.; Bram S.) **17.** w-hoop-ee **18.** infidel **19.** oarsmen (anag.) **21.** talon

No. 248
ACROSS: **1.** pomade (pom + sound of aid) **4.** in for it **9.** cap in hand **10.** as-W-I'm **11.** sidle **12.** all at once (two mngs.) **13.** placard **15.** ex-pert **17.** stolid **19.** for-bear **22.** Whitehall **24.** eaves (i.e. 'eaves) **26.** M(ississippi)-Ouse **27.** pea-souper **28.** stetson **29.** s.-tart-s.
DOWN: **1.** packs-up **2.** moped (two mngs.)

3. dance-hall **4.** indulge **5.** f-'e-ast **6.** rowan-tree **7.** temper (two mngs.) **8.** c-an-ard **14.** attribute (anag. + but-E) **16.** parcel out **18.** dead-pan **19.** Ful(l)-ham **20.** resorts **21.** swamps (M. in anag.) **23.** evens **25.** VI-per

No. 249

ACROSS: **1.** Apache **5.** in-sect **8.** small beer **9.** Com.-i/c **11.** oath **12.** out-patient **13.** tommy-rot **15.** users (two mngs.) **17.** havoc **19.** cru-SA-der **22.** incitement **23.** snip (two mngs.) **25.** trial (two mngs.) **26.** look alive **27.** Hen-bit **28.** to-Mat-o

DOWN: **2.** phantom **3.** Cu'll **4.** executor **5.** irrupt (ru(m) in anag.) **6.** secateurs **7.** compete (Co. + m-pet-e) **8.** short shrift **10.** catastrophe (anag.) **14.** yacht-club (anag. of Chay B(lythe) cult) **16.** print-out **18.** vaccine (a cc in anag.) **20.** dentist **21.** a-mule-(rabbi)t **24.** M-aim

No. 250

ACROSS: **1.** O-void **4.** b(end)-lithe **9.** transom (N-so in tram) **10.** v-an-illa **11.** opine **12.** 'Kidnapped' (kid-napped; R. L. Stevenson's novel) **13.** tin-opener (tin-op + anag.) **14.** ripen **15.** Eiger **17.** archangel **20.** outfitter **22.** Bing (i.e. Crosby)-O **23.** needle(s) **24.** Utopian **25.** Stan-CE **26.** keeps (two mngs.)

DOWN: **1.** out for the count (two mngs.) **2.** oration **3.** distemper (two mngs.) **4.** bump-kin **5.** invader **6.** henna (he + rev. of Ann) **7.** slap-up **8.** cardinal points (i.e. of the compass) **14.** roadblock (anag. + lock) **16.** gather **17.** artisan (anag.) **18.** carouse **19.** Gentile **21.** inlet

No. 251

ACROSS: **1.** sta-P-le **5.** pooh-pooh (rev. of hoop-hoop) **9.** jump-suit **10.** Fa-U(ranus)-st **11.** dining-table **13.** for-E. **14.** signpost **17.** flaming-O **18.** Eire (hidden) **20.** enlightened **23.** viola **24.** nickname **25.** close set **26.** sister (two mngs.)

DOWN: **2.** to-Ur **3.** pipe-dream **4.** E-quin-E **5.** put one's foot in it **6.** off-stage (anag. + (s)e(t)) **7.** plumb (sound of plum) **8.** outmeasure **12.** boll-weevil (anag.) **15.** pleadings **16.** anagrams **19.** snicks (C. in rev. of skins) **21.** looms (two mngs.) **22.** s-m(ere)-ee

No. 252

ACROSS: **1.** mess (two mngs.) **4.** sock (two mngs.) **9.** snorter (anag. + r(aging)) **10.** A-lad-din **12.** boyfriend (anag. in Bond (James)) **13.** knave (sound of nave) **14.** (gao)l-one **15.** snap-dragon **17.** pitch-black (pitch + b-l ack) **20.** stir (two mngs.) **22.** as-hen **23.** al(l)-bat-Ross **25.** carto-O-n **26.** neutral (two mngs.) **27.** be(TT)er **28.** tyke (hidden)

DOWN: **2.** enter (hidden) **3.** s(teak)-urge-on **4.** stand up (anag.) **5.** crackers (two mngs.) **6.** Isabel (AB in anag.) **7.** body-snatcher (at Ch. in anag.) **8.** intern (in + sound of turn) **11.** draughtboard (sound of draft-board) **16.** shin-bone (anag.) **17.** pla-I-ce **18.** L-earner **19.** cab-I-net **21.** result (anag.) **24.** truck (two mngs.)

No. 253

ACROSS: **1.** well-made (well + sound of maid) **5.** damsel (anag.) **9.** obstruct (obs.-truc(k) + t(oll-bar)) **10.** tiff-in **11.** Port Said (port + S-a-id) **12.** nausea (hidden) **14.** in fine form (fine in inform) **18.** easy street (anag. in East) **22.** robber (b(undle) in robe + R) **23.** in-detail **24.** re-lie-d **25.** Aired-ale **26.** el-apse **27.** leverage (anag. + 'e)

DOWN: **1.** W-hoops **2.** lustre (anag.) **3.** m-or-ass **4.** dictionary (diction + anag.) **6.** a-g-it-ated **7.** soft spot (so-f-t + spot) **8.** land-army (land + anag.) **13.** fire-engine **15.** pear-tree (anag.) **16.** Is-a-bell-a **17.** us-here-SS **19.** De-let-e **20.** banana(s) **21.** sleeve ((hippie)s + sound of leave)

No. 254

ACROSS: **7.** called up (all-Ed in cup) **9.** a-Cu-men **10.** flee(t) **11.** stage-coach (two mngs.) **12.** Chop-in **14.** C.-a-noodle **15.** orchid (hidden) **17.** studio(us) **20.** puppy-fat(e) **22.** parade (anag.) **23.** 'Nutcracker' (i.e. nut-cracker) **24.** chit (two mngs.) **25.** re-cede **26.** sun-dries

DOWN: **1.** ballyhoo (anag.) **2.** blue (two mngs.) **3.** odds-on (odd-son) **4.** Hazel-nut **5.** out of order (two mngs.) **6.** pen-c-I-l. **8.** P-ran-ce **13.** pick-pocket (pick = a diamond playing-card; pocket = to pot) **16.** infra-red (anag.) **18.** old-timer (two mngs.; i.e. old-fashioned timepiece) **19.** stakes (sound of steaks) **21.** unused (two mngs.) **22.** par-en-t **24.** Co.-re

No. 255

ACROSS: **1.** c-her-ub **5.** oriole (O + anag.) **9.** lea-N-der (Hero & Leander, classical mythology) **10.** In-ten-d **11.** to the manner born (sound of manor) **13.** Eden (two mngs.) **14.** mouth-organ (two mngs.; i.e. an organ of the body) **18.** pass muster (anag.) **19.** oner (two mngs.) **21.** go to rack and ruin (got-O + anag.) **24.** te-a-Cu-p(our) **25.** intense (hidden) **26.** S.-tone-D. **27.** Tudors (or in anag.)

DOWN: **2.** he-artless **3.** redden (anag. in RN) **4.** Barbar(a)-O-us **5.** onion (two mngs.) **6.** Interpol (anag.) **7.** Lent-O **8.** clothes'-peg (sound of loathes in CP + e.g.) **12.** non-drinker rink in anag.) **15.** the-rapist **16.** gunrunner nag. + runner) **17.** A-m-Eric-an **20.** edited nag.) **22.** treat (two mngs.) **23.** Cup-I'd

. 256
CROSS: **4.** come on (two mngs.) **6.** end-ger **9.** la-di-da (lad-Ida) **10.** nea(r)-t'-ness . earth-tremor ((Etn)a in anag.) **15.** attract ound of a-tract) **17.** zealous (a-lo in Zeus) photocopier (anag.) **22.** coronary (R-on-a-R coy) **23.** Sat-urn **24.** sea-birds (sound of see rev. of drib + S.) **25.** doodle (do + l(over) in le)
OWN: **1.** doodah (do + rev. of had-O) intermezzo (anag.) **3.** bacteria (anag.) **4.** cul--sac (Cu-l(ingered) + rev. of cased) mode-rate **7.** G-W.-en **8.** rush (two mngs.) . retrograde (anag.) **13.** mo-rib-und . estrange (anag.) **16.** appendix (two mngs.) . or-a-to-r(ecite) **20.** (f)acts **21.** Ir.-Ma

. 257
CROSS: **1.** tap-dance (rev. of Pat + (Fre)d anag.) **5.** nimbus (anag.) **9.** ice-cream nag.) **10.** came-RA **11.** at a pinch (a-tap-inch) . s-*t*-**ated** **14.** clip-joints (two mngs.) **18.** polo-ayer (anag.) **22.** reve-a-l **23.** slag-heap (lag in ag.) **24.** rook-I-e(asily) **25.** a-men-able . beluga (anag.) **27.** St.-r-and-ed
OWN: **1.** tri-b.-al **2.** prefab (anag. + fab) a-f(oe)-raid **4.** coal-cellar (anag. in collar) inaction (cf. in action) **7.** b-L-eating **8.** slap-sh **13.** speed limit (anag.) **15.** spare-rib (two ngs.; ref. creation of Eve) **16.** olive-oil (Olive yl, Popeye's girlfriend) **17.** speaking (a in -Peking) **19.** agenda (a-Gen. + rev. of 'ad) . webbed ((Capt.) Webb + Ed) **21.** a-pp-end

. 258
CROSS: **1.** polo (two mngs.; Marco P.) pump (rev. of PM-up) **9.** fearful (anag.) . O-mitt-Ed. **12.** sea-breeze (anag. + sound ease) **13.** Luigi (hidden) **14.** toll (rev. of £-lot) . fly-by-night (i.e. fly, by night) **17.** bell the t (anag.) **20.** crop (two mngs.) **22.** chain (two ngs.) **23.** upper-case **25.** pass out (pass-out) . a-prop-OS **27.** star (rev. of rats) **28.** talk (two ngs.)
OWN: **2.** (c)offer **3.** O-il-well **4.** Pr.-over-b Ma-in-line **6.** off-set **7.** parallel bars (two ngs.) **8.** adrift (anag.) **11.** trigger-happy Trigger' = name of R. Roger's horse) **16.** stand it (two mngs.) **17.** biceps (two mngs.; ref. eight-lifting) **18.** equator (anag.) **19.** asp-halt . please (pleas + (wr)e(stler)) **24.** rural idden)

o. 259
CROSS: **4.** back up (two mngs.) **6.** h-I-jack-er **9.** Russia (Russ + rev. of AI; R. Conway, popular entertainer) **10.** shambles (anag. in she's) **11.** bright spark (two mngs.) **15.** cholera (sound of collar + a) **17.** marquee (rev. of ram + sound of key) **18.** spring a leak (ring-Al in speak) **22.** newcomer (O(xford) in anag.) **23.** scrap-'e **24.** pre-a-Ch.-ER **25.** prim-US
DOWN: **1.** Mun-I-ch **2.** highwayman (high + Ma in anag.) **3.** haymaker (two mngs.) **4.** bareback (sound of bear + back) **5.** cast-iron **7.** K-ill **8.** rest (two mngs.) **12.** starry-eyed (r(esearch) in anag.) **13.** Luke-war-(atheis)m **14.** reckless (hidden) **16.** ensconce (con in anag.) **19.** accord (a + sound of chord) **20.** snap (two mngs.) **21.** Twee(d)

No. 260
ACROSS: **1.** profit (sound of prophet) **5.** jack-al(l) **9.** EP-I-gram **10.** mentor (sound of meant + or) **11.** picture postcard (anag.) **13.** rear (two mngs.) **14.** babe in arms (anag.) **18.** disc-over-Ed. **19.** echo (hidden) **21.** something in hand (two mngs.) **24.** valet-a **25.** evasion (Va. in rev. of noise) **26.** stat-U-e **27.** nudity (anag.)
DOWN: **2.** raincoats (anag.) **3.** far-out (Farou(k) + T(utankhamen)) **4.** temper-a-te **5.** jumbo (two mngs.) **6.** cons-T-an-T **7.** aloha (anag.) **8.** desperados (anag.) **12.** despo-N.-den-t **15.** ever-green (i.e. ivy-bush) **16.**RA-CIA-list **17.** (Michael) Foot-rest **20.** inlaid (in + rev. of dial) **22.** meant (anag.) **23.** I-rate

No. 261
ACROSS: **7.** p-Ed.-ant-i/c **9.** Exeter (ex + anag.) **10.** A-dam **11.** open-letter (landlord = one who lets) **12.** fee-BL-(battl)e **14.** Pr.-ogress **15.** tobies (I in to be + S) **17.** retort (two mngs.) **20.** goosegog (anag. in anag.) **22.** bobbin (bob + rev. of nib) **23.** just in case (two mngs.; i.e. court-case) **24.** gush (us in G(reenwic)h **25.** game-te(rn) **26.** turn tail (turn + sound of tale)
DOWN: **1.** dead-beat **2.** Pa-£-m **3.** at home (a + H(apsburgs) in tome) **4.** well-done (Well done!) **5.** letter-bomb (TT in anag.) **6.** s.-even-s. **8.** creeps (two mngs.) **13.** baby-sitter (two mngs.) **16.** engineer (engine + rev. of re) **18.** tail-spin (two mngs.) **19.** aghast (anag.) **21.** ocular (hidden) **22.** bleary (anag. in by) **24.** Ga.-te

No. 262
ACROSS: **4.** (c.)hiding **6.** blow-over **9.** no g-gin **10.** barnacle (bar + anag.) **11.** fill the bill (two mngs. of bill) **15.** referee (re + E in free) **17.** throw-in (th-row-in) **18.** chimney-pots (anag.) **22.** indecent (in + EC in dent) **23.** mar-in-a **24.** musk-rose (anag.) **25.** slog-an
DOWN: **1.** ins-I's-t **2.** flea-bitten (anag.)

3. swindler (anag. + R) **4.** hang fire (ha-N-g + fire) **5.** dog's life (anag.) **7.** vice (two mngs.) **8.** reed (sound of read) **12.** eye-witness (anag.) **13.** swooning (W in soon + anag.) **14.** ink-stain (anag.) **16.** race-card (ace-car in Rd.) **19.** yearly (earl in Y(aratishk)y) **20.** film (hidden, rev.) **21.** (m)odés(t)

No. 263

ACROSS: **7.** après-ski (anag.) **9.** Sk-inn-y(e) **10.** s-t(ype)-et **11.** rolling-pin (rolling + rev. of nip) **12.** dancer (N(ureyev) in anag.) **14.** Waterloo (anag. in woo) **15.** have on (two mngs.) **17.** adroit (anag. + it) **20.** guerilla (anag.) **22.** ja-lop-y **23.** pilot-light (I-lot in plight) **24.** boot (two mngs.) **25.** Bonn-et **26.** road-race (anag.)
DOWN: **1.** spot-c.-ash **2.** pelt (two mngs.) **3.** usurer (hidden) **4.** assisted (ass + anag.) **5.** finger-bowl (b(asin) in anag.) **6.** in-dig-o(pal) **8.** in-law-s(pliced) **13.** cover point (two mngs.) **16.** oil-cloth (anag.) **18.** top-notch **19.** dagger (anag.) **21.** uni-s(uccess)-on **22.** jets-Am. **24.** barn (anag.)

No. 264

ACROSS: **1.** plum (two mngs.) **4.** moon (two mngs.) **9.** note-pad (anag.) **10.** utensil (anag.) **12.** to the hilt (tot + l in he-hit) **13.** tac-I-t **14.** Hun-K **15.** make amends (anag.) **17.** easy-doe-sit **20.** Enid (rev. of dine) **22.** stall (anag. + ££) **23.** press-stud **25.** redress (i.e. re-dress) **26.** end-'orse **27.** By-Rd. **28.** gang (an in G(odalmin)g)
DOWN: **2.** laps- (strychnin)e **3.** Madeira (made + anag.) **4.** M.-O-untie **5.** overtime (T in anag.) **6.** snatch (two mngs.) **7.** Staten Island (state-N-is-land) **8.** p-L-ates **11.** second-nature **16.** adultery (anag.) **17.** ensure (hidden) **18.** ex-posed **19.** iceberg (i/c + rev. of grebe) **21.** d.-odder **24.** sedan (anag.)

No. 265

ACROSS: **1.** underman (two mngs.) **5.** strain (two mngs.) **9.** serenity (anag.) **10.** asylum (a + (man)y in slum) **11.** neck-lace **12.** stores (two mngs.) **14.** drop a brick (two mngs.) **18.** beauty-spot (anag.) **22.** t(he)-rough **23.** hear hear (he-a-r + he-a-r) **24.** are-N-as **25.** discreet (anag.) **26.** Turner (two mngs.) **27.** imprison (imp + anag.)
DOWN: **1.** unsung (two mngs.) **2.** direct (sound of Dai-wrecked) **3.** R-on-a-Ld **4.** Antichrist (anag.) **6.** test-tube (the 'Tube') **7.** allergic (anag.) **8.** namesake (rev. of E-man + sake) **13.** Spoonerism (anag.) **15.** AB's-tract **16.** saboteur (anag.) **17.** stagnate (rev. of e-tang-ats) **19.** grocer (sound of grosser) **20.** recess (two mngs.) **21.** cretin (hidden)

PART 9

No. 267
ACROSS: 3. pier 5. son 6. KNOCKED 9. a!! 10. dado 14. ABOUT 16. panel 18. BY 19. deed 21. Yule 22. measure 25. paddle 28. Enid 30. troop 32. drive 33. ton 34. lose 35 OLIVER CROMWELL
DOWN: 1. spool 2. fried 4. inclines 5. snappy 7. dabble 8. bobby 11. day 12. duellers 13. macaroni 15. teem 17. lira 19. dukedom 20. supple 22. motto 23. Errol 24. ideal 26. disc 27. deer 29. Nice 31. for

No. 266
A. whiff B. shy C. gaffe D. inn E. loot F. bur G. equerry H. rate I. Thumb J. too K. high L. engine M. goanna N. outer O. Niagara P. Diana Q. ordeal R. lea S. ill T. equal U. rural V. sow
W.S. Gilbert, *The Gondoliers*:
Oh, 'tis a glorious thing, I ween,
To be a regular Royal Queen!
No half-and-half affair, I mean,
But a right-down regular Royal Queen!

No. 268
1. manner 2. nerves 3. Vesper 4. permit 5. mitres 6. resent 7. entice 8. ice-run 9. runnel 10. Nelson 11. sonnet 12. nether 13. herbal 14. ballad 15. ladles 16. lessen 17. Señora 18. orator 19. torrid 20. ridden 21. dental 22. talent 23. entrée 24. reefer 25. ferric 26. richer 27. hermit 28. mitten 29. tender 30. dermal 31. mallet 32. lethal 33. hallow 34. lowest 35. Esther 36. Hermes 37. meshed 38. hedger 39. German

No. 269

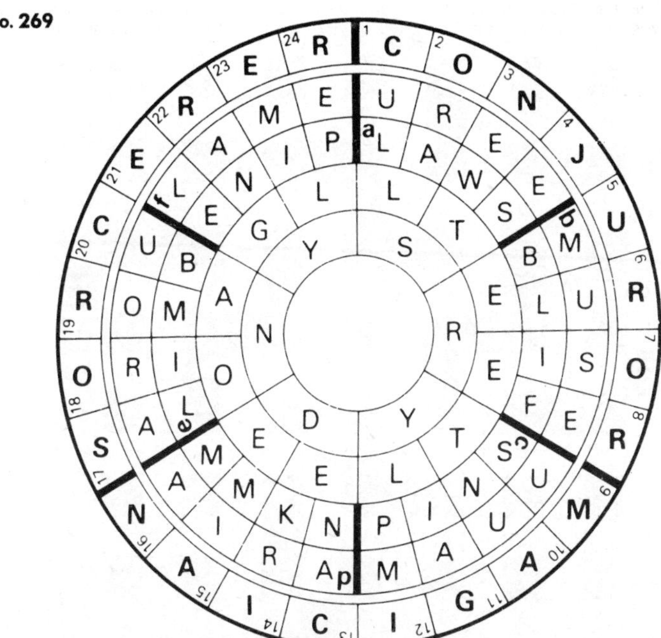

No. 270
DIAGONALLY LEFT: 2. orb 3. tweak 4. toe-nail 5. wad 6. sago pudding 7. sty 8. quell 10. pea 13. sinus 14. dilapidated 16. née 18. mutes 20. don 23. picador 25. tab 26. petal 29. canon 31. red 33. lad 35. dig
DIAGONALLY RIGHT: 1. Bren-gun 2. owe 3. to-dos 4. tag 5. waylaid 6. steed 7. sup 9. baa 11. kinds 12. pin-up 15. lei 17. duped 18. manic 19. lop 21. entered 22. titanic 24. gated 27. salon 28. cad 30. bad 32. tar 34. dog

No. 271
RANKS (in order of clues):
EASTWARD/SHEPHERD/CRUMPETS/SNIGGERS/THIRSTED/BLANKETS/PEERLESS/CROCKERY.
DIAGONAL MOVES: a. salting b. seekers c. tinkers d. holing e. polite f. regard g. clink h. mirth i. pails j. regal k. sling l. trims m. slops n. thong o. chip p. reed q. lard r. seed s. pain t. sees u. sage v. teas
WHITE DIAGONAL: CHECKERS

No. 272
ACROSS: 1. pus 3. cab 5. ash 6. roe 9. assortments 13. partly 15. ebb 17. lariat 19. OCEAN-GOING LINER 20. whale 23. eagle 26. blown 28. limp 30. main 31. tame 32. end 33. Alec 34. ON AN EVEN KEEL
DOWN: 1. pals 2. shore 3. crumb 4. bean 7. voyage 8. deluge 10. steal 11. trail 12. STERN 13. PROW 14. arch 16. brigs 18. anew 21. alto 22. Emma 24. alee 25. lode 26. balk 27. once 29. pen 30. man

No. 274
a. initial b. minimum c. fleeced d. thieves e. waiter f. domain g. infant h. barrow i. singer j. heart k. Heath l. woman m. stick n. water o. rapid p. loot q. heel r. poor s. amen t. yeti u. bent v. dear w. met x. bay y. dry z. sag.
Message: I AM PART OF A CENTRAL HEATING SYSTEM AND WHEN THE WATER INSIDE ME IS HEATED BY A BOILER I RADIATE WARMTH AND KEEP YOUR LIVING-ROOM COMFORTABLE IN WINTER-TIME.

No 275 PLAIN
ACROSS: 1. habit 4. devised 8. sad 9. recurrent 10. alimony 11. imply 13. dotted 15. morrow 18. renal

No. 273

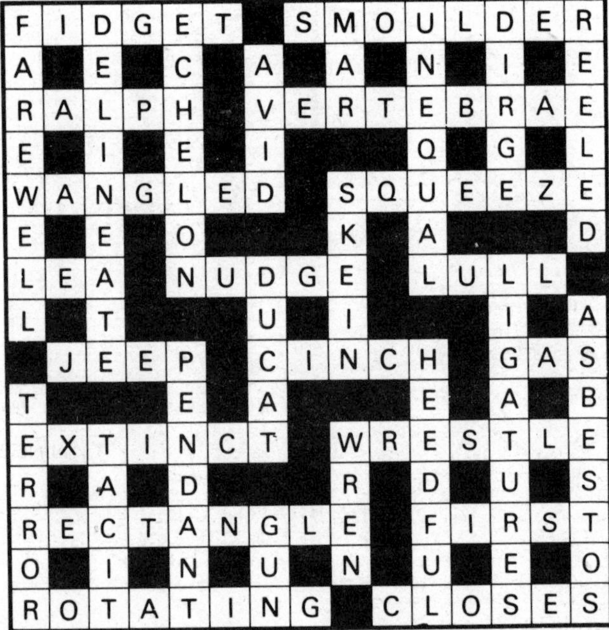

F	I	D	G	E	T		S	M	O	U	L	D	E	R
A		E		C		A		A		N		I		E
R	A	L	P	H		V	E	R	T	E	B	R	A	E
E		I		E		I				Q		G		L
W	A	N	G	L	E	D		S	Q	U	E	E	Z	E
E		E		O				K		A				D
L	E	A		N	U	D	G	E		L	U	L	L	
L		T				U		I				I		A
	J	E	E	P		C	I	N	C	H		G	A	S
T				E		A				E		A		B
E	X	T	I	N	C	T		W	R	E	S	T	L	E
R		A		D				R		D		U		S
R	E	C	T	A	N	G	L	E		F	I	R	S	T
O		I		N		U		N		U		E		O
R	O	T	A	T	I	N	G		C	L	O	S	E	S

No. 275 (continued)

19. umpteen 21. behaviour 23. Exe 24. top-knot 25. seedy
DOWN: 1. husband 2. badminton 3. torso 4. decoys 5. vertigo 6. see 7. ditty 12. persevere 14. enliven 16. wintery 17. put out 18. robot 20. pores 22. hip

No. 275 CRYPTIC

ACROSS: 1. a-mass 4. cove-Red 8. rat (rev. of tar) 9. em-bitters 10. capital (two mngs.) 11. mushy (US-H in my!) 13. todd(y)-le 15. anorak (RA in an-OK) 18. posse (s.s.) 19. cab-l-net 21. character (char + sound of actor) 23. lie (two mngs.) 24. swaddle (anag.) 25. side's
DOWN: 1. apricot (ric(h) in a pot) 2. antipodes (ant-I + anag. of dopes) 3. s-he-et 4. cobalt (BA-L in cot) 5. vitamin (it-a.m. in vin) 6. rye (sound of wry) 7. dusty (anag.) 12. strangled (St.-(w)rangled) 14. leeward (rev. of draw-eel) 16. kittens (Kit + anag. of sent) 17. s-cat-he 18. Pi-c-ts 20. burns (Robert Burns) 22. Ava (hidden)

No. 276

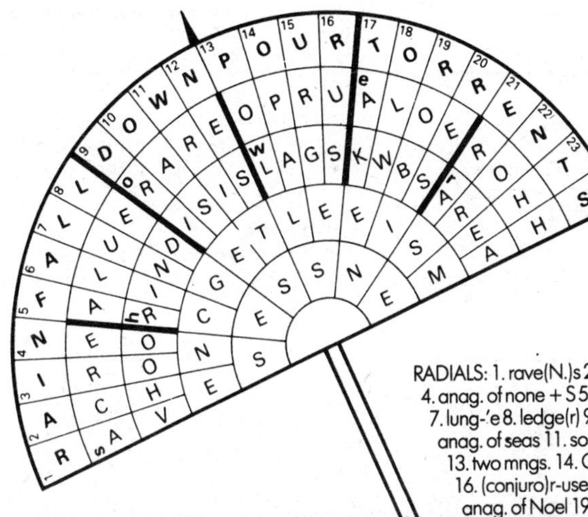

RADIALS: 1. rave(N.)s 2. a-ches(s) 3. two mngs. 4. anag. of none + S 5. fa-R-ce 6. A-lice 7. lung-'e 8. ledge(r) 9. d-r(ain)-ies 10. o(ats) + anag. of seas 11. sound of Ritz 12. nes-t(wo)-s 13. two mngs. 14. O-pal-S 15. (s)urges 16. (conjuro)r-uses 17. TA-ken 18. W. in anag. of Noel 19. robin' 20. hidden 21. e-R.-ase 22. Nor-SE 23. the-me 24. sham-e(xercise) ARCS: s. ac-R.-e h. hidden o. two mngs. w. two mngs. e. a-lo-E. r. a-re-a

No. 277

ACROSS: 1. blade 6. lifer 9. chop 10. area 12. sandal 14. army 16. spectacle 17. pursue 19. elm 20. cheer 22. coma 24. aim 25. nag 26. brass band 27. bet 31. fandango 32. gullet 33. yew 34. elks 35. Edda
DOWN: 1. bloomer 2. lips 3. deans 4. err 5. sharp 7. fractures 8. yea 9. clasp 13. Duce 15. ill 18. season 20. cabbage 21. hire 22. cob 23. managed 25 nanny 28. talk 29. odes 30. rate
Message: A WORD GAME PLAYED FOR AMUSEMENT ONLY

No. 278

ACROSS: 1. cowboy 4. speckles 10. raiment 11. PUDDING 12. seeks 13. murderers 14. MARKETEER 17. apish 19. SHEEP 20. exchanges 21. heatspots 24. table 26. uniting 27. eye-ball 28. ELEPHANT 29. stoker
DOWN: 1. CHRISTMAS 2. WHITE 3. oversleep 5. PAPER 6. cadge 7. loitering 8. signs 9. stampede 15. re-examine 16. recessed 17. apartment 18. hostellers 21. HOUSE 22. SMITH 23. organ 25. BLACK

No. 279

ACROSS: 1. S(H)OWER 4. (H)ARMED 7. PARIS(H) 8. T(H)ANKS 9. riots 10. rooks 11. taken for a ride 15. C(H)ATTY 20. misrepresents 21. exams 23. spoke 24. (H)OLDER 25. (H)AUNTS 26. S(H)IRES 27. S(H)EAT(H)S
DOWN: 1. separate 2. warlocks 3. RUS(H)ES 4. (H)ALTER 5. mandolin 6. desisted 12. nacre 13. (H)OTTER 14. abyss 16. emperors 17. islander 18. insomnia 19. assesses 22. S(H)ORES 23. S(H)EARS

No. 280

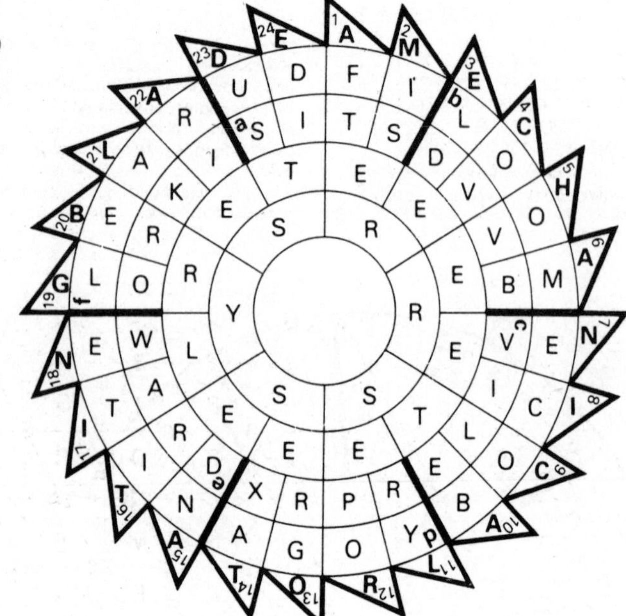

No. 281

ACROSS: 6. I + sound of glue 7. pro + sound of log 9. anag. 10. two mngs. 11. R-egret 13. over-'eats 14. anag. 17. sound of grew + some 20. line-a-r 21. cu-R-t 22. anag. 24. inn in the-St. 25. C.-LA-RA

DOWN: 1. h. in anag. of the wild 2. g-L.-en 3. moment-um 4. to + us-L-e 5. anag. 7. pronoun-cement 8. un-lit 12. re-creating 15. anag. of a call in + E 16. a in anag. of a lesson 18. sound of ruff 19. OS-prey 23. two mngs.

■	1W	■	2G	■	3M	■	■	■	4T	■	5C	■	■	■
■	6I	G	L	O	O	■	7P	R	O	L	O	G	8U	E
■	T	■	E	■	M	■	R	■	U	■	M	■	N	■
9T	H	U	N	D	E	R	O	U	S	■	10P	E	L	T
■	H	■	■	■	N	■	N	■	L	■	L	■	I	■
11R	E	G	12R	E	T	■	13O	V	E	R	E	A	T	S
■	L	■	E	■	U	■	U	■	■	■	T	■	■	■
■	14D	O	C	U	M	E	N	T	15A	R	I	E	16S	■
■	■	■	R	■	■	■	C	■	L	■	O	■	E	■
17G	18R	U	E	S	19O	M	E	■	20L	I	N	E	A	R
■	O	■	A	■	S	■	M	■	I	■	■	■	S	■
21C	U	R	T	■	22P	R	E	C	A	U	23T	I	O	N
■	G	■	I	■	R	■	N	■	N	■	R	■	N	■
24T	H	I	N	N	E	S	T	■	25C	L	A	R	A	■
■	■	■	G	■	Y	■	■	■	E	■	P	■	L	■

No. 282
ACROSS: 1. TENCH 4. THORNBACK 6. COD 7. BREAM 9. DAB 11. CHUB 12. HERRING 13. CRAB 15. PIKE 16. HALIBUT 19. HAKE 22. EEL 23. PERCH 24. RAY 25. BARRACUDA 27. SKATE
DOWN: 1. trouble 2. nun 3. headman 4. tide 5. kids 6. chuckle 8. earlier 10. Barbary 11. cap 14. bee 17. aspires 18. unhouse 20. glib 21. Irma 26. aga

No. 283
ACROSS: 1. beast 4. lip 6. also 8. raise 9. set 10. read 12. elements 13. came to 14. New 16. mould 18. dusky 20. hated 21. heavy 22. gun 23. relics 26. short cut 30. grey 31. air 32. rough 33. felt 34. tip 35. later
DOWN: 1. Burke and Hare 2. alive 3. there 4. lose touch 5. pity 6. aorta 7. stake 11. body-snatcher 15. wet 16. mad 17. death-trap 18. day 19. sag 24. large 25. crypt 27. rural 28. Count 29. last

No. 284
1. sorely 2. pastor 3. assail 4. glance
5. parole 6. pepper 7. diaper 8. glider
9. grille 10. harass 11. sapper
12. peruse 13. murder 14. retire
15. litter 16. lashed 17. savers
18. serene 19. resume 20. meaner
21. tenant 22. wonted 23. valuer
24. vendor 25. endear
26. astare 27. ananas
28. novena 29. furore
30. rodent 31. neater
32. Easter 33. leaned
34. russet 35. tea-urn
36. tourer 37. teller

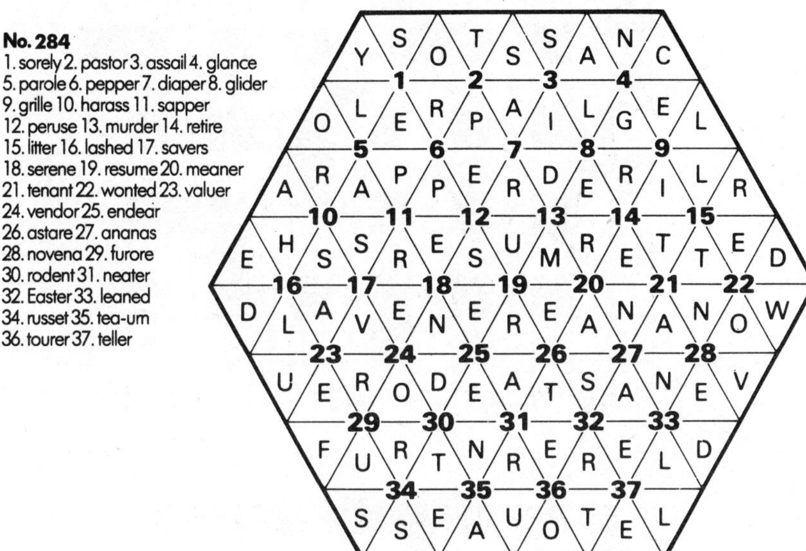

No. 285
ACROSS: (corrected misprints shown in brackets): 1. AMONTILLADO (wine) 10. KNEE-CAPS (bones) 11. DISCOVER (find) 14. FLARE (light) 15. TOSSING (hurling) 16. SATES (gluts) 18. TAPIOCA (pudding) 19. ASSAULT (charge) 23. TITLE (book) 24. TANTRUM (temper) 26. INCAS (kings) 29. PASSOVER (feast) 30. ENTITIES (beings) 31. HEARTLESSLY (pity)
DOWN: 1. audits 2. obsess 3. necks 4. invent 5. leek 6. acclaim 7. data 8. ashes 9. limousine 12. precluded 13. pique 16. spine 17. malaria 20. tassel 21. craves 22. smarmy 23. tired 25. tools 27. cote 28. bait

No. 286
(Correct definitions are shown in brackets)
ACROSS: 1. RIVER (Ganges) 4. STUDY (read) 5. MATCH (suit) 8. crease 11. mellow 15. tap 16. boa 17. RHINE (river) 18. RANGE (rove) 19. rot 21. dot 22. extent 24. chases 25. ANGER (ire) 27. DRAIN (sewer) 28. MEETS (faces)
DOWN: 1. resume 2. VAULT (spring) 3. rhythm 6. asp 7. cub 8. CURVE (bend) 9. EDICT (order) 10. STERN (rear) 12. EARTH (land) 13. LINES (rows) 14. WEEDS (hoes) 20. ton 21. dye 23. tandem 24. cranks 26. GRADE (rank)

No. 287

PART 10

No. 288

ACROSS: 1. aeroplane (anag.) 6. cat-ch. 9. hostile (St.-I in hole) 10. blatant (L. in bat + ant) 11. go-Ur-ds 12. pro-poser 14. addition (a-DD-I + anag. of into) 16. do-OM 19. award (rev. of draw-a) 21. plainsman (pla-I-ns + man) 22. emphysema (E.-MP-Hy. + anag. of same) 23. re-B(attalion)-el 25. eclipse (L in anag. of pieces) 27. cant-rip 29. h-a bit-at 32. Riviera (anag.) 33. no-I-some 34. collect (two mngs.) 36. S-wee-P 38. slantwise (anag.) 40. yell-owing 42. mitre (two mngs.) 43. t(errified)-hug 44. bully off (two mngs.) 48. hand-so-me 50. spider (rev. of re-dips) 53. durable (anag.) 54. (bac)K-he-dive 55. win-c.-e 56. diagnosis (anag.)

DOWN: 1. as high as an elephant's eye (two mngs.; song from 'Oklahoma') 2. re-sound 3. p.-lied 4. (r)aver 5. E.-MB-Ark 6. c-R.-amp 7. transform (anag. of rants + form) 8. h-at-ers 13. comp-L.-ete 15. toddy (rev. of yd.-Dot) 16. don-or 17. BA-lancer 18. an elephant never forgets (anag.) 20. appal (rev. of Pa + pal) 24. bor-N-e 26. Pat-I-O 28. novel (two mngs.) 30. Bri-N-e 31. theistic (he is in TT-i/c) 34. clangour (sound of clanger) 35. exi-S-t 37. prong (p. + sound of wrong) 39. Tamil (hidden) 41. Lo-hen-grin 45. ordains (or + d-a-ins) 46. sh-ad-ow 47. imp-end 49. sabre (anag.) 51. p-ae.-an 52. skua (rev. of auks)

No. 289

ACROSS: **1.** David **4.** wigwam **9.** withers (two mngs.) **10.** Raleigh **11.** In-cas(e) **12.** Offa's Dyke **13.** tongue-tie **14.** finė-d **15,51.** E-Boat Alley **17,29 Down,47.** Screaming Lord Sutch **20.** out-and-out **22.** Heath (two mngs.) **24.** to-nigh-t **25.** Neptune **28.** ibex **33.** osmosis (i(rrigations) in anag.) **34.** elevate **35.** delta (two mngs.) **37.** overt-rain **38.** ruminates (anag.) **39.** chaff **40.** s-kill **42.** 'Moon River' **45.** enshrines (anag.) **48.** t-ER-rier **49.** abiding (two mngs.) **50,27.** 'Nellie Dean'

DOWN: **1.** down in the mouth (two mngs.) **2.** Vatican **3.** Dr.-ess-suit **4.** wash-out **5.** giraffe **6.** atlas **7.** Libyan (Lib. + rev. of nay) **8.** sheep-dog **14.** flash (two mngs.) **16.** Ostend **17.** shoot one's bolt (two mngs.) **18.** retentiveness **19.** Icarus **21.** nuggets (rev. of gun + gets) **23.** heed (sound of he'd) **26.** present **30.** emblem **31.** pan-a-Ma **32.** penny for the guy **36.** Anna-L **39,38.** Christina Rossetti **41.** insure **42.** mongrel **43.** on stage (stag in one) **44.** vitriol **46.** raise (sound of rays)

No. 290

ACROSS: **1.** forge-t(ale)-s **5.** memory (anag.) **8.** re(st)-members **9.** navy (rev. of van + (journe)y) **11.** thaw (anag.) **12.** break cover (sound of brake + cove-R.) **14.** elephant (anag.) **15.** balsa (rev. of a-slab) **17.** RU-men **19.** ship's log (s-hips-log) **22.** anthracite (anag.) **23.** once (rev. of No. + CE) **25.** E-very **27.** stringent (string + anag.) **29.** testate (test + anag.) **31.** p-L-otter **32.** hesitated (he + s-It-ated) **33.** bosun (rev. of sob + un) **35.** w-(indig)o-ad **36.** off-the-cuff **39.** ninepins (N-in rev. of snipe-in) **41.** un-F-it **43.** as-pen **45.** game-some **48.** tale-teller (two mngs.) **50.** opus (rev. of Po(e) + US) **52.** bar-b(arrels) **53.** re-collect **55.** re-call **56.** amnesia (anag. in Asia)

DOWN: **1.** fir (sound of fur) **2.** ram-page **3.** Emma (hidden) **4.** s-hearing **5.** miss-a-£ **6.** man-ic(e) **7.** re-v.-IV-al **10.** great-great-grand-fat-hers **11.** the greatest show on earth (anag.) **13.** shiner (shin + rev. of RE) **15.** bap (hidden) **16.** whet (sound of wet) **18.** mit-R-e **20.** longest (G(ospels) in lone-St.) **21.** ice-sheet (anag.; easterly = E.) **24.** entomb (tom in anag.) **26.** yea-sty **28.** rapidity (anag. + sound of ditty) **30.** s-us-tain **34.** snuff (two mngs.) **37.** fun-D **38.** exuded (ex + anag.) **40.** pun (hidden) **42.** Valencia (Val-E + N-CIA) **44.** p-ill-age **46.** OS-preys **47.** p-lur(e)-al **49.** tibia (rev. of I-bit + a) **51.** G-L(iberators)-en. **54.** tea(l)